Gender, Age and Inequality in the Professions

The literature on gender and professions shows that professional careers continue to be impacted by gender—albeit with important differences among professions and countries. Much less researched is the issue of the significance of gender and age-cohort or generation to professional work.

Gender, Age and Inequality in the Professions explores men's and women's experiences of professional work and careers through an intersectional lens by focusing on the intersection of gender and age. The chapters explore different professions—including Medicine, Nursing, Law, Academia, Information Technology and Engineering—in different Western countries, in the present and over time. Through original research, and critical re-analysis of existing research, each of the chapters explores the significance of gender and age cohort or generation to professional work, with particular attention to professionals just entering professional careers, those building professional careers, and comparisons of men and women in professions across generational cohorts.

The book contributes to literature on inequalities in the professions by demonstrating the ways in which gender and age converge to confer privilege and produce disadvantage, and the ways in which gender inequality is reproduced, and disrupted, through the activities of professionals on the job. The book constitutes a departure point for future research in terms of theoretical perspectives and empirical findings on how gendered and age-related processes are produced and reproduced in particular organizational, professional and socio-cultural contexts. To enhance generational understanding, relationships and collaboration in educational institutions, organizations and professions, the book ends with a section on policy recommendations for educators, professionals, professional organizations as well as policy- and decision-makers. This book will also appeal to students and researchers in the fields of Sociology, Gender Studies, Organizational and Management Studies, Law, Medicine, Engineering and Information Technology as well as related disciplines.

Marta Choroszewicz, PhD, is a postdoctoral researcher in Sociology at the University of Eastern Finland whose research explores patterns of inequality in the professions and organizations.

Tracey L. Adams is a professor of sociology at the University of Western Ontario, Canada who specializes in the sociology of work, occupations and professions.

Routledge Studies in Gender and Organizations
Series Editor: Elisabeth K. Kelan

Although still a fairly young field, the study of gender and organizations is increasingly popular and relevant. There are few areas of academic research that are as vibrant and dynamic as the study of gender and organizations. While much earlier research has focused on documenting the imbalances of women and men in organizations, more recently, research on gender and organizations has departed from counting men and women. Instead research in this area sees gender as a process: something that is done rather than something that people are. This perspective is important and meaningful as it takes researchers away from essentialist notions of gender and opens the possibility of analysing the process of how individuals become women and men. This is called 'gendering', 'practising gender', 'doing gender' or 'performing gender' and draws on rich philosophical traditions.

Whilst Routledge Studies in Gender and Organizations has a broad remit, it will be thematically and theoretically committed to exploring gender and organizations from a constructivist perspective. Rather than focusing on specific areas of organizations, the series is to be kept deliberately broad to showcase the most innovative research in this field. It is anticipated that the books in this series will make a theoretical contribution to the field of gender and organization based on rigorous empirical explorations.

Gender and the Professions
International and Contemporary Perspectives
Edited by Kaye Broadbent, Glenda Strachan, and Geraldine Healy

Postfeminism and Organization
Edited by Patricia Lewis, Yvonne Benschop, and Ruth Simpson

Women and Careers
Transnational Studies in Public Policy and Employment Equity
Marilee Reimer

Gender, Age and Inequality in the Professions
Edited by Marta Choroszewicz and Tracey L. Adams

Gender, Age and Inequality in the Professions

Edited by Marta Choroszewicz and Tracey L. Adams

Routledge
Taylor & Francis Group

NEW YORK AND LONDON

First published 2019
by Routledge
605 Third Avenue, New York, NY 10017

and by Routledge
2 Park Square, Milton Park, Abingdon, Oxon, OX14 4RN

First issued in paperback 2021

Routledge is an imprint of the Taylor & Francis Group, an informa business

© 2019 Taylor & Francis

Library of Congress Cataloging-in-Publication Data
Names: Choroszewicz, Marta, editor. | Adams, Tracey Lynn,
   1966– editor.
Title: Gender, age and inequality in the professions / edited by
   Marta Choroszewicz and Tracey L. Adams.
Description: New York : Routledge, 2019. | Series: Routledge
   studies in gender and organizations | Includes index.
Identifiers: LCCN 2018058617| ISBN 9780815358572
   (hardback) | ISBN 9781351052467 (ebook)
Subjects: LCSH: Sexual division of labor. | Sex discrimination in
   employment. | Women's rights. | Older people—Employment.
Classification: LCC HD6060.6 .G456 2019 | DDC
   306.3/615—dc23
LC record available at https://lccn.loc.gov/2018058617

ISBN 13: 978-0-367-78676-2 (pbk)
ISBN 13: 978-0-8153-5857-2 (hbk)

Typeset in Sabon
by Apex CoVantage, LLC

Contents

Figures

Tables

Contributors

Editors

Marta Choroszewicz, PhD, is a postdoctoral researcher in Sociology at the University of Eastern Finland whose research explores patterns of inequality in the professions and organizations. She completed her PhD on career experiences of women in the legal profession in Finland and Poland. She is currently involved in two projects. The first project explores the links between mobile technologies, intersection of gender and age, work–family reconciliation and career progress in the legal profession. The second project, Data-Driven Society in the Making, focuses on the use of digital data and learning algorithms in healthcare and social welfare services in Finland.

Tracey L. Adams is a professor of sociology at the University of Western Ontario, Canada who specializes in the sociology of work, occupations and professions. Within this broad area, she has two primary areas of research. The first explores work and social inequality, with a focus on gender, in intersection with class, race and age. The second research area is professional work in Canada. This research pays particular attention to professional regulation, profession creation, professional change and inter-professional relations.

Contributors

Isabel Boni-Le Goff has a PhD in Sociology. She is FNS senior researcher at the University of Lausanne. Isabel is interested in gender and gender regimes in the economic field as well as in the contemporary changes at stake in expertise, professions and higher-level occupations. Her fieldwork is both quantitative and qualitative, based on a mixed-methods approach with an interest in comparative and longitudinal studies. She has published articles on executive women's movements in the field of gender equality and on higher-level occupations from a gendered perspective.

Christianne Corbett is a PhD candidate in sociology at Stanford University, where she studies inequality in engineering work environments from a social psychological perspective. Her research focuses on understanding the persistence of gender and race inequality in these settings despite the absence of formal barriers to inclusion in them. Prior to coming to Stanford, Christianne worked as a legislative aide on Capitol Hill and as a mechanical design engineer in the aerospace industry. Christianne holds a master's degree in cultural anthropology from the University of Colorado and bachelor's degrees in aerospace engineering and government from the University of Notre Dame.

Marci D. Cottingham is an assistant professor of Sociology at the University of Amsterdam. Her research examines how emotions are structured by social inequalities, organizations and media communications across the domains of healthcare and biomedical science. Her research has appeared in *Theory and Society, Gender & Society* and *Social Psychology Quarterly* and received support and awards from the American Sociological Association, the National Science Foundation and the Society for the Study of Social Problems.

Janette S. Dill is an associate professor of Sociology at the University of Akron. Her research focuses on changes in work and occupations in today's labor market, particularly for men and women without a college degree. She has recent publications on work in the healthcare sector in *Human Relations, Social Science & Medicine,* and *Gender & Society*.

Jeff Hearn is Senior Professor, Gender Studies, Örebro University, Sweden; Professor of Sociology, University of Huddersfield, UK; Professor Emeritus, Hanken School of Economics, Finland; Professor Extraordinarius, University of South Africa; and Honorary Doctor, Social Sciences, Lund University, Sweden. His work focuses on gender, sexuality, violence, work, organizations, social policy and transnational processes. He is co-managing editor of *Routledge Advances in Feminist Studies and Intersectionality* book series; and co-editor, *NORMA: The International Journal for Masculinity Studies*. Recent books include *Men of the World: Genders, Globalizations, Transnational Times* (Sage, 2015), and the co-edited books *Engaging Youth in Activist Research and Pedagogical Praxis* (Routledge, 2018) and *Unsustainable Institutions of Men* (Routledge, 2018).

Liisa Husu is Professor of Gender Studies, Örebro University, Sweden; Co-Director of GEXcel International Collegium; and Affiliated Researcher, Hanken School of Economics, Finland. Her research focus is on gender in science and academia, and she is active in international research policy and research development. She co-authored the EC report 'Gender and Excellence in the Making' (2004) and was

Rapporteur of the EC report, 'The Gender Challenge in Research Funding' (2009). Other publications include *Sexism, Support and Survival in Academia* (University of Helsinki, 2001); the co-edited books, *Hard Work in the Academy* (Helsinki University Press, 1999), *Leadership Through the Gender Lens* (Hanken School of Economics, 2010), and *Women, Management and Leadership* (Hanken School of Economics, 2011); journal articles; and book chapters.

Fiona M. Kay, PhD, is Professor of Sociology at Queen's University, Canada. Her research interests include gender and the professions, developmental strategies within organizations, and work–life interface over the life course. She is presently engaged in a thirty-year longitudinal study of career pathways among Canadian lawyers. A second study, in collaboration with Elizabeth Gorman, focuses on retention and advancement of racial minorities in corporate U.S. law firms. A third study, in collaboration with Robert Granfield, examines the nature of volunteerism among professionals.

Eugena Kwon is currently a PhD candidate enrolled in the Collaborative Program in Sociology & Migration and Ethnic Relations (MER) at Western University. With a broad research interest in the sociology of work, immigration, population health, and social inequalities, her current work focuses on how structural challenges and barriers to immigrant integration play a role in shaping immigrants' post-migration food choices in Canada.

Nicky Le Feuvre is full Professor of Sociology at the University of Lausanne. She has researched extensively on the implications of the feminisation of higher-level occupations, from a comparative and life course perspective. Besides working on gender and globalization in the legal profession, she is currently director of the Gender & Occupations sub-project of the LIVES National research programme (www.lives-nccr.ch/) and is in charge of the Swiss contribution to an FP7 European research project on gender inequalities in early academic careers (www.garciaproject.eu).

Eléonore Lépinard is Associate Professor and Director of the Institute for Social Science at Université de Lausanne. Eléonore's work is situated in the field of socio-legal studies, gender and politics, gender equality public policies and social movements. Aside from the study of gender and globalization in the legal professions, she currently works on gender quotas in political and economic decision making in France and beyond, and on feminist movements in France and Canada.

Charlotta Magnusson is an associate professor of Sociology at the Swedish Institute for Social Research, Stockholm University, Sweden. Her current research focuses on gender stratification in the labor market, in particular wage, occupational prestige and work conditions. Her work has recently been published in *British Journal of Sociology, Gender Issues* and *Work, Employment and Society*.

Grégoire Mallard is Associate Professor in the Department of Anthropology and Sociology at the Graduate Institute of International and Development Studies, in Geneva. He is the author of *Fallout: Nuclear Diplomacy in an Age of Global Fracture* (University of Chicago Press, 2014) and co-editor of *Contractual Knowledge: One Hundred Years of Legal Experimentation in Global Markets* (Cambridge University Press, 2016), and *Global Science and National Sovereignty: Studies in Historical Sociology of Science* (Routledge, 2008). His recent publications focus on the globalization of the legal profession, the global governance of nuclear trade, postwar financial negotiations and the study of harmonization as a social process.

Sandrine Morel worked as a junior research assistant on the FNS project Gendered Globalization of the Legal Professions. Currently she is a PhD student and a teaching assistant at the University of Lausanne at the Life Course and Inequality Research Center. She is a sociologist interested in life course and parenthood, she studies family and work trajectories, their normative dimensions and their interactions. She tends to keep a quantitative and qualitative approach in her research.

Magnus Nermo is a professor of Sociology and Head of the Department of Sociology, Stockholm University, Sweden. His research focuses on stratification and segregation in Western societies by gender and social class. His work has recently been published in *Acta Sociologica, European Sociological Review* and *Social Indicators Research*.

Patricia Neville is a sociologist with research interests in the sociology of gender, health and professionalism. Her research has been published in such journals as *Critical Social Policy, Journal of Gender Studies, Health Sociology Review* and *European Journal of Dental Education*. She is currently Lecturer in Social Sciences at the Bristol Dental School, University of Bristol, United Kingdom and Theme Lead for Personal and Professional Development. She is overseeing research projects into the impact that social media has on healthcare professionalism and the distribution of ethnicity and gender in the dental profession.

Antero Olakivi is a postdoctoral researcher at the University of Helsinki in the Centre of Excellence in Research on Ageing and Care. His sociological PhD dissertation, *The Relational Construction of Occupational Agency: Performing Professional and Enterprising Selves in Diversifying Care Work* (University of Helsinki, 2018), examined the construction of ethnic and migration-based inequalities in old-age care work in Finland. He has published articles in journals such as *Sociology* *of Health and Illness* and *Journal of Professions and Organization.* He is a member of the editorial team of the journal *Professions and Professionalism.*

Gabriele Plickert is an assistant professor in the Department of Psychology and Sociology at California State Polytechnic University in Pomona. Her research interests include life course sociology, criminology, professionals' work experiences and well-being, and cross-cultural comparisons. Her recent publications include 'Attorneys' Career Dissatisfaction in the New Normal' (with Milan Markovic) in the *International Journal of the Legal Profession* (2018) and 'Depressive Symptoms and the Salience of Job Satisfaction Over the Life Course of Professionals' (with Fiona M. Kay and John Hagan), in *Advances in Life Course Research* (2017).

Sirpa Wrede is a senior lecturer in Sociology at the University of Helsinki and vice-director and team leader at the Centre of Excellence in Research on Ageing and Care. She has carried out research on professions and professionalism since the mid-1990s and has led several related projects funded by Academy of Finland. She has published articles in journals such as *Sociology of Health and Illness* and *Social Science and Medicine.* She holds the title of Docent in Sociology at University of Helsinki. Her chapter is based on her ongoing research collaboration with the Finnish Medical Association, which began in 2015.

Acknowledgments

This book is the result of an intensive and collaborative journey to which many people have contributed along the way. The book dates back to the joint chapter, 'Gender, Diversity and Intersectionality in Professions and Potential Professions: Analytical, Historical And Contemporary Perspectives', which was initiated and put together by Jeff Hearn and his colleagues. As a follow-up, David Varley, Senior Editor at Routledge, proposed to Jeff Hearn to turn the chapter into the book. Jeff Hearn, after discussing the issue with Ingrid Biese, kindly passed on the idea of the book to one of this book's editors. We would like to thank everyone mentioned above for initiating the process.

The book idea got its current shape at the Interim Meeting of RC52 Sociology of Professional Groups at what is now Oslo Metropolitan University in June 2017. This is where we—the book editors—met and intensively started to work on the book proposal.

We are extremely thankful to David Varley, who assisted us with the book proposal and to Megan A Smith, Editorial Assistant at Routledge, who helped us with a book contract. The book benefitted also from the encouraging comments by two anonymous reviewers of the book proposal.

Toward the end of the process, Awish Aslam did marvelous work with editing and formatting the chapters for which we are deeply grateful. Brianna Ascher, Editor at Routledge, and Mary Del Plato, Editorial Assistant at Routledge, provided continuous advice on the manuscript preparation.

Finally, we would like to thank all of the contributors, without whom this book would not happen.

Introduction

1 Introduction
Themes, Objectives, and Theoretical Perspectives

Marta Choroszewicz and
Tracey L. Adams

Introduction

Since the 1990s there have been numerous changes in the world of work owing to globalisation, rising competitiveness, technological progress, organisational change, and marketisation of higher education. These social and economic trends have combined to alter professional work and career prospects. Professionals may be more closely managed and monitored than in previous decades, and they face more precarious work settings. Professions are also transforming from the inside. Elite professions like medicine, law, and engineering were traditionally male-dominated in the West, but in recent decades women have entered these professions in large numbers. In many countries the professional workforce is more ethnically diverse as well, thanks to increased immigration, and the globalisation of the professional labour market. In light of these developments, men and women entering professions today face different workplace and professional environments than their predecessors.

This book explores the experiences of young professionals entering the workforce, and the significance of gender in shaping those experiences and intergenerational dynamics in professions, through contributions from scholars studying professionals in a variety of professions across national settings. There is a large body of research documenting how professional work is gendered (Adams 2010a; Davies 1996; Witz 1992): gender norms and expectations are embedded into the structure of professional jobs and career paths. Less research has focused on the significance of age cohort or generation. However, in light of the significant transformations shaping professional work and professional workers, generational differences in experience are quite likely. With this book, we argue that a gender lens alone is no longer sufficient to capture the experiences of men and women in professions. Rather, it is necessary to adopt an intersectional approach, and explore how age and gender intersect to shape experiences of professional work and careers.

The book includes contributions from researchers in six countries, presenting research conducted on about nine professional groupings, in seven national contexts. Through original research, and critical re-analysis of existing research, each of the chapters in this volume explores the significance of gender and age cohort or generation to professional work, paying particular attention to professionals just entering professional careers, those building professional careers, and comparisons of men and women in professions across generational cohorts. Combined, the chapters demonstrate the importance of looking at the intersection of gender and age/cohort/generation when researching professionals and their work.

From the outset, it is important to emphasise that our perspective in this volume is limited to Western countries (the US, Canada, Nordic countries, and Western Europe) that are characterised by long research traditions on professionals and professional work (Adams 2015). At the same time, we highlight a need for more international and comparative work on the changing nature of professions in these societies through an intersectional lens. By bringing together researchers from across Western countries, this book brings attention to generational issues in the workplace, and develops policy recommendations for workplaces and employing organisations, professional groups, professional education programs, and governments.

In this introductory chapter we provide brief outlines of the theoretical context for the empirical chapters to follow by examining the significance of gender and age cohort to professional work, and by making a case for an intersectional approach to research on professions and professional work. We also outline the key themes of this book and highlight our main contributions. Finally we end the chapter with a summary of the different sections and chapters contained herein.

Professional Work

For decades scholars have debated how best to define professions and professional work. We will not repeat those debates here. Rather we take a more pragmatic approach to defining professions, but one that builds on the substantial body of research on work in this field (Abbott 1988; Freidson 1994, 2001; Johnson 1972; Larson 1977; Macdonald 1995). Professions are traditionally a set of occupations distinguished from others by their high education, complex body of knowledge and skills, their status, and their fiduciary responsibilities (Carr-Saunders and Wilson 1933; Greenwood 1957). Professionals mobilise advanced knowledge to provide important services to the public, states, and societies. Professionals have also been distinguished through their organisation; traditionally many have enjoyed some degree of self-regulation, in society and/or on the job. They have been granted discretion and latitude in the performance of their work. Exactly who is regarded as a professional has varied across time and place; however, in the West, there are considerable similarities across nations. Among the most recognised high-status professions are lawyers, medical doctors and other health professionals, academics, engineers, and others. These are the same groups that are of key focus in the pages of this volume.

Although the work of professionals varies across field and specialisation, the literature has pointed to several key characteristics that are important to note here. First, professionals' work involves drawing on complex, esoteric knowledge to provide often pragmatic solutions to clients. Most professionals have undergone advanced education involving exposure to complex, theoretical ideas, and on-the-job training to acquire practical skills required for effective service delivery. There is an expectation that professionals will continue to learn on the job, and (increasingly) regularly retrain to keep their skills up-to-date.

Second, professional work either directly or indirectly affects the well-being of others. The work of healthcare workers has a direct impact on the health of patients and clients, while the work of engineers has significant public safety implications. The work of lawyers, teachers, academics, and others directly affects the well-being, safety and security, and life prospects of those whom they come in contact with. Not surprisingly, then, the work of professionals has been regulated by codes of ethics and by governments, to ensure that professionals are using their skills responsibly and ethically and are acting to protect the public, rather than do harm (Adams 2010b; Law and Kim 2005). Professionals who fail to uphold their obligations are subject to discipline, which may include suspension, loss of license, and even criminal charges.

Third, professional workers have traditionally possessed a fair amount of autonomy in the conduct of their work (Freidson 2001; Johnson 1972; Larson 1977). The expectation has been that professionals need a degree of freedom in order to draw on their education and training, to meet the complex needs of clients. Historically, as long as professionals met their fiduciary responsibilities to the public, they were granted a considerable amount of leeway, concerning how they did so. They were allowed the freedom to find creative solutions to complex problems.

Fourth, there are internal status hierarchies within professions based on gender, class, and race, and generally a recognised career ladder; those professionals who are highly successful in their work have an expectation of promotion, or at least enhanced recognition (Davies 1996; Tomlinson et al. 2013; Witz 1992).

Fifth, professional workers often have a strong work-oriented identity. Professional work is not simply something professionals do for a living, but it defines who they are as people. Even when they are not working, professional workers identify as professionals.

Finally, all of these characteristics combine to promote a culture of long work hours. Professionals tend to work long hours (Choroszewicz and Tremblay 2018), and doing so is expected to ensure that clients' well-being is met and skills are up-to-date; long hours are required for promotion.

While these characteristics of professional work remain important, professions have experienced substantial change in recent decades, as we noted earlier. Technological change and research advancements have altered the content of professional work, and increased the amount of work needed to keep professionals up-to-date. The popularity of neo-liberal ideologies has encouraged the questioning of professional monopolies, contributing to major changes in professional regulation (Abel 2003; Adams 2017; Evetts 2011, 2013; Noordegraaf 2011; Saks 2015). It has also altered the professional labour market, through its encouragement of globalisation, removal of barriers and protections, and reduced job security. Precarious employment within professions has increased substantially (Francis 2015; Francis and Sommerlad 2009; Kalleberg 2009), making professional careers increasingly fragmented and unsystematic (Biese and Choroszewicz 2018).

Organisational change has also been transformative. In the past, many professionals were employed in workplaces characterised by collegiality, in which professionals held significant leadership positions. Professionals were often managed by other professionals and professional norms guided conduct (Freidson 1986). In recent decades, this has changed, and professionals are closely managed according to managerialist principles now more than ever before (Noordegraaf and Steijn 2013). The introduction of new public management in public-sector organisations means that professionals in this sector, like their counterparts in the private sector, experience more regulations, discipline, and cost-cutting measures. These trends combine to alter the content of professional work, reducing the autonomy and authority of rank-and-file professionals (Livingstone 2018).

Globalisation and internationalisation are also trends affecting professions, expanding professional markets, resulting in larger and more complex work organisations, altering regulatory regimes and the nature of professional work itself, and contributing to a more diverse professional workforce (Faulconbridge and Muzio 2012; Susskind and Susskind 2015). Additionally, technological advances optimise traditional ways in which professionals work; they also actively transform the nature of work itself, and thus the types of tasks performed by professionals (Susskind and Susskind 2015).

Recent changes strike at the very heart of professionalism, affecting professionals' autonomy (Muzio et al. 2013), job security (Kalleberg 2009), promotion opportunities (Tomlinson et al. 2013), and relationships with clients and colleagues (Gustafsson et al. 2018; Hanlon 1998). These changes impose multiple, conflicting pressures on professional workers (Noordegraaf and Steijn 2013). As a result, internal inequalities within professions are exacerbated (Noordegraaf 2013; Waring 2014).

Professionals are increasingly differentiated by gender, race/ethnicity, and age, as well as by status, organisational position, and authority. There is some concern that these divisions could undermine professional collegiality and shared identities. These changes have implications for professional workplaces, as well as professions more broadly. In light of the changing nature of professions, the next sections explore the significance of gender and age to professional work.

Gender and Professions

Feminist scholars have critiqued gender-blind approaches to theorising and studying professions (Crompton 1987; Davies 1996; Witz 1992). Gender is an organising principle that underlies the formation and structure of professions (Acker 1990; Davies 1996; Kuhlmann 2003). Cultural assumptions around femininity and masculinity, and institutionalised gender inequality, were central to the establishment of professions (Adams 2000; Davies 1996: 671). Historically, women in male-dominated professions faced exclusionary mechanisms that aimed to sustain a male monopoly and reinforce male dominance (Witz 1992: 6). Gendered expectations have shaped the division of professional labour (Adams 2000; Davies 1996) and continue to influence professionals' social practices and identities. The gendering of professions takes place even in professions comprised of only women or only men (Hearn et al. 2016). Gendered processes shape professional hierarchies and specialties, and their combined impact, for women in male-dominated fields, has been one of cumulative disadvantage, limiting opportunities for their ability to obtain positions of power, authority, and influence.

Gender theory provides insights as to how gender operates at multiple levels from micro- through meso- to macro-levels (Acker 1990, 2006, 2012; Connell 1987). These frameworks enable us to examine, first, the influence of the state of gender relations in a country (i.e. gender order) on career opportunities of women and men, and second, the influence of the state of gender relations in a particular occupation or organisation (i.e. gender regime) on the development of tasks, work, and the construction of jobs as either 'men's work' or 'women's work' (Bloksgaard 2011; Choroszewicz 2014). This division continues to underpin the numerical domination of certain professions by either women or men, making it difficult for the opposite sex to access them. The gendering of professional work shapes career choices as well as social constructions of professional expertise (Bolton and Muzio 2007). For example, women's professional career choices are informed not only by their sense of what is occupationally advantageous, but also by their beliefs about what careers are appropriate for them, and what careers they will be good at (Choroszewicz 2014). Male-dominated professions are seen to require masculine skills, while many female-dominated professions are seen to utilise feminine skills and qualities. The selective and context-sensitive valorisation of traditionally feminine or masculine skills and qualities can create (and reproduce) niches between professions and among specialties within particular professions (Choroszewicz 2014). Women gain credibility in female-dominated professions and in professional specialties, which are also seen to be easier to combine with family life (Choroszewicz 2014).

Gender is also central to the status of professions (Davies 1996; Riska 2014; Witz 1992). While most archetypical professions were constructed as male-dominated, female-dominated professions have been regarded as semi-professions or non-professions (Hearn 1982). The majority of prestigious and high-status professions have been constructed or organised by men for men (Adams 2000), thereby privileging men in their career progress. Women's inroads into these professions were associated with three interactive dominant strategies:

1. the need to live up to the established masculine ideals of professional roles and behaviours or be channelled to lower-status professions and professional roles (e.g. Adams 2000);
2. the need to convert feminine skills, qualities, and life experience into professionally powerful resources to strengthen their professional credibility (e.g. Riska 2003); and
3. the need to negotiate between, on the one hand, living up to the masculine ideals (sameness) and, on the other hand, cultivating the gendered dispositions expected of them (difference) in their pursuit of professional careers (e.g. Choroszewicz 2014; Simpson et al. 2010).

Today, in Western societies, women no longer face formal barriers to entering traditionally male-dominated professions as they did in decades past. However, despite advancements brought by gender equality legislation and changes within the professions, women are not yet integrated into the professions on an equal basis with men, as the chapters in this volume show.

While women and men are nowadays increasingly found in similar occupations and professions, their experiences in regards to professional activity, career choices and progression, and work–family reconciliation still differ. As a result, women and men professionals are still engaged in different work, different areas of the same work, and/or completing different tasks and responsibilities. They are also assumed to possess, and therefore put emphasis on investing differently in, skills and human capital—aspects that are now even more central to professional success. Women and men may enter professions with clear and often differential ideas of what sorts of career opportunities and specialisations are appropriate for them as women and men (Bloksgaard 2011; Choroszewicz 2014).

While in numerical terms, women's share within professions has increased, in terms of substantive representation, the picture is more complex and less optimistic. Substantive representation refers to how women are represented across top positions—positions of power, prestige, and authority—within the professions (Riska 2008). Women are still under-represented at this level. There are also rising voices arguing that women's progress in professions has stalled in some Western countries (see e.g. Brenner 2014). The analysis of factors, processes, and practices that hold women back in substantive representation are multidimensional and complex, partly because they interlock with other social divisions, such as age and race/ethnicity, and partly because they are tied to specific socio-historical, organisational, and occupational contexts. These all pose particular challenges to current research on gender inequalities in professions.

To sum, gender shapes the organisation and experience of professional work, in complex and changing ways. This volume will contribute to our understanding of the ways in which contemporary professions continue to be gendered projects—in part by drawing attention to the intersection of gender with age, and a life course perspective.

Age, Cohort, and Generation

There has been little attention to the significance of age, cohort, or generation to professions and professional practice; however, with recent shifts to the age composition of the workforce, attention to age in work research has been revived (Kertzer 1983; Krekula 2007; Parry and Urwin 2011: 84; Schalk et al. 2010). This is particularly the case in management and organisational studies research. There has also been increased attention to generational differences in the workplace in recent years, with the entrance of the Millennial generation into the labour market, and emerging public attitudes that Millennial workers differ from their predecessors in many ways. Increased attention to age, cohort, and generation has been encouraged by the emergence of the life course perspective, which emphasises the significance of time, place, and cohort to one's experience of life's major events (Shanahan and Macmillan 2008).

Against misconceptions, 'age' is a complex concept, and it can be applied in diverse ways with numerous meanings and functions. Schalk and colleagues (2010: 78–80) combine some earlier typologies of age, which they organise on a continuum between age as an individual characteristic and as a characteristic of the environment. Among the age categories that they distinguish, the most relevant to the studies in this volume are chronological, organisational, and social ages:

1. Chronological age is an individual characteristic measured by the number of lived years. The distinction between younger and older workers is based on calendar age.

2. Organisational age is measured by the number of years in the same organisation or job. It can also refer to career stage.
3. Social age is a social marker of attitudes, norms, and expectations about appropriate behaviour, characteristics, and lifestyles expected of an individual at different ages.

Research has identified many barriers experienced by young workers in the labour force, including high rates of unemployment, underemployment, and discrimination from being stereotyped as unreliable and low-skilled (Foster 2013; Scheuer and Mills 2017: 49–50). Older workers are also subject to stereotypes and disadvantages in the labour force. Workers over fifty may be stereotyped as inflexible, unable to learn new things, and slower (Riach 2007; Scheuer and Mills 2017: 47–49). Those who lose their jobs in their fifties and sixties have more difficulty obtaining a new job than their younger counterparts (McMullin and Berger 2006). Thus, younger and older workers appear to face more difficulties; it is primarily those in their thirties and forties who seem most advantaged in the labour market (Riach 2007; Scheuer and Mills 2017; Thomas et al. 2014). Nonetheless, this can vary by career. In some jobs—such as those involving technology and computing—younger workers are valorised and by their mid-thirties, workers may be regarded as over-the-hill (Corbett in this volume; McMullin 2011). In contrast, in other careers, like academia, workers may not fully enter the labour market until they are in their thirties, and older workers may be held in high esteem (Hearn and Husu in this volume). Older workers may have the emotional capital needed for a job (Cottingham and Dill in this volume). They may also have more freedom from family responsibilities, and therefore, they tend to emphasise an individual capacity in managing work and family life (Choroszewicz in this volume; Olakivi and Wrede in this volume).

Age also influences career opportunities at career entry (Kay in this volume). The significance of organisational ages may also vary across sector, with loyalty and experience being rewarded in some fields, while in others there may be more benefit to changing jobs and work settings more frequently, to gain varied experience as well as to seek less hostile work environments and specialties (Adams in this volume; Adams and Kwon in this volume). Women are specifically vulnerable to experiencing multiple discrimination because of gender and age, which influences their employment trajectories and decisions to exit the profession (Boni-Le Goff, Le Feuvre, Mallard, Lépinard and Morel in this volume; Plickert in this volume). Women, among top earners, are still more likely to have lower wages than their male colleagues, even in countries with a reputation for gender equality (Magnusson and Nermo in this volume).

Age cohort and generation are also important concepts in research across the social sciences and humanities (Kertzer 1983; Mannheim 1952; Parry and Urwin 2011). 'Cohort' refers to 'a group of individuals born at the same time who are *presumed* to be similar as a result of shared experiences. Only chronological proximity to events and other drivers of difference are assumed to distinguish them from other cohorts' (Parry and Urwin 2011: 84). Different cohorts may have distinct life experiences, as these are shaped by social structures, norms, cultures, and institutions, which prevail at certain historical periods (Elder 1994: 6–7). While this definition of cohort might be similar to the definition of generation, there are some notable differences between these two concepts. Age cohorts are often narrow in size (Parry and Urwin 2011). For example, one might speak of birth cohorts, grouping everyone born in the same year or in a few-year span together, or focus on a cohort of graduates entering the labour force—for instance, everyone graduating from a professional programme in a defined span of time can be said to form a cohort. In contrast, generations are usually much broader, often grouping people born in a twenty-year span of time (Shanahan and Macmillan 2008).

In his 1952 essay, 'The Problem of Generations', Mannheim provides an excellent baseline for research on generations. Mannheim (1952) sees generation as a social location marked by shared birth years and distinctive historical events—common experiences that create a bond among members of the same generation. Categorisations of the major generational categories vary (see e.g. Parry and Urwin 2011: 89; Smola and Sutton 2002); however, four generations have been studied most: The Silent Generation/Traditionalists (born 1925–1945), Baby Boomers (born 1946–1964), Generation X (born 1965–1979), and Generation Y/ Millennials (born 1980–2000). It is believed that the shared events and experiences of these generations provide common ground for them to develop shared values, features, and attitudes.

The reviewed literature suggests that generations differ in terms of their work commitment, working arrangements, and work preferences, as well as attitudes to work–life balance. There are also considerable differences in gender relations at work and in family life, between generations. Generations X and Y are prone to experience more contradictions in the state of gender relations at work and in family models, and may be more conscious of gender equality discourse and policies (Niemistö et al. 2016).

In the literature on generations in the workplace, it is the Millennials (or Generation Y) who have been singled out for special attention (Foster 2016). Millennials tend to be more highly educated than other generations, on average, but upon entering the labour force, they face more precarity and polarised employment opportunities than their predecessors did. As the internet, digital communication technologies, and social media have been present from the start of their lives, they are regarded as 'digital natives' (Milkman 2017: 2). Perhaps because of these characteristics, Millennials are believed to enter the labour force with a different set of expectations, and this has led to criticisms from their colleagues from other generations (Foster 2013). Millennials have been criticised for being disrespectful, uncommitted, and holding unconventional work atti-tudes and behaviours (Laird et al. 2015; Ng et al. 2017). The differences between their approaches to work and those of the generations preceding them are believed to lead to potential workplace conflict and problems (Deyoe and Fox 2011).

Intersectionality, Age, and the Life Course

Intersectional theoretical approaches to social inequality explore how gender, race, and class intersect to shape social practices, organisation, and experience. Although gender, race, and class have each been seen as important structured systems of inequality in society, intersectionality research shows how the three are not separate, but actually 'simultane-ous processes of identity, institutional and social practice' (Holvino 2010: 249). Indeed, gender, race, and class are co-constructed, to the extent that they gain meaning through their interaction in particular organisational, institutional, and social-historical contexts (Acker 2006; Glenn 2002; Holvino 2010). For example, meanings of gender have been shown to vary across race and class, and perceptions of race vary across class and gender (Glenn 2002). To understand intersectionality in organisations, Acker (2006) has coined the term 'inequality regimes' to refer to the processes, practices, actions, and meanings that produce and reproduce class, gender, and racial inequalities in organisations. This concept has been taken up by many other researchers exploring patterns of inequality embedded within organisations.

Yet, research on intersectionality has rarely considered the role of age cohort (Krekula 2007: 163; McMullin 2011). Indeed, Acker (2006: 445) argues that while age is a 'significant basis for inequality' it is 'not . . . as thoroughly embedded in organizing processes as are gender, race, and class.' Moreover, while gender, race—and to some extent social class—are socially constructed, and hence subject to change, they are not as changeable as age, which by definition alters throughout one's lifetime. Nonetheless, it is the case that age intersects with other dimensions of inequality. Moreover, since gender norms, practices, and experiences vary across age, age may, in part, co-construct gender, and possibly other dimensions of inequality as well. To understand people's experiences, it is important to explore the intersection of age with other dimensions of inequality.

Only a limited body of research has explored the intersection of gender and age to document inequalities in the workforce (McMullin 2011). Although in most fields men have been seen to approximate the ideal worker best (Acker 1990), ideal worker norms are also shaped by age (McMullin 2011; Thomas et al. 2014). Those who 'transgress age norms—those who are the "wrong age" either too young or too old to correspond with the "ideal worker" profile' may face marginalisation and even job loss (McMullin 2011; Thomas et al. 2014: 1571). Age- and gender-based assumptions about ability to learn and competence can fundamentally shape opportunities for professional employment, promotion, and career success (McMullin 2011). In light of this literature, it is important to incorporate age into intersectional approaches.

One valuable means of bringing age in is through adopting a life course approach. Life course approaches highlight the importance of social pathways, social contexts, and change over time, and in so doing highlight the centrality of age, cohort, and generation (Elder et al. 2003; Shanahan and Macmillan 2008). The age cohort or generation one is born into, combined with their historical time period, major social events, social institutions and cultural norms, and social position (including social class, race, gender) shapes the course of their lives. Central concepts within the life course approach are 'trajectories' and 'transitions'. Trajectories are patterns of behaviour or achievement that occur over time (Shanahan and Macmillan 2008: 86). Career paths are trajectories, as is child-rearing. Transitions are changes in circumstances or roles. Graduating from school, or obtaining a new job are examples of transitions. Each transition or change is embedded within a broader trajectory, and a broader social context (Ibid). Our experiences of transitions can shape our trajectories. For instance, those embarking on careers during a recession experience this major life course transition quite differently from those who enter the labour force during good economic times and/or times of labour shortage. These initial differences lead to distinct career trajectories. Because transitions and trajectories are patterned and shaped by social-historical context, they vary across age cohort and generation (Elder 1994). The life course perspective thus draws attention to age cohort and generation, encouraging us to explore how individuals' experiences of key life course transitions shape their trajectories (Shanahan and Macmillan 2008).

Bringing intersectionality theory and a life course approach together allows us to not only look at the simultaneous processes and practices constructing gender, class, and racial inequalities, but explore how these vary across time and place, how transitions are implicated, and what trajectories result. Blending these approaches allows us to explore how gender, class, and race structure social pathways, and how our experiences along these pathways change as we age. Moreover, the life course approach brings into focus generational differences in experience. Therefore combining the life course and intersectionality approaches leads to a focus on how the interaction of gender, class, and race may differ across generations and age cohorts. Overall, adopting a life course lens facilitates exploration of the intersection of age, gender, and other dimensions of social inequality.

Drawing on the insights of the life course paradigm, and research on age cohort and generations, one would predict that the experiences of men and women entering professions decades ago would be potentially quite different from those entering more recently. As we have seen, professions have undergone significant changes in recent years, including the expansion of employment in large organisations, increased precarity, deregulation, and increased competition, to name only a few. What do these changes mean for the career trajectories of millennial workers, compared to their predecessors? How do they experience the transition towards establishing professional careers? These are questions to which research on professions has yet to find satisfactory answers.

This Volume: Themes and Objectives

This book explores men's and women's experiences of professional work and careers through an intersectional lens, by focusing on the intersection of gender and age. Gendered and age-related practices and processes are produced and reproduced in particular organisational, professional, and socio-cultural contexts, and they often impact women and men differentially. Each of the chapters acknowledges these influences either directly or indirectly. By examining these processes across professional groupings and national contexts, we enhance our understanding of the successful transition and integration of young professionals into the labour market. The explored cases reveal various logics and inequalities embedded within professions and the organisations in which professionals work, demonstrating cross-cultural similarities and differences. As many contemporary professions are at a crossroads, in terms of the way in which they educate and train their members as well as organise their work (Susskind and Susskind 2015), it is important to understand what the professions can learn from one another in these respects.

We acknowledge that dimensions of inequality other than gender and age are present, but they are not of primary focus here. Rather, our goal is to enhance the literature on the significance of gender to professional work, through a consideration of age and cohort/generation. As we have noted, age has been a largely neglected dimension in the study of professional work, as has the intersection between age and gender. In keeping with the life course perspective we focus predominantly on moments of key life course transitions across professional careers—the transition between school and work, entering the professional labour market, and building careers. Our core objectives in this book are as follows:

- to explore the changing significance of gender to young professionals' experiences and career paths as they enter professional work;
- to explore how gender and age intersect in shaping a matrix of privilege and disadvantage in professions;
- to explore the ways in which gender inequality is both reproduced and undermined through the activities of young professionals, and through their interactions with their more experienced colleagues; and

- to explore professional work cross-nationally (and across age) in Europe, the US, and Canada.

Each of the chapters in this volume addresses at least one of these objectives. Combined, the chapters shed light on the significance of age cohort/generation and gender to professional work, across professions and social context. Although the chapters represent separate studies examining various issues across professions and national contexts, several common themes emerged that deserve highlighting here.

1. Challenges for young professionals entering and building professional careers:
   Several chapters in this volume explore the challenges experienced by Millennials as they seek work and begin working in professions, and as they attempt to build careers. Studies highlight labour market challenges and difficulties embarking on careers (Adams; Kay), challenges with finding supportive mentors and choosing specialties that will allow for some work–life balance (Adams and Kwon), and the difficulties of acquiring the right professional demeanour, including specifically emotional capital and resistance towards stress (Cottingham and Dill; Olakivi and Wrede).
2. Work–family balance challenges within and across generations:
   A few chapters in this volume highlight the ways in which competing pressures of demanding careers and family life are particularly relevant for young men and women professionals who strive for more fluid gender roles in family life and careers. Yet, they are constrained in their efforts by professional ideals and structures, which rest upon traditional gender norms of masculinity and femininity. Studies highlight the influence of national and occupational gender regimes on lawyers' opportunities for work–life balance (Boni-Le Goff et al.), differential employment schedules of men and women lawyers as a function of workplace discrimination (Plickert), and increasing work–family balance challenges for Millennial men (Choroszewicz).
3. The shifting significance of gender to professional work:
   Chapters in this volume suggest that the gendering of professional work varies across time, professional grouping, and place. Men and women entering professions find a different landscape than their predecessors, and some gains have been made reducing the gender gap in earnings (Magnusson and Nermo), and in some instances work–family conflict (Adams); however, gender is still significant as men and women have different labour market opportunities and experiences of work environments (Adams; Corbett; Hearn and Husu), different experiences with social media use (Neville), and make different adjustments before and after they become parents (Boni-Le Goff et al.; Plickert).

Overall, the contributions in this volume provide rich insight into the individual strategies and tactics used by early career professionals to cope with structural inequalities. While these tactics and strategies are important coping mechanisms, in the concluding chapter we argue that they are insufficient to make these professions more inclusive for women and nascent generations of professionals. These strategies are also laborious and often invisible to others—especially to those in privileged positions. While some of these strategies do result in creating fissures in the professional practice, they are also resource-consuming, and thus they might further disadvantage these professionals in their careers.

The Chapters in This Volume

There are three sections in this book, each exploring professionals in different sectors. The first section explores workers in healthcare professions. The second focuses on workers in legal professions. The third considers other professional groups, with one chapter looking across professional groups and the others focused on engineers, information technology workers, and academics, respectively. All of the professional groupings discussed herein have been historically organised along gender lines, most as male-dominated professions, although a few were structured for women. Women have been entering male-dominated professions in recent decades—disrupting gender regimes, but not eliminating them.

The focus of the first section of the book is on health professions. In Chapter 2, Antero Olakivi and Sirpa Wrede examine the cultural and discursive resources that early career and experienced doctors in Finland use for mitigating and mobilising critical interpretations of their work. They show the ways in which the traditional ideals of a male medical profession in Finland are sustained by the inequality regimes that rest on the invisibility and the legitimacy of gendered and age-related inequalities. In Chapter 3, Tracey L. Adams and Eugena Kwon combine a gendered life course perspective with intersectionality to explore the medical specialty choices of young women pursuing medical careers. They find that gender, ethnicity, and age intersect to construct social expectations for womanhood and professional careers, leading women—especially young Asian women—to choose medical specialties perceived as more conducive to family and community life. In Chapter 4, Marci D. Cottingham and Janette S. Dill take up the issue of age-related dynamics and multigenerational conflict in the nursing profession. Their study reveals that younger nurses report feeling negative emotions more intensely compared to their Baby Boomer colleagues. Also, older nurses are more likely to evaluate their own care more highly overall and across a range of specific features of the job. Finally, in Chapter 5, Patricia Neville explores the role of social media, especially Facebook and Twitter, as a platform for young healthcare professionals to reproduce and to challenge inherent sexist assumptions in the profession. Neville also shows the ways in which social media is currently used by female professionals to present alternative and more gender-neutral perceptions about who can be a surgeon.

The second section of the book covers empirical research conducted on lawyers in five national contexts: Canada, the US, France, Switzerland, and Finland. In Chapter 6, Fiona M. Kay examines the factors that sort new lawyers into different work settings as they enter the legal labour market. Her study reveals that age, gender, and law school credentials surface as key determinants for lawyers' first jobs. New lawyers who are older than the typical graduate, women, and racial minorities are more likely to enter the public sector as well as solo practice and small firms than large law firms. In Chapter 7, Isabel Boni-Le Goff, Nicky Le Feuvre, Grégorie Mallard, Eléonore Lépinard, and Sandrine Morel analyse the interactions between gender relations at the societal level and at the occupational level to understand how they shape gendered career outcomes among young lawyers in France and Switzerland. They find that despite a less favourable gender regime and a greater motherhood penalty in Switzerland, Swiss women lawyers enjoy relatively similar career prospects as their French counterparts as a result of greater occupational opportunities to re-enter the profession. In Chapter 8, Gabriele Plickert investigates how perceptions of workplace discrimination shape women's and men's employment schedules across the early stages of their careers. Her research demonstrates that women in their mid-thirties to mid-forties report a relatively high incidence of discrimination, which negatively impacts their employment schedules in contrast to men. In Chapter 9, Marta Choroszewicz examines the ways in which male lawyers negotiate different concepts of fatherhood when they unfold their legal careers. The study shows that barriers that traditionally hindered women's career progress are currently also shared among some young male lawyers who do not necessarily want to organise their lives according to traditional gender norms. This disadvantages these men in their career progression in their organisations.

The third section includes a chapter on the gender wage gap across professions and three chapters that focus on engineers, information technology workers, and academics. In Chapter 10, Charlotta Magnusson and Magnus Nermo examine gender wage differences in highly prestigious professions over the span of forty years in Sweden—a country with a strong reputation for Nordic gender equality. The results reveal that while the share of young women in high-prestige professions and among top earners has increased since the 1960s, the gender wage gap remains relatively unchanged, in contrast to low and middle-high prestige occupations, where it decreased from about 10% to 23%. In Chapter 11, Jeff Hearn and Liisa Husu outline some prominent historical developments in the academic profession, across selected European countries. They argue that despite recent policy developments focusing on the entry into academic careers, a long, extended career entry phase remains dominant, and it specifically disadvantages young female academics. In Chapter 12, Christianne Corbett examines how workplace experiences among men and women technology workers vary at different ages. The study reveals that young men have the most positive experiences, and women of all ages have the least positive experiences. Women are particularly less likely to report the presence of a supportive manager, advancement and development opportunities, and manageable levels of stress. In Chapter 13, Tracey L. Adams explores experiences of discrimination among women in engineering across different age cohorts. Her study reveals that despite new equality initiatives in the Canadian engineering profession, women—especially in the youngest and oldest cohorts—experience sexism and discounting of their skills. To deal with less favourable working conditions, women develop numerous coping strategies including job exit.

In the concluding chapter, we summarise the theoretical contributions of the chapters and formulate an agenda for future research. We also advocate for more joint efforts made by educators, policymakers, professional associations, organisations, professional leaders, and professionals to build more inclusive work environments for women and nascent generations of professionals. The chapter ends with a section on policy recommendations for educators, professionals, professional organisations, as well as policy- and decision-makers. The aim of the final section is to enhance generational understanding, relationships, and collaboration in educational institutions, organisations, and professions.

References

Abbott, AD (1988) *The System of Professions: An Essay on the Division of Expert Labor* (Chicago, IL, University of Chicago Press).

Abel, RL (2003) *English Lawyers Between Market and State: The Politics of Professionalism* (New York, Oxford University Press).

Acker, J (1990) 'Hierarchies, Jobs, Bodies: A Theory of Gendered Organization' 4 *Gender & Society* 139. doi:10.1177/089124390004002002

——— (2006) 'Inequality Regimes: Gender, Class, and Race in Organizations' 20 *Gender & Society* 441, 445. doi:10.1177/0891243206289499

——— (2012) 'Gendered Organizations and Intersectionality: Problems and Possibilities' 31 *Equality, Diversity and Inclusion: An International Journal* 214. doi:10.1108/02610151211209072

Adams, TL (2000) *A Dentist and a Gentleman: Gender and the Rise of Dentistry in Ontario* (Toronto, University of Toronto Press). doi:10.3138/9781442670297

——— (2010a) 'Gender and Feminization in Health Care Professions' 4 *Sociology Compass* 454. doi:10.1111/j.1751-9020.2010.00294.x

——— (2010b) 'Profession: A Useful Concept for Sociological Analysis' 47 *Canadian Review of Sociology* 49. doi:10.1111/j.1755-618X.2010.01222.x

——— (2015) 'Sociology of Professions: International Divergences and Research Directions' 29 *Work, Employment & Society* 154. doi:10.1177/0950017014523467

——— (2017) 'Self-Regulating Professions: Past, Present and Future' 4 *Journal of Professions and Organization* 70. doi:10.1093/jpo/jow004

Biese, I and Choroszewicz, M (2018) 'Creating Alternative Solutions for Work: Experiences of Women Managers and Lawyers in Poland and the USA' in S Taylor and S Luckman (eds), *The 'New Normal' of Working Lives: Critical Studies in Contemporary Work and Employment* (London, Palgrave Macmillan).

Bloksgaard, L (2011) 'Masculinities, Femininities and Work—The Horizontal Gender Segregation in the Danish Labour Market' 1 *Nordic Journal of Working Life Studies* 5. doi:10.19154/njwls.v1i2.2342

Bolton, SC and Muzio, D (2007) 'Can't Live with 'Em; Can't Live Without 'Em: Gendered Segmentation in the Legal Profession' 41 *Sociology* 47. doi:10.1177/0038038507072283

Brenner, H (2014) 'Expanding the Pathways to Gender Equality in the Legal Profession' 17 *Legal Ethics* 261. doi:10.5235/1460728X.17.2.261

Carr-Saunders, AM and Wilson, PA (1933) *The Professions* (Oxford, Oxford University Press).

Choroszewicz, M (2014) 'Managing Competitiveness in Pursuit of a Legal Career: Women Attorneys in Finland and Poland' PhD dissertation (University of Eastern Finland, Joensuu).

Choroszewicz, M and Tremblay, D-G (2018) 'Parental Leave Policy for Male Lawyers in Helsinki and Montreal: Cultural and Professional Barriers to Male Lawyers' Usage of Paternity and Parental Leaves' 25 *International Journal of the Legal Profession* 303. doi:10.1080/09695958.2018.1456435

Connell, RW (1987) *Gender and Power: Society, the Person and Sexual Politics* (Cambridge, Polity Press).

Crompton, R (1987) 'Gender, Status and Professionalism' 21 *Sociology* 413, 428.

Davies, C (1996) 'The Sociology of Professions and the Profession of Gender' 30 *Sociology* 661, 671. doi:10.1177/0038038596030004003

Deyoe, RH and Fox, TL (2011) 'Identifying Strategies to Minimize Workplace Conflict Due to Generational Differences' 4 *Journal of Behavioral Studies in Business* 1.

Elder Jr., GH (1994) 'Time, Human Agency, and Social Change: Perspectives on the Life Course' 57 *Social Psychology Quarterly* 4, 6–7. doi:10.2307/2786971

Elder Jr., GH, Kirkpatrick Johnson, M and Crosnoe, R (2003) 'The Emergence and Development of Life Course Theory' in JT Mortimer and MJ Shanahan (eds), *Handbook of the Life Course* (New York, Kluwer Academic/Plenum Publishers).

Evetts, J (2011) 'A New Professionalism? Challenges and Opportunities' 59 *Current Sociology* 406. doi:10.1177/0011392111402585

——— (2013) 'Professionalism: Value and Ideology' 61 *Current Sociology* 778. doi:10.1177/0011392113479316

Faulconbridge, JR and Muzio, D (2012) 'Professions in a Globalizing World: Towards a Transnational Sociology of the Professions' 27 *International Sociology* 136. doi:10.1177/0268580911423059

Francis, A (2015) 'Legal Education, Social Mobility, and Employability: Possible Selves, Curriculum Intervention, and the Role of Legal Work Experience' 42 *Journal of Law and Society* 173. doi:10.1111/j.1467-6478.2015.00704.x

Francis, A and Sommerlad, H (2009) 'Access to Legal Work Experience and Its Role in the (Re)Production of Legal Professional Identity' 16 *International Journal of the Legal Profession* 63. doi:10.1080/09695950903204961

Foster, KR (2013) 'Generation and Discourse in Working Life Stories' 64 *The British Journal of Sociology* 195. doi:10.1111/1468-4446.12014

────── (2016) 'Generation as a Politics of Representation' 1 *International Journal of Work Innovation* 375. doi:10.1504/IJWI.2016.078642

Freidson, E (1986) *Professional Powers: A Study of the Institutionalization of Formal Knowledge* (Chicago, IL, University of Chicago Press).

────── (1994) *Professionalism Reborn: Theory, Prophecy and Policy* (Cambridge, Polity Press).

────── (2001) *Professionalism: The Third Logic* (Chicago, IL, University of Chicago Press).

Glenn, EN (2002) *Unequal Freedom: How Race and Gender Shaped American Citizenship and Labor* (Cambridge, MA, Harvard University Press).

Greenwood, E (1957) 'The Attributes of a Profession' 2 *Social Work* 45. doi:10.1093/sw/2.3.45

Gustafsson, S, Swart, J and Kinnie, N (2018) ' "They are your testimony": Professionals, Clients and the Creation of Client Capture During Professional Career Progression' 39 *Organization Studies* 73. doi:10.1177/0170840617708001

Hanlon, G (1998) 'Professionalism as Enterprise: Service Class Politics and the Redefinition of Professionalism' 32 *Sociology* 43. doi:10.1177/0038038598032001004

Hearn, J (1982) 'Notes on Patriarchy, Professionalisation and the Semi-Professions' 16 *Sociology* 184.

Hearn, J, Biese, I, Choroszewicz, M and Husu, L (2016) 'Gender, Diversity and Intersectionality in Professions and Potential Professions: Analytical, Historical and Contemporary Perspectives' in M Dent, IL Bourgeault, J-L Denis and E Kuhlmann (eds), *The Routledge Companion to the Professions and Professionalism* (London, Routledge).

Holvino, E (2010) 'Intersections: The Simultaneity of Race, Gender and Class in Organization Studies' 17 *Gender, Work & Organization* 248–249. doi:10.1111/j.1468-0432.2008.00400.x

Johnson, TJ (1972) *Professions and Power* (London, Palgrave Macmillan).

Kalleberg, AL (2009) 'Precarious Work, Insecure Workers: Employment Relations in Transition' 74 *American Sociological Review* 1. doi:10.1177/0003 12240907400101

Kertzer, D (1983) 'Generation as a Sociological Problem' 9 *Annual Review of Sociology* 125. doi:10.1146/annurev.so.09.080183.001013

Krekula, C (2007) 'The Intersection of Age and Gender: Reworking Gender Theory and Social Gerontology' 55 *Current Sociology* 155, 163. doi:10.1177/0011392107073299

Kuhlmann, E (2003) 'Gender Differences, Gender Hierarchies and Professions: An Embedded Approach to the German Dental Profession' 23 *International Journal of Sociology and Social Policy* 80. doi:10.1108/01443330310790525

Laird, MD, Harvey, P and Lancaster, J (2015) 'Accountability, Entitlement, Tenure, and Satisfaction in Generation Y' 30 *Journal of Managerial Psychology* 87. doi:10.1108/JMP-08-2014-0227

Larson, MS (1977) *The Rise of Professionalism: A Sociological Analysis* (Berkeley, University of California Press).

Law, MT and Kim, S (2005) 'Specialization and Regulation: The Rise of Professionals and the Emergence of Occupational Licensing Regulation' 65 *The Journal of Economic History* 723. doi:10.1017/S0022050705000264

Livingstone, D (2018) 'The Proletarianization of Professional Employees' Paper presented at the meetings of the International Sociological Association, Toronto, Canada, July 2018.

MacDonald, KM (1995) *The Sociology of the Professions* (London, Sage).

Mannheim, K (1952) 'The Problem of Generations' in P Kecskemeti (ed), *Essays on the Sociology of Knowledge* (London, Routledge and Kegan Paul).

McMullin, JA (ed) (2011) *Age, Gender, and Work: Small Information Technology Firms in the New Economy* (Vancouver, University of British Columbia Press).

McMullin, JA and Berger, ED (2006) 'Gendered Ageism/Age(ed) Sexism: The Case of Unemployed Older Workers' in TM Calasanti and KF Slevin (eds), *Age Matters: Realigning Feminist Thinking* (New York, Routledge).

Milkman, R (2017) 'A New Political Generation: Millennials and the Post-2008 Wave of Protest' 82 *American Sociological Review* 1–2. doi:10.1177/0003122416681031

Muzio, D, Brock, DM and Suddaby, R (2013) 'Professions and Institutional Change: Towards an Institutionalist Sociology of the Professions' 50 *Journal of Management Studies* 699. doi:10.1111/joms.12030

Ng, ES, Lyons, ST and Schweitzer, L (2017) 'Millennials in Canada: Young Workers in a Challenging Labour Market' in E Parry and J McCarthy (eds), *The Palgrave Handbook of Age Diversity and Work* (London, Palgrave Macmillan).

Niemistö, C, Hearn, J and Jyrkinen, M (2016) 'Age and Generations in Everyday Organisational Life: Neglected Intersections in Studying Organisations' 1 *International Journal Work Innovation* 353.

Noordegraaf, M (2011) 'Risky Business: How Professionals and Professionals Fields (Must) Deal with Organizational Issues' 32 *Organization Studies* 1349. doi:10.1177/0170840611416748

—— (2013) 'Reconfiguring Professional Work: Changing Forms of Professionalism in Public Services' 48 *Administration & Society* 783. doi:10.1177/0095399713509242

Noordegraaf, M and Steijn, B (eds) (2013) *Professionals Under Pressure: The Reconfiguration of Professional Work in Changing Public Services* (Amsterdam, Amsterdam University Press).

Parry, E and Urwin, P (2011) 'Generational Differences in Work Values' 13 *International Journal of Management Reviews* 79. doi:10.1111/j.1468-2370.2010.00285.x

Riach, K (2007) ' "Othering" Older Worker Identity in Recruitment' 60 *Human Relations* 1701. doi:10.1177/0018726707084305

Riska, E (2003) 'The Career and Work of Pathologists: A Gender Perspective' 23 *International Journal of Sociology and Social Policy* 59. doi:10.1108/01443330310790516

——— (2008) 'The Feminization Thesis: Discourses on Gender and Medicine' 16 *NORA—Nordic Journal of Feminist and Gender Research* 3. doi:10.1080/08038740701885691

——— (2014) 'Gender and the Professions' in WC Cockerham, R Dingwall and SR Quah (eds), *The Wiley Blackwell Encyclopedia of Health, Illness, Behavior, and Society* (Chichester, West Sussex: Wiley-Blackwell). doi:10.1002/9781118410868.wbehibs007

Saks, M (2015) *The Professions, State and the Market* (London, Routledge).

Schalk, R, van Veldhoven, M, De Lange, AH, De Witte, H, Kraus, K, Stamov-Roßnagel, C et al. (2010) 'Moving European Research on Work and Ageing Forward: Overview and Agenda' 19 *European Journal of Work and Organizational Psychology* 76, 78–80. doi:10.1080/13594320802674629

Scheuer, CL and Mills, JM (2017) 'Reifying Age-Related Employment Problems Through the Constructions of the "Problematic" Older and Younger Worker' in I Aaltio, AJ Mills and JH Mills (eds), *Ageing, Organisations and Management: Constructive Discourses and Critical Perspectives* (Cham, Switzerland, Palgrave Macmillan) 47–50.

Shanahan, MJ and Macmillan, R (2008) *Biography and the Sociological Imagination: Contexts and Contingencies* (New York, WW Norton and Co), 86.

Simpson, R, Ross-Smith, A and Lewis, P (2010) 'Merit, Special Contribution and Choice: How Women Negotiate Between Sameness and Difference in Their Organizational Lives' 25 *Gender in Management: An International Journal* 198. doi:10.1108/17542411011036400

Smola, KW and Sutton, CD (2002) 'Generational Differences: Revisiting Generational Work Values for the New Millennium' 23 *Journal of Organization Behavior* 363. doi:10.1002/job.147

Susskind, R and Susskind, D (2015) *The Future of the Professions: How Technology Will Transform the Work of Human Experts* (Oxford, Oxford University Press).

Thomas, R, Hardy, C, Cutcher, L and Ainsworth, S (2014) 'What's Age Got to Do with It? On the Critical Analysis of Age and Organizations' 35 *Organization Studies* 1569, 1571. doi:10.1177/0170840614554363

Tomlinson, J, Muzio, D, Sommerlad, H, Webley, L and Duff, L (2013) 'Structure, Agency and Career Strategies of White Women and Black and Minority Ethnic Individuals in the Legal Profession' 66 *Human Relations* 245. doi:10.1177/0018726712460556

Waring, J (2014) 'Restratification, Hybridity and Professional Elites: Questions of Power, Identity and Relational Contingency at the Points of "Professional—Organisational Intersection"' 8 *Sociology Compass* 688. doi:10.1111/soc4.12178

Witz, A (1992) *Professions and Patriarchy* (New York, Routledge), 6.

Section 1

Health Professions

2 Early Career Doctors and In/justice in Work

The Invisibility of Gender in a 'Male' Profession

Antero Olakivi and Sirpa Wrede

Introduction

In 2016, we interviewed 38 doctors at different career stages and in different professional settings in Finland for a study that targeted, among other things, the issue of clinical autonomy (Wrede et al. 2017).[1] When listening to the doctors from a gender perspective, we were somewhat surprised: despite the salient gendered divisions of labour in the Finnish medical field, the interviewed doctors seemed to almost avoid talking about the relevance of gender in their work and careers. To make sense of the invisibility of gender in our interview data, we turned to research on the 'gendering' of organisations. Rather than considering the superficial 'gender neutrality' of our co-constructed interviews to indicate the irrelevance of gender in the medical field, we assumed that all organisations constantly shape gendered inequalities and divisions of labour through policies, practices, culture and interactions (e.g. Acker 1990).

In line with critical studies of work organisation, we assume that, despite the growing proportion of female physicians in younger cohorts, middle-class masculinity continues to dominate over other career and work orientations in Finnish medical culture (also, Davies 1996). This culture of 'male' profession, we argue, values freedom from family responsibilities and thus may have problematic consequences for young doctors, particularly young mothers, whose childcare responsibilities can disproportionally limit their opportunities to perform the expected, normative, middle-class and masculine impressions of themselves as completely devoted to their work. In the context of a numerically 'feminised' profession, we argue that, by not problematising the organisation of work from a gender perspective, doctors can (sometimes tacitly and unwittingly) reproduce the masculinised career context of their profession.

In the following section, we discuss gendered and age-related inequalities within the Finnish medical profession that are expressed in related patterns of segregation within the profession and doctors' reports about work-related concerns and challenges. We then elaborate upon our theoretical position, drawing on the interactionist line of thought in the sociology of professions (see Riska 2010). From this perspective, we claim that while masculine expectations dominate within the culture of the medical profession, the *legitimacy* of the gendered and age-related structures within the profession is an interactional accomplishment and must be constantly negotiated and updated in discursive practice.

Our empirical analysis is presented with two slightly different foci associated with gendered and age-related inequalities in the organisation of work. First, we examine the issue of on-call shifts, which are common at hospitals. Through commitment on-call work, we argue, doctors can perform the 'right' kind of career orientation, the absence of which appears to be a legitimate excuse for non-advancement. Second, we analyse public health centres as a constraining work context, considering the problematic position of young doctors facing stressful and lonesome work and the cultural ideals that highlight individual and masculine endurance in health centres. These two foci are united by their relevance to young female doctors. In Finland, young (i.e. under 35 years of age) and female doctors are overrepresented in public health centres (Parmanne et al. 2016: 25–26). Young and early career doctors also work on call more often than their senior colleagues (Parmanne et al. 2016: 30). Moreover, doctors on call must often work at times that are inconvenient for young women dealing with family responsibilities (Kiianmaa 2012). The two foci allow us to tackle some of the most salient structural inequalities in the medical profession related to gender and age. Our focus on discursive practice allows us to argue that doctors' difficulty (and reluctance) to criticise these inequalities is an aspect of the hegemony of a specific, masculine understanding of medicine that tends to treat the difficulties faced by young and female doctors as inevitable and normal features of a demanding profession. We conclude by considering whether career systems that are built on such cultural 'contracts' are socially sustainable in the long haul.

A 'Feminised' and Numerically Expanding Profession

The male domination in the Finnish medical field may appear paradoxical since the feminisation of medicine (in numerical terms) has such a long history in Finland. The proportion of female doctors increased in Finland earlier than in any other Nordic or Anglo-American country (Riska and Wegar 1993; Riska 2001), and it keeps increasing. Although at the beginning of the 20th century practically all physicians in Finland were men, in 2016 60 per cent of Finnish physicians were women (Parmanne et al. 2016: 8).

Gender segregation, nevertheless, is a persistent feature of the Finnish medical profession. In 1964, Haavio-Mannila noted that, while there was an equal proportion of men and women in most types of medical work, men much more often combined their work with private practice.

She explained the figures by noting that most women doctors held double roles as doctors and as mothers and wives (Haavio-Mannila 1964: 12–14). In the early 1990s, Riska and Wegar (1993: 84) observed that female doctors were most often found in organisational settings characterised by a bureaucratic medical practice, relatively low degree of occupational autonomy, high degree of routinisation, low salary and low professional status compared to their male colleagues. To the authors, these divisions of labour were expressions of institutionalised 'glass ceilings' that hinder women's career advancement in the Finnish medical field (Riska and Wegar 1993). In the 2000s, the career advancement opportunities available to female doctors increased in Finland, causing a growing number of female physicians to hold administration, research and teaching positions. In particular, over the past two decades, the proportion of women serving as chief physicians has grown substantially (Parmanne et al. 2016: 27–29). Yet, the proportion of women among these decision-makers still does not equal the proportion of female practitioners.

In Finland, where medical education has constantly expanded since the Finnish government has sought to encourage more people to become doctors, female doctors are overrepresented in younger cohorts (Parmanne et al. 2016: 6–9). Some of the difficulties faced by female doctors regarding job content and hierarchical positioning may be related more to their early career stage and the patterns of practice associated with this stage than to their gender. In Finland, young doctors (i.e. those under 35 years of age) are overrepresented in public health centres (Parmanne et al. 2016: 26), making them more likely to experience precarious working conditions. On average, doctors working at public health centres report more problems—such as poorly functioning IT machinery, constant time pressure and lack of collegial support—than doctors at other workplaces, such as public hospitals and private clinics (Finnish Medical Association 2016).

Young doctors must work at public health centres; training for all medical specialties requires service at a health centre for nine months. Due to such compulsory elements it is not surprising that young doctors tend to report less autonomy at work than their older colleagues (Finnish Medical Association 2016). Young and female doctors also work while ill more frequently but take more sick leave as well: in 2015, 71 per cent of under 35-year-old female doctors took sick leave during the past 12 months, while only 39 per cent of 55–64-year-old male doctors took sick leave (Finnish Medical Association 2016). Some inequalities are more strongly related to gender than to age; for instance, female doctors tend to have more work overload and a higher risk of burnout than men, regardless of their age and workplace (Finnish Medical Association 2016).

The inequalities affecting young and female doctors described earlier are relatively well-known and have been reported in previous research—and recently, Finnish media (Järvi 2011; Paatero 2018; Piirainen 2018). Critical media coverage might signify a minor disjunction within the hegemonic culture of the medical profession. In particular, the Finnish association representing young doctors is increasingly critical of phenomena linked to gender- and age-related inequalities in medical professions (e.g. Paatero 2018; Piirainen 2018). Despite this criticism, the legitimacy and acceptability of divisions of labour seem to be maintained in the Finnish medical field. Young doctors in health centres and hospitals still report surprisingly low—and similar—levels of dissatisfaction with their work. In a 2013 survey (Sumanen et al. 2015: 45–48), only seven per cent of recently graduated doctors working at health centres and hospitals reported being somewhat or extremely dissatisfied in their current jobs. The majority of respondents (average age, 34) considered their current jobs to be their first choice and expected to hold similar jobs in 2025. Interestingly, the respondents' preferences were significantly gendered: women much more often preferred working at health centres (20 per cent of women versus 11 per cent of men). To an extent, doctors' personal preferences thus aligned with the existing career systems in Finnish medicine.

Based on the observations made earlier, one can speculate that many young doctors learn to adjust their individual expectations to match the options that are socially and practically available to them. For instance, health centres have much less need for on-call work than hospitals (Parmanne et al. 2016: 30). One could speculate that, since women perform a larger share of domestic responsibilities (e.g. childcare and housework) compared to men (Kiianmaa 2012), many young women 'choose' to pursue a career in health centres rather than in hospitals. This apparent alignment between individual expectations and existing career systems is an important source of social legitimacy for any liberal profession; the profession maintains an impression of a division of labour based on the free will and personal choice of individual actors rather than open, explicit and unjust exclusion of certain people (e.g. Olakivi 2018).

Previous commentators (Sumanen et al. 2015: 20) have also identified a culture of individual endurance in the Finnish medical field. In line with Davies' (1996) discussion of medicine as a 'male' profession, ideals of individual endurance can be interpreted as expressions of hegemonic masculinity. The ethos of individual endurance highlights and values doctors' ability to individually manage the difficulties they face. Consequently, this masculine ethos can individualise and privatise gendered and age-related problems in professions that might otherwise receive political and transformative attention. A doctor who talks about problems in her work, including precarious work environments or lack of collegial support, is liable to be stigmatised as an uncommitted or incompetent doctor who lacks the (masculine) abilities of self-management and endurance. Against this cultural background, it is not surprising that the challenges and obstacles faced by young and female doctors are not always explicitly articulated as public concerns that require intervention from professional agencies, not even by young and female doctors themselves.

Theoretical Perspective on Inequality Regimes in Medicine

In line with Acker (2006), gendered and age-related inequalities in the medical profession can be examined as elements of 'inequality regimes', that is, of the social processes and practices that create, make sense of and legitimate inequalities in work. Two dimensions of inequality regimes are particularly relevant to our study: the *visibility* and *legitimacy* of inequalities (Acker 2006). Inequalities are not always publicly visible and recognised as matters that require collective intervention. As Berbrier and Pruett (2006: 261) note, '[a]ny "inequality" may be recognized as real and existing, but still taken for granted as the inevitable, normal, and/ or functional means of distributing wealth, power, prestige, safety, and security, or anything else considered valuable'. Additionally, according to Acker (2006), societal change is more likely for social inequalities with high visibility and low legitimacy and less likely for inequalities with low visibility and high legitimacy.

From the cultural and discursive perspective we adopt in this chapter, the visibility and legitimacy of inequalities depend on the meanings that doctors collectively assign to the problems they—or some of them—face in their work (e.g. Harris 2006). By drawing on collectively recognisable values, narratives and identities as building blocks and resources of discursive practice, doctors can mobilise different interpretations of such problems (see Berbrier and Pruett 2006; Harris 2006). Some interpretations help doctors visualise illegitimate inequalities in their—or their colleagues'—work. Others construct inequalities as legitimate, natural and inevitable features of a demanding profession or diminish the importance of collective intervention by highlighting the importance of doctors' individual endurance. To doctors, some interpretations can be more affectively appealing than others, depending on how the profession articulates its collective values and desirable 'subject positions, or the ways in which professionals should conduct themselves' (Fournier 1999: 285). In a culture that values all actors' private responsibility and individual endurance, doctors' ability to demonstrate such qualities can amplify their sense of dignity and self-respect and, consequently, 'make their work tolerable, or even make it glorious to themselves and others' (Hughes 1984: 342). This can help doctors legitimate and accept environments that might otherwise be difficult to bear morally or materially.

Methods and Materials

Our empirical study involves interviews with 38 doctors in Finland. Half of the interviewees were recently graduated doctors with an average age of 34 years, and the other half were doctors with at least 20 years of clinical experience who were 60 years of age or older. Eighteen of the interviewees were women. We recruited the interviewees via the Finnish Medical Association, mostly by random sampling from the membership register. The interviewees worked at public health centres, public hospitals and private clinics in two large hospital districts in southern Finland. We mainly conducted the interviews at the interviewees' workplaces. The interviews were audio-recorded and transcribed verbatim. The extracts in this chapter were translated by the authors. In the extracts, square brackets indicate removed passages or the authors' additions.

Gender and age were not explicitly topicalised in the interview scheme apart from a question about potential differences in the 'work orientations' of doctors 'at different career stages, at hospitals and health centres'. Other questions and themes included doctors' relations with their colleagues, autonomy at work and work with patients.

In this chapter, we analyse selected parts of the data from a specific gender perspective. First, we analyse extracts in which doctors discuss the pressures and responsibilities of on-call work. Second, we analyse extracts in which doctors discuss the pressures and constraints of work at health centres. Our analysis demonstrates how the (mostly male but also female) doctors in our interviews were able to downplay the visibility of gendered and age-related injustice, to frame the position of young and female doctors as unavoidable, acceptable and tolerable, and to articulate the problems they face as individual, private and apolitical problems that do not require political reform (at least not from *within* the profession). We examine the interviews as examples of discursive practice in which the participants draw on cultural and discursive resources (e.g. values, narratives and identities) to offer collectively recognisable interpretations of their work while maintaining impressions of themselves as good doctors. Although our analysis is based on research interviews, doctors can—or must—draw upon similar (albeit not always the same) cultural and discursive resources in other contexts, including interactions with their colleagues.

Working on Call—Objective Obstacles and 'Personal Preferences'

Young and early career doctors who worked in hospitals often described working on call as a key source of stress (also, Wrede et al. 2017). Compared to work at health centres, hospital work involves more on-call duties, the majority of which are performed by early career doctors. In addition to causing stress, on-call duties can create gendered inequalities and divisions of labour in the medical profession. Many young women have a 'second shift' at home, which may be difficult to manage with the often inconvenient hours of on-call work.

In the interviews, we asked a question about on-call work in the form of a narrative vignette (see Hughes and Huby 2012):

> You are working in a unit in which on-call work is an essential part of the functions. Doctors' collective bargaining contract defines on-call work as a duty of doctors. Because working on call is a duty of doctors, on-call shifts must be divided equally and justly, which is also the view of the [Finnish] Medical Association. Some colleagues in your unit have reasonable causes for not wanting to work on call. This situation creates problems for the division of on-call shifts in the unit. What do you think about the situation?

We asked the interviewees to discuss the vignette from different perspectives. Literally, the vignette invited them to not only elaborate on reasonable causes for not wanting to work on call but also define 'equal' and 'just' distribution of on-call work. According to a cultural ideal often invoked in the interviews, equal and just division of on-call work means *numerical* equality (i.e. all doctors in a unit have an equal share of on-call shifts). This ideal, however, was not blindly supported by most participants; most acknowledged some reasonable causes for not wanting to work on call. A 37-year-old male participant from a private clinic reflects upon these causes.

PARTICIPANT 2: If the reasonable cause is that there is a colleague who has bipolar disorder and staying awake at nights makes her/him[2] mentally unbalanced, then s/he does not work on call. We—other colleagues—take care of it and it's understandable. [. . .] Then, if there is someone who has young children and who just wants to be at home with them and has selected a field [of medicine] that includes working on call, then no-can-do. Then you must work on call. Or you must change your field or workplace. I don't think these are very complex issues in the end. People know that it is part of their job when they select a field in which people work on call. If it doesn't fit your life situation, you must make your own arrangements. For instance, you can work somewhere else when the children are small.

In the interviews, many participants clearly distinguished between cases in which one is *objectively unable* to work on call and one simply *prefers not to* for understandable but illegitimate reasons. Participant 2 constructs this kind of distinction between a doctor with a medical condition and one who has young children. In this line of reasoning, having young children may result in (gendered) divisions of labour in the medical profession that are natural and legitimate because they depend on doctors' private choices, that is, their allegedly private choices to, first, have children and, second, 'be at home with them'.

To some interviewees, however, the above simple and, one might argue, gender-blind way of viewing the demands of on-call work did not seem entirely appropriate. These interviewees gave more nuanced answers to the vignette and more reflexive impressions of themselves but, oftentimes, came to the same conclusion as Participant 2. In the following extract, a 63-year-old male doctor who primarily fulfils an administrative role elaborates on the vignette from multiple perspectives.

PARTICIPANT 14: There are pretty clear rules. There is age and . . . I mean the age after which working on call decreases or ends according to the rules. But, of course, in real life [. . .] there are always those who complain, 'why so much on-call work' and so on. But I don't know. Then it's part of the human resource management skills of the leader to build the kind of unit in which people participate in on-call work in decent ways but in which different life situations are also taken into consideration. There can, of course, be like, for instance, a woman doctor who has recently become a single mother of young children or something like that. I assume that people will understand it [i.e. not working on call] then. But it is a question of leadership, how to take care of it. In general, doctors' willingness to work on call [*päivystyshalukkuus* in Finnish] has decreased.

In the extract, the participant begins by highlighting that there are 'pretty clear rules' but then moves on to make exceptions to these rules because, in 'real life', there are always those who complain about working on call. Instead of describing clear rules, he ends up highlighting the importance of reflexive leadership and consideration of different life situations as a way of solving potential problems. The example of 'a woman doctor who has recently become a single mother of small children' demonstrates a degree of reflexivity and awareness of gendered issues. This may be related to the contemporary demand for doctors, particularly those in supervisory positions, to demonstrate (a degree of) gender awareness in the medical profession and to avoid impressions of exclusion and inequality. The example of a *recent* single mother is, however, clearly marked as a special case that 'people will understand'. Evidently, family responsibilities are not normally understandable and legitimate reasons for not working on call. Finally, at the end of the extract, after demonstrating understanding and reflexivity, the participant invokes a novel theme: contemporary doctors' decreasing willingness to work on call.

Young doctors' (alleged) unwillingness to work on call was a common topic in our interviews with senior doctors. Occasionally, the interviewed doctors demonstrated a degree of sympathy towards such unwillingness and its gendered dimensions. Participant 14, for instance, commented on some women's unwillingness to work on call: 'If you have children at home, then you have some worries going through your mind about those things [i.e. the children] [. . .] and you are away from home, then the desirability of working on call is not that great'. In this line of reasoning, unwillingness to work on call was psychologically understandable but, ultimately, not a professionally legitimate reason to not work on call (or even to reduce the amount of on-call work). Ultimately, the burdens of on-call work were private problems of female doctors' (and their families), not issues that would require collective action. Regardless of the (superficial) reflexivity and understanding that these participants tried to demonstrate (in their talk), when it came to actual calls for transformative action, gender-blind work arrangements remained untouched.

Finally, not all doctors demonstrated understanding of young doctors' (allegedly) decreasing willingness to work on call. For many interviewees, this unwillingness signified young doctors' corrupt interests, lack of professional devotion or inability to manage their private lives (also, Wrede et al. 2017). In the following account, a 61-year-old male doctor from a private clinic considers having young children to not be a reason to avoid working on call.

PARTICIPANT 37: In my youth, when I had just graduated, it [i.e. having young children] wasn't a reason at all for not working on call. People worked on call even when they had young children. Childcare was just arranged in one way or another. It's a contemporary thing, that they [i.e. young doctors] use it as a reason. It is difficult for me to understand, since I don't have children, and if I had, they'd be adults already and I'd have lived through the time when childcare was arranged in such a way that people were able to work on call. I find it difficult to place myself in the position of these present-day fathers and mothers and to view things from their perspective.

In the extract, the participant demonstrates a seemingly genuine inability to understand the contemporary position of young doctors with children. In his youth, childcare was arranged, although the actors who arranged it remain unspecified or taken for granted in the extract. Overall, his account casts a shadow of doubt over young doctors' abilities, ethics and interests, implying they 'use' childcare as a reason, that is, an excuse, for not working on call. This reason, according to Participant 37, is not understandable or legitimate. At the end of the extract, the participant highlights his gender-neutral—or gender-blind—perspective on the issue at stake, mentioning both male and female doctors who use childcare as a reason to avoid working on call. The gendered aspect of the topic is thus tacitly denied.

In this discursive context, it is hardly surprising that young mothers find it difficult to criticise the medical system, which reproduces a culture of hegemonic masculinity. Such criticism is liable to be misinterpreted by senior (and male) doctors. Consequently, many young mothers end up working in seemingly less masculine contexts, such as public health centres.

The Health Centre as a Constraining Work Environment

In comparison to working at hospitals, balancing family and work can be easier while working at health centres, at least in part due to the more limited amount of on-call work. Compared to hospitals, public health centres indeed employ more women and early career doctors. In this section, we examine how young doctors working at public health centres described their work in the interviews, including the problems they encountered. In line with previous research, many young doctors described public health centres as professionally constraining and difficult work environments (also, Wrede et al. 2017). In line with previous research, they were also willing to accept personal responsibility for the problems they faced. In the following extract, a 32-year-old male doctor describes public health centres as workplaces in which doctors have few resources and little support.

INTERVIEWER: Have you noticed any differences between doctors' work orientations, between, for instance, doctors at different career stages, in hospitals, health centres and private practices, or between women and men? And if so, what kinds of differences? [. . .]

PARTICIPANT 24: I feel that young doctors take their work more personally, which usually leads to a greater mental burden. [. . .] A young doctor is usually very careful, very cautious and very thorough. At least that's what I would argue, on average. I am not necessarily saying that this is always the case. But what it leads to is that every patient is potentially dying right now and you must concern yourself with a whole lot of things. [. . .] I cannot say there are any significant overall differences between male and female colleagues. [. . .] But then if you think about hospitals versus health centres, then only a few have liked health centres. Usually it's because of the feeling of insecurity that is much more common in here [i.e. health centres], the lack of resources, that you have a constant hurry, that you do not necessarily get the kind of support that you usually get in special health care, at the lunch table for instance. We do not necessarily have time to eat lunch in here. So, young doctors are normally afraid of health centres because you are alone in there. My own view is that, now, when I have practically only worked in well-functioning health centres, in my opinion it has been amazing and the only burdens there are have been my own constructions. It's me who decides how many patients I meet, and it is me who decides how carefully I examine them.

In the extract, the participant—together with the interviewer—draws on different collectively recognisable interpretations of the position of young doctors at public health centres. On the one hand, he highlights the objective difficulties of his work at a public health centre (i.e. the lack of resources and support). On the other hand, he highlights his own and other young doctors' individual agency: young doctors tend to be mentally overburdened because they are deliberate and devoted and tend to take their work personally—that is, not because of the external and objective pressures they face, but because of their internal and subjective orientations. The extract thus exemplifies the ambivalent position of young and early career doctors at public health centres. On the one hand, young doctors have well-established cultural and discursive resources with which they can mobilise critical interpretations of their position and work at public health centres. On the other hand, the masculine culture of individual endurance can encourage young doctors to emphasise their own agency and responsibility for managing the problems they face—also as a source of pride and prestige. Ultimately, young doctors can end up reproducing a culture that privatises and undermines these problems as their own constructions. Participant 24's ability to bring up problems in his work while simultaneously assuring his audience—and perhaps himself—of the completely manageable and tolerable nature of these problems (at least in the particularised context of 'well-functioning health centres') is striking. Evidently, a good way for young doctors to raise awareness of problems in their work is, paradoxically, to highlight that these problems are not 'real' problems at all—at least not for themselves. Otherwise, young doctors risk losing their credibility as competent, trustworthy and self-managing professionals who can manage demanding work. In such a discursive context, presenting substantial criticism of the organisation of work can be extremely difficult. When voicing out criticism, victim blaming is a constant threat.

In the following extract, a 30-year-old woman doctor describes problems in her work at a health centre, including a lack of resources. Like Participant 24, she highlights the importance of self-management.

INTERVIEWER: Have you noticed any differences between doctors' work orientations, between, for instance, doctors at different career stages, in hospitals, health centre and private practices, or between women and men?

PARTICIPANT 15: Well, I guess differences are inevitable if you think about the people at our workplace, for instance. Of course, young doctors. . . . [. . .] Also, when I had just graduated, the amount of work felt, how should I put it, somehow more overwhelming. Everything is, of course, more difficult [when you have just graduated]. . . . You must concern yourself with everything. And you don't have the kind of touch that you get from experience. [. . .] There can be a kind of insecurity in respect to your own skills. And then, on the other hand, the way you manage with this insecurity. [. . .] Personally, I already belong to specialising [doctors] at this stage [of my career], so it kind of varies day by day. [. . .] It depends on the number of doctors in the roster and a bit on the season, how burdensome the work is. In the wintertime, for instance, when lot of people have the flu and a lot of doctors are away and their kids are sick, and the patients have the same thing, then it can be quite burdensome and tiring. And, when I have talked to my colleagues at this same career stage, it does come up occasionally, that you might want to do something else. Sometimes you think about it, half seriously, that, gosh, I'm gonna switch to another trade and do something completely different.

Like Participant 24, Participant 15 describes her work as potentially burdensome and relates this burden to a particular career stage; she claims that young doctors *inevitably* face more difficulties at work. Like Participant 24, Participant 15 tries to assure her audience—and perhaps herself—that these difficulties no longer concern her since she has learnt to manage her work and insecurity. In this way, she can distance herself from the professionally precarious (and stigmatised) identity of a young doctor. Significantly, after adopting the identity of a specialising doctor in the extract, she seems to receive a whole new right to complain. As a *young* doctor, she needed to concern herself with everything and learn how to manage her work. As a *specialising* doctor, she can complain that her work is burdensome and tiring and ask for more interesting tasks beyond caring for patients with the flu in a precarious context in which doctors are overburdened with private responsibilities (i.e. childcare). As a *specialising* doctor, she can even consider resigning from her profession. Later in the interview, she expresses a fear of stagnation:

PARTICIPANT 15: Specialisation is, of course, nice. But, in a sense, when you have completed your specialisation, then it's not so easy to get anywhere, to work periods in hospitals, train yourself, try something different, acquire knowledge. They would like to keep those specialised doctors stuck here a little bit, stuck in a health centre. At least, people have had that kind of experiences.

The participant does not name any identifiable actor at a health centre or hospital that is keeping her at the health centre. By referring to 'people' in the last sentence, however, she implies that other doctors also experience the problems she describes.

The preceding extracts introduce some of the dilemmas associated with the cultural situation of young doctors working at public health centres. First, among young doctors, working at a health centre is recognised as less prestigious and more precarious than working in a hospital. Second, the identity of a young doctor is easily stigmatised in the medical field. In the interviews, early career doctors often distanced themselves from the stigmatised identity of a young doctor by highlighting their age or career stage as a positive sign of devotion or precision, even at the expense of their own well-being, or by highlighting their ability to manage themselves and their insecurities. In a masculine culture of individual endurance, these professional self-presentations are, evidently, sources of (self-)respect and prestige. For young doctors, they are understandable—and perhaps necessary—discursive strategies. Simultaneously, the constant emphasis on individual endurance can hinder young doctors from critiquing the problems they face. Instead of presenting critique, a good doctor presents self-management. In addition, for many young doctors, it is difficult to name professional or political actors that are responsible for the problems they face. The specific reasons for career stagnation, for instance, are also not always easy to identify.

Discussion and Conclusions

Young and female doctors in Finland face multiple constraints and challenges in their work and careers (also, Wrede et al. 2017). However, our analysis shows that doctors' discursive practice does not always recognise these constraints and challenges as markers of illegitimate, gendered or age-related inequality that self-evidently requires collective intervention. Instead of attributing the difficulties faced by many young and female doctors to the illegitimate structures of a masculine and middle-class profession, doctors' discursive practice tends to construct these difficulties as natural and inevitable features of a demanding profession. Furthermore, doctors' discursive practice tends to highlight people's private and individual responsibility for overcoming the difficulties they face. To many young doctors, individual responsibility, endurance and self-management are key sources of prestige and self-respect and ways to avoid the stigma associated with young doctors.

For individual doctors, highlighting individual endurance is understandable in a discursive context that values such endurance. At the same time, we observe tensions that are relevant to the future of career systems in the Finnish medical field. The social sustainability of a career system that supports the dominant 'male' culture of medical professions is problematic for all doctors who are unable or unwilling to conform to traditional masculine norms, such as freedom from family responsibilities. Furthermore, in the current career system, work at health centres is not highly regarded, and remaining there in the long term is commonly interpreted as career stagnation. This is a situation predominantly faced by female doctors. In a culture that highlights all actors' private responsibility, these women may also lack the resources to mobilise critiques over their slower career progress. In the discursive practice of a 'male' profession, these women are not necessarily considered to be unjustly excluded from higher-ranked and prestigious jobs. Rather than illegitimate results of objective obstacles, their career paths can be considered legitimate results of their personal interests, preferences or lifestyle choices, such as their 'unwillingness' to work inconvenient hours. Men, however, tend to be able to make the choice to have a family without negatively impacting their career advancement. A culture that views family responsibilities as private business does not recognise this discrepancy as a problem that requires a collective response.

The traditional ideals of the 'male' profession of medicine seem to persist. Currently, however, traditional masculine ideals may not be accepted without negotiation and potential counter-arguments. In a recent survey, the ability to balance work and family was revealed to be one of the most important values to Finnish doctors, predominantly those who are young and female (Finnish Medical Association 2018). The way the interviewees discussed dilemmas associated with on-call work, moreover, demonstrated a lack of consensus within the medical profession regarding work–family balance (see Wrede et al. 2017). While the traditional expectations of the 'male' profession of medicine are still powerful, it seems that these expectations can no longer be endorsed without at least superficial demonstrations of reflexivity, without considering alternative ideals, and without potential controversies among doctors in Finland. Also, the disadvantaged position of young doctors in Finland has recently gained increasing media coverage. Clearly, actors in the Finnish medical field must start discussing these issues in greater depth.

Based on our analysis, we can envision alternative outcomes concerning the social sustainability of career systems within the medical field in Finland. First, career systems in the medical field can be made more diverse and inclusive in terms of accommodating diverse family arrangements and combining work at hospitals and health centres. Besides transformation of the structural organisation of work, this change will require evolution of the cultural ideals and expectations of the medical profession. It is likely that some (male) actors who have benefited from the masculine organisation and culture of the medical profession will oppose these changes. Second, the divisions of labour in the medical profession can remain gendered, the career systems can remain exclusive and balancing family and work can remain difficult. In this case, a crucial question is, how does the medical profession maintain the social legitimacy of these divisions of labour and career systems among its members? For how long can young and female doctors remain satisfied and tolerate the difficulties they face in their work and careers? Currently, this legitimacy, satisfaction and tolerance seem somewhat strong, but there is underlying discontent. Whether—or perhaps when—this discontent will result in political action remains to be seen.

Notes

1 Two research assistants, Noora Fischer and Anton Sigfrids, performed the interviews as part of a research project funded by the Finnish Medical Association and independently executed by the University of Helsinki (PI Sirpa Wrede). The work of the first author was also supported by the Ella and Georg Ehrnrooth Foundation and the Academy of Finland (#312310).
2 In Finnish, pronouns are gender neutral.

References

Acker, J (1990) 'Hierarchies, Jobs, Bodies: A Theory of Gendered Organizations' 4 *Gender and Society* 139.
——— (2006) 'Inequality Regimes: Gender, Class, and Race in Organizations' 20 *Gender and Society* 441.
Berbrier, M and Pruett, E (2006) 'When Is Inequality a Problem? Victim Contests, Injustice Frames, and the Case of the Office of Gay, Lesbian, and Bisexual Student Support Services at Indiana University' 35 *Journal of Contemporary Ethnography* 257.
Davies, C (1996) 'The Sociology of Professions and the Profession of Gender' 30 *Sociology* 661.
Finnish Medical Association (2016) 'Lääkärin työolot ja terveys 2015. Kyselytutkimuksen tuloksia'. www.laakariliitto.fi/site/assets/files/1266/l_k_rin_ty_olot_ja_terveys_2015_tuloksia.pdf
——— (2018) Unpublished survey data.
Fournier, V (1999) 'The Appeal to "Professionalism" as a Disciplinary Mechanism' 47 *The Sociological Review* 280.
Järvi, U (2011) 'Naislääkäreillä kivinen tie professoreiksi' 66 *Lääkärilehti* 2228.
Haavio-Mannila, E (1964) *Lääkärit tutkittavina* (Helsinki, University of Helsinki).
Harris, SR (2006) 'Social Constructionism and Social Inequality: An Introduction to a Special Issue of JCE' 35 *Journal of Contemporary Ethnography* 223.
Hughes, EC (1984) *Sociological Eye: Selected Papers* (New Brunswick, Transaction Books).
Hughes, R and Huby, M (2012) 'The Construction and Interpretation of Vignettes in Social Research' 11 *Social Work and Social Sciences Review* 36.
Kiianmaa, N (2012) *Tasa-arvobarometri 2012* (Helsinki, Ministry of Social Affairs and Health).
Olakivi, A (2018) *The Relational Construction of Occupational Agency: Performing Professional and Enterprising Selves in Diversifying Care Work* (Helsinki, University of Helsinki).
Paatero, J (2018) 'Ettei homma tökkisi' 2 *Nuori Lääkäri*. www.nly.fi/artikkeli/ettei-homma-tokkisi.

Parmanne, P, Ruskoaho, J and Vänskä, J (2016) *Lääkärit Suomessa. Tilastotietoja lääkäreistä ja terveydenhuollosta 2016* (Helsinki, Finnish Medical Association).

Piirainen, J (2018) 'Kiusaamista, nöyryyttämistä, solvaamista ja savustamista—nuoret lääkärit kertovat alalla vuosia jatkuneesta asiattomasta käytöksestä' *YLE*. https://yle.fi/uutiset/3-10102659

Riska, E (2001) 'Towards Gender Balance: But Will Women Physicians Have an Impact on Medicine?' 52 *Social Science and Medicine* 179.

Riska, E (2010) 'Health Professions and Occupations' in WC Cockerham (ed) *The New Blackwell Companion to Medical Sociology* (West Sussex, John Wiley & Sons).

Riska, E and Wegar, K (1993) 'Women Physicians' in E Riska and K Wegar (eds) *Gender, Work, and Medicine: Women and the Medical Division of Labour* (London, Sage Publications).

Sumanen, M, Vänskä, J, Heikkilä, T, Hyppölä, H, Halila, H, Kujala, S, Kosunen, E, Virjo, I and Mattila, K (2015) *Lääkäri 2013. Kyselytutkimus vuosina 2002–2011 valmistuneille lääkäreille* (Helsinki, Ministry of Social Affairs and Health).

Wrede, S, Olakivi, A, Fischer, N and Sigfrids, A (2017) *Autonomia ja ammatillisuus käytännön lääkäreiden näkökulmasta* (Helsinki, Finnish Medical Association).

3 'Not That Many Female Med Students Want to Pursue Surgery'

Gender, Ethnicity, and the Life Course in Medical Students' Specialty Choices

Tracey L. Adams and Eugena Kwon

Introduction

In the West, women have been moving into the traditionally male-dominated medical profession in larger numbers (Babaria et al. 2012; Boulis and Jacobs 2008; Heru 2005). In Canada, women currently compose 41% of medical doctors (CIHI 2016). The medical profession is also becoming more ethnically diverse in Canada: more doctors now claim racial/ethnic minority backgrounds (Cooke 2017). The latter trend is encouraged by the immigration of foreign-trained doctors: currently 26% of medical doctors in Canada are foreign-trained (many of these doctors are also women) (Boulis and Jacobs 2008; CIHI 2016; Dolishny 2012). These demographic shifts promise change within the medical profession, but studies show that the ideal image of a medical doctor is still male and White. Women—and especially minority women—continue to face challenges in the medical field (Bhatt 2013; Cassell 1998; Cooke 2017; Murti 2014; Riska 2011; Seemann et al. 2016).

These challenges may be reflected in women medical students' specialty choices. There is evidence that women still shy away from staunchly male-dominated fields like surgery, and instead are drawn to fields viewed as more family-friendly, like family medicine (Cassell 1998; CIHI 2016; Hinze 1999). Moreover, research suggests that this internal sex segregation within the medical profession is not simply the result of preference, but that there are structural forces pushing women away from some medical specialties, and towards others (Heitkamp et al. 2017; Kwon 2017). Studies have highlighted discrimination, hostile work environments, skill discrediting, and lack of mentorship that, combined with the 'clockwork of male careers' (Hochschild 2003), shape women's career pathways and choices (Beagan 2001; Colletti et al. 2000; Heitkamp et al. 2017).

Despite a fairly large body of research exploring women's experiences in medicine, few studies have adopted an explicitly intersectional lens to consider how gender, ethnicity, and age cohort combine to shape the specialty choices of young women embarking on professional careers. This chapter contributes to the literature on women in medicine by combining intersectional approaches with the life course paradigm, to identify the factors affecting medical students' career decision-making. In the first part of the chapter, we provide an overview of our theoretical influences. In the second part of the chapter, we present findings from our interviews with 15 White and Asian women medical students and residents about their specialty choices. Ultimately, we show that women in medical training face structural barriers and gendered life course pressures that shape their specialty choices, but that the experiences of Asian and White women differ slightly, with Asian women reporting more challenges.

Gender and the Life Course

Under the life course paradigm, scholars see the life course as 'age-graded patterns that are embedded in social institutions and history' (Elder et al. 2003: 4). Life course scholars study the social pathways people traverse as they live their lives. These pathways are historically patterned, institutionalised trajectories that carry people through various roles, opportunities, and events, and shape their life experiences (Elder et al. 2003; Shanahan and Macmillan 2008). Along these pathways individuals experience many transitions and key turning-points—for example, finishing school and embarking on a career, or getting married and having a child. One's experiences of these transitions and turning points can shape one's subsequent life trajectories significantly. For example, individuals entering the labour force during an economic downturn will have notably different career and life experiences than those entering when the economy is booming and jobs are plentiful. Those who have children very early in life will have different pathways than those who have children later, or those who have no children at all. Given the importance of social-historical context for transitions and turning points, life course scholars often focus on age cohorts. Cohorts 'link age and historical time' (Elder et al. 2003: 9); those born within a few years of each other experience historical events and key transitions around the same time, at the same age, leading to shared life experiences that can potentially produce commonalities in outlook and opportunities.

This perspective easily lends itself to a study of young woman embarking on medical careers. The women in our study are experiencing a key transition at a time when the medical profession is more welcoming of women than in the past. At the same time, for many of these women, other key transitions are anticipated in the not-too-distant future—getting married, having children, and raising families. In this sense, they may have different experiences than young men entering the profession alongside them. The *gendered life course perspective* (Moen 2011; Scott et al. 2012) is a variation of the life course paradigm that illuminates how women's life trajectories—especially in terms of work and family—may be gendered and shaped differently from men's. Young women entering professions may anticipate that their future family roles will conflict with their work roles. Their career (and family choices) may be made with the aim of minimising work–family conflict. Therefore, gendered expectations across the life course can lead men and women to make different career choices (Moen 2011; Vespa 2009). Women's life course has traditionally been family-oriented, with paid work as a secondary activity (Scott et al. 2012). Even though our society is more gender egalitarian than in the past, women's identities may still remain tied to marriage and motherhood (Sharp and Ganong 2007, 2011). Women pursing professional careers may be highly career-oriented, but family care obligations remain institutionalised as women's work (Moen 2011). Thus, many women pursuing professional careers may anticipate that their family responsibilities will, at least at some point, conflict with career expectations. According to Allison and Ralston (2018), anticipated concerns about work–life balance can alter women's career pathways. In this manner, young women entering highly demanding professional fields, like medicine, may believe it will be too difficult for them to 'do it all,' resulting in them sacrificing career goals, family goals, or both (Gayle et al. 2012; Moen 2011).

Pressures are particularly intense for women, not only because it is expected that they will take the lead with child-rearing, but also because of societal norms concerning *when* they should marry and have children. Marriage and parenthood are seen as essential developmental milestones for transition to complete adulthood, and it is expected that they will be completed according to a socially prescribed timetable (Crosnoe and Muller 2014; Elder et al. 2003; Marshall and Muller 2003). Despite the fact that the life course of today's generation has become less standardised than in the past, there is still an expectation that women will marry and have children in their late twenties and early thirties. Negative sanctions are often imposed for 'offtime' or missed transitions (Elder et al. 2003; Marshall and Muller 2003). Those who follow non-conventional, less-ordered pathways experience greater social stigma (Poortman and Liefbroer 2010); this is especially the case for women (DePaulo and Morris 2005). For example, studies have shown that women who remain single past the normative age for marriage are subjected to negative social stigmas, which can lead to stress (Sharp and Ganong 2011).

For women pursuing professional careers like medicine, the years of core career building coincide with the expected years of family building. Both men and women entering medicine experience this potential role conflict, but women experience more stress from the conflict (DePaulo and Morris 2005). While women may aim to get married and have children between 25 and 35 (Howe 2012; Sharp and Ganong 2007), men are

44   *Tracey L. Adams and Eugena Kwon*

not under the same biological constraints and hence appear to experience less stress and anxiety from delayed marriage and parenthood.

Nevertheless, women in medicine face more than life course constraints. Research has identified discrimination and a masculine work environment as additional barriers (Beagan 2001; Cassell 1998; Cooke 2017). Moreover, women in medicine feel they receive less mentoring and/or fewer professional opportunities than their male counterparts (Colletti et al. 2000). The lack of women mentors in high-status specialties like surgery may deter women from these areas of practice (Baxter et al. 1996; Riska 2011). Structural barriers may combine with life course expectations to stream women into different medical specialties than their male counterparts.

A gendered life course perspective reveals how the social meanings of age and time differ for men and women: their lives run on different social timetables (Settersten 2003). Gendered life courses, along with gendered organisations that disadvantage women, combine to shape women's career experiences and career trajectories. Although research has shown how organisations are not only gendered, but racialised as well, fewer studies have linked intersectional approaches with the life course paradigm.

Intersectionality and the Life Course

Intersectional approaches conceive of gender, race/ethnicity, class, and other dimensions of inequality as 'simultaneous processes of identity, institutional and social practices' (Acker 2006; Holvino 2010). Because these processes are simultaneous, it is difficult to disentangle gender inequalities from racial and class inequalities. Multiple forms of inequality are inextricably bound together, through processes that become institutionalised and embedded within social structures and social practices.

Perhaps one of the most significant insights generated from intersectional approaches is that gender is racialised and race is gendered. This means that cultural expectations about femininity and masculinity can vary by race, ethnicity, class, and age (Espiritu 1997; Glenn 2002). Following this line of inquiry, researchers have shown how expectations and pressures placed on minority men and women in the US and Canada can differ significantly from those placed on majority men and women (Glenn 2002). Experiences can also differ as the intersection of gender, class, and race has implications for access to resources, exposure to discrimination, and labour market opportunities.

Research has rarely linked the life course perspective with intersectionality approaches, but we argue that to understand social pathways and experiences of key life transitions and trajectories accurately, one has to adopt an intersectional lens. Just as the gendered life course perspective holds that the life paths of men and women are distinct, an intersectional life course perspective explores how life course experiences of transitions, turning points, and trajectories are shaped by the intersection of race, class, and gender (as well as other dimensions of inequality like age and sexual orientation). Individuals who share an age cohort may have similar experiences of historical events, but those experiences will be conditioned by their structural location in the class hierarchy, their relative resources, as well as their gender and race.

An intersectional life course approach is useful for understanding how different groups of women experience major life transitions, such as embarking on a professional career, and enables us to draw on a wealth of research highlighting racial differences in professional employment among women. For example, Purkayastha's (2005) research on Asian-Indian immigrant women pursuing professional careers in the US uses the concept of cumulative disadvantage to highlight how the disadvantages that minority women face when entering education programs, and subsequently the labour market, accumulate to lessen their odds of success. Immigrant women are often required to rebuild 'family and community networks' in their new country, which not only requires time and effort, but also may mean that they have a smaller support system than other women attempting to combine family and work life. Immigrant women also face discrimination and disadvantage when seeking advanced education, and in the labour market. At each stage, their disadvantages accumulate, lessening their odds of success (Ferree and Purkayastha 2000; Purkayastha 2005). While all women breaking into professions that have been gendered masculine may face such cumulative disadvantages, more disadvantages accrue to immigrants, racialised minorities, and the working class. These disadvantages are compounded and amplified over time, leading to distinct life course experiences. For minority and/or immigrant women, the result of cumulative disadvantage can be poorer labour market outcomes, and more limited career success.

Research on Asian women in professional careers has identified similar cumulative disadvantages. Asian women may experience more intense family expectations. For example, in China there are strongly negative attitudes towards late marriage: women who do not get married at a normative age are called *sheng nu* which means 'left-over women' (To 2013). There are similar negative attitudes to delayed marriage in other Asian countries such as Korea and Japan. Women who have immigrated from Asia to Canada—or those whose parents have immigrated—may share this viewpoint, which would place extra pressure on Asian women pursuing careers, and considering delaying marriage, that their White counterparts may not experience.

Overall, adopting an intersectional life course lens leads us to explore how expectations around gender and career may differ for White and Asian women pursuing medical careers, and whether these expectations shape their specialty choices.

Methodology

Between the spring of 2014 and spring of 2015 we conducted semi-structured interviews with a sample of 15 Ontario women medical students and residents. We were specifically interested in their medical specialty decision-making, and whether family aspirations influenced their specialty choices. Interviews were semi-structured and were conducted face-to-face. Given the primary aim of the study, we spoke with advanced medical students only (those in year three or four) and recent graduates undertaking residency training—those in the process of making specialty choices, or those who had made a decision about their specialisation recently. To recruit participants we targeted three Ontario, Canada universities with medical schools, putting up posters around campus and notices on Facebook, and advertising in student newspapers. We also engaged in passive snowball sampling in which those interviewed were invited to tell other eligible participants about the study; those interested were asked to contact the researcher(s). The semi-structured interviews were audio-recorded and varied in length from 35 minutes to 50 minutes. Medical students are busy people so we tried to accommodate their schedules by interviewing them at locations convenient to them, and keeping the interviews short. A university ethics board approved the research.

Data analysis was thematic and primarily inductive. As noted, we were especially interested in specialty choices, and the factors shaping women's decision-making. Both authors reviewed the transcripts several times, separately, to identify themes, and then compared notes. Themes respecting life course transitions emerged early on, and the interview data were analysed more thoroughly to explore this aspect. The presence of racial/ethnic differences also emerged from the inductive data analysis. We began to realise that minority students spoke differently about work and family than did their White counterparts. Subsequent analyses focused on racial/ethnic differences around life course transitions.

Eight of our women medical student/resident participants could be classified as Asian: seven had an East Asian background (Korean or Chinese), while one had an Indian background. Seven of our participants were White. Among the racialised minority women, five were first-generation immigrants born outside of Canada, while three were born in Canada, but had at least one immigrant parent. Participants' average age was 27, with an age range between 25 and 30. Table 3.1 provides more information about our participants, listing them by pseudonym and providing their age, background, and medical specialty choice. In the discussion that follows, we discuss our participants' specialty choices, illustrating how the intersection of age cohort, gender, and race/ethnicity shaped their decision-making. We argue that to understand women's experiences one needs to draw on both life course and intersectionality perspectives.

Table 3.1 Participant profiles

White Participants				Asian Participants			
Name	Year of study	Age	Medical specialty of consideration	Name	Year of study	Age	Medical specialty of consideration
Jennifer	Resident	29	Paediatric	Jennie	Third	28	Emergency medicine
Emily	Third	25	Undecided	Tiffany	Resident	26	Radiology
Samantha	Third	25	Family medicine	Jackie	Third	25	Internal medicine
Rachelle	Fourth	27	Internal medicine	Hanna	Resident	28	Emergency medicine
Laura	Fourth	27	Emergency medicine	Monica	Third	26	Undecided
Catherine	Fourth	27	Dermatology	Amy	Fourth	26	Emergency medicine
Lindsey	Resident	30	Anesthesiology	Christina	Third	27	Undecided
				Sarah	Third	29	Family medicine

* *All names are pseudonyms.*

We draw heavily on interview excerpts, which we have edited slightly to make quotations more readable.

Results

We asked women medical students and residents about their career goals, what areas of medicine they had decided to pursue, and what factors shaped their decisions. Overall, a confluence of factors shaped women's specialty choices; however, the ones mentioned most often were personal interests, the influence of faculty and other mentors, and concern for work–life balance. Although the women had much in common, there were some differences by race/ethnicity. Notably, Asian-Canadian women appeared to have less support, and more (and different) pressures, as they attempted to balance work and family. We first highlight the role of mentors and networks on women's career decision-making. Then, we explore family considerations.

The Influence of Medical School Faculty, Mentors, and Networks

Medical school faculty are discouraged from directing students towards specific career paths; yet, faculty and clinical mentors, and the women's networks, strongly influenced their career choices. In the third year of their medical studies, students engage in 'clerkships' where they are exposed to different medical specialties, and learn what practice in these specialties is like. An encouraging or discouraging mentor during this period can be quite impactful. When asked about specialty choices, several participants pointed to specific conversations or experiences that strongly shaped their decision-making.

Jennie's career decision-making was influenced by a male professor. She recounted an exchange:

> Well, once . . . I was talking to one of my professors who specialises in general surgery. I told him that I wanted to pursue surgery, and he was like. . . . 'Don't you think that it might be bit difficult if you are considering having a family later?' He was giving me an impression that . . . if you are considering a family, pursuing surgical field is not a good idea.
> (Jennie, Asian, third year, emergency medicine)

This faculty member led Jennie to believe that women could have a career in surgery, but only by sacrificing having a family. Jennie decided to pursue a different specialisation, one she anticipated would allow more work–life balance: emergency medicine.

For Jackie, it was the culture of surgery that turned her off of the specialty. She felt like she would not belong there. Like Jennie, she recounts a particular incident that shaped her decision-making:

> I think you should have very strong personality to be a surgeon. Like, I was in OR neurosurgery once, and the surgeon was just yelling at the resident, and I was like, if I was that resident, I would walk out crying. I know that I cannot handle that kind of teaching. And it's . . . You know . . . I understand it . . . Because you are operating on someone. . . . Their life is in your hands, and that surgeon is responsible for you and for that patient. So, it's not like I am blaming the surgeon but I just don't know if I have a personality for that.
> (Jackie, Asian, third year, internal medicine)

This episode led Jackie to understand that surgery was not for her. She continued to pursue a different competitive medical specialty, internal medicine, which she viewed as having a more welcoming culture.

In contrast, several of our respondents talked about positive experiences where they had mentors who really helped inform their decisions and contributed to their success. For example, Lindsay talked about a mentor she acquired early on in medical school:

> One of them is a female surgeon and she kind of took me on a shadowing experience . . . and it was that kind of transformative

experience that you anticipate going into med school. . . . That was my second month of med school. And I kept in contact with her. So she was an excellent mentor and excellent teacher. Umm, I think she was one of the reasons that I love general surgery as much as I did anaesthesiology. And I had a hard choice choosing between the two, but she was very formative for me. We did research together. She is the type of person who you want to look up to and you wanna be, because she is so good at what she does. She is so well respected but she is such a genuinely kind person, you know . . . and she gives you opportunities, and she is totally encouraging. . . . So, she was excellent in every way.

(Lindsey, White, resident, anaesthesiology)

Laura talked about the importance of making these kinds of connections during medical school. She said 'it's really competitive to get matched to a specialty of your choice.' She told us about a programme at her school where medical students are connected with a medical doctor in their area and allowed to shadow them with the goal of 'making a relationship and network with this person.' Laura felt that this kind of networking helped her to get a residency in her specialty of choice: emergency medicine. In this manner, Laura and Lindsey had exposure to positive mentors who not only provided guidance and encouragement, but also helped shape their career decision-making.

On analysing our data, we noted that more of our Asian-Canadian participants mentioned negative experiences with faculty, and discussed the lack of female mentors as problematic. With respect to the latter, Monica (Asian, third year, undecided) expressed frustration, and believed that a female mentor would have helped her 'know what challenges there are and what other people have done and how other people have survived through.' In contrast, more of the individuals who described having a strong mentor to help guide them were White. Although we do not claim a representative sample, our findings raise questions about whether minority women have access to the same positive mentorships as White women, and even whether male faculty are less encouraging of minority women. Still, some White women did identify difficulties as well. Emily and Samantha, for example, voiced feelings of isolation and uncertainty. Such feelings led Samantha to think about quitting medical school:

You wouldn't understand how many times I thought of quitting med school. . . [Laughs]. Really. It was so different from what I have imagined before coming here. When I was in undergrad, I thought that once I get into med school, my life would be a paradise from that point on . . . But once I came here . . . I was so lost. . . . Because I didn't know what to do.

(Samantha, White, third year, family medicine)

A lack of networks and mentors was a disadvantage for Samantha, making her medical school experiences difficult. These experiences may have encouraged her choice of family medicine, which some of our participants suggested was almost a default for women. Although some Asian students felt that their lack of mentors and networks might be a disadvantage, most had confidence that they could succeed:

> I don't [have networks] . . . But for me . . . I never feel bothered by it. They do have advantages [people with networks]. I totally agree that they do. . . . But what can you do? The only way to catch up is by working harder to build the network yourself. Getting your ass moving. [Laughs]
>
> (Jackie, Asian, third year, internal medicine)

To summarise, in interviews, both Asian and White women medical students highlighted the importance of mentors and networks as they navigated this major life course transition; however, the White and Asian women in our study had different access to mentors and networks, which, in turn, meant that they had different experiences of this transition. Asian women appeared to face more challenges, which could lead to different career trajectories.

Family Considerations

Many respondents considered their future work–family balance when choosing a specialty. They were well aware that medical careers could be challenging to combine with child-rearing, and some deliberately chose specialties they felt would allow for more work–life balance. Family considerations also emerged in other ways: specifically, some women—especially minority women—sought specialties where they could pursue residencies that would allow them to reside near partners and family members, eschewing specialisations that might require them to leave their communities and live far away from the people and places they loved.

Jennie nicely summarised the relevance of family considerations to many women's specialty choices:

> Women often get married earlier than men. . . . So, while guys choose their medical specialty without much pressure . . . female doctors have to consider their husband's work as well. Women often have to consider various things. So, some choose easier medical specialty to pursue, or even choose specialty depending on which region they want to stay. . . . [In family medicine], the residency period is much shorter, compared to other medical specialties. Many fall into family

medicine because of that. . . . Family . . . is something I need to consider. . . . Like, when would I have a child if I do five years of residency? My boyfriend wants three kids when we get married! [Laughs].

(Jennie, Asian, third year, emergency medicine)

Family considerations led many young women to pursue specialties like family medicine that had shorter residency periods, were available in many different communities, and were seen as easier to combine with child-rearing. Jackie elaborates:

So lot of people do wanna do easy specialties . . . Oh, no . . . Not easy specialties but ones that you get regular hours.

(Jackie, Asian, third year, internal medicine)

Laura agreed that women in medical schools were drawn to family medicine, paediatrics, and other specialties seen as more female-friendly, but felt that women were increasingly drawn to traditionally masculine specialties like surgery. Although family leave policies for residents were good, regardless of specialty, enabling women to take time off to have children, Laura felt that even 'just taking six months off is a huge deal.' She believed that by the time they got back to work after a leave, residents would have 'forgotten everything already' (Laura, White, fourth year, emergency medicine). Hence, many women preferred to push child-bearing back later, but this meant building careers and raising families at the same time.

While most participants spoke at some point about future work–family conflict, family was not necessarily the most important consideration when choosing a specialty. Women also talked about choosing a field that interested them, and where they saw opportunities for career growth. For example, Lindsey explained,

When I was making my decisions it was really between general surgery, which I still really love, and anaesthesiology. And I made this decision about anaesthesiology because of how much I felt like my background fit with it and how much I can kick it further.

(Lindsey, White, resident, anaesthesiology)

Jackie also highlighted the importance of doing something she loved and that would make her happy (Asian, third year, internal medicine).

Yet, many women spoke about achieving 'balance.' They wanted a career that would enable them some degree of work–life balance, and ideally, work–family balance for them in the future. This was a particular concern for our Asian-Canadian participants. Although some of our White participants spoke about wanting balance, Asian medical students in our study voiced considerable unease around work–family balance, and identified family pressures as shaping their career choices.

Some specialties were just not seen as conducive to family life, as Hanna explains:

> Those in surgical specialties. . . . I found it more common to have females to be divorced than to be still married. They all eventually get married but it doesn't mean that they are going to be still married. So it's more common for them to be divorced than anything.
>
> (Hanna, Asian, resident, emergency medicine)

In her search for work–family balance, Hanna seriously weighed both her career and her family options:

> It would be very hard to have a family life if I do a five-year residency, because that would set back me getting married and having kids. . . . Also, I didn't want to get married to a medical doctor because I knew that if I was busy and they are busy too, that means that nobody will be home, and our relationship will suffer. Our children would never have any parents around. So I chose to marry somebody who is not in medicine at all. Moreover, I also decided to go into a medical specialty that is not as time consuming, something that doesn't take forever to get through, like a surgical or a five-year specialty.
>
> (Hanna, Asian, resident, emergency medicine)

The emergency medicine residency can be completed in three years and hence was more suitable for Hanna's life and career goals.

Like Hanna, Jennie's age and life course stage shaped her career decision-making:

> We sort of have to consider our age as well. Well . . . Women do have some pressure about marriage. Like, because we have to residency after our four years of med school.
>
> (Jennie, Asian, third year, emergency medicine)

Both Jennie and Hanna felt age was crucial. Hanna told us that women 'who were older when they got into [med] school' faced tougher decisions.

> What should I do? Should I marry? Should I not marry? [. . .] Should I have a child right now? Should I have a child later? Because if I have a kid, that is going to keep me from being able to go from place to place easily. [. . .] Once you have kids . . . It's hard to move.
>
> (Hanna, Asian, resident, emergency medicine)

For many Asian-Canadian women, age and life course stage were strong considerations shaping their medical specialty choices.

Another consideration, especially for Asian-Canadian women, was the location and availability of residencies. Obtaining a medical residency of their choice is a very competitive process, and aspiring medical doctors in many fields had to be prepared to relocate to find a residency position. However, many expressed anxiety about moving far away from family and community.

> Getting matched in a specialty that you wanna pursue, especially in regions that you would want to live at—is so hard. You basically start again, actually. Med school is just the beginning. Most competitive specialties, it is really difficult to be matched to a place in your preferred place, well, preferred cities for everyone else too (laugh), like Toronto or Vancouver. If you want to pursue a specialty which is very specific . . . You may have to be ready to . . . Pretty much, go anywhere. Even outside Canada. Like, some . . . Actually quite many, eventually go to US, for example.
>
> (Amy, Asian, fourth year, emergency medicine)

Toronto and Vancouver are not just attractive cities because they are two of Canada's largest. These cities are also home to a large number of Asian Canadians. In this interview excerpt, Amy is expressing a desire to be close to other members of her racial/ethnic community. She was not the only one to do so. Christina talked about how her family really wanted her to do a residency in Toronto. When asked why, she explained

> There are a lot of people from my ethnic background in Toronto. . . [My parents] are kind of scared that I don't have any Asian friends here. . . . They want me to get the residency in Toronto because they want me to date a guy with a same ethnic background.
>
> (Christina, Asian, third year, undecided)

Preference or pressure to live in certain locales could limit specialty options. When asked about surgery as a specialty option, Sarah explained that residency location was a serious concern:

> You don't know where you will have to relocate yourself to get a spot in surgery. You really have to go wherever there is a spot for you. So . . . things like this matter.
>
> (Asian, third year, family medicine)

Sarah's specialty choice of family medicine provided her with maximum flexibility with respect to her residency location, increasing her chances of working close to her family, community, and potential marriage partners.

Those women who were partnered spoke about choosing a specialty that would allow them to balance their career pursuits with their partners. Women whose partners were in medicine might choose family medicine or another specialty where residencies were more plentiful, so they could relocate to whatever region their partner's residency was located. Catherine talked about having more flexibility because her partner's career allowed him to move to suit her needs.

Overall, the women embarking on medical careers in our study were at the stage of their life course where they were contemplating major life and career transitions. However, these life course transitions were experienced differently by women from different racial/ethnic backgrounds, because gender and family expectations differed by race and ethnicity. Moreover, Asian women were hesitant to locate away from cities like Toronto and Vancouver, with a higher concentration of racial/ethnic minority populations. They wanted to be closer to their families and to ethnic communities that can support them. In this manner, gender, race/ethnicity, age, and life course stage intersected to shape career decisions. White and Asian women's different experiences of these life course transitions could have significant implications for their subsequent career trajectories. In the final section of this chapter we discuss how these findings can only be understood through combining the life course perspective with an intersectionality approach.

Discussion and Conclusions

By combining intersectionality approaches with the life course paradigm, this chapter extends the current literature, illustrating how gender, race/ethnicity, age, and life course stage intersect to shape women's medical specialty decisions. Many young women we spoke to expressed interest in high-status, demanding specialties, like surgery. However, anticipating work–family conflict, and, in many cases, perceiving a lack of support from mentors and/or their families, these women gravitated towards more family-friendly specialties. Asian and White women's experiences differed in notable ways. Asian-Canadian women in our study had less support from mentors, and felt more (and different) family pressures, resulting in greater anxiety about their medical specialty choices. Cultural attitudes towards gender, marriage, and family may be influential: in some Asian cultures there is pressure for women to marry at a normative age to avoid being labelled *sheng nu* or 'left-over women' (To 2013). However, structural constraints, including the limited availability of residencies, which can force new doctors to move far away from family and friends for further training, and institutionalised racism and a lack of community supports for racialised individuals are also important contributors to these racial/ethnic differences. Community supports may be particularly important to minority women who lack supports within the medical profession.

Previous research has taken a gendered life course approach, revealing how gender norms and stereotypes reproduce gender inequality, in part through cumulative disadvantages that negatively affect women's career trajectories (Moen 2011; Settersten 2003). We have argued that an intersectional life course approach is more fruitful as it highlights the ways in which age, gender, and race/ethnicity intersect to shape advantage and disadvantage over time. Here, we have seen that faculty members, clinical mentors, and social networks combine with differential family considerations to shape career transitions in a manner that could have long-term career implications. We recommend that future research adopt an intersectional life course approach, and suggest there is a need for longitudinal research to determine how educational and early career experiences shape career trajectories over time. Differential pressures in experiences in medical school could lead to long-lasting social inequalities in professional outcomes. Additional research in this area is necessary if we are to produce a future where individuals are not disadvantaged in professional careers due to the intersections of age, gender, race/ethnicity, and other dimensions of social inequality.

References

Acker, J (2006) 'Inequality Regimes: Gender, Class, and Race in Organizations' 20 *Gender & Society* 441. doi:10.1177/0891243206289499

Allison, R and Ralston, M (2018) 'Gender, Anticipated Family Formation, and Graduate School Expectations Among Undergraduates' 33 *Sociological Forum* 95. doi:10.1111/socf.12400

Babaria, P, Abedin, S, Berg, D, and Nunez-Smith, M (2012) ' "I'm too used to it": A Longitudinal Qualitative Study of Third Year Female Medical Students' Experiences of Gendered Encounters in Medical Education' 74 *Social Science & Medicine* 1013. doi:10.1016/j.socscimed.2011.11.043

Baxter, N, Cohen, R and McLeod, R (1996) 'The Impact of Gender on the Choice of Surgery as a Career' 172 *The American Journal of Surgery* 373. doi:10.1016/S0002-9610(96)00185-7

Beagan, B (2001) 'Micro Inequities and Everyday Inequalities: "Race," Gender, Sexuality and Class in Medical School' 26 *The Canadian Journal of Sociology* 583. doi:10.2307/3341493

Bhatt, W (2013) 'The Little Brown Woman: Gender Discrimination in American Medicine' 27 *Gender & Society* 659. doi:10.1177/0891243213491140

Boulis, AK and Jacobs, JA (2008) *The Changing Face of Medicine: Women Doctors and the Evolution of Health Care in America* (Ithaca, NY, ILR Press).

Canadian Institute for Health Information (CIHI) (2016) 'Supply, Distribution and Migration of Physicians in Canada, 2016: Data Tables' (Ottawa, CIHI). www.cihi.ca/en/physicians-in-canada.

56   Tracey L. Adams and Eugena Kwon

Cassell, J (1998) *The Woman in the Surgeon's Body* (Cambridge, MA, Harvard University Press).

Colletti, LM, Mulholland, MW and Sonnad, SS (2000) 'Perceived Obstacles to Career Success for Women in Academic Surgery' 135 *Archives of Surgery* 972. doi:10.1001/archsurg.135.8.972

Cooke, M (2017) 'Implicit Bias in Academic Medicine: #WhatADoctorLooksLike' 177 *JAMA Internal Medicine* 657. doi:10.1001/jamainternmed.2016.9643

Crosnoe, R and Muller, C (2014) 'Family Socioeconomic Status, Peers, and the Path to College' 61 *Social Problems* 602. doi:10.1525/sp.2014.12255

DePaulo, BM and Morris, WL (2005) 'Singles in Society and in Science' 16 *Psychological Inquiry* 57.

Dolishny, VN (2012) ' "Proving Yourself" in the Canadian Medical Profession: Gender and the Experiences of Foreign-Trained Doctors in Medical Practices' MA thesis (University of Western Ontario). https://ir.lib.uwo.ca/etd/880

Elder Jr, GH, Johnson, MK and Crosnoe, R (2003) 'The Emergence and Development of Life Course Theory' in JT Mortimer and MJ Shanahan (eds), *Handbook of the Life Course* (New York, Kluwer Academic/Plenum Publishers).

Espiritu, YL (1997) *Asian American Women and Men: Labor, Laws and Love* (Thousand Oaks, CA, Sage Publications).

Ferree, MM and Purkayastha, B (2000) 'Equality and Cumulative Disadvantage: Response to Baxter and Wright' 14 *Gender & Society* 809. doi:10.1177/089124300014006007

Gayle, GL, Golan, L and Miller, RA (2012) 'Gender Differences in Executive Compensation and Job Mobility' 30(4) *Journal of Labor Economics* 829–872.

Glenn, EN (2002) *Unequal Freedom: How Race and Gender Shaped American Citizenship and Labor* (Cambridge, MA, Harvard University Press).

Heitkamp, DE, Norris, CD and Rissing, SM (2017) 'The Illusion of Choice: Gender Segregation and the Challenge of Recruiting Women to Radiology' 14 *Journal of the American College of Radiology* 991. doi:10.1016/j.jacr.2017.01.021

Heru, AM (2005) 'Pink-Collar Medicine: Women and the Future of Medicine' 22 *Gender Issues* 20. doi:10.1007/s12147-005-0008-0

Hinze, SW (1999) Gender and the Body of Medicine or at Least Some Body Parts: (Re)Constructing the Prestige Hierarchy of Medical Specialties 40 *The Sociological Quarterly* 217. doi:10.1111/j.1533-8525.1999.tb00546.x

Hochschild, AR (2003) *The Commercialization of Intimate Life: Notes from Home and Work* (Berkeley, University of California Press).

Holvino, E (2010) 'Intersections: The Simultaneity of Race, Gender and Class in Organization Studies' 17 *Gender, Work & Organization* 248. doi:10.1111/j.1468-0432.2008.00400.x

Howe, TR (2012) *Marriages and Families in the 21st Century: A Bioecological Approach* (Malden, MA, Wiley-Blackwell).

Kwon, E (2017) ' "For Passion or for Future Family?" Exploring Factors Influencing Career and Family Choices of Female Medical Students and Residents' 34 *Gender Issues* 186. doi:10.1007/s12147-016-9168-3

Marshall, VW and Muller, MM (2003) 'Theoretical Roots of the Life-Course Perspective' in WR Heinz and VW Marshall (eds), *Social Dynamics of the Life Course: Transitions, Institutions, and Interrelations* (Hawthorne, NY, Aldine de Gruyter).

Moen, P (2011) 'From "work–family" to the "gendered life course" and "fit": Five Challenges to the Field' 14 *Community, Work & Family* 81. doi:10.1080 /13668803.2010.532661

Murti, L (2014) *With and Without the White Coat: The Racialization of Southern California's Indian Physicians* (Boca Raton, FL, Universal Publishers).

Poortman, A and Liefbroer, AC (2010) 'Singles' Relational Attitudes in a Time of Individualization' 39 *Social Science Research* 938. doi:10.1016/j. ssresearch.2010.03.012

Purkayastha, B (2005) 'Skilled Migration and Cumulative Disadvantage: The Case of Highly Qualified Asian Indian Immigrant Women in the US' 36 *Geoforum* 181. doi:10.1016/j.geoforum.2003.11.006

Riska, E (2011) 'Gender and Medical Careers' 68 *Maturitas* 264. doi:10.1016/j. maturitas.2010.09.010

Scott, J, Dex, S and Plagnol, AC (eds) (2012) *Gendered Lives: Gender Inequalities in Production and Reproduction* (Northampton, MA, Edward Elgar Publishing Limited).

Seemann, NM, Webster, F, Holden, HA, Moulton, C-AE, Baxter, N, Desjardins, C and Cil, T (2016) 'Women in Academic Surgery: Why Is the Playing Field Still Not Level?' 211 *The American Journal of Surgery* 343. doi:10.1016/j. amjsurg.2015.08.036

Settersten Jr, RA (2003) 'Age Structuring and the Rhythm of the Life Course' in JT Mortimer and MJ Shanahan (eds), *Handbook of the Life Course* (New York, Kluwer Academic/Plenum Publishers).

Shanahan, MJ and Macmillan, R (2008) *Biography and the Sociological Imagination: Contexts and Contingencies* (New York, WW Norton and Co).

Sharp, EA and Ganong, L (2007) 'Living in the Gray: Women's Experiences of Missing the Marital Transition' 69 *Journal of Marriage and Family* 831. doi:10.1177/0192513X10392537

—————— (2011) ' "I'm a Loser, I'm Not Married, Let's Just All Look at Me": Ever-Single Women's Perceptions of Their Social Environment' 32 *Journal of Family Issues* 956. doi:10.1177/0192513X10392537

To, S (2013) 'Understanding Sheng Nu ("Leftover Women"): The Phenomenon of Late Marriage Among Chinese Professional Women' 36 *Symbolic Interaction* 1. doi:10.1002/symb.46

Vespa, J (2009) 'Gender Ideology Construction: A Life Course and Intersectional Approach' 23 *Gender & Society* 363. doi:10.1177/0891243209337507

4 Intergenerational Dynamics Among Women and Men in Nursing

*Marci D. Cottingham and
Janette S. Dill*

Introduction

The gendered nature of the nursing profession has received considerable attention from sociologists (Dill et al. 2016; Williams 1992). The roles of race (Cottingham et al. 2018; Wingfield 2009) and sexuality (Cottingham et al. 2016) have also received some consideration, but age and generational dynamics have been less developed within sociological research on nursing. This is particularly surprising considering that predictions in workforce shortages are specifically linked to the retiring of Baby Boomer nurses (Buerhaus et al. 2006) coupled with increasing health demands of an aging population (Hecker 2001; US Department of Labor Statistics 2018a). Younger, well-trained nurses are increasingly needed to meet demand, yet recent research indicates that they have the highest turnover rate and levels of turnover intention (Lavoie-Tremblay et al. 2010; Tourangeau and Cranley 2006).

Given the diversity of nursing, the profession can shed light on how experiences in an emotionally demanding profession vary across age, generational cohort, and experience levels. Past research has shown that older nurses are significantly more satisfied in their jobs as compared to younger nurses (Widger et al. 2007; Wilson et al. 2008). Leiter et al. (2009, 2010) found that Generation X nurses report higher levels of distress as compared to Baby Boomer nurses, including higher exhaustion, cynicism, turnover intent, and negative physical symptoms. In order to address the high turnover rates of younger nurses, Erickson and Grove (2007) call for more experienced nurses to serve as 'emotional mentors' to younger nurses. Following this call, further research can shed light on the day-to-day negotiations of nurses with variation in experience levels as well as the conflicts that could limit the success of emotional mentorship.

Past research on age and experiences at work among nurses has highlighted the conflict that can emerge between younger and older nurses. Younger nurses can experience bullying on the job (Vessey et al. 2009), including belittling and public shaming perpetuated by more senior nurses as well as physicians. In their qualitative study of intra-professional conflict, Boateng and Adams (2016) find age and race to be particularly salient categories that structure co-worker interactions. Older nurses might refuse to help new nurses or resent interruptions to their work. The recurrent theme in nursing culture is that nurses 'eat their young'. Kelly and Ahern (2008: 916) frame this phenomena as a hangover from '19th century hierarchical traditions'. Turning to the complexity of emotions that nurses confront on the job might additionally identify particular practices that shape conflict between younger and older nurses.

Despite the advances of the sociology of emotion over the last four decades (Bericat 2016), research on the relationship between emotion, age, and generational cohorts has been notably limited. Research on age and emotion tends to focus on old age and emotional changes (Carstensen and Charles 1998), family, marriage, and love (Sumter et al. 2013), or children's emotional development (Andrew 2015; Froyum 2010), with less focus on how age and generational diversity shape emotion in the workplace. One notable exception is recent work on intergenerational communication and emotional labour among nurses (Anderson and Morgan 2017a; Anderson and Morgan 2017b). Anderson and Morgan (2017a) find that the saying that 'nurses eat their young' is used iteratively to construct older and younger nurses as fundamentally distinct and 'positioned age groups against each other' (385). With these distinctions naturalised, the bullying that younger nurses experience is also naturalised and partly justified.

This chapter builds on this past work by using both quantitative and qualitative data to compare differences in nurses' emotional experiences while at work. Combining survey and audio diary data allows us to address both general responses along with situationally specific emotional reflections. This methodological combination aligns with a theoretical framework of emotion practice (Cottingham 2016; Erickson and Cottingham 2014; Erickson and Stacey 2013; Scheer 2012). In this approach, emotions are viewed as relational, not limited to nurses as isolated emotion managers (Burkitt 2017). Individual nurses are always embedded in connections with co-workers, patients, organisational policies, and units. In turn, organisations are shaped by broader cultural beliefs about gender (Ridgeway 2011), race (Evans and Moore 2015), and generational differences (Mannheim 1952).

Distinct emotions emerge from one's ongoing engagement with divergent others and environments. The extent to which an individual can anticipate and meet situational demands with pre-developed skills and resources, the greater likelihood that feelings of comfort, ease, and generally positive emotions will emerge. Friction between internalised dispositions ('habitus' in Bourdieu's 1990 framework, see also Gould 2009; Reay 2015) and situational demands leads to feelings of unease, discomfort, and further negative emotions. Emotion-based skills, resources, and capacities are theorised in this approach as part of a nurse's 'emotional capital' (Cahill 1999; Cottingham 2016; Stacey 2011), which is in turn drawn upon to meet the interactional demands of providing care and comfort to patients, patient family members, and co-workers. Nurses both bring and develop their emotional capital throughout the course of their nursing career as they confront novel demands and develop expertise. Using an emotion practice framework draws our analytical gaze to the ongoing situated practices that make up nursing. This approach can shed light on the emotional complexities of nursing and the generational differences that emerge out of this complexity.

Methods

For investigating the role of intergenerational dynamics in nurses' emotion practice, we draw on survey and audio diary data collected from nurses in two Midwestern hospital systems in the US. For the survey, a complete listing of full-time, direct care registered nurses (RNs) was obtained from the health system's human resources department and written questionnaires in sealed envelopes were distributed to eligible RNs employed within each hospital (N = 1,702). Completed surveys were returned by mail from 762 participants, or 45% of the original eligible sample. This response rate is consistent with other studies among registered nurses (e.g., Lucero et al. 2010). Cases with missing observations were dropped from the analysis; this resulted in a final sample of 730 respondents. The data collection protocols were reviewed and approved by the University of Akron Institutional Review Board.

We use the survey data to look at a variety of outcomes for Millennial and Baby Boomer nurses, including negative and positive emotions experienced at work and self-perceived performance at work. In measuring age, we divide nurses into three age groups: Millennial nurses (age 23–31), mid-career nurses (age 32–50), and Baby Boomer nurses (age 51+). In most of our analyses we focus exclusively on Millennial nurses and Baby Boomer nurses. In our regression analyses, we include a few personal demographic characteristics (gender, race), and some work characteristics that might influence a nurse's experience at work (patient acuity, job tenure). Table 4.1 includes a description of all the measures that we use from the survey data.

A diverse sample in terms of gender, race, and generational cohort was sought for the audio diary data. We targeted all men, all nurses of colour, and all Millennial-aged nurses (born on or after 1980) from the first hospital system. We continued to target these subgroups in a second hospital system. The final audio diary participants included 48 nurses total, including 37 women and 11 men; 38 identified as white, 8 African American, and 2 Asian American. Fifteen participants were born in or after the year 1980. The average age was 44 years old. Participants

Table 4.1 Survey measures

Outcome measures	Response categories
Negative emotions at work (e.g., afraid, angry, anxious, frustrated, guilty, helpless, irritated, sad)	Scale from 'Not at all' (0) to 'Very intensely' (5)
Positive emotions at work (e.g., calm, excited, happy, proud, relaxed, surprised)	Scale from 'Not at all' (0) to 'Very intensely' (5)
Self-perceived performance at work (e.g., showing concern for patients, anticipating patient needs)	(1) Did not provide, (2) Poor, (3) Fair, (4) Good, (5) Excellent
Age	Millennial (age 23–31), mid-career (age 32–50), and Baby Boomer nurses (age 51+)
Female	Female (1) and male (0)
Race	White (0), Black (1), and other minority (1)
Patient acuity in work setting	High patient acuity (1) and low patient acuity (0)
Job tenure	Reported in months

Source: Caring about Relationships and Me Always (CARMA) dataset, 2011.

were given a digital recorder and instructed to make recordings during or after six consecutive shifts. Generally, each nurse was told that the research project focused on the emotional experiences of nurses. They were prompted to provide as much detail as possible in terms of key players, settings, events, and implications of their experiences on the job. Audio diary recordings were transcribed and uploaded to a qualitative data analysis programme (Dedoose). All names used are pseudonyms and participant IDs are provided in parentheses.

Findings: Survey Data

Table 4.2 contains summary statistics for the nurses in our survey sample, by age category: 32% of the sample is between the ages of 23 and 31, 39% is between the ages of 36 and 50, and 29% of the sample is over the age of 50. Nursing is a female-dominated occupation, and our sample, which is around 90% female, largely reflects national gender demographics (US Department of Labor Bureau of Labor Statistics 2018b). Five per cent of the sample is African American, 5% are another minority, and 90% of respondents are white, percentages that are fairly consistent across age categories. About 57% of nurses work in settings with high patient acuity. Millennial nurses have an average job tenure of 41 months, while Baby Boomer nurses have an average tenure of 332 months.

62   *Marci D. Cottingham and Janette S. Dill*

Table 4.2 Demographic characteristics of study sample, by age category

	Millennial	Mid-Career	Baby Boomer
	(Age 23–31) Mean or %	(Age 32–50) Mean or %	(Age 51+) Mean or %
Age	27.3	40.6	57.2
Male	5.2%	12.5%	7.3%
Female	94.8%	87.5%	92.7%
White	91.6%	85.7%	92.1%
African American	2.8%	8.1%	4.8%
Other minority	5.6%	6.2%	3.1%
High patient acuity	69.4%	52.4%	47.1%
Job tenure (in months)	40.7	136.4	332.2
N	251	308	229

Source: CARMA dataset, 2010.

Notes: Respondents included in the 'other minority' category are any respondents that identified as a race/ethnicity other than white or African American.

Table 4.3 contains mean values for emotions that a respondent experienced during the last week while at work and mean values for self-perceived performance at work. In Table 4.3, we include only Millennial nurses (age 23–31) and Baby Boomer nurses (age 51+) to better contrast the experiences of younger and older nurses. Millennial nurses report more negative emotions and less positive emotions at work as compared to Baby Boomer nurses. We find that younger nurses are more likely to report that they experienced being afraid, angry, anxious, frustrated, guilty, helpless, and irritated as compared to older nurses ($p < .05$), as determined by t-tests. Younger nurses report significantly lower mean values for feeling calm and relaxed while at work during the last week as compared to older nurses ($p < .05$).

Millennial nurses also have significantly lower self-perceived performance at work as compared to Baby Boomer nurses across all measures, indicating that Millennial nurses are much more insecure about their ability to meet the demands of their jobs as compared to their more experienced counterparts ($p < .05$). Millennial nurses rate their ability to show concern for patients, anticipate patient needs, explain procedures to patients, demonstrate skill in the provision of care, help calm patient fears, communicate effectively, and respond to patient requests at levels lower than Baby Boomer nurses.

In Table 4.4, we present a regression analysis of scales of the measures described earlier: negative emotions experienced at work, positive emotions experienced at work, and perceived performance at work. We use

Table 4.3 Mean values of emotions and self-rated performance at work, by age category

	Age 21–31	Age 51+
Positive emotions experienced at work in the last week		
Calm	2.996	3.171*
Excited	2.044	1.926
Happy	2.916	3.078
Proud	3.004	3.096
Relaxed	2.360	2.641*
Surprised	1.144	1.005
Negative emotions experienced at work in the last week		
Afraid	0.764	0.404*
Angry	2.016	1.468*
Anxious	1.816	1.336*
Frustrated	3.132	2.894*
Guilty	0.408	0.234*
Helpless	1.229	0.959*
Irritated	2.916	2.413*
Sad	1.152	1.170
Self-rated performance at work		
Showing concern for patients	4.522	4.636*
Anticipating patient needs	4.382	4.565*
Explaining procedures to patients	4.212	4.507*
Demonstrating skills in provision of care	4.410	4.629*
Helping calm patient fears	4.200	4.552*
Communicating effectively	4.348	4.484*
Responding to patient requests	4.368	4.533*
Overall nursing care	4.364	4.575*

Source: CARMA dataset, 2010.

Notes: Only Millennial nurses (age 21–31) and Baby Boomer nurses (age 51+) are included in Table 4.3 to better highlight the differences between younger and older nurses.

* Indicates a significant difference in the mean values of Millennial and Baby Boomer nurses ($p < .05$).

a continuous measure of age and control for a variety of demographic (gender, race) and work characteristics (patient acuity, and tenure). We find that age is negatively related to negative emotions experienced at work ($p < .01$), indicating that older nurses experience fewer negative emotions at work. Positive emotions are not significantly related to age in our regression model, but perceived performance is positively related

Table 4.4 Linear regression models predicting negative emotions, positive emotions, and perceived performance at work

	Negative emotions last week	Positive emotions last week	Perceived performance
	Coeff. (SE)	Coeff. (SE)	Coeff. (SE)
Age	−0.015** (3.38)	0.008 (1.46)	0.006* (2.40)
Sex (reference male) Female	0.035 (0.32)	−0.208 (1.56)	0.009 (0.16)
Race (reference White) Black	−0.082 (0.64)	0.009 (0.06)	0.05 (0.73)
Other minority	−0.161 (1.20)	−0.055 (0.33)	0.11 (1.55)
High patient acuity	0.174** (2.86)	−0.111 (1.46)	0.025 (0.78)
Job tenure (months)	0.000 (1.24)	0.000 (0.82)	0.000 (0.42)
Constant	1.84** (9.74)	2.717** (11.54)	4.19** (41.97)
R^2	0.05	0.01	0.04
N	703	703	696

Source: CARMA dataset, year.

$*p < .05; **p < .01; ***p < .001$

Notes: Respondents included in the 'other minority' category are any respondents that identified as a race/ethnicity other than white or African American.

to age ($p < .05$). Older nurses rate their performance higher as compared to younger nurses.

Findings: Qualitative Diary Data

Findings from the survey data suggest that Millennial nurses report feeling fear, anger, anxiety, shame, frustration, and helplessness more intensely than their Baby Boomer counterparts. Using an emotion practice framework, we can interpret these differences in emotional experience as a result of the ongoing, habitual expectations to which older nurses have, over time, endured and adapted. As the fit between expectation and experience becomes more predictable to experienced nurses, the intensity of felt emotions on the job decreases. With some variation, we find similar examples in audio diary data that suggest that younger and older nurses experience the profession differently.

Millennial Nurses: Feeling Young and Inexperienced

Millennial nurses (age 23–31) in our sample discuss stress as the norm. Good days are often the exceptions. As Megan relays: 'So today overall was a good day, I've had some pretty stressful days, no sleeping cause I can't get things off my mind, but today was a good day and overall very positive' (5002). Ending a shift where a patient died, Melanie has 'mixed feelings' and tries to

> run it through my mind. Did I make the right choice by coming down to a different department? I don't know . . . Just trying to get used to everything; maybe I'll get used to it at some point. Probably not but I'll keep working at it.
>
> (5011)

Getting 'used to everything' in an emotion practice framework means developing the habituated dispositions that match the objective demands of her work.

Melanie contrasts her prior work as an LPN (Licensed Practitioner Nurse) with her current role as an RN (Registered Nurse) in the emergency unit:

> Started working in the emergency room about a month ago. And I like it, but I guess I've seen more people die than I did when [pause] I was a nurse—an LPN for about three years before I became an RN. RN for a year and even during clinicals, I never saw anyone die. Yesterday I had someone come in full arrest. Did CPR. Tried everything and they didn't make it.
>
> (5011)

Melanie uses the phrases 'I don't know' and 'I guess' some 27 times in her diaries and details numerous scenarios where she is unsure how to act. Ending her final diary entry, she returns to the issue of death:

> I guess, I don't know, I'm still getting used to so many patients dying. When I worked on the floor I only had one patient of mine actually pass away and I've—I saw another one which wasn't my patient. I just went in to assist with a few things until the other staff got there to help. So I guess this is just something new for me. And I'm just trying to—kind of getting used to that emotion of, 'okay, wow this patient actually died'.
>
> (5011)

In this quote we see both the intensity of emotion from the job as she relays her shock from a patient's death as well her continued uncertainty on the job ('I guess, I don't know'). Yet Melanie interprets her shock with death as a sign of her emotional investment as a nurse:

> I don't know, but then I try to look at it as . . . well I guess since I actually care about patients that I will work very hard to try and bring them back if they don't seem like they're going to live. So I guess, in a way, it's a good thing.
>
> (5011)

Becoming 'used' to patient death is not merely a matter of becoming emotionally numb, but of maintaining her active concern for her patients while also becoming less jarred by the unexpected loss of a patient.

Other Millennial nurses talk of not 'really know[ing] how to feel' (5022 and 5002) or being 'uncomfortable'. For example, Molly (1301) is uncomfortable with emergency situations, while Ella (1986) is uncomfortable with exerting authority over support staff. Both are in their 20s. Lianna, the youngest nurse in our sample, mentions not knowing what to do in a situation where patients look to her for answers while the power ultimately rests in the hands of the physician. In terms of co-workers, Lianna says that there are 'certain people I am uncomfortable with' (1497). Talk of discomfort can signify a habitus in flux as it encounters novel demands and experiences friction between those demands and the familiar patterns of practice that individuals take for granted. Younger, Millennial nurses, with fewer work experiences, have had less time and exposure to the demands of the job.

Despite this lack of experience and the incongruities between demands and embodied capital (skills, knowledge, and capacities), this does not always mean that Millennial nurses share the same needs in terms of training. For example, Rachel discusses a notably stressful shift in which the distribution of patients was particularly uneven across the nurses on the unit.

> So it wasn't bad, but still, why when everybody has four should one guy have one patient? And I'm sure after the budget meeting we just had that is not gonna make my manager happy. This one RN—the—Luke the guy who only had one patient, he's really nice. He was really helpful. He always offered help to everybody. Anything he could do for you he absolutely would. He didn't hesitate at all but it made me feel guilty to have him help me. I felt guilty when he answered my call lights. I have—I personally have trouble accepting help. I want to do things on my own. I wanna know that I can do them. I want my co-workers to know that I am a strong asset to the team that I'm not the weak link.
>
> (5006)

In this excerpt, Rachel explicitly mentions her interactions with a male co-worker. While the gender of her co-worker does not appear to influence her reaction to the situation, it is clear that her inexperience manifests itself in a desire to be seen as 'strong' and able to tackle the demands of the job independently. Guilt with having to ask for help emerges from her sense of helplessness as a sign of weakness. Adjusting to a teamwork dynamic is a skill that Rachel has yet to develop as a part of her emotion practice on the job.

Differences in experience level do not simply lead to better training or skills. In the case of some Millennial nurses, more experienced, Baby Boomer nurses appear to become too detached from patients and their families. Megan uses the language of 'we' to refer to herself and other newer nurses in contrast to 'nurses that have worked there for a long time'. Reflecting on these differences, she says:

> I just hope and pray that my attitude never changes. I mean, I think I'm pretty much known as being a caring nurse on that floor with my patients—I interact with them, I feel like they're, I don't know, like they're family almost. I get connected to them, to their families. I have conversations. I don't know, I just—I couldn't imagine not caring and I just—I notice a lot of that and it's just pretty sad and I hope the day that I stop caring that's the day that I just quit cause you can't not care in this field.
>
> (5002)

Within this excerpt from Megan we see her making a distinction between herself as a newer nurse and those who seem to have become jaded with the job. Rather than become jaded, she hopes that she can retain her active connection with patients or leave the profession altogether.

The notion of nurses becoming more emotionally distanced from patients over time seems to echo some of the reflections of male nurses. Overall, men talk of learning to reframe the nursing role in a way that creates more emotional distance between themselves and patients and families (see the case of Russell in Cottingham 2015). Young men talk of 'fixing' patients, while older male nurses shift their understanding of their role away from fixing and into technical expertise and providing comfort.

Baby Boomer Nurses: Embodying the Nurse Habitus

While Baby Boomer nurses (age 51+) still struggle with some of the stress and pressures of the job that Millennial nurses describe, they appear to have developed distinct coping strategies that come with the repeated pressures to mould one's habituated disposition to the external demands of the job. For example, Muriel reflects on the tendency of nurses to ruminate on negative experiences on the job. While she initially seems to mimic the sentiments of Millennial nurses, she then speaks at length about the emotion-specific skills (as part of her emotional capital) that she has developed over the course of her 30 years in nursing:

> And I've worked on this for 30 years and you have to learn to just let it go. There are some things that stick with you and that's when I'll find a trusted co-worker or find the head nurses and kind of joke about it a little bit and try to release some of the pressure. At lunchtime sometimes, if it's nice, I'll just take a little walk around outside and just get some fresh air, but at the end of the day, a day like today, even now I'm sitting here thinking of things maybe I'm sure I missed something and what was—and do I need to deal with it and call him and have someone else deal with it or is it something I can let go. And you're left with that almost every day. Days like this when my drive is 40 minutes, I try to blast the radio and try to forget it, but some days like today, I spend the whole time thinking about everything. The whole day running through your mind. The whole day and what did you not do that you should have done, but [I] haven't come up with anything yet. I think the important things are taken care of. I'm home now after nine plus hours.
>
> (1851)

Like Megan and Melanie, Muriel discusses the practice of rumination as an inevitable feature of the job. Yet, she has developed distinct strategies for pulling herself out of a nonproductive spiral of rumination. These include finding trusted co-workers to vent to in order to release the pressure, taking a walk, or blasting the radio during her commute home.

While Millennial nurses cite the need to adjust to novel work experiences as a primary source of stress, Baby Boomer nurses described interruptions to the flow of work as one of their main sources of frustration (3025; 2241; 1929; 1451; 1497 is a Millennial who reports feeling like she annoys her manager when she interrupts). While Millennial nurses seem to experience stress and intense negative feelings as a result of not knowing what to expect, Baby Boomer nurses are more likely to view organisational policy changes, missing equipment, and disruptions to their workflow as sources of stress. Judy, a nurse in her early 60s, discusses changes in meal policies. While in the past, food trays would come at specific times for breakfast, lunch, and dinner, patients are now free to order their meals when they wish:

> Now trays arrive on the floors at all different times. We have to, you know—there's some medicines that we have to give to the patients on an empty stomach and you walk in the room and they—they have a breakfast or a meal sitting in front of them. So then you have to

re-time the medicine in your head that you—you get it to them before their lunch comes up next time. And some medicines you know are—are just timed. They have to be eight hours apart and this is, you know—these menus are interruptive to OUR routine.

(1451)

Similarly, Marge highlights residents as a source of interruption during the intake process that can have potentially grave consequences:

[T]he residents are coming in at 6:30 too to pre-op a patient, and you could be talking to a patient, or a family member, and basically swallow and they interject and just talk like you're not even there, they just interrupt, which is so rude to begin with. And it's just so disruptive, you may—because you're interrupted, a piece of information, a very valuable piece of information may get missed.

(1929)

Marge highlights the potential implications of missing critical information when residents interrupt their conversations with patients.

In addition to residents and hospital policy changes, Millennial nurses were also seen as sources of interruption. Discussing a particular conflict with a younger nurse, Violet relays her views of Millennial nurses:

This particular nurse is in her probably late twenties and of the generation that my children are [laughter]. And that—I think they [are] pretty much wrapped up in getting things done on their time schedule and not truly understanding that the world does not revolve around them. I know that this is very presumptuous for me to say but that's how I was feeling at the time. This particular nurse doesn't follow the protocol that the rest of us do, which is when an order needs to be done by the doctor—which sometimes there can be up to 50 in a week—there is a specific place where we put these charts when the order comes due of when a new order needs to be written so that the doctor can do this at his convenience, not interrupting patient care throughout the day. But usually at the end of the day when we no longer have patients and he and I can sit and review the orders if there's anything specific.

(3025)

Older nurses can see younger nurses as unable to manage time and more likely to manipulate the scheduling to get more time off (1929). Older nurses can refer to the younger nurses that they are mentoring in patronising terms: Nora refers to her mentee (a new RN) as her 'little helper' and Violet admits that she must continually remind herself that the younger nurses are not her 'children'.

When it comes to disruptions, the training of newer nurses (or 'pre-ceptorship' as it is called in nursing) can be an additional source of annoyance and frustration. While the preceptor–preceptee relationship should be one of mentorship and guidance, teaching new nurses can be viewed as an additional burden that older, more experienced nurses have to shoulder (1851, 1940). As Muriel notes, 'it's taxing to have some-one constantly say "why did you do that?"' (1851). The taxing nature of teaching, though, stems from the now automatic and nonconscious nature of how she works. Muriel elaborates:

> [A]nd I had to think about it because I don't think about it. I had to actually do it and say, 'I guess I do' because it's not something you do consciously. I've just been doing it for so many years it just auto-matically happens. So all of those tiny little things that they question especially when they're fresh out of the gate, and everything is new to them. The new girls generally see every little thing you do and question you about it. And that's a good thing and I think I came up with the good explanations for what I do and why I do it. And she actually, for someone whose just been there for four days scrubbing, she is doing as well as you can expect. And she has a nice attitude—wants to get in there and learn and that's a refreshing thing and it helps with the whole process. It kind of lessens your stress a little bit when you're teaching someone. You don't want to feel like you're having to pull them through it and they're at least attempting to engage and try to learn.
>
> (1851)

Additionally, Muriel highlights one aspect of the work environment that appears to be unique to young women in nursing: the issue of sexual harassment. As she explains:

> [S]ome of these the surgeons can be very intimidating, especially some of the older ones. They feel this is their domain. Plus you're with them all the time and you know and when you're working, they're there [. . .] And I think the young nurses, especially the younger ones I think, I see the ones that come in later in life who come in from a different career or another area of nursing are bet-ter able to deal with them. But for me I think it's just that I've dealt with them for so long and I come from an era where sexual harass-ment or harassment of any kind was hardly even spoken of. And the young kids coming in today, it is very much part of our society, and some can be taken aback by the attitudes of some of surgeons towards them and the people they work with. And it's hard to tell them or explain to them how to deal with it. I think they just have to—they, first of all, I think you either have to be able to do it or

you can't. I mean, I think you find out early on if you're meant for the OR [operating room].

(1851)

Both of these reflections from Muriel richly highlight the extent to which she has adopted the taken-for-granted practices of being a nurse and the processes of practical adaptation within an emotion practice approach. The nurse habitus has been fully attuned to the procedural expectations to such an extent that performing her tasks becomes second nature. Her frustration with mentoring a new nurse stems from the need to interrupt her well-worn, nonconscious practices and instead enact them consciously, thinking through how and why she performs her duties in a particular way. This takes effort and emotional energy that might otherwise be channelled into patient care.

In her second quotation here, Muriel highlights the entrenched gendered dynamics of OR nursing that she has come to take for granted ('it's hard to tell them or explain to them how to deal with it'), but that she sees younger nurses struggle to accept. While she might morally decry sexual harassment in the workplace, she also believes that tolerating the attitudes and behaviours of older male surgeons is simply part of the job. And yet, with the rise of the #metoo movement to challenge sexual harassment (Chira 2018), her claims raise questions about when female nurses should adapt to the job and when they should challenge the very expectations to which Baby Boomer nurses have adapted and, indirectly, accepted. 'Emotional mentorship', as Erickson and Grove (2007) highlight in their research, should go beyond younger nurses simply adopting the tried and tested practices of their experienced colleagues, but to also provide a safe relationship in which dialogue between Millennial and Baby Boomer nurse might foster solidarity and the potential to challenge some of the expectations placed on nurses in today's healthcare environment. Muriel's final quote also highlights the distinction between biological age, generational cohort, and levels of experience that are somewhat confounded in our qualitative data. According to Muriel, middle-aged and older women (non-Millennials) who enter nursing later in life seem to be well adapted to the gender norms of tolerating male surgeons' harassment, despite having limited experience as nurses. This suggests that there are expectations of the job that go beyond nursing to include norms of female acquiescence to male demands. Such norms might vary across generational cohort or age.

Discussion and Conclusion

Survey data from a generationally diverse sample of men and women in nursing revealed striking differences between Millennial and Baby Boomer nurses. Millennial nurses reported feeling a range of emotions more intensely than their Baby Boomer counterparts. Additionally, Baby Boomer nurses reported significantly fewer negative emotions on the job than their Millennial counterparts, controlling for tenure. Higher levels of satisfaction have been linked to working longer in a specific unit or hospital (Bjørk et al. 2007; Li and Lambert 2008), but our findings suggest that the effect of age has an impact that is beyond that of tenure in a job. Older nurses also rate their quality of care higher than younger nurses, suggesting that they are more confident in their skills, while younger nurses are insecure.

Using data from audio diaries, we find additional evidence of differences in emotional experiences and confidence levels between Millennial and Baby Boomer nurses. While Baby Boomer nurses have distinct coping strategies as part of their emotional capital, Millennial nurses discuss rumination, stress, and a lack of confidence in themselves as nurses. Lacking the specific emotional capital needed to meet the demands of the job, Millennial nurses have yet to embody the nurse role in a way that allows for a smooth fit with the environment. Baby Boomer nurses, as more experienced and adapted to the demands of the profession, highlight interruptions as their main frustration on the job. The reflections from Violet, Muriel, and others highlight the potentially negative views that Baby Boomer nurses can have of Millennial nurses as well as the processes by which mentoring younger nurses exacts emotional energy from older nurses who otherwise perform nursing tasks routinely without conscious effort.

Using an emotion practice approach (Erickson and Stacey 2013; Scheer 2012), notions of habitus, emotional capital, and practice can shed light on the discrepancies between Millennial and Baby Boomer nurses. Through continuous exposure to the technical and emotional demands of nursing practice, older nurses develop the emotional capital needed to cope with the stress-induced rumination, grief, and sexual harassment that they encounter. While the nurse habitus is continuously in flux, older nurses develop a 'feel for the game' that goes beyond articulation. Indeed, the act of mentoring younger nurses forces them to consciously articulate practices that generally operate at the level of nonconscious habit. Younger nurses, in their effort to learn, interrupt the practical flows of their mentors in ways that can unintentionally bubble into conflict. Yet, it is only through these interruptions and the ongoing trial and error of younger nurses' practices that will hone the habitus and lead to the development of embodied capital needed for expertise.

Our findings highlight the need to contextualise discussions of age, generational differences, and experience levels in nursing with a comprehensive understanding of the emotional complexities of the profession. The training of new Millennial nurses highlights challenges within the profession. New nurses require support and mentorship if they are to remain. Yet, new nurses can also push back against the expectation that they become emotionally numb to the death of patients or tolerant of sexual harassment from surgeons. While policies might be instituted to provide additional time to older nurses to train the next generation, additional time does not necessarily mean that conflict can or should be fully eradicated. Indeed, conflict can be a productive force for challenging accepted practices in the profession and the wider workplace climate. The case of sexual harassment is one example of a professional norm that Millennial nurses, no matter how long they remain in nursing, might be loath to accept. In this way, individuals can exert agency and resist rather than merely adapt to situational demands accepted by prior generations.

References

Anderson, LB and Morgan, M (2017a) 'An Examination of Nurses' Intergenerational Communicative Experiences in the Workplace: Do Nurses Eat Their Young?' 65 *Communication Quarterly* 377. doi:10.1080/01463373.2016.1259175

—— (2017b) 'Embracing the Opportunities of an Older Workforce: Identifying the Age-Based Strategies for Coping with Emotional Labor' 3 *Work, Aging and Retirement* 403. doi:10.1093/workar/waw039

Andrew, Y (2015) '"I'm Strong Within Myself": Gender, Class and Emotional Capital in Childcare' 36 *British Journal of Sociology of Education* 651. doi:10.1080/01425692.2013.835711

Bericat, E (2016) 'The Sociology of Emotions: Four Decades of Progress' 64 *Current Sociology* 491. doi:10.1177/0011392115588355

Bjørk, IT, Samdal, GB, Hansen, BS, Tørstad, S and Hamilton, GA (2007) 'Job Satisfaction in a Norwegian Population of Nurses: A Questionnaire Survey' 44 *International Journal of Nursing Studies* 747. https://doi.org/10.1016/j.ijnurstu.2006.01.002

Boateng, GO and Adams, TL (2016) '"Drop dead . . . I need your job": An Exploratory Study of Intra-Professional Conflict Amongst Nurses in Two Ontario Cities' 155 *Social Science & Medicine* 35. doi:10.1016/j.socscimed.2016.02.045

Bourdieu, P (1990) *The Logic of Practice* (Stanford, CA, Stanford University Press).

Buerhaus, PI, Donelan, K, Ulrich, BT, Norman, L and Dittus, R (2006) 'State of the Registered Nurse Workforce in the United States' 24 *Nursing Economics* 6.

Burkitt, I (2017) 'Decentering Emotion Regulation: From Emotion Regulation to Relational Emotion' 10 *Emotion Review* 167. doi:10.1177/1754073917712441

Cahill, SE (1999) 'Emotional Capital and Professional Socialization: The Case of Mortuary Science Students (and Me)' 62 *Social Psychology Quarterly* 101.

Carstensen, LL and Charles, ST (1998) 'Emotion in the Second Half of Life' 7 *Current Directions in Psychological Science* 144. doi:10.1111/1467-8721.ep10836825

Chira, S (2018) 'Numbers Hint at Why #MeToo Took Off: The Sheer Number Who Can Say Me Too' *New York Times* 21 February 2018. www.nytimes.com/2018/02/21/upshot/pervasive-sexual-harassment-why-me-too-took-off-poll.html

Cottingham, MD (2015) 'Learning to "Deal" and "De-escalate": How Men in Nursing Manage Self and Patient Emotions' 85 *Sociological Inquiry* 75. doi:10.1111/soin.12064

——— (2016) 'Theorizing Emotional Capital' 45 *Theory and Society* 451. doi:10.1007/s11186-016-9278-7

Cottingham, MD, Johnson, AH and Erickson, RJ (2018) ' "I Can Never Be Too Comfortable": Race, Gender, and Emotion at the Hospital Bedside' 28 *Qualitative Health Research* 145. doi:10.1177/1049732317737980

Cottingham, MD, Johnson, AH and Taylor, T (2016) 'Heteronormative Labour: Conflicting Accountability Structures Among Men in Nursing: Heteronormative Labour' 23 *Gender, Work & Organization* 535. doi:10.1111/gwao.12140

Dill, JS, Price-Glynn, K and Rakovski, C (2016) 'Does the "Glass Escalator" Compensate for the Devaluation of Care Work Occupations? The Careers of Men in Low-and Middle-Skill Health Care Jobs' 30 *Gender & Society* 334. doi:10.1177/0891243215624656

Erickson, RJ and Cottingham, MD (2014) 'Families and Emotions' in JE Stets and JH Turner (eds), *Handbook of the Sociology of Emotions: Volume II* (New York, Springer).

Erickson, RJ and Grove, WJC (2007) 'Why Emotions Matter: Age, Agitation, and Burnout Among Registered Nurses' 13 *Online Journal of Issues in Nursing* 1. doi:10.3912/OJIN.Vol13No01PPT01

Erickson, RJ and Stacey, C (2013) 'Attending to Mind and Body: Engaging the Complexity of Emotion Practice Among Caring Professionals' in AA Grandey, JM Diefendorff and DE Rupp (eds), *Emotional Labor in the 21st Century: Diverse Perspectives on Emotion Regulation at Work* (New York, Routledge).

Evans, L and Moore, WL (2015) 'Impossible Burdens: White Institutions, Emotional Labor, and Micro-Resistance' 62 *Social Problems* 439. doi:10.1093/socpro/spv009

Froyum, C (2010) 'The Reproduction of Inequalities Through Emotional Capital: The Case of Socializing Low-Income Black Girls' 33 *Qualitative Sociology* 37. doi:10.1007/s11133-009-9141-5

Gould, DB (2009) *Moving Politics: Emotion and ACT UP's Fight Against AIDS* (Chicago, IL, University of Chicago Press).

Hecker, DE (2001) 'Occupational Employment Projections to 2010' 124 *Monthly Labor Review* 57.

Kelly, J and Ahern, K (2008) 'Preparing Nurses for Practice: A Phenomenological Study of the New Graduate in Australia' 18 *Journal of Clinical Nursing* 910. doi:10.1111/j.1365-2702.2008.02308.x

Lavoie-Tremblay, M, Paquet, M, Duchesne, M-A, Santo, A, Gavarancic, A, Courcy, F, et al. (2010) 'Retaining Nurses and Other Hospital Workers: An Intergenerational Perspective of the Work Climate' 42 *Journal of Nursing Scholarship* 414. doi:10.1111/j.1547-5069.2010.01370.x

Leiter, MP, Jackson, NJ and Shaughnessy, K (2009) 'Contrasting Burnout, Turnover Intention, Control, Value Congruence and Knowledge Sharing Between Baby Boomers and Generation X' 17 *Journal of Nursing Management* 100. https://doi.org/10.1111/j.1365-2834.2008.00884.x

Leiter, MP, Price, SL and Spence Laschinger, HK (2010) 'Generational Differences in Distress, Attitudes and Incivility Among Nurses: Generational

Differences Among Nurses' 18 *Journal of Nursing Management* 970. https://doi.org/10.1111/j.1365-2834.2010.01168.x

Li, J and Lambert, VA (2008) 'Job Satisfaction among Intensive Care Nurses from the People's Republic of China' 55 *International Nursing Review* 34. https://doi.org/10.1111/j.1466-7657.2007.00573.x

Lucero, RJ, Lake, ET and Aiken, LH (2010) 'Nursing Care Quality and Adverse Events in US Hospitals: Nursing Care Quality' 19 *Journal of Clinical Nursing* 2185. https://doi.org/10.1111/j.1365-2702.2010.03250.x

Mannheim, K (1952) 'The Problem of Generations' in P Kecskemeti (ed), *Essays on the Sociology of Knowledge* (London: Routledge and Kegan Paul).

Reay, D (2015) 'Habitus and the Psychosocial: Bourdieu with Feelings' 45 *Cambridge Journal of Education* 9. doi:10.1080/0305764X.2014.990420

Ridgeway, C (2011) *Framed by Gender: How Gender Inequality Persists in the Modern World* (New York, Oxford University Press).

Scheer, M (2012) 'Are Emotions a Kind of Practice (and Is That What Makes Them Have a History)? A Bourdieuian Approach to Understanding Emotion' 51 *History and Theory* 193. doi:10.1111/j.1468-2303.2012.00621.x

Stacey, C (2011) *The Caring Self: Work Experiences of Home Care Aides* (Ithaca, NY, Cornell University Press).

Sumter, SR, Valkenburg, PM and Peter, J (2013) 'Perceptions of Love Across the Lifespan: Differences in Passion, Intimacy, and Commitment' 37 *International Journal of Behavioral Development* 417. doi:10.1177/0165025413492486

Tourangeau, AE and Cranley, LA (2006) 'Nurse Intention to Remain Employed: Understanding and Strengthening Determinants' 55 *Journal of Advanced Nursing* 497. https://doi.org/10.1111/j.1365-2648.2006.03934.x

U.S. Department of Labor, Bureau of Labor Statistics (2018a) 'Labor Force Statistics from the Current Population Survey'. www.bls.gov/cps/cpsaat11.htm

———— (2018b) 'Occupational Outlook Handbook: Registered Nurse' www.bls.gov/ooh/healthcare/registered-nurses.htm

Vessey, JA, DeMarco, RF, Gaffney, DA and Budin, WC (2009) 'Bullying of Staff Registered Nurses in the Workplace: A Preliminary Study for Developing Personal and Organizational Strategies for the Transformation of Hostile to Healthy Workplace Environments' 25 *Journal of Professional Nursing* 299. doi:10.1016/j.profnurs.2009.01.022

Widger, K, Pye, C, Cranley, L, Wilson-Keates, B, Squires, M and Tourangeau, A (2007) 'Generational Differences in Acute Care Nurses' 20 *Nursing Leadership* 49. https://doi.org/10.12927/cjnl.2007.18785

Williams, CL (1992) 'The Glass Escalator: Hidden Advantages for Men in the "Female" Professions' 39 *Social Problems* 253. doi:10.1525/sp.1992.39.3.03x0034h

Wilson, B, Squires, M, Widger, K, Cranley, L and Tourangeau, A (2008) 'Job Satisfaction among a Multigenerational Nursing Workforce' 16 *Journal of Nursing Management* 716. https://doi.org/10.1111/j.1365-2834.2008.00874.x

Wingfield, AH (2009) 'Racializing the Glass Escalator: Reconsidering Men's Experiences with Women's Work' 23 *Gender & Society* 5. doi:10.1177/0891243208323054

5 'Male'ficence or 'Miss'understandings?

Exploring the Relationship Between Gender, Young Healthcare Professionals, Social Media, and Professionalism

Patricia Neville

Introduction

Historically healthcare has been conceptualised as masculinist (Adams 2005, 2010), with women being actively prohibited from entering some fields, like medicine and dentistry, until the early twentieth century. Women who wanted a career in healthcare at that time were funnelled into specific roles and professions, such as nursing, which came with lower status (Adams 2010). Despite this 'dominant gender order' (Lazar 2005, 2007; De Simone and Scano 2017), the past five decades have seen an increase in the number of women entering healthcare professions, including those that were considered the traditional preserve of men (Hedden et al. 2014). Currently women make up 42% of the world's workforce, and in healthcare they account for 75% of the workforce (Human Resources for Health: Global Resource Center 2008). Forty per cent of practising physicians in the West are female (Arrizabalaga et al. 2014: 363); 32% of all graduate physicians worldwide are female (Hedden et al. 2014); and 58% of medical school enrollees in Canada are female (Hedden et al. 2014: 1). In 2013, 63% of dental students and 49% of registered dentists in the EU/EEA were female (Council of European Dentists 2015: 33, 39). These workplace statistics indicate that healthcare has undergone a process of feminisation (Adams 2005; Brocklehurst and Tickle 2011; Gross and Schäfer 2011), namely a numerical increase of women in healthcare, including medicine (Heru 2005; Riska 2008, 2011) and dentistry (Adams 2005; Neville 2017a; Waylen et al. 2017).

For some, the changing gender composition of the healthcare professions signifies that hegemony has been overturned and gender equality has been achieved. For the current Millennial workforce and the incoming Generation Z professionals, gender equality in the workplace is recognised as a 'vital and non-negotiable right' (Ernst & Young 2016: 9).

However, Reskin and Roos (1990) remind us that feminisation can be a complicated process and that the increased numbers of women do not automatically ensure the successful integration of women into healthcare professions. The literature identifies structural and cultural barriers encountered by women who want to progress in a healthcare career (George 2007; Newman 2014; Newman et al. 2016). It has long been recognised that the organisational structure of healthcare, as in other fields, presents structural difficulties for women juggling family and a career (Langer et al. 2015: 1186). For instance, more men are practicing medicine across the World Health Organisation (WHO) region than women, with the exceptions of the UK, the Nordic region, and some Eastern European countries. Yet, there are more women than men in medical school (George 2007; Langer et al. 2015). Female dentists are more likely to work part-time and take career breaks than their male counterparts (Ayers et al. 2008: 347). The most popular reason women take a career break is to care for children, whereas men typically use career breaks to find a new job, to pursue study, or out of personal choice (Ayers et al. 2008: 348). Most women (61%) take on postgraduate training before having children, unlike men (34%) (Ayers et al. 2008). Moreover, a woman's choice of speciality is often determined by location and proximity to family (Saeed et al. 2008; McKay and Quiñonez 2012). These gender differences have led some to suggest that feminisation poses challenges to the healthcare workforce in the coming decades (e.g. Brocklehurst and Tickle 2011).

Research has also identified a sex pay gap and sex segregation within healthcare. There is a lack of women leaders in global health (Talib et al. 2017), in senior posts or managerial positions (Arrizabalaga et al. 2014; Human Resources for Health: Global Resource Center 2008). Furthermore, a recent UK headcount survey reported that women are over-represented in dental public health (54%), paediatric dentistry (59%), and special care dentistry (85%), whereas a greater proportion of men have careers in oral and maxillofacial surgery (73%), orthodontics (68%), periodontics (73%), and restorative dentistry (72%) (Dental Schools Council 2018).

As restrictive as these structural constraints are, more damning are the cultural barriers that female healthcare professionals encounter. It is commonly assumed that the increase of women in healthcare will change the profession's values and practices (Riska 2001; Adams 2010). For instance, US research claims that the rigid masculine norms of dentistry have become more accepting of women entering the profession (Rosenberg et al. 1998). However, in medicine, it has been well documented that female doctors adopt 'male professional norms' for social acceptance. This change creates issues regarding professional communications (e.g. Schéle et al. 2011: 2). Such observations reveal the gender stereotypes that female healthcare professionals encounter that actively limit their everyday working lives. Gender stereotyping has also been found to influence choice of college course and career (Newman et al. 2016: 14), and several surveys attest to the continued prevalence of sexual harassment in medicine, both during training and when in practice (Mathews and Bismark 2015: 189; Newman et al. 2016: 14).

Despite the ongoing feminisation of healthcare (Dacre 2011; De Simone and Scano 2017), a 'strong gender asymmetry' persists (Davidson and Burke 2016; De Simone and Scano 2017), shaping and modifying women's professional experiences. Such everyday work realities are unacceptable in general, but especially so to the current Millennial workforce, who have high expectations and are keen to challenge what they consider to be outdated workplace norms. These occupational realities are also unsettling for the incoming Generation Z, who value and champion diversity and inclusion in all aspects of their lives (Ernst & Young 2016: 5, 11). Despite the progressive work style and expectations of today's young professionals, it is interesting to observe how entrenched and stubbornly persistent gender discrimination is in healthcare. The lacklustre institutional response to problems may be, in part, attributed to the rhetoric of gender blindness that permeates the discourse of professional education and professionalism more generally. Numerous authors remind us that our construction of professionalism is rooted in androcentric ideals, which are also middle class, White, and Victorian (Adams 2010; Schleef 2010). Furthermore, the aim of professional education is the production of homogenous practitioners (Larson 1977). One way to ensure this is for professional education to dismiss and actively discourage the understanding that social variables such as gender, age, class, and ethnicity have a bearing on professional practice.

Though the rhetoric of feminisation pronounces the increased intake of women into medicine and dentistry to be unproblematic, it obscures the fact that these professions retain a patriarchal value system that needs to be addressed and tackled. I object to the way the discourse of healthcare professionalism dismisses and silences women's experiences of gender stereotyping, discrimination, and inequality in healthcare. Inspired by the recent hashtag movements and their effect of raising awareness of everyday gender inequalities, I contend that social media can be considered a means of raising awareness of the insidious sexism in healthcare and the challenges that women face as they try to progress their careers within a masculinist work culture (see De Simone and Scano 2017). In this way, young professionals use social media to 'crack the gender equality code' that they encounter in their workplaces (Ernst & Young 2016: 11). Two recent case studies will be introduced and discussed, and a feminist analysis will be undertaken to uncover the persistence of misogyny, sexism, and gender discrimination in healthcare in the twenty-first century. In keeping with the ideals of feminist analysis, policy and activism outcomes will also be presented for consideration.

Digital Feminism, Social Media, and Healthcare Professionalism: A Note on Method

The aim of this chapter is to explore women's experiences of everyday sexism in the healthcare professions and to present a feminist analysis of two recent social media events to illuminate the underlying tensions in the profession for women: misogyny, sexism, and gender discrimination. A feminist approach has been taken because the values of feminism mirror the values of this research and its researcher: to challenge the status quo and question the gender hierarchies, male privilege, and power imbalances inherent in healthcare (Kangere et al. 2017: 901).

Feminism can be defined as 'a movement to end sexism, sexist exploitation, and oppression' (hooks 1984: 26). Feminism allows us to investigate how gender inequalities are implicated in the relationships of women and men, and also traces where these inequalities emanate from at a structural/macro-systems level and how they impact on the lifeworld/micro-systems level (Locke et al. 2018: 5) of women. Increasingly we find feminism turning its attention to digital spaces, recognising such spaces as settings where 'issues of privilege, difference and access' (Baer 2016: 18) can be found and studied. 'Digital feminism' (Baer 2016: 18) recognises that digital spaces can be positive and negative for feminist conversations and debates (Turley and Fisher 2018: 128). This ambiguity reflects wider distinctions in digital research and debates about whether digital media can be considered inherently democratic, transcending social categories and distinctions, or if in fact they reproduce and re-problematise existing gender relations (Duffy 2015: 710). There is also a recognition that cyberspace is gendered (Locke et al. 2018: 4) and that a 'matrix of sexism' defines the online world (Stubbs-Richardson et al. 2018: 94). For instance, a 'gender digital gap' exists globally, with the proportion of women using the internet worldwide 12% lower than the proportion of men using this technology (International Telecommunications Union 2017). While there are slightly more women than men using the internet in the Americas (67% women, 65% men), in Europe the gender digital gap favours men (83% men, 76% women) (Statista 2018a). Furthermore, a recent US study of 4,248 adults found that 41% of respondents had been subjected to online harassment, such as name-calling. A further 18% experienced more severe forms of online harassment, including physical threats, sexual harassment, or stalking (Duggan 2017). While men experienced more online harassment than women, for women, the focus of the harassment was sexual in nature (Duggan 2017).

The gendered nature of the online world is also evidenced in social media. Social media, by definition, are online technologies that provide the ability for community building and interaction, allowing people to interface and to share, create, and consume online content (boyd and Ellison 2007; Locke et al. 2018: 3). Social media achieves its impact because of its discreet set of characteristics, namely, that it is inherently 'social, participatory, locative, algorithmic, interactive, affective and entangled with bodies' (Locke et al. 2018: 3). Since the 2010s there has been an increase in the use of social networking sites (SNS) and blogs to raise awareness of issues relating to hegemony and sexism (Baer 2016). Understandably, there has been recent growth in feminist social media research. Feminist approaches to social media are multiple and evolving. Currently, we can categorise feminist social media research according to the following subject matters: investigations into the relationship between the social variables of actors and their online interactions (e.g. Banet-Weier 2011); undertaking a feminist analysis of the values encoded in social media technologies and computer design (e.g. Bardzell 2010; Wacjman 2010); exploring the ways institutions and political decision making are shaped by social media practices (e.g. Papacharissi 2010; Taylor 2014); and researching 'the ways online interactions over particular social media platforms coincide with existing inequalities and hierarchies situated in specific communities' (Korn and Kneese 2015: 708).

This chapter aligns itself with the latter subject matter and takes as its starting point the recognition that social media can be 'a promising tool for spreading feminist discourse' (Kangere et al. 2017: 899). Particularly effective in this area have been hashtag movements like #EverydaySexism and #GamerGate where Twitter hashtags were used as tools to combat misogyny in everyday life and in the gaming community, respectively (Bates ND; Korn and Kneese 2015: 708). Hashtag activism involves creating and using hashtags as 'a way of exposing the prejudice faced by people on a daily basis, while sharing and reacting to it, and provoking responses' (Turley and Fisher 2018: 128). These online activities are taken to represent 'shouting back' against 'hegemony, misogyny and sexism' (Turley and Fisher 2018: 128). This 'hashtag feminism' has also been found to result in 'changed modes of communication, different kinds of conversations and new configurations of activism across the globe, both online and offline' (Baer 2016: 18).

I recognise the potential that 'digital platforms' have to articulate ideas about gender, healthcare, and sexism, and in so doing allow for new forms of protest or 'shouting back' against gender hegemony. I will shortly present two case studies that I believe illustrate some of these ongoing tensions within healthcare professions. However, there are limitations to this research method. From a feminist perspective, it is important to remember that digital space is not a utopia for the feminist cause. By raising awareness about gender issues the resultant visibility can lead to an increase of 'misogynistic and sexist narratives' being communicated online, which in turn can be used to 'shame' women and uphold inequalities in the offline/real world (Turley and Fisher 2018: 129). As a result, the feminist online activist can be victimised or trolled through social media online (Turley and Fisher 2018: 129) or harassed and bullied (Boynton 2012). Furthermore, it is important to match hashtag activism with offline activism to publicise the issue (Turley and Fisher 2018: 129); however, sometimes this is difficult to do.

At a more methodological level, there are also disadvantages with analysing social media 'stories'. In some cases, social media events can dilute or simplify complex issues on gender inequality to appeal to the majority. As a result, we should approach these case studies with some caution, as they cannot give comprehensive coverage to the issues at play, probably only highlighting one or two issues at a time (Kangere et al. 2017: 901). Another limitation of social media stories is the fact that they have an explosive timeline: quickly emerging onto the digital sphere, having their 15 minutes of fame or traction, and then disappearing again (Kangere et al. 2017: 901). Despite the selective and transient nature of social media events, it will be maintained that social media platforms are accessible, creative, expressive, and participatory (Kangere et al. 2017: 901), and so they can breathe new life into the topic of sexism in healthcare. What follows are two case studies of specific online events: a Facebook incident to illustrate how social media can breed misogyny and a hashtag movement that challenges the sexism endemic within healthcare.

Facebook, Cyber VAWG, and Misogyny

There are approximately 4.2 billion internet users in the world (55% of the world's population) (Internet World Stats 2018), and with 2 billion users Facebook is the world's most popular social networking site (Statista 2018b). Facebook is also popular among healthcare students. For instance in their survey of 682 healthcare professional students, White et al. (2013) found that 93% of respondents used Facebook, with the majority (76%) checking their account at least twice a day, and 39% checking it at least five times a day. The first Australian survey of healthcare professional students also found high social media usage, especially with Facebook (Usher et al. 2014: 99). The ubiquity of Facebook has resulted in this social media platform becoming implicated in the unprofessional behaviour of healthcare students. Studies have found that healthcare students have used Facebook to breach patient confidentiality in various postings (Thompson 2010), engage in online relationships with patients (Nyangeni et al. 2015), and write disrespectful comments about colleagues and employers (Chretien et al. 2009; Hall et al. 2013). Neville (2017b) found that most of the Fitness to Practise cases investigated and upheld by the General Dental Council over a three-year period in the UK involved Facebook posts. As a result, Facebook, as a participatory social networking site, provides an opportunity to explore how the norms, values, and behaviours of professionalism are interpreted and constructed by today's young healthcare professionals.

A recent case in Canada demonstrates the role that Facebook can play in revealing and problematising implicit sexist assumptions about gender in professional education programmes. In 2014, the School of Dentistry at Dalhousie University in Halifax, Canada, became embroiled in a social media scandal concerning the Facebook activities of its Year 4 male students. Thirteen of the 26 male dental students created a 'Class of DDS 2015 Gentlemen' Facebook group. There, male students voted on which female classmates they would like to have 'hate sex' with and joked about using chloroform on women. In another post, a woman was shown in a bikini with the caption, 'Bang until stress is relieved or unconscious' (Hunter et al. 2015). The female students (21 in total) lodged a formal complaint about the derogatory remarks posted online about them, and a full departmental and university investigation was launched (Hunter et al. 2015). The 13 men in question were removed from the programme as the academic investigation was undertaken. The investigating committee decided that the students in question should undergo a restorative justice programme and write and read a full letter of apology to their classmates, before they could rejoin the year (Hunter et al. 2015).

A feminist analysis of this social media event highlights three issues for discussion. At its most obvious, we can interpret this event as further evidence of how 'men have turned on women online' (Jane 2017: 1) using 'the rhetoric of sexualised, gendered violence' (Jane 2017: 2) in their posts. Sadly, 'gendered cyberhate' (Jane 2017: 5) has been part of the internet since its inception and is on the increase. In 2015, the UN created the category of 'cyber VAWG' defined as 'cyber violence against women and girls' to highlight this as an issue. Though this starts online, it has offline implications (UN Broadband Commission for Digital Development Working Group on Broadband and Gender 2015: 1). The UN outlines six categories of cyber VAWG: hacking, impersonation, surveillance/tracking, harassment/spamming, recruitment, and malicious distribution (UN Broadband Commission for Digital Development Working Group on Broadband and Gender 2015: 22).

The 'gendered hate speech' (Jane 2017: 2) that the male dentistry students used is also worrying as it calls into question the inclusivity of professional programmes. The cohort's brutish assertion of hegemonic masculinity can be interpreted as a male backlash (Faludi 1991) against the feminisation of dentistry and a reassertion of male dominance in response to their experience of being in the minority. Such gendered power plays are interesting to observe because of the gender–power nexus that operates within medicine and healthcare more generally. Hierarchy in healthcare is multifaceted, operating vertically and horizontally 'by both their disciplines and levels of authority' (Hughes and Salas 2013: 529). Healthcare students are located on the lowest rank of the hierarchy, and experience the most acute of these power asymmetries. Numerous studies have identified the various ways in which 'hierarchically-laden behaviours' and their emotional and performance-based outcomes define medical culture (Braithwaite et al. 2016: 8). Intimidation, humiliation, and harassment are often cited as the common pedagogic tools used by faculty in most undergraduate and specialist training medical programmes (e.g. Lempp 2009; Crowe et al. 2017: 70–71). Sexual harassment is part of this continuum (Mathews and Bismark 2015: 189). As a result, we can interpret this social media event as evidence of the gender conflict and power imbalances that permeate healthcare student culture, especially in professional programmes.

Last, this story can be interpreted as evidence of a success for feminist activism in which this negative experience was turned into a moment of activism and gender awareness building. While the offending students were sanctioned by the institution, it is important to note that some of the female students were upset that a restorative justice approach was taken, interpreting it as a 'softer' line of sanctioning than could have been adopted by the institution (Hunter et al. 2015). The Facebook posts contained threats of sexual violence. Can a verbally delivered apology really make amends for such gendered hate speeches against classmates? There are echoes of the bourgeois assumptions of professionalism again here, where an apology seems like the 'gentlemanly' thing to do to restore the 'honour' and 'reputation' of the 'delicate' and 'offended' female classmates. By remediating the issue in this way, it reframes the problem of misogyny as something that is cultural, and therefore attributable to certain rogue individuals, rather than something that is structural and systemic in nature. As a result, there is a real risk that the consciousness-raising potential of this awful event may be lost out of a desire to protect the institution. This case reminds us that cyber VAWG can occur in any workplace and educational setting, and that institutions need to recognise it as a new category of harmful workplace experience that will need to be monitored and checked for in relation to school policies on professionalism and acceptable behaviours (see Sojo et al. 2016).

#Hashtagging Patriarchy

The previous case study illustrates how social media can act as an echo chamber for online misogyny. However, I have already remarked that social media can also act as a launchpad for calling out gender inequalities and 'shouting back' against patriarchy. While the Dalhousie University Facebook incident presents gender as a socio-cultural construction, open to contrasting interpretations, the hashtag movement #ILookLikeASurgeon presents gender as a structural reality, with lifeworld implications for women working in medicine. The hashtag movement #ILookLikeAS-urgeon will also be used to demonstrate the potential of social media to raise gender awareness in the medical profession.

The hashtag movement #ILookLikeASurgeon is 'an online campaign celebrating women in surgery' (Logghe et al. 2017). It has currently inspired 150,000 tweets, 35,000 users, and up to 1 billion impressions online (Logghe et al. 2017). Its aim is to highlight the barriers women face in surgery, and to challenge the gendered construction of surgeons. It calls for a more inclusive model of surgery (Logghe et al. 2017). As Log-ghe et al. (2017) have written, 'the hashtag underlines the need to create a new surgeon ideal'. It hopes to change popular perceptions about what a surgeon is, increase the number of women working in surgery, and have a positive impact on patient outcomes (Logghe et al. 2017). This hashtag movement has garnered much attention within medicine in the US and internationally. For instance, one spinoff has been the 'Women in Surgery Africa' Twitter account (Logghe et al. 2017). The hashtag movement was also mentioned by Caprice Greenberg in her 2017 presidential address to the Association for Academic Surgeons in the US (Logghe et al. 2017).

The creation of the hashtag #ILookLikeASurgeon was directly influenced by another hashtag movement, #ILooklikeAnEngineer. This hashtag was created by a software engineer, Isis Anchalee, in response to the negative feedback she received after being featured in an advertising campaign for her employer (UNC Healthcare and UNC School of Medicine 2015). Most of the negative comments challenged the veracity of the campaign, stating that they did not believe she was a software engineer working at that company (UNC Healthcare and UNC School of Medicine 2015). Her story was featured in *The New York Times* on 5 August 2015. Heather Logghe, a surgical trainee, read this story and, after a conversation with female colleague Dr Sara Scarlet, decided to write a tweet in response (UNC Healthcare and UNC School of Medicine 2015): 'Hashtag Aims to Break Gender Stereotypes in engineering—Is 'Ilooklikeasurgeon next?' In her tweet she posted a photograph of herself and her young daughter. She also wrote a blog post entitled, '#ILook-LikeASurgeon Tweet it. Own it. Be the role model you always wanted but never had' (Logghe 2015). This hashtag went viral after a few days and the original blog was read 7,000 times, culminating in several guest female bloggers adding their voices to this issue (UNC Healthcare and UNC School of Medicine 2015). The story was picked up by various US and international news outlets, including the *Today Show* and *BBC Trending* (UNC Healthcare and UNC School of Medicine 2015).

The hashtag #ILookLikeASurgeon was resurrected in April 2017. On 4 April 2017, the cover of *The New Yorker* was designed by Malika Favre. The artwork presented the perspective of a patient on a surgical table, looking up at four gowned and masked faces overhead. The purpose of the cover was, according to the artist, 'to capture a patient's feeling of vulnerability' (Savedge 2017). However, when the magazine cover was seen by Dr Susan Pitt, who was on her way to the American Association of Endocrine Surgeons' conference, she tweeted the magazine cover to some of her female colleagues using the hashtag #ILookLikeASurgeon, challenging all recipients to reproduce this image with their female colleagues (Hughes 2015). This challenge went viral and was taken up by female surgeons in Mexico, Brazil, Saudi Arabia, Istanbul, and Ireland (Savedge 2017). Overall, it resulted in 30,000 tweets using the hashtag (URMC 2017).

What is the significance of this hashtag movement? First, it reminds us of the short but frenzied social life of a hashtag movement, how one tweet can spark a viral sensation. Using Symplur software, Hughes (2015) found that the hashtag generated 128 million impressions, 40,000 individual tweets, and 7,900 participants in its initial months. It has been retweeted in 75 countries and in 20 languages (Hughes 2015). From its inception, this hashtag aligned itself with a feminist agenda. According to its originator, Dr Logghe, its aim was to be affirmative and political: 'I like the hashtag in the first person. As woman surgeons, whether we are in our first year of training or an emeritus professor, it's most important that we ourselves believe we "look" like surgeons. Because we do' (Logghe 2015). The online growth of the hashtag has a consciousness-raising effect, challenging gendered perceptions and highlighting the structural inequalities that persist within surgery. #ILookLikeASurgeon reminds us that women are seriously under-represented in surgery. In the US, only 19% of surgeons are female (Savedge 2017). In the UK, the figure is closer to 10% (Garner and Bowbrick 2015). The reasons for the low representation of women in surgery reflect the gendered nature and macho culture of surgery (Peters and Ryan 2014), as well as the incompatibility of the work schedule with family life (e.g. Sund 2017). However, what can a hashtag do to effect change in these structural and cultural factors?

An important issue in adopting a feminist approach to this investigation concerns how and in what ways can we translate these observations into action and change for women and men working in healthcare (Kangere et al. 2017: 902). One of the key aspects of feminist scholarship in social media is that online activism needs to be matched by offline organisation and activism if it is to gain any ongoing improvements. I noted that the hashtag movement generally inspired individual responses from female surgeons, staging and posting photos rather than collective responses. While it also inspired the creation of a 'Women in Surgery' Twitter account in Africa, there does not appear to be much offline activism. This is not always the outcome for hashtag movements. For instance, in January 2016 the #LikeALadyDoc hashtag movement in the UK emerged in response to a sexist newspaper article written by Nigel Lawson, in *The Sunday Times* (2016). Entitled 'The one sex change on the NHS that nobody has been talking about' (Lawson 2016), the article critiqued the feminisation of medicine and openly attributed the growing number of female medics and their over-representation in part-time contracts as one of the main failings of the National Health Service (NHS). Understandably, there was swift reaction to this article online, culminating in the establishment of the #LikeALadyDoc hashtag, used by women medics as they posted their reactions to the article (Grounsell 2016). Posts included recalling pioneering women in medicine, documenting their love of their job, and the challenge of long working hours alongside family responsibilities. Interestingly, Roshana Mehdian, one of the original contributors to the hashtag, created another hashtag, #PinkWednesday, inviting NHS employees to wear pink to work in solidarity with their female colleagues and to post their photos online on 20 January 2016 (Haysomjan 2016). #PinkWednesday was a success, attracting support from NHS staff and non-NHS staff in solidarity with women in healthcare, and garnered media attention as far away as Australia (Grounsell 2016; Haysomjan 2016).

This is one example of where a hashtag movement can result in offline activism. However, more needs to be done to sustain public and sectoral interest in gender inequality and workplace sexism. Digital feminism proposes that a hashtag movement needs to be supported by an offline network or group who will continue to work and garner attention on this issue (Kangere et al. 2017; Korn and Kneese 2015). Ideally, an offline interest group needs to be established, one that will be concerned with the issue of gender inequality in healthcare and its divisive effects. The remit of this group or groups could be twofold: to support and encourage further research on the gender inequalities within healthcare, as well as to lobby professional bodies and regulators on gender inequality as a critical issue for healthcare in the twenty-first century. This important upstream policy work could also be supported by further research by digital feminists studying the online activism of female medics. In this way, digital feminism could help advance its activist agenda, as well as the recognition of the positive impact of social media as a means of sharing opinions and creating debate and discussion.

Concluding Comments

These cases are a timely reminder of the 'pervasive, structural nature' of sexism and gender inequality in healthcare by 'linking the specific local case to larger narratives of inequality' (Baer 2016: 18). Approaching social media as a means of exploring and making visible the endemic nature of gender inequality and discrimination in healthcare provides an opportunity to present an alternative viewpoint on social media that is commonly promoted in the literature, namely that it is a vehicle for unprofessionalism. Social media can capture and amplify these sexist undertones and bring them to public light. The outcomes will be to raise awareness of the inherent sexism in healthcare, especially when we consider how 'gender neutral' the rhetoric of feminisation is. There is a naïve assumption that feminisation has been accompanied by a cultural shift. While the numbers of women in healthcare professions are increasing, there is still much to be done regarding the values, norms, and beliefs within healthcare, to move away from the androcentric model of professionalism. Calls for such a paradigm change will benefit both women and men healthcare workers, as Millennials of all genders are openly concerned with flexibility and maintaining a healthy work–life balance (Ernst & Young 2016: 8). This chapter recommends that the healthcare establishment pays more attention to the online activism of healthcare professionals and recognises the need for the institution to address its implicit, unconscious or otherwise, gender biases. As the number of women continues to increase in healthcare, and in light of Millennial workers' expectation of flexibility, we need to ensure that healthcare is a progressive and inclusive work environment for all.

References

Adams, TL (2005) 'Feminization of Professions: The Case of Women in Dentistry' 30 *Canadian Journal of Sociology* 71. doi:10.1353/cjs.2005.0018
——— (2010) 'Gender and Feminization in Healthcare Professions' 4 *Sociology Compass* 454. doi:10.1111/j.1751-9020.2010.00294.x
Arrizabalaga, P, Abellana, R, Viñas, O, Merino, A and Ascaso, C (2014) 'Gender Inequalities in the Medical Profession: Are There Still Barriers to Women Physicians in the 21st Century?' 28 *Gaceta Sanitaria* 363. doi:10.1016/j.gaceta.2014.03.014
Ayers, KMS, Thompson, WM, Rich, AM and Newton, JT (2008) 'Gender Differences in Dentists' Working Practices and Job Satisfaction' 36 *Journal of Dentistry* 343, 347–348. doi:10.1016/j.jdent.2008.01.012
Baer, H (2016) 'Redoing Feminism: Digital Activism, Body Politics, and Neoliberalism' 16 *Feminist Media Studies* 17–18. doi:10.1080/14680777.2015.1093070
Banet-Weier, S (2011) 'Branding the Post-Feminist Self: Girls' Video Production and YouTube' in MC Kearney (ed), *Mediated Girlhoods: New Explorations of Girls' Media Culture*, 277–294 (New York, Peter Lang).
Bardzell, S (2010) 'Feminist HCI: Taking Stock and Outlining an Agenda for Design' in *Proceedings of CHI'10: World Conference on Human Factors in Computing Systems*. http://wtf.tw/ref/bardzell.pdf
Bates, L. 'The Everyday Sexism Project'. www.everydaysexism.com.
boyd, dm and Ellison, NB (2007) 'Social Network Sites: Definition, History, and Scholarship' 13 *Journal of Computer-Mediated Communication* 210. doi:10.1111/j.1083-6101.2007.00393.x
Boynton, P (2012) 'Getting the Press We Deserve: Opportunities and challenges for Innovative Media Practice' 22 *Feminism & Psychology* 536.
Braithwaite, J, Clay-Williams, R, Vecellio, E, Marks, D, Hooper, T, Westbrook, M, et al. (2016) 'The Basis of Clinical Tribalism, Hierarchy and Stereotyping:

A Laboratory-Controlled Teamwork Experiment' 6 *British Medical Journal Open* 1, 8. doi:10.1136/bmjopen-2016-012467

Brocklehurst, P and Tickle, M (2011) 'Planning a Dental Workforce for the Future for the National Health Service in the United Kingdom: What Factors Should Be Accounted For?' 71 *Health Education Journal* 340. doi:10.1177/0017896911398815

Chretien, KC, Greysen, SR, Chretien, J-P and Kind, T (2009) 'Online Posting of Unprofessional Content by Medical Students' 302 *Journal of the American Medical Association* 1309. doi:10.1001/jama.2009.1387

Council of European Dentists (2015) *EU Manual of Dental Practice 2015* (Wales, CED) 33, 39. www.cedentists.eu/library/eu-manual.html

Crowe, S, Clarke, N and Brugha, R (2017) ' "You do not cross them": Hierarchy and Emotion in Doctors' Narratives of Power Relations in Specialist Training' 186 *Social Science & Medicine* 70. doi:10.1016/j.socscimed.2017.05.048

Dacre, J (2011) 'Women and Medicine' 41 *The Journal of the Royal College of Physicians of Edinburgh* 350.

Davidson, MJ and Burke, RJ (2016) *Women in Management Worldwide: Progress and Prospects* (Burlington, VT, Gower).

De Simone, S and Scano, C (2017) 'Discourses of Sameness, Unbalance and Influence: Dominant Gender Order in Medicine' July 2017 *Journal of Gender Studies* 1. doi:10.1080/09589236.2017.1357541

Dental Schools Council (2018) *A Survey of Dental Clinical Academic Staffing Level* (London: DSC). www.dentalschoolscouncil.ac.uk/wp-content/uploads/2018/08/clinical-academic-survey-dental-2018.pdf

Duggan, M (2017) 'Online Harassment 2017' *Pew Research Center* 11 July 2017. www.pewinternet.org/2017/07/11/online-harassment-2017/

Duffy, BE (2015) 'Gendering the Labor of Social Media Production' 15 *Feminist Media Studies* 710. doi:10.1080/14680777.2015.1053715

Ernst & Young (2016) *Next-Gen Workforce: Secret Weapon or Biggest Challenge?* (Ernst & Young), 5, 9, 11. www.ey.com/Publication/vwLUAssets/ey-next-gen-workforce-secret-weapon-or-biggest-challenge/$FILE/ey-pdf-next-gen-workforce-secret-weapon-or-biggest-challenge.pdf

Faludi, S (1991) *Backlash: The Undeclared War Against American Women* (New York, Crown).

Garner, A and Bowbrick, V (2015) 'Suturing the Surgical Gender Gap' 350 *British Medical Journal* h964. doi:10.1136/bmj.h964

George, A (2007) *Human Resources for Health: A Gender Analysis*. Paper commissioned by the Women and Gender Equity Knowledge Network (Geneva, World Health Organization).

Gross, D and Schäfer, G (2011) ' "Feminization" in German Dentistry: Career Paths and Opportunities—A Gender Comparison' 34 *Women's Studies International Forum* 130.

Grounsell, L (2016) '#LikeALadyDoc: Female Doctors Hit Back at Sexist Claims That Staffing Issues in Hospitals Are Caused by "part-time" Working Mothers Who "put their families first" ' *Daily Mail Australia* 1 February. www.dailymail.co.uk/femail/article-3425932/Female-doctors-social-media-hashtag-LikeALadyDoc.html#ixzz5GEIxd5oV

Hall, M, Hanna, L-A and Huey, G (2013) 'Use and Views on Social Networking Sites of Pharmacy Students in the United Kingdom' 77 *American Journal of Pharmaceutical Education* 9. doi:10.5688/ajpe7719

Haysomjan, S (2016) 'British Doctors Are Fighting Back Against a Sexist Article with This Hilarious Hashtag' 19 January 2016. https://mashable.com/2016/01/19/like-a-lady-doc-hashtag/#uRprFB9muGq8

Hedden, L, Barer, ML, Cardiff, K, McGrail, KM, Law, MR and Bourgeault, IL (2014) 'The Implications of the Feminization of the Primary Care Physician Workforce on Service Supply: A Systematic Review' 12 *Human Resources for Health* 32. doi:10.1186/1478-4491-12-32

Heru, AM (2005) 'Pink-Collar Medicine: Women and the Future of Medicine' 22 *Gender Issues* 20. doi:10.1007/s12147-005-0008-0

hooks, b (1984) *Feminist Theory: From Margins to Center* (Boston, MA, South End Press).

Hughes, KA (2015) *#ILookLikeASurgeon Goes Viral: How It Happened* (Chicago, IL, Bulletin of the American College of Surgeons). www.bulletin.facs.org/2015/11/ilooklikeasurgeon-goes-viral-how-it-happened/

Hughes, AM and Salas, E (2013) 'Hierarchical Medical Teams and the Science of Teamwork' 15 *American Medical Association Journal of Ethics* 529.

Human Resources for Health: Global Resource Center (HRH GDC) HRH Global Resource Center (2008) 'Resource Spotlight: Gender and Health Workforce Statistics' (HRH GRC). www.hrhresourcecenter.org/gender_stats.html

Hunter, K, Maxwell, E and Brunger, F (2015) 'Misogyny in Health Professions? An Analysis of the Dalhousie Dentistry Scandal' 4 *Bioéthique Online* 1. doi:10.7202/1035508ar

International Telecommunications Union (ITU) (2017) *ICT Facts and Figures 2017* (Geneva, ITU). www.itu.int/en/ITU-D/Statistics/Documents/facts/ICTFactsFigures2017.pdf

Internet World Stats (2018) 'World Internet Usage and 2018 Population Statistics' 3 June2018. www.internetworldstats.com/stats.htm

Jane, EA (2017) *Misogyny Online. A Short (and Brutish) History* (Los Angeles, Sage), 1, 2, 5.

Kangere, M, Kemitare, J and Michau, L (2017) 'Hashtag Activism: Popularizing Feminist Analysis of Violence Against Women in the Horn, East and Southern Africa' 17 *Feminist Media Studies* 899, 901–902. doi:10.1080/14680777.2017.1350526

Langer, A, Meleis, A, Knaul, FM, Atun, R, Aran, M, Arreola-Ornelas, et al. (2015) 'Women and Health: The Key for Sustainable Development' 386 *The Lancet* 1165, 1186. doi:10.1016/S0140-6736(15)60497-4

Larson, MS (1977) *The Rise of Professionalism* (Berkeley, University of California Press).

Lawson, D (2016) 'The One Sex Change on the NHS That Nobody Is Talking About' *The Sunday Times* 17 January 2016. www.thetimes.co.uk/article/the-one-sex-change-on-the-nhs-that-nobody-has-been-talking-about-3fq9053kcn9

Lazar, MM (2005) *Feminist Critical Discourse Analysis* (London, Palgrave Macmillan).

—— (2007) 'Feminist Critical Discourse Analysis: Articulating a Feminist Discourse Praxis' 4 *Critical Discourse Studies* 141. doi:10.1080/17405900701464816

Lempp, H (2009) 'The Medical School Culture' in C Brosnan and BS Turner (eds), *The Handbook of the Sociology of Medical Education* (Abingdon, Oxford, Routledge), 71, 88.

Locke, A, Lawthom, R and Lyons, A (2018) 'Social Media Platforms as Complex and Contradictory Spaces for Feminisms: Visibility, Opportunity, Power, Resistance and Activism' 28 *Feminism & Psychology* 3. doi:10.1177/0959353517753973

Logghe, H (2015) '#ILookLikeASurgeon Tweet It. Own It' *Allies for Health Blog* 7 August. www.alliesforhealth.blogspot.com/2015/08/ilooklikeasurgeon-tweet-it-own-it.html?m=1

Logghe, H, Jones, C, McCoubrey, A and Fitzgerald, E (2017) '#ILookLikeASurgeon: Embracing Diversity to Improve Patient Outcomes' 359 *British Medical Journal* j4563. doi:10.1136/bmj.j4653

Mathews, B and Bismark, MM (2015) 'Sexual Harassment in the Medical Profession: Legal and Ethical Responsibilities' 203 *The Medical Journal of Australia* 189. doi:10.5694/mja15.00336

McKay, JC and Quiñonez, CR (2012) 'The Feminization of Dentistry: Implications for the Profession' 78 *Journal of the Canadian Dental Association* 1.

Neville, P (2017a) 'An Observational Analysis of Recent Female Dental Enrolment Figures in the Republic of Ireland' 21 *European Journal of Dental Education* 235. doi:10.1111/eje.12206

—— (2017b) 'Social Media and Professionalism: A Retrospective Content Analysis of Fitness to Practise Cases Heard by the GDC Concerning Social Media Complaints' 223 *British Dental Journal* 353. doi:10.1038/sj.bdj.2017.765

Newman, C (2014) 'Time to Address Gender Discrimination and Inequality in the Health Workforce' 12 *Human Resources for Health* 5. doi:10.1186/1478-4491-12-25

Newman, C, Ng, C, Pacqué-Margolis, S and Frymus, D (2016) 'Integration of Gender-Transformative Interventions into Health Professional Education Reform for the 21st Century: Implications of an Expert Review' 14 *Human Resources for Health* 14. doi:10.1186/s12960-016-0109-8

Nyangeni, T, du Rand, S and van Rooyen, D (2015) 'Perceptions of Nursing Students Regarding Responsible Use of Social Media in the Eastern Cape' 38 *Curationis* 1. doi:10.4102/curationis.v38i2.1496

Papacharissi, Z (2010) *A Private Sphere: Democracy in a Digital Age* (Cambridge, Polity Press).

Peters, K and Ryan, M (2014) 'Machismo in Surgery Is Harming the Speciality' 348 *British Medical Journal* g3034. doi:10.1136/bmj.g3034

Reskin, B and Roos, PA (1990) *Job Queues, Gender Queues: Explaining Women's Inroads into Male Occupations* (Philadelphia, Temple University Press).

Riska, E (2001) 'Towards a Gender Balance: But Will Women Physicians Have an Impact on Medicine?' 52 *Social Science & Medicine* 179.

—— (2008) 'The Feminization Thesis: Discourses on Gender and Medicine' 16 *NORA – Nordic Journal of Feminist and Gender Research*. doi:10.1080/08038740701885691

—— (2011) 'Gender and Medical Careers' 68 *Maturitas* 264. doi:10.1016/j.maturitas.2010.09.010

Rosenberg, HM, Cucchiara, AJ and Helpin, ML (1998) 'Dental Students' Attitude to Gender Roles' 47 *Social Science & Medicine* 1877.

Saeed, S, Jimenez, M, Howell, H, Karimbux, N and Sukotjo, C (2008) 'Which Factors Influence Students' Selection of Advanced Graduate Programs? One Institution's Experience' 72 *Journal of Dental Education* 688.

Savedge, J (2017) 'Female Surgeons Around the World Recreate New Yorker Cover' *Mother Nature Network* 12 April 2017. www.mnn.com/health/healthy-spaces/blogs/female-surgeons-around-world-recreate-new-yorker-cover

Schéle, I, Hedman, L and Hammarström, A (2011) 'Shared Ambiguity But Different Experiences and Demands among Dental Students—A Gender Perspective' 8 *Qualitative Research in Psychology* 1. doi:10.1080/14780880902874231

Schleef, D (2010) 'Identity Transformation, Hegemonic Masculinity and Research on Professionalization' 4 *Sociology Compass* 122. doi:10.1111/j.1751-9020.2009.00265.x

Sojo, VE, Wood, RE and Genat, AE (2016) 'Harmful Workplace Experiences and Women's Occupational Well-Being: A Meta-Analysis' 40 *Psychology of Women Quarterly* 10. doi:10.1177/0361684315599346

Statista (2018a). 'Internet Usage Rates Worldwide in 2017, by Gender and Region' (Statista). www.statista.com/statistics/491387/gender-distribtion-of-internet-users-region/

——— (2018b) 'Most Famous Social Network Sites Worldwide as of January 2018, Ranked by Number of Active Users (in millions)' (Statista). www.statista.com/statistics/272014/global-social-networks-ranked-by-number-of-users/

Stubbs-Richardson, MS, Rader, NE and Crosby, AG (2018) 'Tweeting Rape Culture: Examining Portrayals of Victim Blaming in Discussions of Sexual Assault Cases on Twitter' 28 *Feminism & Psychology* 90,108. doi: 10.1177/0959353517715874

Sund, M (2017) 'UEMS: Survey on Women In Surgery Europe (WISE)' Presentation, Copenhagen 6 May 2017. www.uems.eu/__data/assets/pdf_file/0004/48712/Sund,-M.-WISE-survey-1.pdf

Talib, Z, Burke, KS and Barry, M (2017) 'Women Leaders in Global Health' 5 *The Lancet Global Health* e565. doi:10.1016/S2214-109X(17)30182-1

Taylor, A (2014) *The People's Platform: Taking Back Power and Culture in the Digital Age* (New York, Metropolitan Books).

Thompson, C (2010) 'Facebook—Cautionary Tales for Nurses: Nurses Need to be Wary About What They Post on Social Networking Sites' 16 *Nursing Journal of New Zealand* 26.

Turley, E and Fisher, J (2018) 'Tweeting Back While Shouting Back: Social Media and Feminist Activism' 28 *Feminism & Psychology* 128–129. doi:10.1177/0959353517715875

Korn, JU and Kneese, T (2015) 'Guest Editors' Introduction: Feminist Approaches to Social Media Research: History, Activism, and Values' 15 *Feminist Media Studies* 707–708. doi:10.1080/14680777.2015.1053713

UN Broadband Commission for Digital Development Working Group on Broadband and Gender (2015) 'Cyber Violence Against Women and Girls: A World-Wide Wake-Up Call', 1, 22. en.unesco.org/sites/default/files/gender-report2015final.pdf

UNC Healthcare and UNC School of Medicine (2015) 'UNC Hospitals Resident Physician Launches #ILoolLikeASurgeon' *UNC Healthcare and UNC School of Medicine Newsroom* 31 August 2015. www.news.unchealthcare.org/news/2015/August/ilooklikeasurgeon

University of Rochester Medical Center (URMC) (2017) '#ILookLikeASurgeon: Female Surgical Residents Reflect on Training at URMC' 20 June 2017. www.urmc.rochester.edu/news/story/4800/ilooklikeasurgeon-female-surgical-residents-reflect-on-training-at-urmc.aspx

Usher, K, Woods, C, Glass, N, Wilson, R, Mayner, L, Jackson, D, et al. (2014) 'Australian Health Professions Student Use of Social Media' 21 *Collegian* 95, 99. doi:10.1016/j.colegn.2014.02.004

Wacjman, J (2010) 'Feminist Theories of Technology' 34 *Cambridge Journal of Economics* 143. doi.org/10.1093/cje/ben057

Waylen, A, Barnes, O, Kenyon, P and Neville, P (2017) 'Can Motivations for Studying Dentistry Inform Us About Gender and BME Differences in Dental Academic Careers?' 222 *British Dental Journal* 13. doi:10.1038/sj.bdj.2017.22

White, J, Kirwan, P, Lai, K, Walton, J and Ross, S (2013) ' "Have you seen what is on Facebook?" The Use of Social Networking Software by Healthcare Professional Students' 3 *British Medical Journal Open* e003013. doi:10.1136/bmjopen-2013-003013

Section 2
Legal Professions

6 Launching Careers in Law
Entry to First Jobs After Law School

Fiona M. Kay

Introduction

The progression from student to employed professional marks an important transition—a launch point—for the fulfilment of career aspirations. Researchers in the sociology of the life course have paid particularly close attention to this transition phase for careers (Mayer 2004). Research demonstrates that first occupational job has a direct and substantial impact on the longer trajectory of status attainment (Verwiebe et al. 2016). Those who fail to obtain favourable first jobs are at risk for delayed entry to career tracks, extended periods of unemployment, and wage penalties (Yu and Chiu 2014).

In the context of the legal profession, first jobs play a crucial role in determining law graduates' career paths. For example, an Australian study of 600 New South Wales lawyers revealed that career patterns of lawyers are heavily influenced by the nature of their first legal job. There appears to be little opportunity for movement between lawyer types (property, litigation, commercial, and generalist) (Tomasic 1983). More recently, Dinovitzer and Dawe (2016) examined the sorting of lawyers into settings (e.g. big firms, solo practice, government) and sectors (e.g. private versus public) in Canada and the US. They argue that this sorting fundamentally shapes the opportunities afforded to lawyers over the course of their careers (Dinovitzer and Dawe 2016: 83).

Numerous studies suggest the sorting of law graduates into settings is influenced by socio-demographic factors in addition to law school credentials (Dinovitzer and Dawe 2016; Hagan and Kay 1995; Kay and Gorman 2008; Gorman and Kay 2016; Sommerlad 2015; Webley et al. 2016). Sociological research more generally shows that the likelihood of landing a job hinges on graduates' demographic and socio-economic background "which serves as a powerful sanctioning mechanism for whatever personal aspirations and preferences actors may have" (Dobrev 2005: 806). This chapter builds on prior work by: 1) tracing the demographic distribution of new lawyers across sectors and settings in their first jobs; 2) assessing the contribution of educational credentials, motivations, and economic climate in determining job attainment in various organisational contexts; and 3) exploring occasions for early assessment of job candidates during apprenticeship. Drawing on a survey of law graduates in Canada, this chapter analyses factors shaping who enters where in the profession and why.

Socio-Demographic Background and Job Prospects

Age and Cohort

Age has received little attention in the literature on lawyers' careers, but studies of other professions suggest a younger profile tends to be preferred (Abrams et al. 2016). Theories of ageism demonstrate that people have implicit preferences for young over old (Gringart et al. 2005). Youth is associated with competence and potential. Furthermore, older law graduates are more likely to be discriminated against when there is a stereotypical mismatch between a candidate's perceived age and the characteristics of a particular position, such as a junior associate in a law firm or an entry-level government lawyer (Posthuma and Campion 2009). Other research suggests that those in positions to hire new lawyers may have a greater preference for younger candidates if the investment is viewed as long- rather than short-term, as is the case for associates in law firms versus summer students (Abrams et al. 2016).

A larger body of research has examined cohorts entering the profession. Attention has tended to focus on birth cohorts and generational differences (Glass 2007; Yu and Miller 2005). Although generations are typically defined based on biological age or birth year, a recent study suggests that people also think of generations in terms of other definitions, including life stage and shared experiences (Urick et al. 2017). Graduation from law school, call to the bar, and entry to practice represent shared experiences, and membership in a particular bar admission cohort has implications for hiring prospects. The decades of the 1990s and early 2000s were especially tumultuous. Law graduates entering practice in the early 1990s confronted a struggling economy, mergers and dissolution of firm partnerships, and globalisation of large corporate law firms (Galanter and Henderson 2008). Law graduates entering practice in the early 2000s encountered increased demand for entry-level positions in law firms, but also a restructuring of large law firms (Ackroyd and Muzio 2007) characterised by shrinking ranks of equity partners (Henderson 2011) and a growth of contract and staff lawyers, which derailed many lawyers from partnership tracks (Sterling and Reichman 2016). The legal labour market became increasingly precarious (Milkman 2017), and even more so with the 2008 economic downturn (Markovic and Plickert 2018). There is reason to anticipate that young lawyers entering practice during these two decades encountered significant challenges in their search for entry-level positions.

Gender, Race, and Social Class

Studies of hiring show gender differences emerge early on in professional careers. In the US, women report taking first jobs in government, public interest, or other non-firm settings more frequently than men (Hull and Nelson 2000; Sandefur 2007). In a study of Toronto lawyers, women were less likely than men to take first positions in law firms and more than twice as likely as men to enter jobs in government (Hagan and Kay 1995). In a more recent study of Canadian lawyers, men were more likely than women to start out in solo practice and small- to medium-sized firms (52% versus 47%), while women were more likely than men to start their careers in public practice (27% versus 17%) (Dinovitzer and Dawe 2016: 93). Some studies suggest that young men and women are drawn to different employment settings because of differences in family caregiving roles (Aiken and Regan 2016; Dau-Schmidt et al. 2009; Dinovitzer et al. 2009). Thus, women move into the public sector and work settings other than law firms because these jobs are more family-friendly and promote better work–life balance (Reichman and Sterling 2002; Sommerlad 2016).

Women's distributions across practice settings do not appear entirely attributable to personal preferences. In a British Columbia study of new lawyers, Brockman (1992) found that women were less likely than men to be interviewed for articling positions with law firms and less likely to obtain the positions they had ranked as first or second choice. In a study of 770 offices of large US law firms in the mid-1990s, Gorman (2005) observed that firms where hiring criteria were more stereotypically masculine (e.g. qualities such as aggressiveness and leadership) hired more men, whereas firms with more stereotypically feminine hiring criteria (e.g. qualities such as friendliness and willingness to cooperate) hired more women. These studies suggest gender bias on the part of organisational decision-makers (see also Rice and Barth 2016).

Race and ethnicity also matter for entry to careers. Research shows that the career-entry phase following university graduation poses ethnicity-specific hindrances in various professions (Verwiebe et al. 2016) and ethnic discrimination in hiring decisions persists (Zschirnt and Ruedin 2016). In a US study, researchers found even among graduates of an elite law school, African-American, Hispanic, and American-Indian lawyers are less likely than their white counterparts to start their careers in private practice (Lempert et al. 2000). A US survey of new law graduates conducted in 2000 found Black and Hispanic law graduates are more likely to start in the public sector compared with whites (Dinovitzer and Dawe 2016: 97). A survey of new Canadian lawyers conducted in 2010 found Black, Southeast-Asian, and Asian lawyers are more likely to work in the public sector compared with whites (Dinovitzer and Dawe 2016: 93). Government employment has been subject to greater regulation with respect to equity, so it is perhaps not surprising that this sector offers improved opportunities for women and racial minorities (Kay et al. 2006). Within the private sector, law firm resources shape diversity hiring. In a study of more than 1,300 US law offices, Gorman and Kay (2010: 233) found that firms with more resources at their disposal seem to be more able or more inclined to pursue ethnic diversity in hiring: minority presence rises with firm size, firm gross revenues, and firm profits per partner.

In addition, studies reveal the continuing role that social class plays after the completion of higher education, as students enter the labour market and compete for jobs (Dinovitzer 2011; Rivera and Tilcsik 2016; Torche 2011). Entry to the elite law schools remains reserved primarily for students from middle- to upper-class backgrounds (Sommerlad 2016; Webley et al. 2016), regardless of gender or race. Graduates with social class privilege together with the upper-class eloquence cultivated in elite law schools are sought after by recruiters in the big law firms (Rivera 2012; Sommerlad 2015; Sterling et al. 2007; Wilkins et al. 2007). Even for graduates of non-elite law schools, cues indicating higher social class background can be influential in hiring. In interviews with lawyers in England and Wales, Sommerlad (2011) and Webley et al. (2016) observed that large law firms' recruitment strategies prioritise symbolic and cultural capital, through the use of application forms that rely heavily on open questions that target extracurricular activities. In a résumé audit study, Rivera and Tilcsik (2016) sent out applications about fictitious students at selective but not elite law schools to 316 law firm offices in 14 US cities, randomly assigning signals of social class background and gender to otherwise identical résumés. They found that those who display markers of higher social class are significantly more likely than other candidates to be invited to interview for top law firm jobs (Rivera and Tilcsik 2016).

Motivations and the Economy

What about aspirations—how do these drive early career choices among law graduates? Studies acknowledge that individual preferences are important to career-relevant decisions that will take law graduates in different professional directions. Yet, less is known about these early stages in the supply-side process and why graduates make the choices they do (Aiken and Regan 2016). Nonetheless, it is well documented that most students start law school with a set of altruistic ideas, but become indifferent upon graduating, and join fellow alumni at law firms (Heinz,

Nelson et al. 2005; Pan 2015). In a study of University of Wisconsin law school graduates, Erlanger, Cahill, Epp, and Haines found that while over half of the respondents expressed interest in public interest law before beginning law school, only 13% pursued a job in legal aid, as a public defender, or in a non-profit organisation (1996: 851). Pan summarises this shift in aspirations as follows: "As agents of their own professional indoctrination, law students alter their career goals by rationalising a need for high-quality training, and the availability of creative and meaningful work—goals met by an initial firm trajectory" (2015: 151).

Finally, the larger economic environment may have a hand in shaping law students' job prospects upon graduation and bar admission. Studies of education-to-work transitions often identify macro-level economic conditions as the main culprit for a decline in job opportunities. During periods of economic downturn, new entrants to the labour market are likely to face increased difficulty locating promising jobs, or any jobs at all (Adediran et al. 2017; Yu and Chiu 2014). Notably, the 2008 economic downturn led one-third of US law firms to implement hiring freezes and one-quarter reduced their lawyers' salaries (Merritt 2015: 1073).

Data and Methods

Data for this study were drawn from a survey of lawyers in Ontario, Canada. Ontario is home to the largest proportion of lawyers (39%) in Canada (Federation of Law Societies of Canada 2014). The survey was conducted in the autumn of 2009. The sample consists of a stratified random sample of lawyers from the membership records of the Law Society of Ontario (formerly, the Law Society of Upper Canada). The sample is stratified by gender, to include equal numbers of men and women called to the Ontario Bar between 1990 and 2009. This near 20-year span was selected to pay close attention to the early years of lawyers' careers. The lawyers in this study entered law practice during an era that saw a steep rise in women's representation and a growing presence of racial and ethnic minorities in the profession (Law Society of Upper Canada 2015). Questionnaires were mailed directly to respondents' places of employment. The survey, with two reminders, received a 47% response rate (N = 1,270).

Measures

The dependent variable employs a nominal measure of practice setting, comprised of four categories reflecting sector and firm size. Practice settings are divided into public and private sectors. The latter includes solo practice, *small firms* of less than 10 lawyers, *mid-sized firms* of 10–74 lawyers, and *big firms* of 75 or more lawyers. Independent variables include socio-demographics: *gender* (coded as a dummy variable) and

100 Fiona M. Kay

race (racial minority = 1).[1] The role of age in predicting first job settings is considered with a dummy variable that taps whether the lawyer was of an *atypical age* at time of bar admission (1 = atypical age). The typical new lawyer is young: 70% are in their 20s at bar admission; 24% are in their 30s, and only 6% are over 40. Bar admission cohorts are divided into two decades in this study: 1990–1999 (coded 0) and 2000–2009 (coded 1). In our sample, 43% of the lawyers entered the profession during the 1990s and 57% during the 2000s. Family background consists of two measures: *father's education* and *occupation*. Father's education is a dummy variable indicating whether lawyer's father holds a university degree. Father's occupation is a dummy variable indicating whether lawyer's father is/was a business owner or professional.

Two variables are included to assess law graduates' credentials, including a measure *of law school GPA* and *law school ranking*. Law school GPA is coded along a seven-point scale from 1 = D (50–59%) to 7 = High A (A+; 90–100%). Law school ranking is coded as a variable with three tiers, defined by Maclean's law school rankings (2013). This ranking employs a combined score of graduate quality (based on elite firm hiring, national reach, Supreme Court clerkships, and faculty hiring) and faculty quality (based on faculty journal citations). In the regression models the third-tier schools serve as the reference category. *Education debt* is a dummy variable that indicates whether respondents' education debt is among the top quartile reported in the sample. Early *career motivations* are based on a series of 10 questions that asked respondents to rank the importance of possible career priorities. A factor analysis was used to extract three motivational factors: desire to make *work central* to one's life, desire to promote *social justice*, and desire for *work–life balance*. Finally, *unemployment rate* consists of an interval measure of the provincial unemployment rate at the time of bar admission.

Results

Characteristics of Law Graduates Across Job Settings

Most new lawyers are young (e.g. in their 20s); however, 30% of the lawyers in our sample are older (over 30 years of age at time of bar admission). Differences in the ages of new lawyers correlate with initial practice settings (see Table 6.1). Older law graduates are more likely to start their careers in solo offices or small firms compared with law graduates in their 20s (38% versus 26%), while younger graduates more often land in mid-sized firms (24% versus 21%), and big firms (35% versus 23%). Older law graduates are also more likely to start in the public sector (13% versus 9%). The timing of entry to practice has less impact, at least for recent cohorts. Whether lawyers entered the profession in the 1990s versus the first decade of the 2000s did not drastically shift where they

Table 6.1 Demographics of law graduates by first jobs (row percentages)

First Job	Solo and Small Firm (%)	Mid-Size Firm (%)	Big Firm (%)	Public (%)	Business and Other (%)	Total	p Level
Age							p < .001
Typical	26.3	24.0	35.3	8.8	5.6	100.0	
Atypical	38.2	20.8	23.4	12.8	4.8	100.0	
Cohort							N.S.
1990–1999	32.5	21.6	28.8	11.1	6.1	100.0	
2000–2009	28.0	24.2	33.8	9.2	4.8	100.0	
Gender							p < .001
Male	34.9	23.0	28.8	7.6	5.6	100.0	
Female	24.5	23.1	34.8	12.5	5.0	100.0	
Race							N.S.
White	28.8	24.0	31.7	10.0	5.5	100.0	
Racial minority[a]	37.3	16.7	32.0	10.0	4.0	100.0	
Overall	29.9	23.1	31.7	10.0	5.3	100.0	

Notes: N = 1,179

[a] Includes Asians, Blacks, Southeast-Asians, and other ethnic/racial minorities (e.g. First Nations, Latinos, blended races).

secured jobs. The more recent bar admission cohort (e.g. 2000–2009) is larger than the cohort a decade earlier (57% of lawyers in our sample are in the recent cohort), however, no statistically significant differences are observed among first job settings of lawyers across these two cohorts.

At entry to first jobs, gender differences emerge with reference to sectors of practice. About 13% of women begin in the public sector compared with 8% of men. Most law graduates embark on careers in private practice, although a greater share of men compared with women (87% versus 82%) start in the private sector. The distribution of men and women also varies across firm sizes. For example, 35% of men compared with 25% of women start their careers in solo practice or small law firms. About an even percentage of men and women enter mid-size firms (23%), while more women than men enter big law firms (35% versus 29%).

The distribution of racial minorities across sectors of practice and firm sizes shows less contrast than is seen in the distribution of men and women across these sectors and workplaces. Slightly more racial minorities than whites start in solo practices and small firms (37% versus 29%), and more whites than minorities start in mid-size firms (24% versus 17%). Meanwhile, an equal share of minorities and whites enter big firms (32%) and the public sector (10%). These differences in racial representation across sectors and firms are not statistically significant.

In total, 15% of the lawyers in the survey self-identify as racial minorities. Across all four demographics—age, cohort, gender, and race—similar percentages of new lawyers embark on careers in business and other pursuits (4–6%).

The Impact of Social Class and Law School Standing

Pathways to different sectors of practice and firm sizes reveal the importance of family socio-economic standing and law school credentials (see Table 6.2). Big law firms hire graduates with grades significantly higher than those of graduates starting out in solo practice or small firms. Big firms also hire predominantly from first-tier law schools (41%), while a large share of law graduates starting in solo practice or small firms herald from third-tier law schools (47%). Beyond grades and law school prestige ranking, the social backgrounds of law graduates also matter. Among lawyers from this near 20-year span of bar admissions, 40–59% have university-educated fathers. The majority of new recruits to big law firms (57%), as well as to the public sector (59%), and business (56%), have university-educated fathers, while 40% of lawyers starting out in solo practice and small firms have university-educated fathers. Taken together, the patterns observed are consistent with prior research that indicates a convergence of elite background and strong academic credentials for those working in big law firms (Dinovitzer and Dawe 2016).

Multinomial Models: Factors Most Salient to Initial Job Hiring

The bivariate findings suggest socio-demographics, family background, and credentials matter for entry to the legal labour market. I turn next to the results of multinomial regression models to assess the *relative* effects of factors predicting the sorting of law graduates into practice settings. In these models, I investigate the likelihood of entering each setting in contrast to working in mid-size firms of 10–75 lawyers (see Table 6.3). For ease of interpretation, coefficients are parameterised to relative risk ratios (Hilbe 2009: 300).

The attributes that increase the prospect of starting out as a sole practitioner or joining a small law firm (compared to a mid-sized firm) are being a racial minority and having a desire to pursue social justice issues. Being older than the typical law school graduate increases the likelihood of starting in small firms and solo practice (though the effect is marginally significant). The likelihood of working in these settings decreases with each increment in law school GPA. Not surprisingly, having more law school debt steers law graduates away from these smaller practice settings compared with the attraction of higher-paying mid-size firms.

Table 6.2 Key descriptive statistics by first jobs (column percentages)

First Job	Solo/Small Firm	Mid-Size Firm	Big Firm	Public	Business and Other	Total	p Level
	%/Mean	%/Mean	%/Mean	%/Mean	%/Mean	Total	p Level
Atypical ge	38.6	29.0	24.3	39.0	33.3	31.6	p < .001
Cohort 2000–2009	54.3	60.7	61.8	53.4	52.4	57.9	NS
Women	40.1	48.9	53.5	61.0	46.0	48.8	p < .001
Racial minorities	15.9	9.2	12.8	12.7	9.5	12.7	NS
Father BA or higher	40.3	48.5	56.7	58.5	55.6	50.0	p < .001
Father business/prof.	56.5	59.2	58.6	54.2	61.9	57.9	NS
Law school GPA	4.5	4.9	5.3	4.9	4.6	4.9	
Law school rank							
Tier 1	27.8	27.9	41.4	36.4	36.5	33.5	p < .001
Tier 2	24.7	27.2	24.1	22.9	20.6	24.7	NS
Tier 3	47.4	45.0	34.5	40.7	42.9	41.8	p < .001
Law school debt	21,863.20	26,248.06	23,421.91	22,986.60	20,286.11	23,230.95	p < .001
Total N	352	272	374	118	63	1,179	

Notes: N = 1,179

Table 6.3 Multinomial logistical regression of first practice setting

	Solo/Small Firm	Big Firm	Public	Business and Other
Atypical age	1.42†	0.94	1.68*	0.97
	(0.26)	(0.19)	(0.41)	(0.31)
Cohort 2000–2009	1.01	0.87	1.00	.99
	(0.22)	(0.19)	(0.30)	(0.37)
Female	0.78	1.24	1.67*	1.00
	(0.13)	(0.21)	(0.39)	(0.29)
Racial minority	1.70*	1.43	1.50	0.95
	(0.46)	(0.40)	(0.54)	(0.46)
Father BA or higher	0.78	1.47*	1.94**	1.32
	(0.14)	(0.27)	(0.50)	(0.41)
Father business/prof.	0.98	0.87	0.63†	0.96
	(0.18)	(0.16)	(0.16)	(0.30)
Law school GPA	0.58***	1.77***	0.89	0.64**
	(0.06)	(0.19)	(0.12)	(0.11)
Law school rank				
Tier 1	0.91	2.00***	1.36	1.30
	(0.18)	(0.40)	(0.36)	(0.42)
Tier 2	0.99	1.13	0.93	0.87
	(0.21)	(0.24)	(0.27)	(0.32)
Law school debt	0.68*	0.69†	0.80	0.67
	(0.14)	(0.14)	(0.22)	(0.24)
Motivations				
Work centrality	0.95	0.87†	0.84	1.19
	(0.08)	(0.08)	(0.09)	(0.16)
Work–life balance	1.13	0.66***	1.05	1.21
	(0.13)	(0.08)	(0.16)	(0.24)
Social justice	1.53***	0.62***	1.80***	1.21
	(0.15)	(0.06)	(0.25)	(0.20)
Unemployment rate	0.99	0.92	1.11	1.06
	(0.07)	(0.07)	(0.10)	(0.12)
Constant	22.84***	0.12**	0.24	0.76
	(19.13)	(0.11)	(0.28)	(1.05)

Notes: N = 1 179. Comparison category for dependent variable is mid-size firms of 10–75 lawyers. Relative risk ratios displayed. Standard errors in parentheses. Excluded category for law school rank is third quarter. Standardised scores used in motivation scales. †$p < .10$, *$p < .05$, **$p < .01$, ***$p < .001$; Log likelihood = –1 500.60; LR χ^2 = 418.76, df = 56, $p < .001$.

In contrast, the attributes that increase the likelihood of working in big firms (compared to mid-sized firms) are high law school GPA and graduation from a first-tier law school. Family background is also influential, even when controlling for a host of factors. Law graduates with university-educated fathers are more likely to start out in big law firms. Early career motivations are also significant: both a desire for social justice and work–life balance decrease the likelihood of working in a big firm. Work centrality (i.e. work is the most important thing in one's life), while marginally significant, decreases the likelihood of working in a big firm. One might expect applicants to large firms to place work above all else, given the intense work demands reputed to characterise these firms (Plickert and Sterling 2017; Sommerlad 2016). However, the motivations for entering large firms may have less to do with work centrality, and more to do with desires for compensation (Aiken and Regan 2016) and prestige (Dinovitzer and Dawe 2016). Having more law school debt, while only marginally significant, slightly reduces the likelihood of working in big firms compared with mid-size firms. One might assume that law graduates are drawn to big firms in pursuit of the tremendous starting salaries and with the goal of rapidly paying down debt. The bivariate analysis, however, shows new hires in big firms, on average, carry less law school debt than law graduates starting in mid-size firms.

The predictors of starting one's career in the public sector are remarkably different from the factors leading to the private sector. Law graduates who are an atypical age are 68% more likely to enter the public sector than mid-size firms. Women are also more likely to start out in the public sector. Interestingly, having a father with a university education significantly increases the odds of working in the public sector (OR = 1.94, $p < .01$), though having a father who is a professional or business owner decreases those odds (the latter effect is only marginally significant). Lawyers expressing an interest in social justice are 80% more likely to start their careers in the public sector than in mid-size firms.

The final focal category of business and other settings consists of a diverse range of settings where lawyers work. The category includes, for example, lawyers working as corporate in-house counsel, as managers and consultants, and small business owners. The diversity of work contexts leads to weaker effects. Law graduates with higher GPAs are less likely to enter business and other settings than mid-size firms. Neither demographic background nor career motivations predict whether new lawyers embark on careers in business or settings outside more traditional private and public sectors.

Across all the possible practice settings, the level of unemployment holds little influence on where new lawyers work. Nonetheless, it is possible, even likely, that high unemployment at time of law school graduation bodes poorly for new lawyers, reducing their opportunities for work regardless of setting. Poor economic times compel new lawyers to accept jobs that are not their first preference, or to take work on a contract basis, or work with poor job security (Merritt 2015; Markovic and Plickert 2018).

Sorting Before First Jobs?

Thus far, this chapter has examined factors sorting new lawyers into sectors and settings as they enter the legal labour market. However, it is possible that law firms, and other employers of new lawyers, create opportunities to recruit and assess potential job candidates prior to their first full-time jobs. In the US, for example, law firms hire the overwhelming majority of their new associates through summer internship programs (Ginsburg and Wolf 2004; NALP 2014). The National Association for Law Placement (NALP) 2013 survey reveals that law firms offered a full-time position to 92% of their summer associates (2014). As a result, summer associateships at big firms are coveted positions that, in most cases, can be converted to full-time job offers (Rivera and Tilcsik 2016). In the Canadian context, law students seek summer employment with law firms, but the more significant stage is the articling programme required by provincial Law Societies.[2] The programme is mandatory to the licencing process and is designed to assist law graduates to prepare for entry-level practice. Articles provide law graduates not only with useful work experience, but also with network contacts that enhance their employability (Fuller and Stecy-Hildebrandt 2014). On the other side, employers use these temporary positions to screen candidates, offering permanent positions to those who perform well (McGinnity et al. 2005). Do articles offer the same gateway to law firm jobs that summer internships do in the US?

The majority of Ontario law graduates article in private law practice (85%). Among law graduates articling in a big law firm, nearly 80% (78.9%) successfully secure full-time employment in a big firm (see Table 6.4). The pattern is similar but less pronounced compared to the summer associate to full-time job pathway in the US. There is some job movement, with 8% of lawyers articling in big firms moving to mid-size firms, and 7% to solo practice and small firms. Only 2% of those who article in big firms move to public practice, and 4% move to business and other settings. A strong pattern of retention exists among those completing articles in small firms or with a sole practitioner. Most of these lawyers (82%) stay in small firms or set up their own solo practice. In contrast, variable destinations await lawyers articling in mid-size firms: nearly 60% stay in mid-size firms, but 22% move on to solo practice or small firms, and 10% are hired in big firms. By contrast, only 56% of graduates articling in the public sector remain there for full-time jobs, while 33% move to private practice: 15% to solo practice and small firms, 7% to mid-size firms, and 11% to big firms.

Table 6.4 Cross-tabulation of first jobs by articling placement (row percentages)

First Jobs:	Solo/Small Firm	Mid-Size Firm	Big Firm	Public	Business and Other	Total
	%	%	%	%	%	
Articles:						
Solo/small firm	**82.02**	8.99	1.87	4.87	2.25	100%
Mid-size firm	21.70	**58.65**	10.26	3.23	6.16	100%
Big firm	6.94	7.71	**78.92**	2.31	4.11	100%
Public	15.07	6.85	10.96	**55.48**	11.64	100%
Business and other	27.78	22.22	30.56	11.11	**8.33**	100%

Notes: N = 1,179; Pearson χ^2 = 1,400.0, df = 16, p < .001. Bolded figures represent a match (e.g. consistency) between articling placement and first job.

A further 12% proceed from articles in the public sector to work in business and other settings.

In sum, articling placement does not predict with certainty lawyers' first full-time job destinations. Nonetheless, articling provides a promising gateway to full-time jobs, particularly in big firms (79%) and solo practice and small firm settings (82%). In contrast, career trajectories that follow articling in mid-size firms are more diverse, with considerable movement across sectors and settings. There is even less continuity from articles to full-time jobs for lawyers articling elsewhere. Law graduates who article in the public sector or in business and other settings are less likely to stay in these settings for their first full-time jobs (56% and 8%, respectively). These results suggest that the sorting of lawyers into sectors and settings begins prior to first jobs—with articling after law school and perhaps as early as summer employment during law school.

Conclusion

This chapter aimed to answer this question: what factors explain the sorting of lawyers into different sectors and practice settings after graduation from law school? I examined new lawyers' first full-time jobs after law school across a near 20-year cohort of lawyers in Ontario, Canada. Results demonstrate that the socio-demographic characteristics of new lawyers and their law school credentials surface as key determinants in this sorting process. Age also influences career entry, with new lawyers who are older than the typical graduate being more likely than their younger counterparts to enter the public sector, as well as solo practice and small firms. There were no significant differences in the initial job destinations of lawyers across the two decades of bar admission cohorts. Law graduates from both these decades entered a legal labour market characterised by precarious work; their experiences are more alike than dissimilar (see Yu and Miller 2005). Women are more likely than men to start their legal careers in the public sector, while considering a host of factors such as law school GPA, law school prestige, family background, and career motivations. Race also matters for entry to first professional jobs. Racial minorities are more likely than whites to begin their careers in small firms or as sole practitioners, controlling for several career-related determinants.

Family background shapes early career paths: lawyers with university-educated fathers are more likely to enter big firms, as well as the public sector. Lawyers who excelled in law school (i.e. had a high GPA) and graduated from top-tier law schools are recruited to big law firms. Heavy law school debt steers new lawyers away from entering small law firms or from establishing a solo practice. Motivations also emerge as power-ful drivers. New lawyers with a desire to pursue social justice issues are more likely to enter the public sector and, within the private sector, to join small firms or to start their own solo practice. Not surprisingly, new lawyers with a desire to pursue social justice issues and those who place a priority on work–life balance are less likely to begin their careers in big law firms.

The social mechanisms anticipated in the literature on professions pro-vide a strong explanation of movement into public versus private sectors of practice, and job entry to law firms of different sizes. However, we know far less about what encourages new lawyers to pursue careers out-side traditional law practice in business and other settings. More research is needed to explore unconventional career lines.

The first full-time job after law school represents the launch of a pro-fessional career, with immense consequence for a lawyer's subsequent career trajectory (Dinovitzer and Dawe 2016; Yu and Chiu 2014). This chapter suggests that an intermediary stage—a bridge between law school and first jobs—has been overlooked in the research literature. Employers of lawyers, particularly the big law firms, tap opportunities to preview potential candidates for these full-time (and potentially more permanent) jobs through the apprenticeship stage of articling, and perhaps even ear-lier through summer employment positions for law school students. Some organisational settings (e.g. big firms, small firms, and solo practice) are characterised by continuity of many young lawyers from articles to job hiring. In these contexts, getting 'a foot in early' is crucial to one's future career prospects. Meanwhile, other organisational settings (e.g. mid-size law firms and public sector) display considerable in-flow and out-flow of lawyers across sectors and firm sizes from apprenticeship to full-time job hiring. Future research should examine the hiring of law students into summer positions and articling stages, and the streaming of lawyers from these temporary positions to full-time jobs following law school. Do patterns of attrition exist for specific socio-demographic groups? What social mechanisms underlie retention across these trial periods in early professional careers? Answers to these questions will further advance knowledge of the pivotal transition from advanced degree education to professional careers.

Funding

This study was funded by a research grant from the Social Sciences and Humanities Research Council of Canada (SSHRC) and with the cooperation of the Law Society of Ontario. The views expressed in this chapter are those of the author and do not necessarily reflect the views of the Law Society of Ontario.

Notes

1 Racial minorities represented 13% of the near 20-year cohort (1990 to 2009 bar admissions). Included are Asians (4.7%), Blacks (2%), Southeast-Asians (5%), and other ethnic/racial minorities (e.g., First Nations, Latinos, blended races) (1.7%).
2 Today, in Ontario, law graduates are required to complete one of two experiential training paths: the Articling Program or the Law Practice Program (LPP). The Articling Program requires candidates to work for 10 consecutive months with an approved Articling Principal. The LPP consists of a four-month training program and a four-month work placement. Lawyers in the present study articled in the era prior to the introduction of the dual experiential training system. See www.lsuc.on.ca/articling/.

References

Abrams, D, Swift, HJ and Drury, L (2016) 'Old and Unemployable? How Age-Based Stereotypes Affect Willingness to Hire Job Candidates' 72 *Journal of Social Issues* 105. doi:10.1111/josi.12158

Ackroyd, S and Muzio, D (2007) 'The Reconstructed Professional Firm: Explaining Change in English Legal Practices' 28 *Organization Studies* 729. doi:10.1177/0170840607073077

Adediran, AO, Hagan, J, Parker, P and Plickert, G (2017) 'Making the Best of a Bad Beginning: Young New York Lawyers Confronting the Great Recession' 9 *Northeastern University Law Journal* 259.

Aiken, JR and Regan, MC (2016) 'Gendered Pathways: Choice, Constraint, and Women's Job Movements in the Legal Profession' in S Headworth, RL Nelson, R Dinovitzer and DB Wilkins (eds), *Diversity in Practice: Race, Gender, and Class in Legal and Professional Careers* (Cambridge, Cambridge University Press).

Brockman, J (1992) 'Gender Bias in the Legal Profession: A Survey of Members of the Law Society of British Columbia' 17 *Queen's Law Journal* 91.

Dau-Schmidt, KG, Galanter, MS, Mukhopadhaya, K and Hull, KE (2009) 'Men and Women of the Bar: The Impact of Gender on Legal Careers' 16 *Michigan Journal of Gender & Law* 49.

Dinovitzer, R (2011) 'The Financial Rewards of Elite Status in the Legal Profession' 36 *Law & Social Inquiry* 971. doi:10.1111/j.1747-4469.2011.01258.x

Dinovitzer, R and Dawe, M (2016) 'Early Legal Careers in Comparative Context: Evidence from Canada and the United States' 23 *International Journal of the Legal Profession* 83, 93, 97. doi:10.1080/09695958.2015.1113971

Dinovitzer, R, Nelson, RL, Plickert, G, Sandefur, R and Sterling, JS (2009) *After the JD II: Second Results from a National Study of Legal Careers* (Chicago, IL, The American Bar Foundation and the NALP Foundation for Law Career Research and Education).

Dobrev, SD (2005) 'Career Mobility and Job Flocking' 34 *Social Science Research* 800, 806. doi:10.1016/j.ssresearch.2005.01.002

Erlanger, HS, Cahill, M, Epp, CR and Haines, KM (1996) 'Law Student Idealism and Job Choice: Some New Data on an Old Question' 30 *Law & Society Review* 851. doi:10.2307/3054120

Federation of Law Societies of Canada (2014) '2013 Statistical Report'. http://docs.flsc.ca/STATS2013ReportFINAL.pdf

Fuller, S and Stecy-Hildebrandt, N (2014) 'Lasting Disadvantage? Comparing Career Trajectories of Matched Temporary and Permanent Workers in Canada' 51 *Canadian Review of Sociology* 293. doi:10.1111/cars.12049

Galanter, M and Henderson, W (2008) 'The Elastic Tournament: A Second Transformation of the Big Law Firm' 60 *Stanford Law Review* 1867.

Ginsburg, T and Wolf, JA (2004) 'The Market for Elite Law Firm Associates' 31 *Florida State University Law Review* 909.

Glass, A (2007) 'Understanding Generational Differences for Competitive Success' 39 *Industrial and Commercial Training* 98. doi:10.1108/00197850710732424

Gorman, EH (2005) 'Gender Stereotypes, Same-Gender Preferences, and Organizational Variation in the Hiring of Women: Evidence from Law Firms' 70 *American Sociological Review* 702. doi:10.1177/000312240507000408

Gorman, EH and Kay, FM (2010) 'Racial and Ethnic Minority Representation in Large U.S. Law Firms' 52 *Studies in Law, Politics, and Society* 211, 233. doi:10.1108/S1059-4337(2010)0000052010

——— (2016) 'Which Kinds of Law Firms Have the Most Minority Lawyers? Organizational Context and the Representation of African-Americans, Latinos, and Asian-Americans' in S Headworth, RL Nelson, R Dinovitzer, and DB Wilkins (eds), *Diversity in Practice: Race, Gender, and Class in Legal and Professional Careers* (Cambridge, Cambridge University Press).

Gringart, E, Helmes, E and Speelman, CP (2005) 'Exploring Attitudes Toward Older Workers Among Australian Employers: An Empirical Study' 17 *Journal of Aging & Social Policy* 85. doi:10.1300/J031v17n03_05

Hagan, J and Kay, F (1995) *Gender in Practice: A Study of Lawyers' Lives* (Oxford, Oxford University Press).

Heinz, JP, Nelson, RL, Sandefur, RL and Laumann, EO (2005) *Urban Lawyers: The New Social Structure of the Bar* (Chicago, IL, University of Chicago Press).

Henderson, WD (2011) 'Three Generations of U.S. Lawyers: Generalists, Specialists, Project Managers' 70 *Maryland Law Review* 373.

Hilbe, JM (2009) *Logistic Regression Models* (Boca Raton, FL, Chapman & Hall), 300.

Hull, KE and Nelson, RL (2000) 'Assimilation, Choice, or Constraint? Testing Theories of Gender Differences in the Careers of Lawyers' 79 *Social Forces* 229. doi:10.1093/sf/79.1.229

Kay, FM and Gorman, E (2008) 'Women in the Legal Profession' 4 *Annual Review of Law and Social Science* 299. doi:10.1146/annurev.lawsocsci.4.110707.172309

Kay, FM, Masuch, C and Curry, P (2006) 'Growing Diversity and Emergent Change: Gender and Ethnicity in the Legal Profession' in EA Sheehy and S McIntyre (eds), *Calling for Change: Women, Law and the Legal Profession* (Ottawa, ON, University of Ottawa Press).

Law Society of Upper Canada (2015) *Annual Report 2014* (and 1991 and 2009 reports) (Toronto, ON, The Law Society of Upper Canada). www.annual report.lsuc.on.ca

Lempert, RO, Chambers, DL and Adams, TK (2000) 'Michigan's Minority Graduates in Practice: The River Runs through the Law School' 25 *Law & Social Inquiry* 395.

Maclean's Magazine (2013) 'How Do Canadian Law Schools Compare?' *Maclean's Magazine* 19 September 2013. www.macleans.ca/education/uniandcollege/2013-law-school-rankings

Markovic, M and Plickert, G (2018) 'Attorneys' Career Dissatisfaction in the New Normal' 25 *International Journal of the Legal Profession* 147. doi:10.10 80/09695958.2018.1456437

Mayer, KU (2004) 'Whose Lives? How History, Societies, and Institutions Define and Shape Life Courses' 1 *Research in Human Development* 161. doi:10.1207/s15427617rhd0103_3

McGinnity, F, Mertens, A and Gundert, S (2005) 'A Bad Start? Fixed-Term Contracts and the Transition from Education to Work in West Germany' 21 *European Sociological Review* 359. doi:10.1093/esr/jci025

Merritt, D (2015) 'What Happened to the Class of 2010? Empirical Evidence of Structural Change in the Legal Profession' 3 *Michigan State Law Review* 1043, 1073.

Milkman, R (2017) 'A New Political Generation: Millennials and the Post-2008 Wave of Protest' 82 *American Sociological Review* 1. doi:10.1177/0003122416681031

National Association of Law Placement (NALP) (2014) *Perspectives on Fall 2013 Law Student Recruiting* (Washington, DC, NALP). www.nalp.org/uploads/PerspectivesonFallRec2013.pdf

Pan, Y-YD (2015) 'Becoming a (Pan)ethnic Attorney: How Asian American and Latino Law Students Manage Dual Identities' 30 *Sociological Forum* 148, 151. doi:10.1111/socf.12149

Plickert, G and Sterling, J (2017) 'Gender Still Matters: Effects of Workplace Discrimination on Employment Schedules of Young Professionals' 6 *Laws* 28. doi:10.3390/laws6040028

Posthuma, RA and Campion, MA (2009) 'Age Stereotypes in the Workplace: Common Stereotypes, Moderators, and Future Research Directions' 35 *Journal of Management* 158. doi:10.1177/0149206308318617

Reichman, NJ and Sterling, JS (2002) 'Recasting the Brass Ring: Deconstructing and Reconstructing Workplace Opportunities for Women Lawyers' 29 *Capital University Law Review* 923.

Rice, L and Barth, JM (2016) 'Hiring Decisions: The Effect of Evaluator Gender and Gender Stereotype Characteristics on the Evaluation of Job Applicants' 33 *Gender Issues* 1.

Rivera, LA (2012) 'Diversity Within Reach: Recruitment Versus Hiring in Elite Firms' 639 *The Annals of the American Academy of Political and Social Science* 71. doi:10.1177/0002716211421112

Rivera, LA and Tilcsik, A (2016) 'Class Advantage, Commitment Penalty: The Gendered Effect of Social Class Signals in an Elite Labor Market' 81 *American Sociological Review* 1097. doi:10.1177/0003122416668154

Sandefur, RL (2007) 'Staying Power: The Persistence of Social Inequality in Shaping Lawyer Stratification and Lawyers' Persistence in the Profession' 36 *Southwestern University Law Review* 539.

Sommerlad, H (2011) 'The Commercialisation of Law and the Enterprising Legal Practitioner: Continuity and Change' 18 *International Journal of the Legal Profession* 73. doi:10.1080/09695958.2011.619852

—— (2015) 'The "Social Magic" of Merit: Diversity, Equity, and Inclusion in the English and Welsh Legal Profession' 83 *Fordham Law Review* 2325.

—— (2016) ' "A Pit to Put Women In": Professionalism, Work Intensifiction, Sexualisation and Work–life Balance in the Legal Profession in England and Wales' 23 *International Journal of the Legal Profession* 61. doi:10.1080/0969 5958.2016.1140945

Sterling, JS, Dinovitzer, R and Garth, B (2007) 'The Changing Social Role of Urban Law Schools' 36 *Southwestern University Law Review* 389.

Sterling, JS and Reichman, N (2016) 'Overlooked and Undervalued: Women in Private Law Practice' 12 *Annual Review of Law and Social Science* 373. doi:10.1146/annurev-lawsocsci-120814-121705

Tomasic, R (1983) 'Social Organisation Amongst Australian Lawyers' 19 *Journal of Sociology* 447. doi:10.1177/144078338301900305

Torche, F (2011) 'Is a College Degree Still the Great Equalizer? Intergenerational Mobility across Levels of Schooling in the United States' 117 *American Journal of Sociology* 763. doi:10.1177/144078338301900305

Urick, MJ, Hollensbe, EC and Fairhurst, GT (2017) 'Differences in Understanding Generation in the Workforce' 15 *Journal of Intergenerational Relationships* 221. doi:10.1080/15350770.2017.1329583

Verwiebe, R, Seewann, L, Wolf, M and Hacioglu, M (2016) ' "I have to be very good in what I do": Marginalisation and Discrimination in the Career-Entry Phase—Experiences and Coping Strategies among University Graduates with a Migrant Background in Austria' 42 *Journal of Ethnic and Migration Studies* 2459. doi:10.1080/1369183X.2016.1169160

Webley, L, Tomlinson, J, Muzio, D, Sommerlad, H and Duff, L (2016) 'Access to a Career in the Legal Profession in England and Wales: Race, Class, and the Role of Educational Background' in S Headworth, RL Nelson, R Dinovitzer and DB Wilkins (eds), *Diversity in Practice: Race, Gender, and Class in Legal and Professional Careers* (Cambridge, Cambridge University Press).

Wilkins, DB, Dinovitzer, R and Batra, R (2007) 'Urban Law School Graduates in Large Law Firms' 36 *Southwestern University Law Review* 433.

Yu, H-C and Miller, P (2005) 'Leadership Style: The X Generation and Baby Boomers Compared in Different Cultural Contexts' 26 *Leadership & Organization Development Journal* 35. doi:10.1108/01437730510575570

Yu, W-H and Chiu, C-T (2014) 'Off to a Good Start: A Comparative Study of Change in Men's First Job Prospects in East Asia' 37 *Research in Social Stratification and Mobility* 3. doi:10.1016/j.rssm.2013.11.001

Zschirnt, E and Ruedin, D (2016) 'Ethnic Discrimination in Hiring Decisions: A Meta-Analysis of Correspondence Tests 1990–2015' 42 *Journal of Ethnic and Migration Studies* 1115. doi:10.1080/1369183X.2015.1133279

7 Do Gender Regimes Matter?

Converging and Diverging Career Prospects Among Young French and Swiss Lawyers

Isabel Boni-Le Goff, Nicky Le Feuvre, Grégoire Mallard, Eléonore Lépinard and Sandrine Morel

Introduction

Women now represent the majority of lawyers practising in most European countries (Schultz and Shaw 2003), but their entry into the legal profession has followed a specific timeline in each country. The feminisation of the legal profession is usually accompanied by a radical transformation of the market for legal services (Hearn et al. 2016) and by the general expansion of the population of lawyers (Le Feuvre and Walters 1994). It is generally recognised that these structural changes have led to more intense competition not only between increasingly specialised lawyers, but also between lawyers and other legal professions, resulting in a widening gap between the most prosperous and the most precarious lawyers in an increasingly internally fragmented legal labour market (Rosen 1999; Sommerlad 2016). Although we would not subscribe to any idea of a direct causal link between occupational segmentation and the feminisation process, there is obviously a gender dimension to the structural changes taking place within European legal professions. Attrition rates during the early stages of a legal career are high—particularly so for women (Kay et al. 2016). Even in countries with a long history of women's presence at the Bar, like France (Boigeol 2003), the career prospects of female lawyers remain globally less promising than those of their male counterparts.

In this chapter, we attempt to untangle the mechanisms behind the contrasting career outcomes of male and female lawyers by focusing on the results of a comparative study of early career stage lawyers in France and Switzerland, two countries characterised by different timelines of women's entry into the legal profession and by contrasting gendered labour market participation patterns. Women now make up more than half of all the practising lawyers in France, and they are more numerous than men in the youngest age groups, close to 65% (Ordre des Avocats de Paris 2013), while women make up 29% in the Swiss legal profession as a whole (Fédération Suisse des Avocats 2017) and represent half the lawyers entering the Bar since the early 2000s. We analyse and compare the combined influence of societal-level gender regimes and occupational career structures on women's and men's early career paths in the two countries. After reviewing various conceptions of the notion of 'gender regime', we first provide indicative evidence of direct and indirect effects of national gender regimes on women's career patterns and attrition rates in each country, which suggest that Swiss women face more barriers to entry to the legal profession than their French counterparts, in large part due to stronger constraints placed on mothers in Switzerland. Second, we show that the internal structure of the legal profession in Switzerland partially compensates for the apparently less favourable career opportunities offered to young female Swiss lawyers, as compared to their French counterparts. We show that by combining the analysis of national gender regimes and occupational career structures, we can explain counter-intuitive results, like the fact that Swiss women lawyers, although *less likely* to remain in the profession overall, are *as likely* as French women to attain equity partnership status within the same time frame and are even *more likely* to attain non-equity partnership status within five to nine years at the Bar than their French counterparts. Our findings suggest that the Swiss and French national gender regimes help more French women lawyers remain employed as lawyers than Swiss women lawyers after five to nine years in the profession. However, the occupational career structures in Switzerland and France are such that for those women who remain lawyers for an extended period of time in Switzerland, the conditions are relatively similar as in France, if not better. In other words, the national gender regimes in Switzerland and France may affect the quantity of women lawyers duly employed, but not the quality of their job prospects. We conclude by underlining the insights gained from cross-national comparative studies of gender inequalities in professional labour markets.

Theoretical Framework: Defining the Notion of 'Gender Regime'

The term 'gender regime' is used in at least two different sociological literatures. Firstly the term has been used by authors such as Joan Acker (1994, 2006, 2009) or Raewyn Connell (2006) to describe the institutionalisation of gender (or intersectional) inequalities in organisation settings, particularly working environments. As such, it provides useful insights into meso-level mechanisms of reproducing gender hierarchies and inequalities in different types of organisations. Connell identifies four dimensions of what she calls "the overall pattern of gender relations within an organisation" (2006: 839). These include a) the gender division of labour and the designation of particular occupations or activities as being particularly (un)suitable to either men or women; b) the gender division of power, including the ways in which authority is exercised and legitimised along gender lines; c) gendered emotions, meaning the ways in which feelings of solidarity, attraction, and repulsion are expressed by and in relation to gendered individuals and groups; and d) gender culture and attitudes, referring to prevailing symbols and beliefs about gender (Connell 2006: 839). This fourfold grid provides what she calls a "template for describing any organisation's gender regime, as well as a framework for data collection in interviews and observation" (Connell 2006: 839). According to Connell, "a local gender regime may reproduce, but in specific ways may also depart from, the wider gender order (i.e., the whole societal pattern of gender relations)", which is also considered to be multidimensional (Connell 2006: 839).

This definition of gender regimes at the organisational level stands in contrast to a second body of literature, which uses the notion of gender regime to designate precisely what Connell calls the 'gender order', in order to carry out cross-national comparative research that focusses on the macro-societal or national level gender regimes (Pascall and Lewis 2004; Walby 2004). Building on gendered typologies of welfare states (Craig and Mullan 2010; Lewis 1992; Orloff 1996), this conceptualisation of 'gender regime' captures the various social structures and normative expectations that shape gender relations and gender roles in a given society, at a given moment in time. From this perspective, Gillian Pascall and Jane Lewis (2004) identify five key dimensions of gender regimes that shape institutions and normative expectations of men and women at different points in their life course and that can be targeted through social policies. These are similar to the dimensions of meso-level gender relations identified by Connell (2006) and include the gender divisions of "paid work, care work, income, time and voice" (Pascall and Lewis 2004: 373). This framework captures the institutional and the cultural dimensions of gender relations (Boni-Le Goff and Le Feuvre 2017), including what have been called 'family policy regimes' (Ferragina 2017) at the national or societal level.

In this chapter, we argue that understanding the construction of gender inequalities and early career stage attrition rates in the legal profession requires a focus on the intersecting influences of societal gender regimes and occupational career structures. Together with research that has shown how organisational processes and culture reproduce gender hierarchies (Acker 1994, 2006), research on national gender regimes has also produced a wealth of insightful knowledge about the normative environments within which specific occupations operate (Orloff 1996; Walby 2004; Pascall and Lewis 2004). But relatively little is known about the interplay between macro-level societal gender regimes and the specific meso-level professional gender scripts (Crompton and Le Feuvre 2000; Le Feuvre and Lapeyre 2005) of a given occupation or profession, nor about how they combine to shape gendered aspirations and career patterns. This is the line of research that we would like to push forward.

Methods: Case Selection and Data Collection

In our study, France and Switzerland were selected for comparison precisely because they offer very different national gender regimes. Table 7.1 compares France and Switzerland on the basis of Pascall and Lewis'(2004) gender regime model and situates the two countries on the five dimensions of the model (namely paid work, care, income, time, and voice).

The Swiss national gender regime has been described as 'neo-maternalistic' (Giraud and Lucas 2009), and is based on a modified male breadwinner model, where mothers of young children are expected either to withdraw temporarily from the labour market or to shift to less demanding part-time jobs and to have limited professional aspirations (Le Goff and Lévy 2016). In contrast, the French national gender regime can be described as 'hybrid', with a high rate of full-time working mothers and high levels of subsidised childcare solutions, but also policies enabling women to opt out of employment entirely when their children are under school age (Gregory and Milner 2011).

To collect data on the effects of gender regimes on career prospects of young women and men lawyers in France and Switzerland, we adopted a mixed methods approach combining quantitative and qualitative data, focusing on the careers of lawyers who entered the Bar after 1998, in France and in the French-speaking region of Switzerland. The quantitative part of our research is based on a web survey exploring questions about current and previous work experiences, daily working practices, career aspirations, as well as personal and family life.

The survey instrument was administered in France, between March and July 2016, in collaboration with the French National Bar Council (Conseil National des Barreaux) and the Paris Bar (Ordre des Avocats de Paris) and in Switzerland, between May and June 2016, in collaboration with the Bar organisations in Geneva (Ordre des Avocats de Genève) and Lausanne (Ordre des Avocats Vaudois). Our sample is made up of 1,345 respondents: 982 from the Paris Bar and 311 from the Geneva Bar and the Lausanne Bar (see Table 7.2).

Our sample is not fully representative. For instance, as shown in Table 7.2, the French women lawyers to men lawyers ratio in our survey is 67–33%, which is close to the average national ratio in the youngest age groups (Ordre des Avocats de Paris 2013), but in Switzerland the women to men ratio is 58–42%, which is further from the overall ratio that can be observed in Switzerland. These issues of representativeness are however balanced by the fact that response rates for our surveys were extremely high—with more than half the targeted population in French-speaking Switzerland having responded.

Table 7.1 Swiss and French national gender regimes

	Paid Work	Care Work	Income[3]	Time[3]	Voice[3]
France	**Hybrid dual earner/ mostly female career model**[1] Widespread access to qualified jobs; glass ceiling	Partial externalisation Widespread (free/subsidised) childcare solutions[1] State support for families Unequal division domestic labour	Moderate gender pay gap Higher in qualified professions	Women's (almost) full-time and continuous employment patterns Short working week	**Rank 9** Political empowerment ranking
Switzerland	**Modified male breadwinner model**[2] Limited access to managerial and professional jobs	Limited and expensive childcare solutions Short school hours[2] Almost no state support for working mothers Unequal division of domestic labour	Moderate gender pay gap Higher in qualified professions	Women's part-time and discontinuous employment patterns Long working week	**Rank 28** Political empowerment ranking

Source: Pascall and Lewis (2004)

Notes:
1 Gregory and Milner (2011);
2 Giraud and Lucas (2009)
3 World Economic Forum Global Gender Gap Report (2017)

Table 7.2 Quantitative survey

	Switzerland	France	Total
Women	210 (58%)	663 (67%)	873 (65%)
Men	153 (42%)	319 (33%)	472 (35%)
Total	311	982	1,345

Table 7.3 Qualitative interviews

(N = 44)	Switzerland (N = 19 interviewees)	France (N = 25 interviewees)
Women	14	15
— living with a partner	13	14
— having one child or more	5	10
Men	5	10
— living with a partner	4	9
— having one child or more	4	8

We also conducted 44 semi-structured interviews, between September 2015 and July 2017 (see Table 7.3). Using a biographical approach, the interviews gave us the opportunity to understand the longitudinal dynamics involved in lawyers' careers and to identify the resources needed to achieve professional success, notably to reach partnership positions. Indeed the methodological and epistemological rationale of a small qualitative sample is to provide a relevant illustration of the sociological processes we intend to study, rather than statistical metrics with a perfect match with the entire social group put under scrutiny. However, when selecting interviewees, we paid particular attention to selecting participants with a diverse range of life experiences (with some interviewees having children and others not), as well as the whole spectrum of practice settings (solo practice, small, medium, or big firms), and job positions (associate or 'collaborateur', solo practitioner, non-equity, and equity partner). We also made sure to interview lawyers practising in different areas of the law. The sex ratio of our qualitative sample (66%) mirrors the sex ratio of our quantitative sample (65%).

In both our quantitative and qualitative samples, we targeted lawyers at an early career stage. The survey respondents' mean age is 34 years old, while interviewees' mean age is 37 years old. With these caveats in mind, we proceed to present our results. In the following sections, we use both quantitative and qualitative data to compare the Swiss and French lawyers' career patterns and to shed light on the different social processes shaping inequalities and gendered career prospects in both countries.

The Dual Effect of Gender Regimes in the Shaping of Early Career Patterns

Two distinct signs of the effects of national gender regimes on lawyers' careers can be identified from the interview and survey responses. The first relates to the 'motherhood effect' in each country, whereas the second relates to gendered strategies to delay parenthood in order to optimise the chances of early career progression.

The Differential 'Motherhood Effect' on Female Lawyers' Careers

The first effect of national gender regimes is a rather indirect and antici-patory one. Both our quantitative and qualitative data show that in Switzerland a more significant share of young female lawyers leave the legal profession before the birth of their first child. In both countries, our survey shows that a higher proportion of young female (43%) than male (33%) lawyers report planning to leave the Bar in the short or medium term, and that the proportion is higher in Switzerland. Despite the fact that 76% of the Swiss female lawyers and 74% of their male colleagues are satisfied with their job, while just over half of our French respondents (51% of the female lawyers, and 55% of their male counterparts) are satisfied with their career choice, in France, 45% of women and 33% of men intend to leave the Bar in the short to medium term, as against 49% of women and 33% of men in Switzerland. These estimates can be seen as conservative, as our quantitative survey was only aimed at lawyers still affiliated to a Bar, so we did not capture the view and experience of young French and Swiss women who had already left the Bar. The very low proportion of Swiss women lawyers over the age of 35 (24% of the women were in this age category in Switzerland, as against 38% for the French female sample) also provides indirect evidence of these early exit practices and of truncated female career paths in the Swiss case.

Our qualitative data provided more information about the mechanisms involved in women's early exit in the Swiss context. For young female Swiss lawyers, starting to plan a family seemed to almost automatically trigger a decision to opt out of the Bar. For instance, Anne-Sophie, a 31-year-old former lawyer who had left the Bar a year before our interview and who was working as a court clerk at the time of the interview, insisted on the intensity of work–life conflict that lawyers faced after the transition to motherhood. In her opinion, the family life she had planned with her husband—a lawyer working in a non-governmental organisation—required her to quit after just four years of legal practice.

> It's true that I want to start a family, but . . . from my point of view . . . that just wasn't possible with the kind of life I was living.

It was far too complicated, and, to be honest, I didn't fancy spending my time juggling with court hearings, which always last longer than planned, and the creche, and the grandparents, and the child being ill. No, that wasn't my dream life at all, really not! And going part-time wasn't . . . either . . . I would have just ended up fitting a full-time job into four days a week, instead of five.

Anne-Sophie's account typically reflects the normative Swiss gender regime described earlier. In the course of the interview, she never mentions any potential involvement of her husband in managing childcare on a daily basis.

Despite similarly long working hours in both countries (with an average of 49.7 working hours per week in France and 46.5 hours in the Swiss context for our survey respondents), female lawyers in France spoke very differently about work–life conflict issues. Although they evidently faced a greater 'mental burden' and 'competing devotions' (Blair-Loy 2003) in managing the work–family interface than their male colleagues, French women lawyers rarely envisaged reducing their working hours or sacrificing their career due to motherhood. Murielle, a 40-year-old lawyer, a solo practitioner, and a mother of two young children, is typical of our French interviewees. Despite facing many practical childcare problems, which led her to organise her professional appointments around her children's complicated day-care schedule, she had never envisaged working part-time or leaving the Bar.

The way in which the male lawyers talked about the division of domestic and parental labour and about their partners' professional perspectives also revealed clearly different gender norms and expectations in each country. Three-quarters of the married Swiss male lawyers we interviewed presented the fact that their spouse had reduced her professional aspirations after the birth of their children as a 'natural choice'. For instance, Thomas, a father of two and co-founder and partner of a prosperous law firm, insisted on the fact that his wife, a physics academic who was now working part-time, had always had limited ambitions and was 'much more patient with the children' as he said.

THOMAS: My wife is absolutely devoid of ambition. She is anti-ambitious. Truly. Literally. She is a researcher, she works for . . . I think it is a research fund. It is in Zürich. She works part-time, 50% or 60% I do not know. She partly works at home. She does not have to go to Zürich very often.
INTERVIEWER: How are the housework and parental work divided?
THOMAS: It is awful [laughs]. It is awful. I am a bad father [laughs]. Here is the thing. She does absolutely everything at home. . . . Well, I do take care of the children quite often but all the domestic work I do too little. She sometimes reproaches me with this.

On the contrary, 9 out of the 10 French men we interviewed expressed support for dual-earner household arrangements. While these men were often not taking an equal share of housework or childcare in practice, their explicit support of their partner's career and their effort to be a 'really good husband' (Connell 2005) are indicative of the shift in contemporary French gender norms, especially among qualified workers, to a normative dual-career gender regime (Marry 2014).

For Adrien, a 41-year-old partner in a small law firm in Paris, married to a full-time European public servant, and a father of two children aged 8 and 10, it is important that there should be no exclusive area in the division of domestic labour and parenting:

> I take care of our two children every morning and we alternatively collect the kids in the evening. There is no exclusive area for one of us, because my wife herself has a job, she is rather passionate about it, and she works a lot, rather more than I.

These differences were also reflected in the adoption of specific living arrangements: 87% of the married male lawyers in France have a spouse who is working full-time, compared to only 59% of their Swiss counterparts. However, similar proportions of French and Swiss female lawyers (90% and 92%) were living in dual-earner households, with both partners working full-time. This suggests that the living arrangements of French male and female lawyers are more alike than in the Swiss case, where married men continue to benefit from the domestic availability of their spouses at strategic points in their career, while their women colleagues do not.

Delaying Parenthood

The second effect of national gender regimes in the shaping of early career patterns involves the differential timing of parenthood in Switzerland and France. Lawyers see parenthood as a problematic experience in both countries and this is related to the 'long hours culture' (Sommerlad 2002) of the legal profession, with heavy consequences for work–life conflict and family life. Studies have shown that former 'male bastions' like the legal profession tend to promote a certain type of bread-winning father with no daily involvement in family life (Hagan and Kay 2010), leading to the idea that parenthood is incompatible with 'good lawyering' and to the ultimate discrimination against mothers, whatever their domestic arrangements.

In France and Switzerland too, lawyers appear to delay parenthood. Even if women respondents are slightly younger than men, both in France and Switzerland (mean age is 34 years for French women versus 36 for French men, and 32 years for Swiss women versus 34 for Swiss men), 68% of women and 76% of men are over 30 years old. However, two-thirds of our sample (64% of the women and 61% of the men) have no children. In addition, a significant proportion of respondents with children thought that becoming a parent had a negative impact on their career. For instance, in our sample, when questioned about the different consequences experienced while becoming a parent, 14% of the female lawyers with children and 2% of the male lawyers with children declared that their career progression and promotion had been hampered by them becoming parents, and 20% of the mothers and 9% of fathers felt that their commitment to the job had been questioned.

Swiss female lawyers are nevertheless more likely to be childless than their French counterparts among our sample. In France, just over 60% of the male and female lawyers were childless, as compared to 72% of the Swiss female lawyers and only 63% of their male counterparts. These results tend to confirm that Swiss women lawyers face greater objective and subjective obstacles to starting a family and practising law. Hence a greater proportion of them appear to favour delaying motherhood, or ultimately remaining childless. These results are consistent with national demographic data on the age of the first childbearing and the gap between the two countries (in France the mean age for having a first child is 28 years old while it is 31 in Switzerland) (Eurostat 2015). However, beyond the influence of societal gender regimes that we can identify in our empirical data, it also appears that the career structures of the legal profession shape the career options of male and female lawyers in different directions in each of these countries. This is why we emphasise the need to cross-examine the effects of national macro-level characteristics of gender regimes with the career structures in both countries in order to explain the shape of gender inequalities.

When Societal Gender Regimes Meet Occupational Gender Regimes

Occupational Gender Regimes in France and Switzerland

Given the historically higher rate of feminisation of the legal profession (Boigeol 2003) and the more systematic support provided to working mothers in France (Gregory and Milner 2011), we expected that French female lawyers would experience better career prospects (i.e., higher rates of access to partnership status) than their Swiss counterparts (Bydzovsky 2014), and that irrespective of the country, men would overall have better chances to become partners than women. The early stages of Swiss and French lawyers' careers follow three main paths, not all equal in status. Most lawyers start working for a limited period of time (usually one to five years) as junior associates in a small-, medium-, or large-scale law firm. After that, a first option generally considered to be the least desirable involves a career conversion and consists of leaving the Bar, either to work in another legal occupation (e.g., as a court clerk, magistrate, or in-house counsel), or to take a break from employment entirely. A second option is to set up in solo practice. A third option entails becoming a partner in a law firm. This third option may either happen through internal promotion processes in the same firm where a lawyer had previously worked as an associate or through recruitment and promotion to another law firm. The partnership career path may either lead to an equity or non-equity partnership, the former requiring capital investment in the firm and promising much higher income and organisational power over time than non-equity partnership, a recently developed job position designed by firms to recognise seniority and to offer alternative career prospects to senior/skilled lawyers. Of course—and this is confirmed by our interviews—among the three options, partnership (particularly equity partnership in a large-scale law firm), is considered the most successful—and the most economically rewarding—career option.

Due to the well-documented 'glass-ceiling effect' in the legal profession (Décideurs 2014; Kay et al. 2016; Sommerlad 2002), we expected our female respondents to have lower and slower access to partnership positions than their male counterparts, especially equity partnership, and this was indeed the case. We found that whereas women made up 65% of our whole sample, they represented only 48% of equity partners, and only 28% of partners in the largest and most prestigious international law firms (see Table 7.4).

In order to explore the role played by two variables (gender and country) on the career progressions (and on the probability to be a partner or to be a solo practitioner), we performed several logistic regressions (see Tables 7.5 and 7.6). As these logistic regressions do not offer a complete statistical model as they test only two independent variables (gender and country) on the variable 'job position', they should be considered as a first level of statistical exploration rather than a complete explanatory model. Nonetheless the logistic regression provided evidence that, irrespective of their country of residence, the likelihood of becoming a partner for men with five or more years at the Bar is two times higher than those of becoming a partner for their female counterparts (odds ratio = 2.094, see Table 7.5), whereas gender has no statistically significant effect on the chances of entering solo practice (see Table 7.6).

In our sample, we find that women do make up a larger share of equity partners in law firms in France (51%) than in Switzerland (42%). Nonetheless the gap between the proportion of Swiss and French women lawyers reaching partnership status was smaller than we initially expected, due to the effects of national gender regimes mentioned in the previous section. A more detailed analysis of our data revealed another counterintuitive result. In our sample, the relative chances of becoming a partner are statistically higher for Swiss women lawyers than for their French

Table 7.4 The glass ceiling effect in Swiss and French legal professions

(N = 1345)	Switzerland	France	Total
% of women/total associates	63%	70%	68%
in large international firms (> 30 lawyers)	58%	66%	64%
% of women/total sole practitioners	46%	69%	64%
% of women/total			
non-equity partners	49%	54%	51%
in large international firms	50%	40%	42%
% of women/total equity partner	42%	51%	48%
in large international firms	0%	33%	28%

Table 7.5 Logistic model for the dependent variable 'to be a partner'. Effect of country and gender

Dependent Variable: Job Position (To Be a Partner)	Odds Ratios (Standard Errors in Brackets)
Lawyers with five years of seniority or more	
Country (to be a French lawyer)	0.553**(0.214)
Sex (to be a man)	2.094***(0.226)
Lawyers with five to nine years seniority	
Country (to be a French lawyer)	0.354**(0.356)
Sex (to be a man)	1.539(0.360)
Lawyers with 10 years and more seniority	
Country (to be a French lawyer)	0.579(0.280)
Sex (to be a man)	2.071**(0.256)

Database: Respondents living in marital life (N = 962)

Notes: ** $p < 0.01$; *** $p < .001$

counterparts, and this is particularly true for those women with fewer than 10 years at the Bar. At this stage in their careers, the likelihood of achieving (equity or non-equity) partnership status decreases by 66% for French women lawyers as compared to their Swiss counterparts (odds ratio = 0.343, see Table 7.7). In contrast, French female lawyers are twice as likely as their Swiss counterparts to become solo practitioners, with a less statistically significant effect (odds ratio = 2.064, see Table 7.8).

In light of these results, we now explore the processes behind these slightly ambivalent gendered career mechanisms, which reveal that the French legal profession has a higher proportion of women, including in partnership positions, but that the lower proportion of Swiss female lawyers staying at the Bar has nonetheless better overall career prospects than French female lawyers. In the following section, we consider the interplay of gender norms and practices with the structural characteristics of the national legal labour markets and question the effects of respective career structures.

Table 7.6 Logistic model for the dependent variable 'to be solo practitioner'. Effect of country and gender

Dependent Variable: Job Position (To Be a Solo Practitioner)	Odds Ratios (Standard Errors in Brackets)
Lawyers with five years of seniority or more	
Country (to be a French lawyer)	**1.584***(0.227)
Sex (to be a man)	0.876(0.200)
Lawyers with five to nine years seniority	
Country (to be a French lawyer)	**1.741˙**(0.325)
Sex (to be a man)	0.897(0.299)
Lawyers with 10 years and more seniority	
Country (to be a French lawyer)	1.469(0.283)
Sex (to be a man)	0.910(0.243)

Database: Respondents living in marital life (N = 962)

Notes: ˙ *p* < .10
* *p* < .05
Additional notes:
a) We have constructed two dichotomous variables on job positions: the first dichotomous variable distinguishes two groups of job positions 'to be a partner'/ 'not to be a partner' (Tables 7.5, 7.7 and 7.11), the second variable distinguishes two groups of job positions 'to be a solo practitioner'/'not to be a solo practitioner' (Tables 7.6, 7.8 and 7.12). b) As the logistic coefficients are not immediately interpretable, the odds ratios are reported. Odds ratios can be interpreted as the effect of one unit change in the independent variable on the predicted odds ratio when the other variables in the model held constant.
Interpretation of odds ratios:

Example from Table 7.5, lawyers with five years seniority or more:

—The odds of being a partner are about 0.55 times lower (odds ratio < 1) for a French lawyer than for a Swiss lawyer, meaning that the odds decrease by 45%.
—The odds of being a partner are about 2.09 times higher (odds ratio > 1) for a man than for a woman, meaning that the odds increase by 109%.

Table 7.7 Logistic model for the dependent variable 'to be a partner'. Effect of country for women lawyers

Dependent Variable: Job Position (To Be a Partner)	Odds Ratios (Standard Errors in Brackets)
Women lawyers with five to nine years seniority	
Country (to be a French lawyer)	0.343*(0.470)
Women lawyers with 10 years and more seniority	
Country (to be a French lawyer)	0.390*(0.396)

Database: Women respondents in marital life (N = 617)

Notes: * *p* < .10

Table 7.8 Logistic model for the dependent variable 'to be a solo practitioner'. Effect of country for women lawyers

Dependent Variable: Job Position (to be a solo practitioner)	Odds ratios (Standard errors in brackets)
Women lawyers with five to nine years seniority	
Country (to be a French lawyer)	2.064*(0.426)
Women lawyers with 10 years and more seniority	
Country (to be a French lawyer)	2.184*(0.416)

Database: Women respondents in marital life (N = 617)

Notes: * p < .10
Additional notes: In Tables 7.7 and 7.8, we explore the odds for a woman lawyer 'to be a partner' (resp. 'to be a solo practitioner') (dependent variables) in relation to her country (to be French/to be Swiss) (independent variable).

Occupational Structure and Access to Partnership in France and Switzerland

When trying to explain how much more difficult it is for French and Swiss women lawyers to access a partnership position, it is key to pay attention to the career structure in both countries. Our qualitative data suggests that the restructuring of legal markets and the shrinkage of partnership positions (Galanter and Henderson 2008) does not seem to have progressed to the same extent in France and in Switzerland, leading to contrasting financial rewards and promotion opportunities in each country.

First, the Swiss legal labour market (Geneva and Lausanne) seems to offer proportionally more partner positions than the French (Parisian) one. The French legal labour market is composed of a greater share of solo practitioners (24% versus 15% in Switzerland) and large-scale law firms (21% versus 15% in Switzerland), whereas the Swiss legal profession has a higher proportion of small- or medium-sized firms (66% versus 47% in France), offering relatively more partner positions than in big firms (see Table 7.9). Hence, the Swiss occupational structure appears to be less competitive and this may serve to reduce the glass-ceiling effect to a certain extent.

As a result of the structural characteristics of the profession in each country, being a Swiss lawyer increases the chances of having partner status with a greater proportion of lawyers (30%) in (non-equity or equity) partner positions than in France (17%) (see Table 7.10). A structural gap between the two countries still remains even if we add 'counsels' and 'of counsels'[1]—two types of senior position more frequent in France, and situated between 'associate' and 'non-equity partner' positions in terms of status and prestige—to 'non-equity partners' (19% versus 12%

Table 7.9 Types of law firms among Swiss and French lawyers living in couple with 5–18 years seniority

N = 621	Solo firm	Small firm (2–10 lawyers)	Medium firm (11–29 lawyers)	Big firm (over 29 lawyers)
Total				
—Switzerland	19%	45%	21%	15%
—France	32%	31%	16%	21%
Women				
—Switzerland	15%	48%	22%	15%
—France	34%	32%	21%	13%
Men				
—Switzerland	24%	41%	20%	15%
—France	28%	30%	19%	23%

Table 7.10 Job positions among Swiss and French lawyers living in couple with 5–18 years seniority

N = 621	Associate (% in line)	Solo Practitioner (% in line)	Non-equity Partner (% in line)	Equity Partner (% in line)	Other (Counsel, Of Counsel)
Total					
—Switzerland	46%	22%	18%	12%	2%
—France	43%	32%	5%	13%	7%
Women					
—Switzerland	53%	19%	18%	8%	2%
—France	46%	33%	3%	10%	8%
Men					
—Switzerland	39%	26%	16%	18%	1%
—France	36%	29%	7%	19%	9%

in France). On the contrary, in our French sample solo practitioners are proportionally more numerous. So, despite the lack of societal-level support for working mothers, women lawyers in Switzerland are relatively more likely to have partner status (albeit as non-equity partners) than their French counterparts, primarily because the internal structure of the legal labour markets differs considerably between the two countries.

The qualitative material that we collected also suggests that exit from the Bar does not have the same long-term consequences in both countries. In France, this seems to be a definitive move, whereas a subsequent return to lawyering is believed by certain women lawyers to be much easier to achieve in Switzerland. In the Swiss context, the entry, exit, and eventual return of female lawyers to legal practice is facilitated by the existence of 'bridges' between other sectors of the legal labour market. This means that a temporary move into alternative and often less prestigious legal jobs (e.g., court clerk) does not prevent a subsequent return to lawyering. Although such permeable boundaries around the legal profession may encourage a significant number of Swiss women to leave the Bar at some point, they do not preclude women's subsequent return to lawyering, at least according to our women interviewees. This is less likely in the French legal labour market, where any exit appears to be definitive. Anne-Sophie—mentioned earlier—has recently come back to lawyering and has joined a medium-size firm as an equity partner, after having had her first child and having spent two years as a court clerk in Lausanne. We can also cite the case of Séverine, a former associate now working as an in-house counsel, who decided not to follow the partner track after working for five years in an associate position at one of the most prestigious business law firms in Switzerland. Due to what she described as the excessively competitive atmosphere surrounding the partner promotion process, she left the law firm to become 'an in-house counsel' in the Lausanne office of a multinational company. However, inspired by the example of former female colleagues who have set up in private practice, she firmly intends to return to lawyering in the future—something she believes is a real possibility, which explains why she left in the first place.

Second, there would also seem to be a difference in the timing of access to partner status in these two countries. According to our logistic regression testing the effect of the variables country and sex on job positions, the likelihood to achieve (equity or non-equity) partnership status within five to nine years of joining the Bar decreases by 65% for French lawyers as compared to their Swiss counterparts (odds ratio = 0.354, see Table 7.5). So, we could say that within the first 10 years of practice, Swiss lawyers are more likely than their French counterparts to reach partner status, simply because lawyers tend to become partners earlier in their career in Switzerland than in France. However, the structural differences between France and Switzerland are more salient for women than for men. For male lawyers with five or more years at the Bar, there are no significant country differences in the chances of becoming a partner or a solo practitioner (see Tables 7.11 and 7.12). Hence the country differences in the chances of being a partner may be mainly related to the differential maternity effect and delaying parenthood strategies mentioned earlier.

The differences in the structure of legal labour markets and in the timing of promotion to partnership influence the relative optimism of Swiss and French lawyers, as far as their long-term career prospects are concerned. A sense of worsening economic conditions over time is deeply entrenched among younger lawyers in France, whereas this is less the case in Switzerland. While 75% of Swiss respondents declare they are satisfied or very satisfied with their professional choice of becoming a lawyer, the share of satisfied or very satisfied French lawyers drops to 53%. Thus, Laurent, a

Isabel Boni-Le Goff et al.

Table 7.11 Logistic model for the dependent variable 'to be a partner'. Effect of country for men lawyers

Dependent Variable: Job Position (To Be a Partner)	Odds Ratios (Standard Errors in Brackets)
Men lawyers with five to nine years seniority	
Country (to be a French lawyer)	0.369(0.367)
Men lawyers with 10 years and more seniority	
Country (to be a French lawyer)	0.837(0.388)

Database: Men living in couples (N = 345)

Additional notes: In Tables 7.11 and 7.12, we explore the odds for a man lawyer 'to be a partner' (resp. 'to be a solo practitioner') (dependent variables) in relation to his country (to be French/to be Swiss) (independent variable).

Table 7.12 Logistic model for the dependent variable 'to be a solo practitioner'. Effect of country for men lawyers

Dependent Variable: Job Position (To Be a Solo Practitioner)	Odds ratios (Standard Errors in Brackets)
Men lawyers with five to nine years seniority	
Country (to be a French lawyer)	1.333(0.516)
Men lawyers with 10 years and more seniority	
Country (to be a French lawyer)	0.962(0.401)

Database: Men living in couples (N = 345)

47-year-old practicing as an 'of counsel', describes the intergenerational inequalities of the French legal profession in graphic detail. According to him, older generations of French lawyers are eager to sell their shares in law firms at prices that younger lawyers cannot afford, both because of a general economic downturn and because of the demographic expansion of the profession in recent years.

> The younger generations say to the older ones: "Hang on there, you've made pots of money over the years and now you want even more? Dream on! We've only ever known a legal market that will never enable us to live as richly as you did, and now you want us to subsidise your retirement? Don't count on us for that!"
>
> (Laurent)

The more pronounced generation gap in the French context is linked to a much less favourable demographic and economic situation compared to the one in Switzerland. We hypothesise that, for women, the generation penalty facing the younger lawyers in France tends to reduce the potential benefits of the more egalitarian societal gender regime. In comparison, the less favourable gender regime in Switzerland is balanced by a more buoyant economic climate and by the perception—true or false—of a flexible entry and exit (and re-entry) structure of the legal labour market.

Conclusion

By focusing on one specific profession, we are able to shed new light on the interactions between national gender regimes and specific occupational structures and on how the interactions of these two levels of sociological mechanisms produce unpredictable gendered career outcomes. Our approach enables us to show that despite a highly conservative societal gender regime, Swiss female lawyers ultimately enjoy relatively equal career prospects as their French counterparts—if not slightly better prospects for those who remain in the profession, despite the strong pressures to exit that are exerted by an adverse national gender regime. The qualitative part of our study sheds some light on the potential positive effect of apparently more permeable boundaries between lawyering and other legal professions on Swiss women's careers, by making it possible to return to lawyering after a period of time spent in alternative occupations, or even out of the labour market. However, additional research should be done to offer a more systematic investigation of this effect.

Our study also suggests that solo practice in France may represent a functional alternative to abandoning the legal profession altogether (as in the Swiss case), but that both these alternatives ultimately limit women's access to the most prestigious and well-remunerated positions in the Swiss and French legal labour market hierarchy. Overall, our research calls for more systematic comparison of the evolution of legal professions thanks to robust survey instruments and complemented with qualitative research. In so doing, sociologists of legal professions could generate systematic findings that could then be replicated to the study of other professions, leading to more dialogue across sociologists of professions.

Note

1 The position 'of counsel' can have different professional meanings in the French or Swiss law firms. In some French law firms, former partners become 'of counsel' when they retire but maintain part-time legal activity.

References

Acker, J (1994) 'The Gender Regime of Swedish Banks' 10 *Scandinavian Journal of Management* 117. doi:10.1016/0956-5221(94)90015-9.x

——— (2006) 'Inequality Regimes: Gender, Class and Race in Organizations' 20 *Gender and Society* 441. doi:10.1177/0891243206289499.x

——— (2009) 'From Ceilings to Inequality Regimes/ Du plafond de verre aux régimes d'inégalité' 51 *Sociologie du Travail* 199. doi:10.1016/j.soctra.2009.03.004.x

Blair-Loy, M (2003) *Competing Devotions: Career and Family Among Women Executives* (Cambridge, MA, Harvard University Press).

Boigeol, A (2003) 'Male Strategies in the Face of Feminization of the Profession: The Case of the French Judiciary' in U Schultz and G Shaw (eds), *Women in the World's Legal Professions* (Oxford, Hart Publishing).

Boni-Le Goff, I and Le Feuvre, N (2017) 'Professions from a Gendered Perspective' *Oxford Research Encyclopedia of Business and Management*. doi:10.1093/acrefore/9780190224851.013.89

Bydzovsky, C (2014) 'L'Ordre des Avocats de Genève' *Anwalts Revue de l'Avocat* 1 *Thema/Question du Jour* 11. http://anwaltsrevue.recht.ch/

Connell, RW (2005) 'A Really Good Husband: Work/Life Balance, Gender Equity and Social Change' 40 *Australian Journal of Social Issues* 369. doi:10.1002/j.1839-4655.2005.tb00978.x

——— (2006) 'Glass Ceilings or Gendered Institutions? Mapping the Gender Regimes of Public Sector Worksites' 66 *Public Administration Review* 837, 839. doi:10.1111/j.1540-6210.2006.00652.x

Craig, L and Mullan, K (2010) 'Parenthood, Gender and Work-Family Time in the United States, Australia, Italy, France, and Denmark' 72 *Journal of Marriage and Family* 1344. doi:10.1111/j.1741-3737.2010.00769.x

Crompton, R and Le Feuvre, N (2000) 'Gender, Family and Employment in Comparative Perspective: The Realities and Representations of Equal Opportunities in Britain and France' 10 *Journal of European Social Policy* 1334. doi:10.1177/a014365

Décideurs Magazine (2014) 'Parité dans les Cabinets d'Avocats: Peut Mieux Faire' 88. www.magazine-decideurs.com/univers/droit-regulation

Eurostat (2015) 'People in the EU: Who Are We and How Do We Live' *EuroStat Statistical Books* (Luxembourg, Publications Office of the European Union). https://ec.europa.eu/eurostat/documents/3217494/7089681/KS-04-15-567-EN-N.pdf doi:10.2785/406462

Fédération Suisse des Avocats (FSA) (2017) 'Mitgliederstatistik SAV 2006–2016—Statistiques des Membres FSA' *Anwalts/Revue de l'Avocat* April 2017, 190. http://anwaltsrevue.recht.ch/

Ferragina, E (2017) 'Does Family Policy Influence Women's Employment? Reviewing the Evidence in the Field' *Political Studies Review* 1. doi:10.1177/1478929917736438.x

Galanter, M and Henderson, W (2008) 'The Elastic Tournament: A Second Transformation of the Big Law Firm' 60 *Stanford Law Review* 1867.

Giraud, O and Lucas, B (2009) 'Le Renouveau des Régimes de Genre en Allemagne et en Suisse: Bonjour Néo-Maternalisme?' 46 *Cahiers du Genre* 17. doi:10.3917/cdge.046.0017

Gregory, A and Milner, S (2011) 'Fathers and Work-Life Balance in France and the UK: Policy and Practice' 31 *International Journal of Sociology and Social Policy* 34. doi:10.1111/lasr.12214.x

Hagan, J and Kay F (2010) 'The Masculine Mystique: Living Large from Law School to Later Life' 25 *Canadian Journal of Law and Society/Revue Canadienne Droit et Société* 195. doi:10.1108/01443331111104797

Hearn, J, Biese, I, Choroszewicz, M and Husu, L (2016) 'Gender, Diversity and Intersectionality in Professions and Potential Professions: Analytical, Historical and Contemporary Perspectives' in M Dent, IL Bourgeault, J-L Denis and

E Kuhlmann (eds), *The Routledge Companion to the Professions and Professionalism* (London, Routledge).

Kay, F, Alarie, S and Jones, A (2016) 'Undermining Gender Equality: Female Attrition from Private Law Practice' 50 *Law and Society Review* 766. doi:10.1111/lasr.12214

Le Feuvre, N and Lapeyre, N (2005) 'Les "scripts sexués" de carrière dans les professions juridiques en France' 3 *Work, Knowledge & Society/Travail, savoirs et sociétés* 101–126.

Le Feuvre, N and Walters, P (1994) 'The Legal Professions in Britain and France: A Comparative Perspective on the Dynamics of Occupational Feminization' in Y Lucas and C Dubar (eds), *Genèse et Dynamique des Groupes Professionnels* (Lille, Presses Universitaires de Lille).

Le Goff, J-M and Lévy, R (eds) (2016) *Devenir Parent, Devenir Inégaux: Transitions à la Parentalité et Inégalités de Genre* (Geneva, Éditions Seismo).

Jane, L (1992) 'Gender and the Development of Welfare Regimes' 2(3) *Journal of European Social Policy.*

Marry, C (2014) 'Inégalités dans le Couple et Sentiment d'Injustice. Les Paradoxes de L'égalité Contemporaine' in F Dubet (ed), *Inégalités et Justice Sociale* (Paris, La Découverte).

Ordre des Avocats de Paris (2013) *Femmes au Barreau en 2013: Rapport de l'Observatoire de l'Egalité* Special Edition, March (Paris: Le Bulletin du Barreau de Paris). http://dl.avocatparis.org/com/bulletins_en_pdf/Bulletins_2013/Special_femmes.pdf

Orloff, AS (1996) 'Gender in the Welfare State' 22 *Annual Review of Sociology* 51. doi:10.1146/annurev.soc.22.1.51

Pascall, G and Lewis, J (2004) 'Emerging Gender Regimes and Policies for Gender Equality in a Wider Europe' 33 *Journal of Social Policy* 373. doi:10.1017/S004727940400772X

Rosen, R (1999) ' "Proletarianizing" Lives: Researching Careers' 33 *Law and Society Review* 703. doi:10.1017/S004727940400772X

Schultz, U and Shaw, G (eds) (2003) *Women in the World's Legal Professions* (Oxford, Hart Publishing).

Sommerlad, H (2002) 'Women Solicitors in a Fractured Profession: Intersections of Gender and Professionalism in England and Wales' 9 *International Journal of the Legal Profession* 213.

—— (2016) ' "A Pit to Put Women In": Professionalism, Work Intensification, Sexualisation and Work-Life Balance in the Legal Profession in England and Wales' 23 *International Journal of the Legal Profession* 61. doi:10.1080/0969 5958.2016.1140945

Walby, S (2004) 'The European Union and Gender Equality: Emergent Variety of Gender Regimes' 11 *Social Politics* 4. doi:10.1093/sp/jxh024

World Economic Forum (2017) 'The Global Gender Gap Report. 2017' *Insight Report* (Geneva, World Economic Forum) 2 November. http://www3.weforum.org/docs/WEF_GGGR_2017.pdf

8 A Life Course Approach to Workplace Discrimination and Employment

Evidence From a US National Sample of Women and Men Lawyers

Gabriele Plickert

Introduction

Over the past three decades, the number of women entering the legal profession has significantly increased in the US. Yet, regardless of the influx of women across a wide range of legal practice settings, research continues to show that women, compared with men, still face greater challenges in advancing their legal career (Dau-Schmidt et al. 2009; Epstein et al. 1995; Hagan and Kay 2010; Kricheli-Katz 2012; Rhode 2011; Williams and Richardson 2011). Research overwhelmingly suggests that among the difficult challenges facing women, balancing expectations of high-status careers with responsibilities at home figures prominently. For example, prior research provides evidence that women pay a penalty in labour market outcomes when they become mothers (Budig 2003; Budig and England 2001). Studies focusing on employment exits and returns show that motherhood intersects with inequalities in earnings and promotion in comparison to employed professionals with no children (Budig and Hodges 2010; England et al. 2016). More generally, persistent gender differences in the legal profession are explained by work environments that interfere or deviate from one's personal life goals/events (e.g., marriage and children) (Hagan and Kay 2010; Reichman and Sterling 2002; Wallace 2001).

Some studies on job-related stressors and well-being have also investigated the impact of workplace discrimination (e.g., discrimination based on gender, race, or age) to further understand the complexities of persistent inequalities among various groups of working professionals (Becker 1980; Gee et al. 2007; Hampton and Heywood 1993). For example, Hampton and Heywood (1993) found that perceptions of gender discrimination were predictive of disparities in wages among physicians. Other researchers have examined the relationship between perceived discrimination and labour force participation. These studies suggest an indirect effect of discrimination on employment, stability, and wages (Becker 1980). Scholars have demonstrated that perceptions of discrimination are linked to an array of inequalities (e.g., income, employment participation, career opportunities, and advancement) and well-being (Gee et al. 2007; Mays et al. 2007; Williams et al. 2003). However, we still have a limited understanding of *how* perceptions of workplace discrimination shape women's and men's employment schedules across the stages of their careers, especially in the legal profession.

This chapter investigates how trajectories of employment schedules, the comparison between full-time and part-time work, are a function of workplace discrimination and how this relationship varies for women and men lawyers. The incorporated life course perspective (see also Elder et al. 2003; Marshall and Mueller 2003) shapes the current research in several ways. First, the present study explores workplace discrimination linked to the ages of lawyers across the first ten years of their careers and examines whether experiences of discrimination are important for employment schedules across career stages. Second, the present study examines how workplace discrimination is embedded within legal workplaces, roles, and norms, and suggests that exposure to workplace discrimination varies not only by age, but also by experiences and decisions surrounding personal life events (e.g., marriage, having a child). Thus, the perception of workplace discrimination would vary not only by age, but also by the timing and intensity of family responsibilities (e.g., birth of child[ren] and child caregiving responsibilities) in the context of demanding work schedules. To better understand the trajectories of full-time employment compared to part-time work among legal professionals across stages of their career, this chapter addresses the following questions: (1) How do trajectories of employment change with respect to the experience of workplace discrimination—by gender, race, religion, disability, or sexual orientation (combined) and by family responsibility? (2) To what extent do work characteristics (i.e., workplace authority, firm size, and practice setting) and socio-demographic attributes (i.e., gender, marital status, children at home) shape the trajectories of employment?

Data derive from three waves of a nationally representative US panel study of lawyers for a ten-year period of their careers (see also Dinovitzer et al. 2009). Using only responses to all three waves of the study, the findings discussed in this chapter include 2,035 lawyers in full-and part-time employment with repeated measurement information from data collected between 2002 and 2013. Lacking in the research literature are data that track employment and perceptions of workplace discrimination in the context of lawyers' professional and personal lives. Taking advantage of the detailed information collected on workplace discrimination and specific workplace characteristics (i.e., firm size, practice setting), across three time points over a ten-year span of law practice, provides a more focused investigation on how age and workplace discrimination impact women's and men's employment schedules.

Experiences of Discrimination Across the Life Course

The life course entails a sequence of events and roles that the individual engages in over the course of their professional and personal life (Giele and Elder 1998). The occurrence of events is marked by the timing, duration, spacing, and sequencing. For instance, women's employment is influenced by the birth of a child, meaning the age of the mother (timing) determines the birth and consequences that follow, regarding work and personal life circumstances. Lasting effects, like the birth of a child, are events that can be best described as trajectories. Trajectories are pathways that summarise the cumulative experiences of individuals with respect to an outcome (Elder et al. 2003), such as employment schedules. Trajectories can also reveal the mechanisms by which the accumulation of events can generate long-term consequences with different outcomes for different groups of individuals. Thus, focusing on age-related reporting across years of legal practice informs us as to *when* the timing of events (work and personal) matters for women's and men's employment schedules. Moreover, it allows for the disentangling of circumstances at work and/or at home that may promote or hinder professionals' workforce participation.

Experience of discrimination in the workplace has become an important measure of inquiry to explain persistent differences in performance between mothers and childless women, as well as fathers and childless men (Budig and England 2001; Plickert and Sterling 2017).

Discrimination can be defined as the actions arising from institutions and individuals that unfairly treat and systematically harm members of socially marginalised groups (Feagin and McKinney 2003). However, unfair treatment by an employer, as revealed by preferences for male employees over female employees, is sometimes part of a daily routine and is not necessarily defined and experienced as discrimination by individuals (Ridgeway 1997; Rosen and Martin 1998). Despite individual variations in experience and definitions of unfair treatment or discrimination, research shows that perceptions of discrimination represent an objective experience, including the awareness about the reason for the experience (Gee et al. 2007; Kessler et al. 1999). Overall, experiences of unfair treatment, adverse circumstances, and discrimination are reported frequently in survey research. For example, Kessler and colleagues (1999) found that 33% of a nationally representative sample experienced a major incident of discrimination in their lifetime, while 61% experienced incidents of discrimination on a daily basis.

Furthermore, experiences of discrimination in the workplace have been linked to a greater likelihood of distress and a decline in emotional well-being, especially among women (Pavalko et al. 2003). Perceived discrimination not only adversely affects health outcomes, but also impedes equity in the workplace, and thus negatively affects individuals' employment and, more broadly, individuals' career pathways (Kessler et al. 1999).

The literature exploring careers over the life course suggests that the relationship between age and negative workplace experiences is higher among younger lawyers (those in their thirties) compared to professionals in their mid-life (those in their mid-forties) (Garcia-Manglano 2015). Among the few studies that do examine discrimination effects on employment profiles across the life course, findings show that shifts in employment are the result of professional experiences, preferences, and constraints, meaning that events such as marriage or children influence the launching of one's early career (Garcia-Manglano 2015). In fact, discriminatory experiences in concert with poor health have been associated with less attachment to work, particularly during women's childbearing years.

Another reason for this age pattern is explained by the co-occurrence of lower job satisfaction with higher depressive symptoms, which is particularly prominent during the early years of professional careers (Plickert et al. 2017; Yang 2007). The early career stages are especially stressful because during this period, young professionals work to develop specialised skills and establish a professional plan that allows for upward mobility. Despite these early stressful career experiences, Plickert and colleagues (2017) found that career trajectories improve around the mid-40s to early 50s among all lawyers regardless of their different experiences earlier in their career (see also Yang 2007). These positive late-life trajectories are the result of improvements in authority and control in the workplace and the establishment of positive intimate relationships (Plickert et al. 2017).

With respect to gender inequality in the legal profession, one frequently cited explanation is the notion that women are less motivated and committed to their careers than men (Budig and Hodges 2010; Coontz 1995; Epstein 1981; Gough and Noonan 2013; Kuo 2005). Stereotyped beliefs and adverse experiences result in women receiving less challenging assignments than their male counterparts (Epstein 1992; Hagan and Kay 2007). These assumptions are embedded in the argument that centres on masculinity in the workplace. Especially in the legal profession, the image of masculinity is perpetuated by individuals working long hours to show dedication to the workplace (Kuo 2005; Webley et al. 2016). In comparison, women face stereotypes of being perceived as less committed to their work and therefore unable to fulfil an expected *ideal* workload (Epstein et al. 1995; Rhode 2011). Employers are likely to have an exaggerated view of women—especially mothers—that may potentially hinder women in their efforts to succeed in an adverse work environment (Yu and Kuo 2017). Thus, while employers' expectations are tied to job devotion, occupational competitiveness, and full-time schedules, these *static* expectations of employers may potentially interact adversely with life events (e.g., having a child and experiencing discrimination upon return to work) and negatively impact the employment trajectories of those who assume primary child caregiving responsibilities.

Overall, events of discrimination refer to unfair treatment that is commonly based on age, gender, race, and ethnicity—to name a few. Thus, considering general workplace discrimination and discrimination based on family responsibilities may provide unique insights into persistent inequalities in the legal profession and discrimination more generally. Taken together, exposure to and consequences of general workplace discrimination and/or family responsibility discrimination will vary by age, gender, and other life events (e.g., birth of child[ren]) and thus influence employment schedules across careers.

Survey Data and Method

The data used to examine trajectories of workplace discrimination are drawn from a nationally representative panel survey of US law school graduates, the After the JD study (AJD). This study started with a random sample of more than 5,000 US women and men lawyers who began their careers in 2000, and were surveyed in 2002–03, 2007–08, and 2012–13 (see Dinovitzer et al. 2009; Plickert and Dinovitzer 2007; Nelson and Plickert 2014). The AJD study longitudinally tracks the professional careers of lawyers and examines their professional identities, personal roles, and responsibilities. The sample includes lawyers from eighteen legal markets, ranging from the four largest markets (i.e., New York City, the District of Columbia, Chicago, and Los Angeles) to fourteen smaller metropolitan areas or entire states. The first wave (AJD1) consists of 4,538 eligible respondents, with a response rate of 71%. The second wave (AJD2) obtained responses from 3,705 respondents, including 70% of the respondents to AJD1 and 27% of those who were eligible but did not respond to the first wave. In total, AJD2 consists of responses from 51% of eligible sample members. The third wave (AJD3) surveyed only those individuals who had previously responded to either AJD1 or AJD2. Thus, AJD3 obtained completed surveys from 2,862 respondents, for a response rate of 53% among those individuals who previously responded to either one or both of AJD1 or AJD2. In all three waves, the race/ethnicity status of attorneys was oversampled (see Dinovitzer et al. 2009) minority attorneys (e.g., African-American, Hispanic, and Asian) were oversampled (see Dinovitzer et al. 2009).

To investigate the effects of perceived general workplace discrimination and discrimination based on family responsibilities on the employment trajectories of women and men, I use the final analytical sample, which includes 2,035 lawyers, with repeated measurement information from data collected across three waves, between 2002 and 2013. The distribution between women and men is about equal (50%) across the three waves. For parental status across the three waves, women lawyers have somewhat fewer children (19% AJD1, 52% AJD2, and 66% AJD3) compared to their male colleagues (31% AJD1, 60% AJD2, and 73% AJD3). The detailed information on life course transitions collected from lawyers across ten years of legal practice with a wide range of ages (28–48 years)[1] make this an ideal data source to explore the dynamics of workplace discrimination on employment schedules among this group of professionals.

Before examining the relationship between age, employment, and discrimination over time, the relationship between age and employment status is established. Two sets of models are explored. The first two models examine employment trajectories as a function of general workplace discrimination. The second two models investigate employment trajectories as a function of family responsibility discrimination. These model steps allow for the assessment of variation in employment characteristics based on discrimination and in the presence of controls.

A population-average logit model (Fitzmaurice et al. 2004; Rabe-Hesketh and Skrondal 2005) was estimated. The predicted probabilities, also referred to as marginal probabilities, are population averages (rather than predicted probabilities for individuals) for given levels of the predictors (Rabe-Hesketh and Skrondal 2005). Thus, the marginal probabilities refer to predicted probabilities of general workplace discrimination and family responsibility discrimination for respondents with a given set of characteristics.

Measurement of Key Variables

The outcome measure, *employment schedule*, is a binary outcome, contrasting those currently employed full-time to those currently employed part-time.

Age is a significant independent measure in the analysis of employment trajectories. Thus, at each wave, age is measured by calculating the date of the first survey minus each respondent's date of birth. Given that the literature suggests that the relationship between age and experience of discrimination should be higher among younger lawyers (those in their thirties) compared to professionals in mid-life (those in their mid-forties) (Garcia-Manglano 2015), the statistical models examine age and age-squared.

Workplace discrimination captures two types of discrimination: one defined as general discrimination, and the other defined as family responsibility discrimination. Both types of discrimination are binary independent measures, indicating whether a respondent reported experiencing discrimination at work over the years of their career. For general workplace discrimination, respondents answered that they have experienced discrimination based on race, religion, ethnicity, gender, disability or sexual orientation—referred to in this chapter as *general workplace discrimination* (WPD). About 35% of the final analytical sample provided a response indicating they had experienced WPD.

Family responsibility discrimination (FRD) refers to respondents' experiences of adverse consequences at work as a result of having children. In the final analytical sample of ADJ1, approximately 25% of professionals became a parent, which increased to 56% in ADJ2, and to 69% in ADJ3. Overall, about 48% of the entire parent sample responded to at least one form of FRD. This time-variant measure of FRD is composed of three items: (1) commitment to work, (2) performance, and (3) ideal worker expectations. The survey asked respondents whether they had been questioned by an employer about their *commitment to work*. About 19% reported being questioned about their commitment to work after five years of legal practice and about 27% after ten years. *Performance* is an indicator that refers to adverse experiences as a result of having had a child including (1) delay of promotion, (2) loss of seniority, (3) loss of clients, (4) loss of income, and/or (5) loss of challenging assignments ($\alpha = 0.70$). Similar to the responses to questions about commitment to work, responses to adverse experiences with performance are at 17% in their early years of practice, increasing to 22% ten years later. The final item refers to the *ideal worker expectation*, which includes responses concerning experiences of (1) work pressure while on parental leave and/ or (2) unreasonable workload following parental leave ($\alpha = 0.63$). This item received the most frequent responses across respondents' years of practice (22–23%).

Measuring WPD quantitatively in surveys poses a challenge (Yu and Kuo 2017). Studies that describe lawyers' work and the imbalance between work and family have yet to explore the impact of structural discriminatory factors when describing the dynamics between women and men lawyers at work. Recent work using lab experiments and qualitative responses has shown that employers evaluate women with children less favourably than men or women without children (Correll et al. 2007; Fuegen et al. 2004; Kay et al. 2013). Extending these experiences of general WPD and FRD to the legal profession, it is assumed that over the course of legal careers, both types of discrimination will directly affect women's work schedules, especially mothers, but will have less impact on men's or father's work schedules (see also Fuegen at al. 2004; Plickert and Sterling 2017).

Satisfaction

Two scales were created to capture dimensions of satisfaction. The first, *satisfaction with substance of work*, includes the following five items: satisfaction with (1) level of responsibility you have, (2) opportunities for building skills, (3) tasks you perform, (4) substantive area of your work, and (5) intellectual challenge of your work. Responses range from 1 = highly dissatisfied to 7 = highly satisfied ($\alpha = 0.90$).

Prior studies demonstrate the importance of job satisfaction on work experience and work attitudes (Sloan 2012). The second scale, *satisfaction with control over work*, includes two items: (1) control one has over the amount of work one does, and (2) control one has over how one does the work. While greater responsibilities may foster job satisfaction, it is likewise possible that greater workload leads to demanding work schedules that may potentially increase job dissatisfaction and heightened levels of depression, often affecting women who bear greater caregiving responsibilities (Moen et al. 2013).

The analysis also includes a measure of *depression*, indicating whether or not respondents reported feelings of depressive symptoms during the last two survey periods. These symptoms are included because depressed individuals are more likely to be at risk of perceiving discrimination. Hence, individuals who experience discrimination are more prone to depression over time (Gee et al. 2007; Pavalko et al. 2003).

Practice Settings

A series of dummy codes were created including eight separate measures: (1) solo, (2) small firm size of less than 21 lawyers, (3) firm size of 21–100 lawyers, (4) firm size of 101–250 lawyers, (5) firm size of 251 and more lawyers, (6) government or public interest, (7) non-profit legal sector or education, and (8) business. In the analyses, solo practice serves as a reference group.

Individual Background Characteristics

The time-invariant measures include gender, race/ethnicity, and law school tier. Because perceptions of discrimination are found to vary by gender and race/ethnicity (Kasschau 1977; Kessler et al. 1999), the statistical models control for both. *Gender* is coded 1 for women and 0 for men. For respondents' *race/ethnicity*, "Minority," coded 1, contrasts with "White," coded 0. Respondents' *law school rank* includes five tiers: (1) top ten schools, (2) top 11–20 schools, (3) schools ranked 21–100, (4) schools ranked 101–37, and (5) schools ranked 138–78. The rank order of these five categories is based on the groupings of law schools published by *U.S. News and World Report* in 2003. Previous studies have shown that in the US, law school ranking is significantly associated with type of practice, income, and promotion—that is—graduates from top-tier schools experience greater opportunities initially, as compared to graduates from lower-tier schools (Moriss and Henderson 2008). The final models also include *marital status* as a time-varying control, contrasting currently married, remarried, and cohabiting to never married or currently not cohabiting respondents. The second time-varying control, *number of children*, ranges from zero to four, and includes those children who currently reside in the household and are under the age of 18.

Results

Experiences of Discrimination Across Age and Gender

For employment schedules, the descriptive data show that the majority of lawyers are employed full-time (98%) at the beginning of their career. Full-time employment slightly declines to 92% after five years of work and continues to drop after ten years (90%). The variation in full-time employment over the years is primarily due to gender differences. On average 96% of women work full-time at the start of their career (in their early thirties); however, five years into their career (in their mid-thirties) full-time employment declines to 86%, and to about 82% when women are in their mid-forties, with about ten years of practice. In comparison, the majority of male respondents (98–99%) work full-time throughout the same years of practice. Noticing these gender differences in employment schedules, it is meaningful to assess to what extent these trajectories vary by age and experiences of discrimination.

With respect to discrimination, patterns of reported general WPD show variation by age and gender. About 40% of female lawyers reported experiences of WPD in their thirties, with an increase to 50% in their forties. Among male lawyers, reports of WPD are relatively similar across all ages—at about 20%, only increasing to 29% in their early forties (see Figure 8.1).

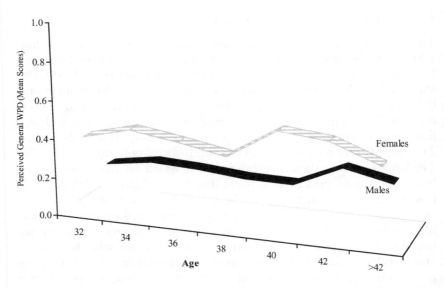

Figure 8.1 Perceived experiences of general workplace discrimination (WPD) among US lawyers, by age and gender (2002–2013)

Source: AJD 2002–03, 2007–08, and 2012–13.

Notes: General WPD includes the combined experiences discrimination by gender, race, ethnicity, religion, disability, or sexual orientation.

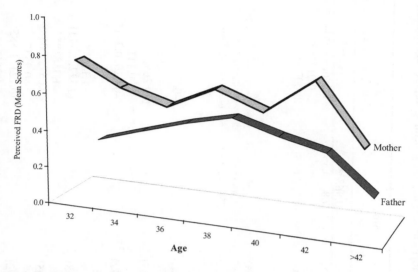

Figure 8.2 Perceived experiences of family responsibility discrimination (FRD) among US lawyers, by age and gender (2002–2013)

Source: AJD 2002–03, 2007–08, and 2012–13.

Notes: FRD data are collected only for those respondents with children and include the following experiences: (1) questioned about commitment to work; (2) adverse experience in performance (i.e., delay of promotion, loss of seniority, loss of office clients, loss of challenging assignments, loss of income); and (3) ideal worker expectation (i.e., pressure to work while on parental leave, unreasonable workload).

In comparison to general WPD, reports of FRD show frequent experiences for young mothers in their early thirties (77%), slightly declining between their mid-thirties and early forties (50–60%), and significantly increasing again for women in their mid-forties (80%). Across a ten-year career span, the majority of women lawyers with children have experienced discrimination because of child caregiving responsibilities. In contrast, 40% of fathers report FRD in their early thirties, increasing to 48% around age thirty-eight, and significantly decreasing to 14% around their forties (see Figure 8.2). While fathers also report experiences of FRD at their work, the likelihood of such experiences remains significantly lower across their careers, as compared to mothers. The descriptive data suggest a unique pattern of age-related reporting for both types of discrimination, specifically affecting women and mothers.

Age-Related Reporting of General Workplace Discrimination on Employment

In Table 8.1 the first two models (1a and 1b) refer to trajectories of employment as a function of general WPD. The first model estimates the

Table 8.1 Population-average fixed effects models predicting age variation in employment schedules by general workplace discrimination and family responsibility discrimination

	Model 1a (Population Average)	Model 1b	Model 2a	Model 2b (Population Average)
Age	-0.740*** (0.959, -0.522)	-0.834*** (-1.097, 0.571)	-0.863*** (-1.168, -0.558)	-0.934*** (-1.286, -0.581)
Age-squared	0.009*** (0.006, 0.012)	0.010*** (0.007, 0.014)	0.011*** (0.007, 0.015)	0.012*** (0.007, 0.017)
Experience of Discrimination				
General WPD	0.326** (0.097, 0.556)	-0.464 (-1.183, 0.254)	–	–
FRD	–	–	-1.483*** (-1.776, -1.189)	-1.992*** (-3.018, -0.966)
Satisfaction with				
Substance of work		0.057 (-0.050, .164)		0.051 (-0.088, 0.190)
Control over work		0.009 (-0.138, 0.157)		- 0.064 (-0.265, 0.137)
Depressive Symptoms		0.068 (-0.036, 0.172)		0.111 (-0.020, 0.241)
Practice Setting[a]				
Small firm size 2–20		1.372*** (0.923, 1.818)		1.117*** (0.522, 1.711)
Firm size 21–100		1.540*** (0.985, 2.095)		1.358*** (0.657, 2.058)
Firm size 101–250		1.094*** (0.496, 1.692)		0.853* (0.121, 1.585)
Firm size 251+		1.348*** (0.851, 1.846)		1.266*** (0.612, 1.920)

Government or public interest		2.228*** (1.738, 2.719)	1.796*** (1.154, 2.439)
Non-profit or education		1.807*** (1.313, 2.301)	0.693* (-0.006 1.392)
Business		1.263** (0.248, 2.279)	1.647*** (0.975, 2.319)
Controls			
Female		-2.685*** (-3.116, -2.255)	-3.594*** (-4.541, -2.646)
Nonwhite		0.261 (-0.023, 0.544)	0.034 (-0.312, 0.379)
Married		-1.052* (-1.466, -0.638)	-0.697* (-1.302, -0.092)
Children in household		0.683*** (0.603, 0.772)	-0.087 (-0.302, 0.127)
Law school tier		0.004*** (0.002, 0.007)	0.006*** (0.003, 0.009)
Discrimination Female*[b]		0.824* (0.055, 1.593)	1.394** (0.302, 2.486)
Constant	19.06***	19.81***	22.63***
LR chi²	358.34***	457.39***	386.19***
N	5985	5985	3681
Pseudo R²	0.129	0.200	0.253

Source: AJD 2002–03, 2007–08, and 2012–13.

Notes: *p < .05; **p < .01; ***p < .001, two-tailed test, 95% confidence intervals are shown in brackets.
[a] Comparison group for practice setting is solo practice.
[b] The interaction between discrimination*female refers to general WPD *female in Model 1b and to FRD *female in Model 2b.

probability of employment as a function of age, including a quadratic association of age, and WPD. The quadratic association with age is statistically significant, meaning that full-time employment initially declines and then slightly improves with age. Also, experiences of WPD affect employment schedules (see also Figure 8.3a). Model 1b adds controls for job satisfaction, depressive symptoms, and practice setting, as well as personal characteristics including gender, race, marital status, and children residing at home. Many of these covariates are associated with the likelihood of part-time work over full-time employment. For example, married women with children who experience general WPD are less likely to be employed full-time in comparison to their male counterparts with children. The significant interaction speaks to the differences in employment schedules between women and men by experiences of general WPD.

Figure 8.3a illustrates the predicted levels of full-time employment over part-time work. The findings show that the most notable gender differences in employment status appear with reports of general WPD after

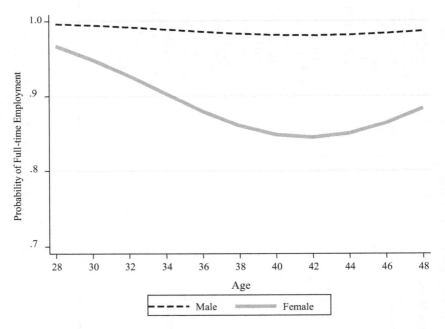

Figure 8.3a Predicted probabilities for trajectories of employment schedules among US lawyers by perceived general WPD

Source: AJD 2002–03, 2007–08, and 2012–13. Average age of participants by survey waves: AJD1 = 31 years (age range 27–42); AJD2 = 36 years (age range 32–47); and AJD3 = 41 years (age range 37–48).

Notes: Perceived general WPD includes the combined experiences discrimination by gender, race, ethnicity, religion, disability, or sexual orientation.

age 38. For women, the probability of full-time work declines with the beginning of their early career years, reaching a low in their early forties, and remaining steady until about their mid-forties. Only in their mid-forties, women's probability of full-time work seems to rise again. These fluctuations in women's employment trajectory suggest that women are either more exposed or more sensitised to experiences of WPD than their male colleagues. In contrast, for men, the experience of general WPD does not significantly alter their full-time employment trajectory.

While various dimensions of job satisfaction have been found to offset adversities at work (Plickert et al. 2017), the current findings suggest that higher levels of job satisfaction do not decrease the experience of general WPD. Regardless of firm size, practice setting, and dimensions of satisfaction, general WPD negatively impacts women's employment schedules. However, for men with and without children employed in similar work settings, the effect of general WPD does not impact their full-time work schedule.

Age-Related Reporting of Family Responsibility Discrimination on Employment of Parents

Models 2a and 2b, in Table 8.1, examine experiences of FRD and their impact on work schedules among mothers and fathers. As part of the survey design, responses to FRD are provided by lawyers who assume the role of a parent. Model 2a estimates the probability of full-time employment as a function of age, age-squared, and FRD. The quadratic association of age is significant as well as the experience of FRD, meaning that employment schedules change over time. For example, mothers who experience FRD are less likely to work full-time. In fact, full-time employment decreases by about 20% as a result of experiences with FRD—this trajectory begins as soon as women start their career and shifts upward beginning at age 40 (see Figure 8.3b). Interestingly, assumed protective factors do not have their anticipated effects. For example, low depression and high job satisfaction should buffer against adverse experiences (Plickert et al. 2017). However, the findings in Models 2a and 2b suggest that experiences of FRD further widen the differences in employment schedules among young professionals, even for those who report few depressive symptoms and high job satisfaction.

Figures 8.3a and 8.3b illustrate differences in predicted probabilities of employment across age of young lawyers comparing women and men and mothers and fathers. The pattern shows support for differences by age and gender. The quadratic effect of age on employment status indicates that beyond experiences of both types of discrimination, additional characteristics may impact these employment trajectories. Overall, the inclusion of practice setting and organisational size does not change the likelihood of transitioning from full-time to part-time employment. In

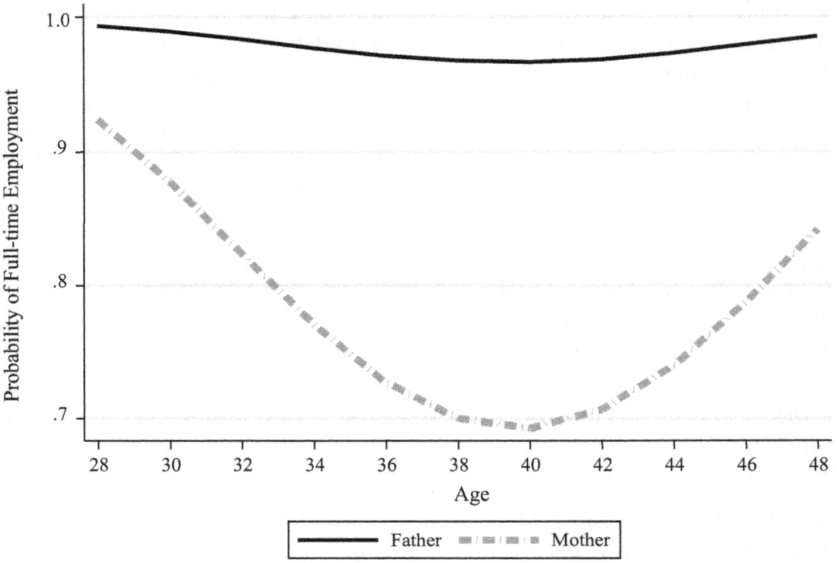

Figure 8.3b Predicted probabilities for trajectories of employment schedules among US lawyers by perceived FRD

Source: AJD 2002–03, 2007–08, and 2012–13. Average age of participants by survey waves: AJD1 = 31 years (age range 27–42); AJD2 = 36 years (age range 32–47); and AJD3 = 41 years (age range 37–48).

Notes: Perceived FRD displays the combined experiences of respondents with children and includes the following: (1) questioned about commitment to work; (2) adverse experience in performance (i.e., delay of promotion, loss of seniority, loss of office clients, loss of challenging assignments, loss of income); (3) ideal worker expectation (i.e., pressure to work while on parental leave, unreasonable workload).

fact, all practice settings show greater odds for full-time employment, as compared to solo practice.

Overall, the findings indicate that over the life course general WPD negatively affects women's employment. However, the most notable difference in employment schedules is the result of FRD. Particularly, mothers in their mid-thirties show a greater likelihood of part-time employment—this is a critical time period, which coincides with their mid-career stage when opportunities and decisions for professional advancement take place.

Conclusion

Research has shown that experiences of discrimination in the workplace negatively impact individuals' well-being and their employment status (Gee et al. 2012; Mays et al. 2007; Williams et al. 2003). Yet, less explored are the effects of discrimination across the life course of legal professionals (Gee et al. 2012). While it is challenging to detect experiences of unfair treatment, everyone can be at risk of experiencing general WPD or FRD at some point in their career (Ensher et al. 2001). Although the current findings point to differences in the strength of the relationship between perceived general WPD and employment status compared to perceived FRD and employment, both types of discrimination suggest the potential for long-term workplace inequality developed from discriminatory experiences.

While everyone is at risk of experiencing some form of discrimination at work, the current research showed that among lawyers, women were more likely than men to engage in part-time employment (short- or long-term) over the course of their career as a result of perceived discrimination. While women's experiences of general WPD only moderately affected their full-time employment schedule, experiences of FRD considerably impacted women's full-time employment schedule, in particular women with child caregiving responsibilities. In contrast, similar experiences of perceived WPD or FRD did not have a significant effect on men's employment schedules across the ten years of their careers explored here.

With regard to job satisfaction and emotional well-being, the findings showed no significant association with unfair treatment or experiences of discrimination, and thus no effects on changes in employment. However, this does not mean that experiences of discrimination are not affected by levels of job satisfaction or depressive symptoms, as have been reported in previous work on age discrimination or racial employment discrimination (Gee et al. 2007; Hirsh and Lyons 2010).

In light of these stark differences in employment schedules between women and men lawyers, discriminatory experiences, similar to the work–life–family conflict, could be interpreted as a continuing *women's issue* instead of a *workplace issue*. Across the first ten years of their careers, women are more likely to experience general WPD in their late forties, perhaps corresponding to ageism and sexism of "older" workers and their declining potential for career advancement (Duncan and Loretto 2004). In comparison, experiences of FRD are prominent when mothers are in their mid-thirties to early forties, matching the timing and onset of childbearing for many US women lawyers (Plickert and Hagan 2011). Women who assume the role of the primary child caregiver continue to face greater challenges in legal workplaces that give value to employees who are willing to work long hours and prioritise work over family life (Epstein et al. 2014). Thus, the likelihood for women with children to be employed part-time over full-time significantly varies to a greater extent with the experience of FRD in the workplace.

What are potential solutions? Provision of part-time work schedules and/or other forms of flexible work arrangements have been recurrently proposed to balance the work-life–family conflict primarily experienced by women with children (Correll et al. 2007; Epstein et al. 2014). While these arrangements might work for some individuals, it does not seem that there is one alternative pathway, or preferable choice, that will accommodate employment schedules to fit *all* legal professionals. Epstein and colleagues (2014) emphasise that women select part-time schedules often as a way of managing the increasing demands of professional time at work and caregiving responsibilities at home. Adding discriminatory workplace experiences to the work-life–family conflict more likely leads women (not men) to work part-time.

Consequently, part-time schedules may be solutions—within the control of the lawyer themselves—that allow women to escape adverse workplace experiences. However, these circumstances may cause another dilemma by heightening women's peripheral status in the workplace, thus fostering less secure bonds with the employer and festering inequalities in the workplace. Part-time employment may suffice as a short-term fix; however, without any long-term solutions these alternative schedules only continue to foster disparities between women and men in the profession.

Instead of self-sufficient solutions of flexible work schedules mainly retaining women, other more fruitful approaches may be pursuing interventions that cultivate changing *all* employers' and employees' attitudes. These could include more inclusive approaches about alternative employment schedules and decisions regarding caretaking responsibilities, for example. Because institutional changes tend to be resistant to legal reforms (Albiston 2007), these interventions will require long-term involvement of all members of an organisation before significant changes can be expected (O'Connor and Cech 2018). Ideally, the long-debated implementation of a national family leave policy in the US could expedite organisational change efforts by focusing on the diverse needs of *all* employers and employees who wish to adjust their work schedules for *any* caregiving responsibilities.

FRD continues to be particularly relevant to women's employment trajectories. However, employment trajectories—in this chapter over a ten-year career period—also show that it is the balance between work and personal life that is essential, especially for women who are interested in returning to full-time work. Perceived FRD impacts trajectories of employment; however, women's childcare responsibilities shift (i.e., child[ren] transitioning from childhood to adolescence) while many women are in their forties, and this creates opportunities for women to return to full-time employment and pursue career advancement. These findings about work-related improvements later in the life course (see Plickert et al. 2017) suggest that the age-related reporting of work experiences and personal life-choices/events are better understood through a life course lens, instead of cross-sections. Therefore, it remains essential to improve research strategies to effectively facilitate solutions to the challenges women and men face in an era of accelerating workplace changes with greater levels of diversity.

The job expectations of millennials already challenge the expectations of prior generations with regard to attitudes and work-life–family preferences (Garcia-Manglano 2015). Understanding these generational dynamics, in addition to the individual challenges and preferences women and men face, will offer an understanding beyond static policies and temporary flexible work arrangements.

Note

1 Average age of participants by survey waves: AJD1 = 31 years (age range 27–42); AJD2 = 36 years (age range 32–47); and AJD3 = 41 years (age range 37–48).

References

Albiston, C (2007) 'Institutional Perspectives on Law, Work and Family' 3 *Annual Review of Law Social Science* 397. doi:10.1146/annurev. lawsocsci.3.081806.112803

Becker, BE (1980) *Perceived Discrimination, Work Attitudes, and Labor Market Experience* (Washington, DC, U.S. Department of Labor, Employment and Training Administration).

Budig, MJ (2003) 'Are Women's Employment and Fertility Histories Interdependent? An Examination of Causal Order Using Event History Analysis' 32 *Social Science Research* 376.

Budig, MJ and England, P (2001) 'The Wage Penalty for Motherhood' 66 *American Sociological Review* 204. doi:10.2307/2657415

Budig, MJ and Hodges, MJ (2010) 'Differences in Disadvantage: Variation in the Motherhood Penalty Across White Women's Earnings Distribution' 75 *American Sociological Review* 705. doi:10.1177/0003122410381593

Coontz, PD (1995) 'Gender Bias in the Legal Profession: Women "See" It, Men Don't' 15 *Women Politics* 1. doi:10.1300/J014v15n02_0

Correll, S, Benard, S and Paik, I (2007) 'Getting a Job: Is There a Motherhood Penalty?' 112 *American Journal of Sociology* 1297. doi:10.1086/511799

Dau-Schmidt, KG, Galanter, MS, Mukhopadhaya, K and Hull, KE (2009) 'Men and Women of the Bar: The Impact of Gender on Legal Careers' 16 *Michigan Journal of Gender & Law* 49.

Dinovitzer, R, Nelson, RL, Plickert, G, Sandefur, R and Sterling, JS (2009) *After the JD II: Second Results from A National Study of Legal Careers* (Chicago, IL, The American Bar Foundation and the NALP Foundation for Law Career Research and Education). www.law.du.edu/documents/directory/publications/ sterling/AJD2.pdf

Duncan, C and Loretto, W (2004) 'Never the Right Age? Gender and Age-Based Discrimination in Employment' 11 *Gender, Work & Organization* 95. doi:10.1111/j.1468-0432.2004.00222.x

Elder Jr, GH, Johnson MK and Crosnoe, R (2003) 'The Emergence and Development of Life Course Theory' in JT Mortimer and MJ Shanahan (eds), *Handbook of the Life Course* (New York, Kluwer Academic/Plenum Publishers).

England, P, Bearek, J, Budig, MJ and Hodges, MJ (2016) 'Do Highly Paid, Highly Skilled Women Experience the Largest Motherhood Penalty?' 81 *American Sociological Review* 1161. doi:10.1177/0003122416673598

Ensher, EA, Grant-Vallone, EJ and Donaldson, SI (2001) 'Effects of Perceived Discrimination on Job Satisfaction, Organizational Commitment, Organizational Citizenship Behavior, and Grievances' 12 *Human Resource Development Quarterly* 53. doi:10.1002/1532-1096(200101/02)12:1<53::AID-HRDQ5>3.0.CO;2-G

Epstein, CF (1981) *Women in Law* (New York, Basic Books).

—— (1992) 'Tinkerbells and Pinups: The Constructions and Reconstruction of Gender Boundaries at Work' in M Lamont and M Fournier (eds), *Cultivating Differences: Symbolic Boundaries and the Making of Inequality* (Chicago, IL, University of Chicago Press).

Epstein, CF, Sauté, R, Oglensky, B and Gever, M (1995) 'Glass Ceilings and Open Doors: Women's Advancement in the Legal Profession' 64 *Fordham Law Review* 291.

Epstein, CF, Seron, C, Oglensky, B and Sauté, R (2014) *The Part-Time Paradox: Time Norms, Professional Life, Family and Gender* (New York, Routledge).

Feagin, JR and McKinney, KD (2003) *The Many Costs of Racism* (Lanham, MD, Rowman & Littlefield).

Fitzmaurice, GM, Laird, NM and Ware, JH (2004) *Applied Longitudinal Analysis* (Hoboken, NJ, Wiley-Interscience).

Fuegen, K, Biernat, M, Haines, E and Deaux, K (2004) 'Mothers and Fathers in the Workplace: How Gender and Parental Status Influence Judgments of Job-Related Competence' 60 *Journal of Social Issues* 737. doi:10.1111/j.0022-4537.2004.00383.x

Garcia-Manglano, J (2015) 'Opting Out and Leaning In: The Life Course Employment Profiles of Early Baby Boom Women in the United States' 52 *Demography* 1961. doi:10.1007/s13524-015-0438-6

Gee, GC, Walsemann, KM and Brondolo, E (2012) 'A Life Course Perspective on How Racism May Be Related to Health Inequities' 102 *American Journal of Public Health* 967. doi:10.2105/AJPH.2012.300666

Gee, GC, Pavalko, EK and Long, JS (2007) 'Age, Cohort and Perceived Age Discrimination: Using the Life Course to Assess Self-reported Age Discrimination' 86 *Social Forces* 265. doi:10.1353/sof.2007.0098

Giele, JZ and Elder Jr, GH (eds) (1998) *Methods of Life Course Research: Qualitative and Quantitative Approaches* (Thousand Oaks, CA, Sage).

Gough, M and Noonan, M (2013) 'A Review of the Motherhood Wage Penalty in the United States' 7 *Sociology Compass* 328. doi:10.1111/soc4.12031

Hagan, J and Kay, FM (2007) 'Even Lawyers Get the Blues: Gender, Depression, and Job Satisfaction in Legal Practice' 41 *Law & Society Review* 51. doi:10.1111/j.1540-5893.2007.00291.x

—— (2010) 'The Masculine Mystique: Living Large from Law School to Later Life' 25 *Canadian Journal of Law and Society* 195. doi:10.1017/S0829320100010383

Hampton, MB and Heywood, JS (1993) 'Do Workers Accurately Perceive Gender Wage Discrimination?' 47 *Industrial and Labor Relations Review* 36. doi:10.1177/001979399304700103

Hirsh, E and Lyons, CJ (2010) 'Perceiving Discrimination on the Job: Legal Consciousness, Workplace Context, and the Construction of Race Discrimination' 44 *Law & Society Review* 269.

Kasschau, PL (1977) 'Age and Race Discrimination Reported by Middle-Aged and Older Persons' 55 *Social Forces* 728. doi:10.1093/sf/55.3.728

Kay, FM, Alarie, S and Adjei, J (2013) 'Leaving Private Practice: How Organizational Context, Time Pressures, and Structural Inflexibilities Shape Departures from Private Practice' 20 *Indiana Journal of Global Legal Studies* 1223. doi:10.2979/indjglolegstu.20.2.1223

Kessler, RC, Mickelson, KD and Williams, DR (1999) 'The Prevalence, Distribution, and Mental Health Correlates of Perceived Discrimination in the United States' 40 *Journal of Health and Social Behavior* 208. doi:10.2307/2676349

Kricheli-Katz, T (2012) 'Choice, Discrimination, and Motherhood Penalty' 46 *Law & Society Review* 557. doi:10.1111/j.1540-5893.2012.00506.x

Kuo, S-CG (2005) 'Rethinking the Masculine Character of the Legal Profession: A Case Study of Female Legal Professionals and Their Gendered Life in Taiwan' 13 *American University Journal of Gender, Society Policy, and the Law* 25.

Marshall, VW and Mueller, MM (2003) 'Theoretical Roots of the Life-Course Perspective' in WR Heinz and VW Marshall (eds), *Social Dynamics of the Life Course: Transitions, Institutions, and Interrelations* (New York, Aldine de Gryter).

Mays, VM, Cochran, SD and Barnes, NW (2007) 'Race, Race-Based Discrimination, and Health Outcomes Among African Americans' 58 *Annual Review of Psychology* 201. doi:10.1146/annurev.psych.57.102904.190212

Moen, P, Fan, W and Kelly, EL (2013) 'Team-Level Flexibility, Work—Home Spillover, and Health Behavior' 84 *Social Science and Medicine* 69. doi:10.1016/j.socscimed.2013.02.011

Moriss, AP and Henderson, WD (2008) 'Measuring Outcomes: Post-Graduation Measures of Success in the U.S. News & World Report Law School Rankings' 83 *Indiana Law Journal* 791.

Nelson, RL and Plickert, G (2014) 'Introduction to AJD3' in R Dinovitzer, BG Garth, R Nelson, G Plickert, R Sandefur, J Sterling and D Wilkins (eds), *After the JD III: Third Results from a National Study of Legal Careers* (Chicago, IL, The American Bar Foundation and The NALP Foundation for Law Career Research and Education). www.americanbarfoundation.org/uploads/cms/documents/ajd3report_final_for_distribution.pdf

O'Connor, LT and Cech, EA (2018) 'Not Just a Mothers' Problem: The Consequences of Perceived Workplace Flexibility Bias for All Workers' 61 *Sociological Perspectives* 808. doi:10.1177/0731121418768235

Pavalko, EK, Mossakowski, KN and Hamilton, VJ (2003) 'Does Perceived Discrimination Affect Health? Longitudinal Relationships between Work Discrimination and Women's Physical and Emotional Health' 44 *Journal of Health and Social Behavior* 18. doi:10.2307/1519813

Plickert, G and Dinovitzer, R (2007) *Technical Addendum of the After the JD First Results Report* (Chicago, IL, The American Bar Foundation and The NALP Foundation for Law Career Research and Education). www.americanbarfoundation.org/uploads/cms/documents/weighted_ajdreport_9.6.07.pdf

Plickert, G and Hagan, J (2011) 'Professional Work and the Timing of Family Formation Among Young Lawyers in US and German Cities' 18 *International Journal of the Legal Profession* 237. doi:10.1080/09695958.2011.679801

Plickert, G, Kay, F and Hagan, J (2017) 'Depressive Symptoms and the Salience of Job Satisfaction Over the Life Course of Professionals' 31 *Advances in Life Course Research* 22. doi:10.1016/j.alcr.2016.11.001

Plickert, G and Sterling, J (2017) 'Gender Still Matters: Effects of Workplace Discrimination on Employment Schedules of Young Professionals' 6 *Laws* 1. doi:10.3390/laws6040028

Rabe-Hesketh, S and Skrondal, A (2005) *Multilevel and Longitudinal Modeling Using Stata* (College Station, TX, Stata Press).

Reichman, NJ and Sterling, JS (2002) 'Recasting the Brass Ring: Deconstructing and Reconstructing Workplace Opportunities for Women Lawyers' 29 *Capital University Law Review* 923.

Rhode, DL (2011) 'From Platitudes to Priorities: Diversity and Gender Equity in Law Firms' 24 *Georgetown Journal of Legal Ethics* 1041.

Ridgeway, CL (1997) 'Interaction and the Conversation of Gender Inequality: Considering Employment' 62 *American Sociological Review* 218.

Rosen, LN and Martin, L (1998) 'Psychological Effects of Sexual Harassment, Appraisal of Harassment, and Organizational Climate among U.S. Army Soldiers' 163 *Military Medicine* 63. doi:10.1093/milmed/163.2.63

Sloan, MM (2012) 'Unfair Treatment in the Workplace and Worker Well-Being: The Role of Coworker Support in a Service Work Environment' 39 *Work and Occupations* 3. doi:10.1177/0730888411406555

Wallace, JE (2001) 'Explaining Why Lawyers Want to Leave the Practice of Law' in JV Hoy (ed), *Legal Professions: Work, Structure and Organization* (London, JAI Publishing House).

Webley, L, Tomlinson, J, Muzio, D, Sommerlad, H and Duff, L (2016) 'Access to a Career in the Legal Profession in England and Wales: Race, Class and the Role of Educational Background' in S Headworth, RL Nelson, R Dinovitzer, and DB Wilkins (eds), *Diversity in Practice: Race, Gender, and Class in Legal and Professional Careers* (Cambridge, Cambridge University Press).

Williams, DR, Neighbors, HW and Jackson, JS (2003) 'Racial/Ethnic Discrimination and Health: Findings from Community Studies' 93 *American Journal of Public Health* 200. doi:10.2105/AJPH.93.2.200

Williams, JC and Richardson, V (2011) 'New Millennium, Same Glass Ceiling? The Impact of Law Firm Compensation Systems on Women' 62 *The Hastings Law Journal* 597.

Yang, Y (2007) 'Is Old Age Depressing? Growth Trajectories and Cohort Variations in Late-Life Depression' 48 *Journal of Health and Social Behavior* 16. doi:10.1177/002214650704800102

Yu, W and Kuo, J (2017) 'The Motherhood Wage Penalty by Work Conditions: How Do Occupational Characteristics Hinder or Empower Mothers?' 82 *American Sociological Review* 744. doi:10.1177/0003122417712729

9 Fathers in Private Law Practice in Finland

Reconciling Work and Family Life for Male Lawyers From Different Generations

Marta Choroszewicz

Introduction

The question of work–life reconciliation has been a central topic of debate for several decades and is still more often attributed to professionally active women than men (Smithson and Stokoe 2005). More specifically, the debate is attributed to those women who prevail in male-dominated professions, such as the legal profession, due to their challenges in reconciling a demanding career with family life (see Bacik and Drew 2006; Biese and Choroszewicz 2018; Choroszewicz 2014). To retain women lawyers in private law practices, some law firms have been increasingly adopting organisational solutions to assist female employees to achieve a balanced combination of family life and legal careers (Choroszewicz 2016; Walsh 2012). Yet, these solutions have been constructed as feminine solutions and can be accompanied by misconceptions of career commitment (Thornton and Bagust 2007). At the same time, prerequisites for career progress continue to be tailored for unencumbered male workers, and thus result in the reproduction of gendered norms and hierarchies in law firms and the legal profession (Choroszewicz 2014, 2016).

However, less is known about how the reconciliation of work and family life is experienced by different generations of men who work in male-dominated professions. This issue emerges as important to study now, due to changes in family policies and attitudes to the participation of fathers in family life. This is specifically topical for Finnish fathers, whose parenting rights have been strengthened through an ongoing process since the 1970s as an incentive for enhancing gender equality in the family and in the labour market (Ylikännö et al. 2014: 103). The statistics show that paternity leave is becoming fairly popular among Finnish fathers—particularly, the first part of the leave that can be taken at childbirth (Salmi and Lammi-Taskula 2014: 306).

The new discourse on active and involved fatherhood has slowly extended to also encompass executive positions in Finland (Kangas et al. 2017), and internationally has further included the legal profession

(Collier 2013, 2015). Collier (2013: 424) notices that 'many men may be seeking different kinds of relationships with their children from previous generations', yet they might be professionally pressured to scrutinise their wants and needs regarding their participation in family life. While motherhood is considered a social duty, fathers' involvement in family life has a more voluntary character, even in Finland (Vuori 2009). Achieving a proper balance between work and family life is central to the concept of new fatherhood put forward by Johansson and Klinth (2008), yet, men's opportunities for embracing this new fatherhood can be hampered because of their work environments. In the case of the legal profession, studies show that the culture of long working hours, tight deadlines, and few accommodations at the workplace for caregiving responsibilities reinforce the traditional gender order with a male breadwinner (Thornton 2016a: 31). While breadwinner fatherhood is no longer the only alternative available to men, its prevalence in the work environment can imprint negatively on men's opportunities to reconcile their work and family life.

This study advances our understanding of the work–life reconciliation of Finnish male lawyers by capturing the ideas that male lawyers of two different generations have concerning the balance between their legal careers and fatherhood. The male lawyers' narrations of their reconciliation of work and family life demonstrate that male lawyers belonging to Generation Y are particularly torn between the breadwinner fatherhood norm and their wants and needs to be involved as fathers. Baby Boomer male lawyers sustain traditional masculine ideology that imprints negatively on organisational change to provide men with more opportunities to reconcile work with an equal parenting role.

The Cultural Context for Fathers in Finland

In Finland, as in other Nordic countries, family policies have aimed to encourage and support a dual-earner/dual-caregiver family model, in which both spouses combine childcare with breadwinning (Leira 2006). Finnish families receive legislated state support in the form of subsidised maternity, paternity, and parental leave (KELA 2018). The Finnish State also provides extensive public childcare, which guarantees parents access to good quality and affordable childcare during daytime hours till around 5 p.m. Yet, in the case of high-status professions that are characterised by intensive and often unpredictable working schedules, such as the legal profession, public childcare is not enough to assist parents in reconciling childcare with a demanding career (Choroszewicz 2014, 2016).

Paternity leave that is non-transferable to mothers dates back to 1978 (Lammi-Taskula 2008), and represents a long-standing political attempt to promote gender equality by facilitating greater participation of Finnish fathers in early childcare. Eerola (2014) notes that a more gender-balanced division of childcare is not only the goal of family policies, but also a cultural norm of parenting in Finland. In the 2000s, paternity leave has been extended so that paternity leave nowadays covers nine weeks and is paid at 70–75% of the income (KELA 2018). Fathers can take up to three weeks of paternity leave while their spouse is on maternity leave, and the remaining weeks must be used after maternity leave ends and before the child is two years old. Fathers can also share the 26-week-long parental leave with their spouses.

Despite these incentives, the use of parental leave in Finland remains gendered. In 2012, three weeks of paternity leave for birth was taken by 84% of fathers, with the remaining six weeks of paternity leave taken by 32% of fathers (Salmi and Lammi-Taskula 2014: 306). The further parental leave of 26 weeks was taken by only 2–3% of fathers—a trend that has remained stable since 1995 (Salmi and Lammi-Taskula 2014: 306). Mothers' primacy in childcare is also reflected in the fact that Finnish fathers tend to take their leave as late as possible, that is, when children are between one and two years old (Tilastokeskus 2017).

While between 1987 and 2010 the time spent with children by Finnish fathers has almost doubled, the gendered division of childcare time between fathers and mothers has remained stable for two decades (Ylikännö et al. 2014). This situation is partly sustained by a high level of horizontal and vertical gender segregation of the Finnish labour market, despite the high women's employment rate, which is among the top in the EU (Eurostat 2017). Finnish women are more likely to work in precarious and temporary positions (Nätti and Väisänen 2000) and men in administration and business (Pulkkinen 2005). Women's salaries also tend to be lower than men's, so they more frequently choose to stay at home in order to care for small children (Julkunen 2010: 117–119). Even when working in demanding positions, Finnish women still carry the main responsibility for domestic work and childcare (Choroszewicz 2014; Heikkinen et al. 2014). As a result, breadwinning retains an important social position for Finnish fathers (Salmi and Lammi-Taskula 2014).

The Ideal of Flexible Lawyer and Discourses on Fatherhood Across Generations

Private law practice continues to rest on the ideal of a flexible lawyer. This is underpinned by the assumption that lawyers who are truly committed to their legal careers will display an ability to prioritise work demands over the demands of private life (Choroszewicz 2016: 129). Living up to this ideal is regarded as a free choice or an individual capacity that originates from extreme motivation and devotion to legal work. Yet, what is less often emphasised is that this type of commitment rests upon a structurally conditioned ability to sacrifice any suggestion of a personal life (Thornton 2016b), or that someone else must carry most of the family responsibilities. While this ideal applies equally to all lawyers, men have traditionally had more opportunities to live up to this expectation due to their limited roles in household work and childcare. This ideal has been more problematic for women, and thus imposes harder choices on women in terms of career and family, due to their primary role in family life (Meyerson and Fletcher 2000: 129).

The ideal of a flexible lawyer has taken on a new dimension with the ever-increasing commercialisation and fragmentation of the profession. Lawyers are increasingly exposed to the clients' influence and control over their work, and this means unlimited availability to enquiries from clients. Bergman and Gardiner (2007: 401) explain that availability entails human capacity and potential to be available in time and space to meet the needs of others. This expectation is easier to execute today, with the use of mobile technology that facilitates work spillover into family time, especially for professionals in high-status professions and positions (Schieman et al. 2009).

The new ideal of the flexible lawyer is in line with the traditional masculine ideology and thus a clear dichotomy between gender roles in the family: a female caregiver and homemaker, and a male breadwinner providing financially for the family. Male lawyers are still more often regarded as the main earners and thus they may progress faster in their careers as they are not expected to take paternity or parental leave. While the ideal of the flexible lawyer may sustain 'breadwinner fatherhood' as a norm in the legal profession, Kangas and colleagues (2017) demonstrate three additional types of discourses concerning fatherhood that are prevalent among male managers who work as fathers in Finland: 'uncommitted fatherhood', the 'best bits of fatherhood', and 'hands-on fatherhood'.

For a breadwinning father, family life is organised around his career demands. He is constantly absent from family life, with the exception of holidays (Kangas et al. 2017: 22). However, he appreciates his wife's greater devotion to family life. The discourse of uncommitted fatherhood also involves a distant and absent father who, in contrast to the former discourse, has no regrets for his absence from family life. Additionally, this discourse includes a double burden assigned to uncommitted fathers' wives, who are presented as being responsible for both their own careers and family life (Kangas et al. 2017: 23–24). The two remaining discourses on fatherhood—the best bits of fatherhood and hands-on fatherhood— draw to a larger extent on the new fatherhood and manhood ideology (see e.g. Holter 2007; Johansson and Klinth 2008). The discourse wherein the father acknowledges the best bits of fatherhood includes some limited adjustments from the side of a father's career to the family life situation.

The father participates more actively in his children's lives, but he is still an elective parent who chooses the most pleasant elements of parenting, such as participation in children's hobbies, outdoor activities, and games (Kangas et al. 2017: 24–25). In contrast, the discourse concerning the hands-on father refers to an independent parent who takes an active role in all parenting activities. He adapts his career to his family life to live up to the expectations of shared parenthood (Kangas et al. 2017: 25–26). While the best bits of fatherhood provides the potential for more fluid gender roles in the family, it is hands-on fatherhood that rests on fully fluid gender roles in which both spouses are equal parents who juggle childcare and work to a similar extent.

The availability and use of the previously described discourses on fatherhood may vary for different generations of male lawyers—Baby Boomers (born between 1946 and 1964), Generation X (born between 1965 and 1979), and Generation Y (born 1980 and after)—due to differences in shared social and historical circumstances (see Choroszewicz and Adams 2019, in this volume; Smola and Sutton 2002). Generations may differ also in their attitudes to work and parenting, as well as the availability of paternity leave that is non-transferable to the mother (Choroszewicz and Tremblay 2018), which can influence their abilities to comply with the ideal of a flexible lawyer. By applying the ideal of the flexible lawyer and the four fatherhood discourses to the analysis of fictionalised stories, it is possible to capture generational differences in gender relations within the family and at the workplace, which shape the male lawyers' wants, opportunities, and experiences of reconciling a legal career with family life.

Data and Methods

This chapter is based on the methodology introduced by Susie Orbach (2002) in her book *The Impossibility of Sex* and further developed by Anthony Elliott and Charles Lemert (2006) in *The New Individualism: The Emotional Costs of Globalization*. These authors apply a fictionalised case method in which data are combined to create fictionalised stories to ensure the anonymity of the participants of their studies as well as to capture the most relevant, multifaceted, and shared experiences of their subjects in a few illustrated narratives. I have also used this method in a joint article to illustrate the shared experiences of female US managers and Polish lawyers who opt out of mainstream career patterns to adopt alternative solutions for work (Biese and Choroszewicz 2018).

This chapter is based on the analysis of fictionalised stories of two male Finnish lawyers: 58-year-old Ilkka, who is a partner in a middle-sized law firm, and 35-year-old Eliel, who works as a senior associate in a large law firm. The stories originate from a postdoctoral comparative study on work–life reconciliation of male lawyers in Helsinki and Montreal that covers in total 35 interviews with male lawyers. The stories presented in this chapter are based on 21 interviews with Finnish attorneys from 2016.

The interviewees ranged from 32–67 years of age. One interviewee worked as solo practitioner, one in a legal aid office, and the remaining 19 in law firms. Six interviewees worked as associates or counsels and 13 were partners in law firms. Two interviewees worked in law firms employing 10 or fewer lawyers, eight worked in medium-sized law firms employing between 11 and 60 lawyers, and nine worked in law firms employing 61 or more lawyers. All participants were either married or cohabiting, and all had children whose ages ranged from a couple of months to 24 years old.

A comparative case study approach enables an in-depth understanding of the cases analysed and provides in-depth insights into experiences, behaviours, processes, and patterns with their relation to the context in which they take place (Hartley 1994). The illustrative stories of Ilkka and Eliel demonstrate differential experiences of reconciling professional and family lives of two male lawyers who belong to two different generations, Baby Boomers and Generation Y. Ilkka's story is constructed from interviews with 13 partners in law firms and counsels who were 40 years old or older, and thus they belong to the Baby Boomer generation and Generation X. They also comprise a professional elite in law firms and thus have influence on professional and organisational norms. These interviewees did not take any paternity leave, but they might have taken some days or weeks off at the birth of their children. Their narratives include a more distant and less present role as fathers. Eliel's story is constructed from interviews with seven junior and senior associates, and a junior partner, who were under 40 years old and thus belong to Generation Y and late Generation X. Each of these interviewees took at least a part of their entitled paternity leave and they expressed wants towards participating in their children's lives from the very beginning. While there was some variation between the interviewees classified under each story, the aim is to highlight most prominent differences in experiences between lawyers of two generations: Baby Boomers and Generation Y. Lawyers belonging to Generation X were divided into either the first or second generational groups according to the similarities found in their attitudes to paternity leave, work, and work–life balance. While these two stories do not allow for generalisations, due to the convenience sampling method, the study adds to the current debate on generational differences in work–life reconciliation, fatherhood, and career progress in male-dominated professions and work environments.

The Cases of Two Male Lawyers

The Story of Ilkka, a Partner in a Middle-Sized Law Firm

Ilkka is 58 years old, married, and has three children who are 10, 20, and 24 years of age. When the first two children were born he did not take any paternity leave. However, he might have taken a couple of days off in 2007, when his last child was born. His family life has been based on the assumption that his wife, as an employee and as a woman, has access to better entitlements to parental leave, so she could stay home for about one and a half or two years with each child. Family life has been always important to her, and he stresses that she did not mind doing it. He recalls that, back then, the attitudes were different towards fathers. He also needed to grow his law practice and get clients. He emphasises that one can be a good father even without taking paternity leave. For example, he has been very involved in his children's hobbies, for instance transporting the children to and from their activities. Nowadays he is very engaged in his youngest child's hobby, hockey. He travels with him to different hockey games on the weekends. He also plays hockey himself once a week. As two of his children are already grown up, nowadays he has more time for work and doing hobbies. Legal work is like a hobby for him—a well-paid hobby, he stresses.

His typical working days start at about 6 or 6:30 a.m. and end around midnight. After he wakes up, he checks his emails to see whether there is something that he needs to react to immediately. Then he wakes his 10-year-old son and eats breakfast with him. Around 8:30 a.m. he goes to the office and stays there until about 7 p.m. He is normally involved in about seven to 10 ongoing legal cases, so the days are busy. He usually has a few client meetings, some internal meetings, and communication with clients by phone and email. After he gets home around 7 or 8 p.m., he takes a two-to-three hour break to be with his family and play some sports. Afterwards he may work an extra one or two hours to draft documents or reply to important emails or phone calls. He has become used to this late evening work, so he does not have a bad conscience about it. He is continuously in work mode; his phone is always on even during holidays, so that any of his clients can reach him anytime.

He claims that being a lawyer is all-consuming work: it stays with you no matter where you are. It is not a profession that you can do for only eight hours, and if you do so, you will not master it to the highest level. He admits that with mobile technology the expectation of 24/7 availability has increased, especially for law firm partners who need to meet client expectations. If his client wants something to be done by the next morning, it is his responsibility to deliver it. The speed of replies and need for swift replies has also increased. He feels that he has to respond immediately to clients' enquiries; otherwise they might go to another law firm. He concludes that this is business, and that you have to keep your phone on if you want to stay in the game.

When he recalls the time his children were young, he admits that he invested most of his time developing his career. Even today he feels that paternity leave is not so relevant for law firm partners, but rather for junior lawyers. He notices that nowadays his younger colleagues go on paternity leave more willingly. No one has anything against it, and it is their right. He also recognises that young people today value free time, hobbies, and their work–life balance much more. He also thinks that they do not want to do as much work as is needed in the profession. Sometimes he needs his associates to stay longer at work, or when they work on a deal they need to be available to him by phone in the evenings.

The Story of Eliel, a Senior Associate in a Large Law Firm

Eliel is 35 years old, married, and has one child who is three years old and a second who is due in five months. When his first child was born, he spent a total of four months at home. He took two weeks off work after childbirth, and when the child was about one year old and his wife returned to work he took the remaining two and a half months of paternity leave, plus annual holiday. He planned his paternity leave for the slower period at work. He feels that for his generation, it is acceptable to take some length of paternity leave. However, taking the full nine weeks of paternity leave or longer is less common, at least in his firm. He was compensated at his full salary level for his leave, which is rather uncommon for law firms.

His typical day starts around 7 a.m. and ends at 11 p.m. He usually helps his daughter to get ready for nursery and he drives her there on the way to work. He arrives at the office around 8:30 or 9 a.m. and he works intensively until about 5 p.m. He is at home by 6 p.m. at the latest. His wife is in charge of picking up their daughter from the nursery. Approximately once a week he needs to stay at work until 7 or 8 p.m. He prefers to do that than to go home for a couple of hours and resume working after their child is asleep. This does not work for him, as he is too tired to work late in the evenings. He tries to maintain a clear division between work and family life—at least to the extent that it is possible. Yet, he has his phone on while he is at home so that he is available in case of an emergency at work.

His working day lasts around 8–10 hours. While he is at work, he works efficiently so that he can leave the office on time to be with his family. If he does not have client meetings at lunch time, he eats in his office. If he needs to stay longer at work, he informs his wife in advance. In case of an emergency at work or when his child is sick, Eliel and his wife draw on help from their parents, friends, or a nanny. His workplace also offers childcare in case of emergencies. They have used this facility twice. However, it needs to be arranged at least a day in advance, and they usually only notice that their child is sick and requires a day off early in the morning.

Before having a child, he worked a lot in the evenings. Now he starts the day earlier, so that he can end it earlier. There is also less time for socialising and hobbies. There is lot of balancing between work and family demands. When he has a demanding project at work, the schedule can be very tight, but when there is no project, he has more flexibility. He can also work from home, but he does it rarely. However, he finds it difficult not to think about work when he leaves the office. Earlier, it was not such a problem, but now that he has a child, he finds it more difficult.

When he recalls his paternity leave, he says he enjoyed it. It was less stressful and more predictable compared to his work. It enabled him to get to know his child better and become an independent parent. Yet, he also missed being a lawyer. He has not made his mind about the length of his second paternity leave. He wonders how a second, longer paternity leave could affect his career, because he is currently considering taking on more responsibility at work. When he becomes more senior, he knows he will have more direct responsibility for his clients, and the number of phone calls in the evenings will probably increase as a result. He will also have more responsibility in the firm to recruit new clients and find new projects. He expects that it will become more challenging to spend time with his family and take care of his children.

Generational Differences in Work–Life Reconciliation

The stories of Ilkka and Eliel demonstrate the interviewees' different ideas and practices of fatherhood (see Eerola 2014). Ilkka belongs to the

Baby Boomer generation, which is characterised by their strong commitment to their work and their employers; Eliel—born at the beginning of 1980s—belongs to Generation Y, which is considered the Internet generation that values personal life and free time (Niemistö et al. 2016: 357). While for Ilkka the dominant available discourse on fatherhood has been breadwinning, Eliel has grown up in a society permeated with the discourse of a new fatherhood. Thus, taking paternity leave was natural for him, even though in his workplace he was one of the pioneers in doing it. Being at a relatively early stage of his career, Eliel felt he could take paternity leave without damaging his career. Yet, he is no longer sure about taking paternity leave now, when he considers his opportunities for further career progress. His superiors are more likely to share Ilkka's views on being constantly available for work, as reflected in the ideal of the flexible lawyer and facilitated by mobile technology (Thornton 2016a).

Ilkka takes the ideal as an indicator of not only a career commitment but also of professional suitability. Like the rest of his generation, he has worked hard to get to the top of his workplace. This is also what he expects of his subordinates who want to stay in the firm and make a career. The work organisation in his firm supports traditional, linear, and unbroken career models as well as a breadwinning family model (Biese and Choroszewicz 2018; Choroszewicz and Tremblay 2018). Ilkka's family model has followed the traditional gender order. While he stresses his wife's interest in family life and commitment to childcare, he only became more active in his children's upbringing as they grew older and he could support them in cultivating their hobbies and sports.

Ilkka has been available for his legal work to the extent that the ideal of the flexible lawyer assumes. Relying on his own experience, he believes that living up to this ideal is a matter of individual choice. Yet, his choice was facilitated by the particular structural circumstances of a more traditional family model, in which his wife took on the primary role in childcare and family life. After 30 years in the profession, tight schedules and long working hours at the office and at home have become the norm for him (see Thornton 2016a, 2016b).

As mentioned by Eliel, some law firms in Finland offer a set of services to their employees, including cleaning, grocery, laundry, meals, and childcare services (Carlsson 2016). Childcare services appear to be the most crucial for lawyers with small children, yet Eliel's story suggests that these services could be better organised if only professional elite of law firms would be aware of the need for it. For instance, Ilkka, as a law firm partner, holds a powerful position in his organisation to make necessary organisational changes to accommodate the increasing needs and wants of fathers with regard to work–life reconciliation. Yet, his perspective is limited to his own personal experience, which aligns with traditional gender order.

While Ilkka's story is permeated with a mixture of both 'breadwinning' and 'the best bits of fatherhood' (Kangas et al. 2017), the new reality in which his younger male colleagues unfold their careers and engage with childcare might be less familiar to him. They are more likely to have spouses with careers that are equally demanding and financially rewarding. For instance, Eliel's wife is a manager herself, and thus she could not afford to be longer than a year away from work on maternity leave. Her return to work was a good opportunity for Eliel to spend time alone with their child. Thus, his involvement in early childcare was motivated by both circumstances and his urge to bear an equal share of responsibility for childcare (see Holter 2007). As an example of a hands-on father, he is in charge of morning chores, as he can better control his morning work schedule. He also tries to be home on time in the evenings to accompany his wife in the evening childcare activities. To be able to be actively involved in childcare and family life, Eliel needs to maintain a clear structure in his working day and a temporal and spatial boundary between work and family life. While work spillover into family life is typical for people in higher-status professions, maintaining a work–family division is easier for employees in less senior positions with lower earnings (Schieman et al. 2009: 984). Due to his leadership position, Ilkka is used to the blurring of both spheres and work spillover into his family life. This is made possible for him due to few family demands and a separate office space in his home.

While Baby Boomers' generational attitudes to work and life are shaped by traditional gender roles, this is less common for later generations, who are influenced to a greater extent by awareness of gender equality (Niemistö et al. 2016) and a new fatherhood discourse (Holter 2007; Johansson and Klinth 2008). Yet, their egalitarian views and attitudes may clash with gendered work realities that are created and sustained by, for example, Ilkka's generation (Choroszewicz and Tremblay 2018). While Ilkka tolerates his younger colleagues' different attitudes towards work–life balance, he is convinced that these do not work in their profession, and thus he is rather unwilling to change the professional norms so that they could work better for Eliel's generation. In contrast, Eliel's generation of men are under more pressure with regard to their participation in housework and childcare (Ylikännö et al. 2014). However, their superiors at work do not necessarily understand these new pressures, which they have not experienced themselves, and thus they are more likely to consider Eliel's greater involvement in childcare and family life as indicators of less commitment to and interest in career development.

Eliel and his peers might still aspire to career development, but with less family sacrifices. They do not necessarily want to make their work all-consuming, nor do they often have opportunities to do so because of their different family models, which contrast to those held by previous generations. Eliel observes his superiors' around-the-clock work and wonders whether it is something he wants to commit to. Eliel expects that as he advances in his career, he will experience more challenges in participating in family life—similar to the challenges that professional women have experienced for decades as they have been torn between intensive parenting and the world of formal work (Blair-Loy 2003). In light of Ilkka's comments about the need to be hard-working and constantly available in the legal profession, Eliel's concern about the negative impact of sequential, relatively long paternity leave is realistic. By taking longer paternity leave, Eliel would act in contradiction to the ideal of the flexible lawyer.

Conclusion

The results indicate the ways in which gender relations are shaped at the micro level in a male-dominated profession, within the Nordic dual-earner/dual-caregiver family model. This is captured through the fictionalised stories of Ilkka and Eliel, which reflect the generational differences in family models, fatherhood practices, and attitudes to work–life balance. The results demonstrate that Finnish male lawyers' lesser involvement in childcare is linked to the traditional masculine ideology that prevails in the legal profession and hampers male lawyers' opportunities to engage more actively in childcare and family life. This ideology is sustained by the professional elite, currently consisting of a majority of male representatives of Baby Boomers and Generation X, who have more traditional views on gender relations in family life and on attitudes towards work and a work–life balance (e.g. Wallace 2006). In the lawyers' working environments, fathers' roles are still understood more in terms of breadwinning and securing the family's welfare, rather than caregiving. While women lawyers have been recently provided with flexible work arrangements and part-time work to assist them in devising their own means of combining work and family life (Choroszewicz 2016), male lawyers continue to be professionally pressured to live up to the ideal of a flexible lawyer, and thus they may experience difficulty in building a new narrative describing them as involved fathers. Ilkka's perception of his wife's greater interest and entitlement in carrying out caregiving responsibilities reflect the stand of many contemporary employers who consider motherhood inevitable (Vuori 2009), while fathers remain ghosts in the organisational machine (Burnett et al. 2013).

The findings reported here have theoretical implications for understanding the persistence of gender inequality and gender segregation within private law practice and the legal profession in general. The results unpack the ideal of the flexible lawyer that rests upon the gendered dynamics of identity formation as a lawyer and as a father (see also Collier 2018). The results also advocate for the revision of this ideal, so that it better fits the experiences and expectations of the younger generation of not only young women lawyers but also young male lawyers, who want to organise their private lives differently compared to their older colleagues. Further research should elaborate on the limitations of this study and examine heterogeneity within generations in terms of gender roles as well as ideas and practices among parenthood, fatherhood, and motherhood. There is also a need to study generational differences in the context of the ongoing restructuring of professions and organisations. Generation Y's attitudes to work and achieving a work–life balance might be specifically shaped by an organisations' lower commitment to their employees and the growth of precarious employment across industries.

References

Bacik, I and Drew, E (2006) 'Struggling with Juggling: Gender and Work/Life Balance in the Legal Professions' 29 *Women's Studies International Forum* 136. doi:10.1016/j.wsif.2006.03.006

Bergman, A and Gardiner, J (2007) 'Employee Availability for Work and Family: Three Swedish Case Studies' 29 *Employee Relations* 400–401.

Biese, I and Choroszewicz, M (2018) 'Creating Alternative Solutions for Work: Experiences of Women Managers and Lawyers in Poland and the USA' in S Taylor and S Luckman (eds), *The 'New Normal' of Working Lives: Critical Studies in Contemporary Work and Employment* (London, Palgrave Macmillan).

Blair-Loy, M (2003) *Competing Devotions: Career and Family Among Women Executives* (Cambridge, MA, Harvard University Press).

Burnett, SB, Gatrell, CJ, Cooper, CL and Sparrow, P (2013) 'Fathers at Work: A Ghost in the Organizational Machine' 20 *Gender, Work & Organization* 632. doi:10.1111/gwao.12000

Carlsson, M (2016) *Ruuhkavuosien ratkomisopas: luovia ratkaisuja ruuhkavuosien johtamiseen* (Helsinki, Tietosanoma).

Choroszewicz, M (2014) 'Managing Competitiveness in Pursuit of a Legal Career: Women Attorneys in Finland and Poland' PhD dissertation (University of Eastern Finland, Joensuu).

——— (2016) 'Women Attorneys and Gendering Processes in Law Firms in Helsinki' 53 *Sosiologia* 122, 129.

Choroszewicz, M and Adams, TL (2019) 'Introduction' in M Choroszewicz and TL Adams (eds), *Gender, Age and Inequality in the Professions* (New York, Routledge).

Choroszewicz, M and Tremblay, D-G (2018) 'Parental Leave Policy for Male Lawyers in Helsinki and Montreal: Cultural and Professional Barriers to Male Lawyers' Use of Paternity and Parental Leaves' 25 *International Journal of the Legal Profession* 303. doi:10.1080/09695958.2018.1456435

Collier, R (2013) 'Rethinking Men and Masculinities in the Contemporary Legal Profession: The Example of Fatherhood, Transnational Business Masculinities, and Work-Life Balance in Large Law Firms' 13 *Nevada Law Journal* 410, 424.

——— (2015) 'Naming Men as Men in Corporate Legal Practice: Gender and the Idea of "Virtually 24/7 Commitment" in Law' 83 *Fordham Law Review* 2387.

——— (2018) 'Fatherhood, Gender and the Making of Professional Identity in Large Law Firms: Bringing Men into the Frame' *International Journal of Law in Context*, 1. doi:10.1017/S1744552318000162

168   Marta Choroszewicz

Eerola, P (2014) 'Nurturing, Breadwinning, and Upbringing: Paternal Responsibilities by Finnish Men in Early Fatherhood' 17 *Community, Work and Family* 308. doi:10.1080/13668803.2014.933774

Elliott, A and Lemert, C (2006) *The New Individualism: The Emotional Costs of Globalization* (London, Routledge).

Eurostat (2017) *Statistics Explained: Employment Statistics* (Luxembourg, EuroStat). www.ec.europa.eu/eurostat/statistics-explained/index.php/Employment_statistics

Hartley, JF (1994) 'Case Studies in Organizational Research' in C Cassell and G Symon (eds), *Qualitative Methods in Organizational Research: A Practical Guide* (London, Sage).

Heikkinen, S, Lämsä, A-M and Hiillos, M (2014) 'Narratives by Women Managers About Spousal Support for Their Careers' 30 *Scandinavian Journal of Management* 27. doi:10.1016/j.scaman.2013.04.004

Holter, ØG (2007) 'Men's Work and Family Reconciliation in Europe' 9 *Men and Masculinities* 425. doi:10.1177/1097184X06287794

Johansson, T and Klinth, R (2008) 'Caring Fathers: The Ideology of Gender Equality and Masculine Positions' 11 *Men and Masculinities* 42. doi:10.1177/1097184X06291899

Julkunen, R (2010) *Sukupuolen järjestykset ja tasaarvon paradoksit* (Tampere, Vastapaino), 117–119.

Kangas, E, Lämsä, A-M and Heikkinen, S (2017) 'Father Managers (Un)Doing Traditional Masculinity' in A Pilińska (ed), *Fatherhood in Contemporary Discourse: Focus on Fathers* (Newcastle upon Tyne, Cambridge Scholars Publishing), 22–26.

KELA (2018) 'Quick Quide for Families with Children' (The Social Insurance Institution of Finland). www.kela.fi/web/en/families

Lammi-Taskula, J (2008) 'Doing Fatherhood: Understanding the Gendered Use of Parental Leave in Finland' 6 *Fathering* 133. doi:10.3149/fth.0602.133

Leira, A (2006) 'Parenthood Change and Policy Reform in Scandinavia, 1970s-2000s' in AL Ellingsæter and A Leira (eds), *Politicising Parenthood in Scandinavia: Gender Relations in Welfare States* (Bristol, Policy Press).

Meyerson, DE and Fletcher, JK (2000) 'A Modest Manifesto for Shattering the Glass Ceiling' 78 *Harvard Business Review* 126, 129.

Nätti, J and Väisänen, M (2000) 'Työajat ja työsuhteet kotitaloudessa' in A Lehto and N Järnefelt (eds), *Jaksaen ja joustaen: artikkeleita työolotutkimuksesta* (Helsinki, Statistics Finland).

Niemistö, C, Hearn, J and Jyrkinen, M (2016) 'Age and Generations in Everyday Organizational Life: Neglected Intersections in Studying Organisations' 1 *International Journal Work Innovation* 353, 357. doi:10.1504/IJWI.2016.078645

Orbach, S (2002) *The Impossibility of Sex: Stories of the Intimate Relationship Between Therapist and Patient* (New York, Touchstone).

Pulkkinen, P (ed) (2005) *Gender Equality in Finland 2004* (Helsinki, Statistics Finland).

Salmi, M and Lammi-Taskula, J (2014) 'Policy Goals and Obstacles for Fathers' Parental Leave in Finland' in GB Eydal and T Rostgaard (eds), *Fatherhood in the Nordic Welfare States: Comparing Care Policies and Practice* (Bristol, Policy Press), 306.

Schieman, S, Milkie, MA and Glavin, P (2009) 'When Work Interferes with Life: Work-Nonwork Interference and the Influence of Work-Related Demands and Resources' 74 *American Sociological Review* 966, 984. doi:10.1177/000312240907400606

Smithson, J and Stokoe, EH (2005) 'Discourses of Work–life Balance: Negotiating "Genderblind" Terms in Organizations' 12 *Gender, Work & Organization* 147. doi:10.1111/j.1468-0432.2005.00267.x

Smola, KW and Sutton, CD (2002) 'Generational Differences: Revisiting Generational Work Values for the New Millennium' 23 *Journal of Organization Behaviour* 363. doi:10.1002/job.147

Statistics Finland (2017) *Isät tilastoissa 2017* (Helsinki, Statistics Finland). www.tilastokeskus.fi/tup/tilastokirjasto/poimintoja-tilastovuodesta.html/isat-tilastoissa-2017

Thornton, M (2016a) 'The Flexible Cyborg: Work–life Balance in Legal Practice' 38 *Sydney Law Review* 1, 31.

——— (2016b) 'Work/Life or Work/Work? Corporate Legal Practice in the Twenty-First Century' 23 *International Journal of the Legal Profession* 13. doi:10.1080/09695958.2015.1093939

Thornton, M and Bagust, J (2007) 'The Gender Trap: Flexible Work in Corporate Legal Practice' 45 *Osgoode Hall Law Journal* 773.

Vuori, J (2009) 'Men's Choices and Masculine Duties: Fathers in Expert Discussion' 12 *Men and Masculinities* 45. doi:10.1177/1097184X07306720

Wallace, JE (2006) 'Work Commitment in the Legal Profession: A Study of Baby Boomers and Generation Xers' 13 *International Journal of the Legal Profession* 137. doi:10.1080/09695950600961293

Walsh, J (2012) 'Not Worth the Sacrifice? Women's Aspirations and Career Progression in Law Firms' 19 *Gender, Work & Organization* 508. doi:10.1111/j.1468-0432.2012.00607.x

Ylikännö, M, Pääkkönen, H and Hakovirta, M (2014) 'Time Use of Finnish Fathers—Do Institutions Matter?' in GB Eydal and T Rostgaard (eds), *Fatherhood in the Nordic Welfare States: Comparing Care Policies and Practice* (Bristol, Policy Press), 103.

Section 3

Further Professions

10 Forty Years of Gender Inequality Among Men and Women in High-Prestige Occupations— Does the Story Differ Among the Young?

Charlotta Magnusson and
Magnus Nermo

Introduction

Swedish society has changed dramatically since the 1960s, both in the labour market and in the family sphere. The most central structural changes in the labour market are the substantial increase of jobs with high skill requirements (le Grand et al. 2001), educational expansion (Schofer and Meyer 2005), and the shift in jobs from manufacturing to services (Schettkat and Yocarini 2006). These changes, together with a dramatic increase in the female labour force (Blau and Kahn 2017; Olivetti and Petrongolo 2014), imply that both the occupational structure and the composition of employees in the labour market are different compared to the 1960s. They also imply that women's work life has changed the most due to increased participation and time in paid labour, decreased time in unpaid labour, increased levels of education, and increased participation in high-skilled occupations.

These changes in women's work life have taken place gradually where young women have increased their education level over time. This suggests that the labour market may differ for young women today compared to well-established workers. It is also likely that work-life conditions faced by young women during the late 1960s and the 1970s differ in comparison to the conditions that young women face today. Entering male-dominated, high-skilled, and prestigious occupations probably implied different work conditions in the 1960s compared to entering similar occupations in more recent times. For example, today high-prestige occupations are occupied by both men and women (Magnusson 2009). Interestingly, and perhaps surprisingly, we know little about whether young women's career opportunities in high-prestige occupations have changed since the 1960s.

Moreover, despite the growing number of women in both higher education and high-skilled occupations, a gender wage gap persists in Sweden and elsewhere (e.g., Blau and Kahn 2017; Boye et al. 2017). It is clear that the gender wage gap in Sweden is more salient in qualified

174   *Charlotta Magnusson and Magnus Nermo*

occupations (Boye et al. 2017), at the upper-end of the wage distribution (Albrecht et al. 2003), and in high-prestige occupations (Magnusson and Nermo 2017). However, we lack knowledge on whether this gender inequality varies by age, that is, whether it is different among the young and/or has evolved in another way for young employees over time. The overall purpose of this chapter is therefore to fill this void and study changes in the gender wage gap, particularly among young men and women over time. Thus, the comprehensive question raised in this chapter is whether gender wage inequality among young employees is larger or smaller today compared to the 1960s and 1970s.

In the following, we present a brief and explorative overview of women's allocation and careers (in terms of wages) in highly prestigious occupations and among top earners in Sweden between 1968 and 2010. In particular, we investigate wage differences between young men and women in highly prestigious occupations and whether these associations vary over time. Sweden's history of high rates of educated women, and a relatively long period of high female labour force participation, make it an interesting country to study.

Paid and Unpaid Labour in Sweden Over Time

During the past 40 or 50 years, Sweden has transformed from a 'male breadwinner' society to a society characterised by dual-earner families. Thus, Sweden has long had a large welfare system and active policies to help men and women combine work and family (Korpi et al. 2013). Simply stated, one can argue that there are especially two major changes during this time that most likely have had a strong impact on young women's career opportunities: i) the expansion of family-friendly policies and ii) the gender integration of high-qualification occupations.

Family-friendly policies were introduced stepwise in the 1970s and the 1980s. The first of these policies was the individual taxation system, introduced in 1971, which led to stronger incentives for a more equal division of paid work between spouses. This reform was followed in 1974 by the parental leave insurance policy, which gave both parents equal rights to paid parental leave. Today, Swedish family policies provide parents with extensive paid parental leave (480 paid days in total that can be used until the child turns 8 years old or finishes first grade at school), access to subsidised public childcare, and the option to reduce their work time when their children are young.[1] In all, these policies have allowed parents to combine family and work, and have made it possible for mothers to enter the labour market. The employment rate, especially among mothers with young children, is also much higher in Sweden compared to other countries (Thévenon 2011). In all, it may appear reasonable to assume that these changes should have contributed to an increase of young women's career opportunities over time.

The second major structural change, the upgrading of occupational skill level, has led to an increased share of women in higher education and in high-prestige occupations. Women's improvement in human capital since the 1960s has been remarkable. Women have increased their enrolment in higher education at a much higher level than men, and from the late 1970s, women have outnumbered men in tertiary education (Universitetskanslersämbetet 2016). Women have also increased their human capital in terms of both work hours and labour market experience in the past several decades. The average work time per week for women increased from 30 hours in the mid-1970s to 36 hours in 2010 (Boye and Evertsson 2014).

Given women's relative increase of human capital (education and work experience), we would assume that gender inequality decreases over time, especially among the young. Together with increased opportunities to combine family life with working life, women's improvement in education and inroads into high-prestige occupations are important changes that theoretically imply a decrease in gender inequality over time.

However, the shift to dual-earner families, in which both partners may face problems combining paid and unpaid work, may also present new challenges for women (and men) in the labour market. Although parental benefits are offered to both parents, in reality, it is still women who take the lion's share of all parental leave days (Duvander and Viklund 2014). Part-time work is also much more common among mothers than fathers. Among women with two children under the age of 17, where the youngest is aged 3–5 years, 40% worked part-time in 2018. The corresponding figure for men is only 8% (Statistic Sweden 2018). The use of family-friendly policies also varies between individuals, according to both level of education and occupation. Low-educated women work part-time to a larger extent than women with higher education. In 2010 about 60% of all women working part-time had less than secondary education (Lanninger and Sundström 2014).

Even if Sweden is often characterised by a 'universal breadwinner model', it has also been described as a 'universal caregiver model', where not only women but also men are involved in family care work (see Fraser 1994). Thus, Sweden, as compared to other countries, is unique in the sense that fathers have been entitled to parental leave days since the 1970s. The father's share of used parental leave days has increased from approximately 0.5% of all days in 1974 to approximately 23% in 2010 (Duvander and Johansson 2012). There is, however, significant variation among fathers in the amount of parental leave days used, where some fathers use a large part of the parental leave, while others barely take any. The father's outtake increases as educational level rises, while the reverse pattern is found among mothers (Försäkringskassan 2011); meanwhile, parents in high-skilled occupations tend to share parental leave days equally. Consequently, women in these occupations take fewer days than women in other occupational groups, and men more days compared to men in other occupations (Försäkringskassan 2016).

The female labour force participation rate in Sweden has been notably high for a long time, but the labour market is still markedly segregated by gender. The relatively high rate of gender segregation in the Swedish labour market is reflected in the fact that men work in the manufacturing industry to a large extent, while women are largely employed in the public health care industry and in social services (SOU 2004). However, even if the level of segregation in the Swedish labour market is high, it is not extreme from a cross-national comparative perspective (Halldén 2014; Nermo 2000). Sweden has, however, often been pointed out as a country with an extremely gender-segregated labour market, and researchers have emphasised that gender-egalitarian family policies, such as those in Sweden, not only lead to greater gender equality, in the sense that most women are economically active, but also have certain non-egalitarian consequences because female employees are disadvantaged through inferior career prospects (see e.g., Mandel and Semyonov 2005). Thus, critics argue that these policies increase the gendered nature of the labour market, where women are trapped in female-dominated occupations, and that the policies contribute to the underrepresentation of women in supervisory positions (Mandel and Semyonov 2005). Moreover, the gender wage gap increases, especially in high-skilled occupations (Gupta et al. 2008). Critics further assert that these policies exacerbate statistical discrimination:[2] employers know that women generally take long parental leave and have primary responsibility for the care of sick children. However, empirical studies (e.g., Gash 2009; Petersen et al. 2014) indicate no or only a small motherhood wage penalty in countries with family policies that support maternal employment. Furthermore, Grönlund and Magnusson (2016) did not find any support for a larger gender wage gap among highly skilled employees in Sweden than in countries characterised by other welfare regimes.

In all, the conflicting findings regarding family-friendly policies make it difficult to predict how the wage gap among young men and women in high-prestige occupations has varied over time in Sweden. Thus, it is possible that family-friendly policies make it easier for young women to combine work and family life and thereby decrease the gender wage gap in this group over time. However, it may also be the case that family-friendly policies have instead exacerbated the gender wage gap in high-skilled occupations, resulting in a larger wage gap among young men and women today than in the late 1960s. The latter would then be explained by mothers being, on average, absent from work more often than fathers, due to family responsibilities. Thus, this absence is assumed to be especially negative for wages in high-skilled or high-prestige occupations often characterised by, for example, high availability, overtime work, and business travel—that is, work conditions that are harder to combine with family duties (Magnusson and Nermo 2017; Williams 2000).

The main focus of this chapter is on high-prestige occupations. However, the empirical section is structured by contrasting high-prestige occupations with low- and middle-prestige occupations. These two occupational groups differ quite substantially from each other in terms of the occupational structure as well as the ease of balancing family responsibilities. High-prestige occupations are often characterised by high skill requirements, and most require a university degree (e.g., civil engineers, psychologists, and lawyers). Low/middle-prestige occupations are obviously a more mixed group consisting of both occupations with low skill requirements (e.g., clerks, waiters, and bus and tram drivers) and occupations that require higher education (e.g., nursing and midwifery professionals). High-prestige occupations are largely gender integrated today, while low/middle-prestige occupations often are either male- or female-dominated occupations (Magnusson 2009). This pattern has changed somewhat over time. In particular, high-prestige occupations that were often male dominated in the 1960s have become more gender integrated due to the inflow of women rather than an outflow of men (England 2010; Nermo 1999). It is, as mentioned earlier, more common to share the parental leave more equally among highly educated parents. Fathers' use of parental leave days is higher in high-prestige occupations. Given that mothers with a low education level take longer parental leave than highly educated mothers, it is likely that mothers in low/middle-prestige occupations also take more parental leave days. It is also more common for less educated women to work part-time, which implies that women in low/middle-prestige occupations perform more part-time work than other women.

These assumptions are confirmed by our data: for all time periods studied, the share of part-time work among women is larger in low/middle-prestige occupations as compared to high-prestige occupations. High-prestige occupations are characterised by work conditions that are harder to combine with family responsibilities to a larger extent than low/middle-prestige occupations (Magnusson and Nermo 2017). The relationship between family-friendly policies and prestigious occupations is complex. For men, it is more common to use parental leave policies in high-prestige occupations. For women, it may instead be somewhat easier to combine family life with work life in low/middle-prestige occupations. The implications of this for gender equality are thus not easily disentangled.

The increase in women's labour force participation not only affects the composition of the labour force but also the pattern of selection of women in paid labour. Thus, a high female labour force participation rate may imply a higher share of women with low productivity, while a low female participation rate instead may imply a selection of highly productive women because mostly highly skilled women tend to be employed (cf Jurajda and Harmgart 2004). According to this perspective, the gender wage gap is assumed to be smaller when the rate of female participation is low. Thus, in line with this reasoning, we would expect that gender wage gap in high-prestige occupations has increased since the late 1960s.

Taken together, the parallel changes in paid and unpaid labour, combined with the critique raised against the family-friendly policies in Sweden, result in opposing expectations of trends in young women's career opportunities. Thus, while improvement in women's labour market attachment speaks to less gender inequality, the perspective that highlights the negative side effects of family-friendly solutions asserts more gender inequality in the labour market, especially in high-prestige occupations.

In the next section, we attempt to shed light on this issue by empirically investigating changes over time in the gender wage gap among young men and women in high-prestige occupations. First, we explore trends in young men's and women's employment and allocation in high-prestige occupations, in comparison with all employees in the labour market. Thereafter, we investigate trends in the gender wage gap in high and low/middle-prestige occupations for young employees and all employees, respectively. Last, we investigate changes over time in the share of women among top earners.

Empirical Analysis

The empirical analyses are based on the Swedish Level of Living Survey (LNU), which is a nationally representative survey of 0.1% of the Swedish population between the ages of 18[3] and 75. The LNU has been conducted six times since 1968. In the present study, we use data from all six waves: 1968, 1974, 1981, 1991, 2000, and 2010. The samples used for each year consist of employees aged 18–65 working at least five hours per week. To gather sufficient observations in the analyses of young men and women in high-prestige occupations, we needed to pool the surveys pairwise: 1968–74, 1981–91, and 2000–10. These analyses include a control for the survey year.

Being young is a relative concept, and here we define men and women as young when they are between 25 and 40 years old. The lower age limit is because high-prestige occupations often require a university degree.

The dependent variable is the logarithm of *hourly wage*. Using a logarithmic dependent variable in an OLS regression, a change by one unit in the independent variable produces a certain percentage change in the dependent variable (Allison 1999).[4] When information on hourly wages is missing, other types of pay (such as daily, weekly, or monthly pay) are recalculated into hourly wages. The wage variable includes bonuses, piece-rate, other earnings benefits, and compensation for over time.

Occupational prestige is measured by Treiman's Standard International Occupational Prestige Scale (SIOPS). SIOPS is based on national populations' subjective valuations of occupations from 60 countries, integrated into an international scale (Treiman 1977). Studies of occupational prestige have shown that these ratings are stable over time and place, and that occupational prestige is highly correlated with both education and earnings (Wegener 1992); prestige can also be understood as a measure of occupational skill level. The prestige scale is continuous and ranges from 13 to 78, but is used here as a dichotomous variable that distinguishes between high respective to low/middle prestige. *High-prestige occupations* are defined as having a value above 56 in SIOPS. Occupations with a prestige value below 56 are referred to as low/middle prestige. In 1968, a prestige score of 56 corresponds to around the 85th percentile and above in the prestige distribution. This division implies that less than 15% of the individuals in the 1968 sample were employed in occupations that we define as high prestige. Examples of high-prestige occupations include physicians, university professors, lawyers, and engineers. Occupations are classified according to the International Standard Classification of Occupations (ISCO-88).

Top earners is defined as individuals whose wages are at the 80th percentile and above in the wage distribution.

To adjust for gender differences in human capital, *education* (years), *work experience*, and the square of work experience are considered in all regression analyses. As the labour market is markedly segregated by gender, where men and women tend to work in different sectors, all regression analyses include a dummy variable for work in the *public sector*.

The Results

Descriptive Statistics

Table 10.1 shows the development of key characteristics of men and women in the labour market from 1968 to 2010. The table shows descriptive statistics for all employees in our sample and separately for young men and women. There has been an increase in log wages for both men and women, but throughout the period, men have significantly higher log wages than women.[5] This is true for all employees as well as for young employees.

In the beginning of the time period, men's prestige mean value was significantly higher than women's, but since 2000 there has been no statistically significant gender difference in average occupational prestige. The average occupational prestige is higher for young men and women than for all employees. The gender differences in average prestige among young men and women are only statistically significant in 1968 and 1974. Afterward, there are no significant gender differences in occupational prestige

180   *Charlotta Magnusson and Magnus Nermo*

Table 10.1 Descriptive statistics of employees by gender, from 1968 to 2010

	1968	1974	1981	1991	2000	2010
Men						
Log wage (mean)	2.4	3.0	3.7	4.4	4.8	5.1
Young men	2.5	3.0	3.7	4.4	4.8	5.1
Prestige (mean)	40.2	41.0	40.9	41.4	43.9	44.7
Young men	42.3	42.6	42.0	40.7	43.4	44.2
Education (mean)	8.7	9.9	10.7	11.7	12.6	13.5
Young men	9.4	10.8	12.0	12.4	13.1	14.2
Public sector (per cent)	21.2	25.9	30.0	29.0	25.7	23.7
Young men	22.1	23.5	31.6	28.9	17.8	17.8
Work experience (mean)	21.6	20.6	20.1	20.1	20.2	21.4
Young men	14.8	13.4	13.3	11.8	11.4	11.2
N (per cent)	1730 (60.6)	1677 (56.8)	1753 (52.4)	1654 (50.0)	1500 (51.1)	1263 (52.4)
Women						
Log wage (mean)	2.1	2.7	3.5	4.2	4.6	5.0
Young women	2.2	2.8	3.5	4.3	4.6	5.0
Prestige (mean)	35.8	36.7	38.2	39.4	42.6	44.6
Young women	39.1	38.7	40.2	40.2	43.8	45.4
Education (mean)	8.7	9.7	10.3	11.5	12.8	14.0
Young women	9.5	10.5	11.3	12.4	13.5	14.9
Public sector (per cent)	44.1	52.8	60.8	61.3	56.1	54.4
Young women	47.9	54.0	64.5	58.7	46.0	50.3
Work experience (mean)	14.6	14.5	15.4	16.8	19.3	20.9
Young women	11.4	10.6	11.4	11.0	11.0	11.2
N (per cent)	1126 (39.4)	1277 (43.2)	1594 (47.6)	1657 (50.1)	1434 (48.9)	1147 (47.6)

Source: LNU 1968, 1974, 1981, 1991, 2000, 2010.

Notes: Significant gender differences are bold ($p = < 0.05$).

among the young. Both men and women increased their education level in the studied period. In 1968, both genders had an average of nine years of schooling, but by 2010, this figure had increased to approximately 14 years for women and 13.5 years for men. Women's work experience increased by more than six years during the same period, and since the early 2000s, there has been no statistically significant gender difference in work experience. The share of employed women in the public sector is much larger than that of men across the entire time period, both when comparing all employees and when comparing young men and women only.

Sweden Over Time

The previously mentioned important structural change of a dramatic inflow of women into paid work is evident in Figure 10.1 The substantial gender difference in labour market participation in the 1960s and 1970s decreased dramatically in the following decades, and since the early 1990s, women's and men's labour market activity has been almost on par. In 1968, approximately 50% of all women and 84% of all men were active in paid labour; in 2010, over 70% of all women and approximately 80% of all men participated in the labour market.

If we look at young men's and women's activity in our sample over time (Figure 10.2), we see that young women's participation in paid labour increased more quickly compared to the average participation (cf. Figure 10.1). The lower participation rate among young women in 2000 and 2010 is because those on parental leave have a separate category for these years, but most of them are engaged in paid labour when not on parental leave. In Figure 10.2, we see the dramatic decrease of full-time homemakers among young women from approximately 40% in 1968 to a marginal 1% in 2010. Thus, the shift from a 'male breadwinner society' to 'dual-earner families' is clearly shown in this figure. In line with educational expansion, the share of students has increased significantly among young men, but this increase is even more salient among young women. In 1968, approximately 2% of young women in our sample

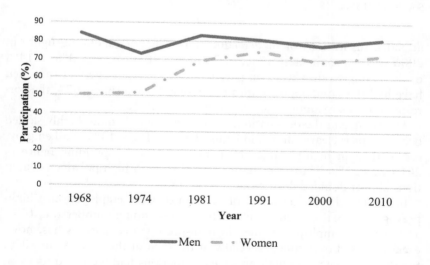

Figure 10.1 Participation in paid work among men and women in Sweden, aged 18–65[a] (1968–2010)

Source: LNU 1968, 1974, 1981, 1991, 2000, 2010.

[a] In the first three waves of LNU (1968, 1974, and 1980) the lower age bound was 15.

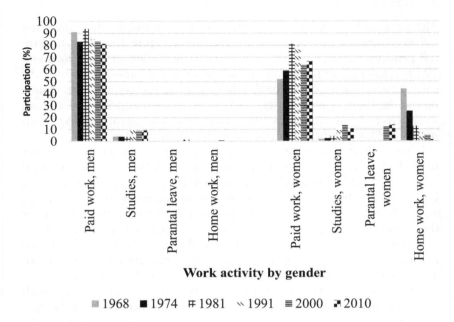

Work activity by gender

▨ 1968 ■ 1974 ♯ 1981 ⦁ 1991 ≡ 2000 ⚐ 2010

Figure 10.2 Work activity among young men and women in Sweden, aged 25–40 (1968–2010)

Source: LNU 1968, 1974, 1981, 1991, 2000, 2010.

attended institutions of higher education. The corresponding figure in 2000 was approximately 13%. In 2000 and 2010 roughly 3% to 14% of the young women were on parental leave. Despite the fact that men have had the same opportunities for parental leave since 1974, the corresponding share among men was only 1% in 2010.

The change in the occupational structure towards more highly skilled occupations is clearly shown in Figure 10.3. In 1968, 13% of all employees worked in high-prestige occupations. The corresponding figure in 2010 was 22%. Thus, the share of employees in high-prestige occupations almost doubled during this time period.

In the late 1960s, only 7% of all women were employed in a high-prestige occupation. Among men, the corresponding number was 16%. The share of employed women in high-prestige occupations has, however, increased over time, especially at the turn of the century. In 2000, the share of women in high-prestige occupations had increased to 18%, and 10 years later, this share had increased to 22%. The corresponding shares among men increased in the same period from 16% to 21%. This means that in 2010 the share of women who worked in high-prestige occupations exceeded the same share among men.

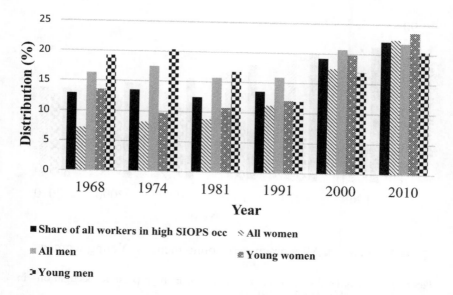

Figure 10.3 Gender distribution of men and women in high-prestige occupations in Sweden (1968–2010)

Source: LNU 1968, 1974, 1981, 1991, 2000, 2010.

Notes: Occupational prestige is measured by Treiman's Standard International Occupational Prestige Scale (SIOPS).

If we instead look at how the share of young men and women in high-prestige occupations have evolved over time, the pattern differs somewhat. Overall, the share of young women in high-prestige occupations, compared to the same share for all employed women, has been somewhat larger throughout the periods under study. The difference was largest in 1968, when 13.5% of young women but only 7.4% of all women worked in high- prestige occupations. In 2010, the share of young women employed in a high-prestige occupations had increased to 23.6%. The corresponding trend for young men has been relatively stable over time and only increased marginally from 19.2% in 1968 to 20.4% in 2010.

The next step is to focus on high-prestige occupations and to compare the shares of men and women in these occupations. It is evident in Figure 10.4 that the gender composition in high-prestige occupations has changed dramatically over the period studied. In 1968, almost eight out of 10 employees in high-prestige occupations were men, but in 2010, these occupations were gender integrated. This is also true if we look at the gender distribution in high-prestige occupations among young men and women.

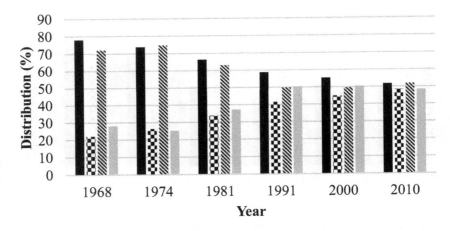

■ All men   ⚒ All women   ⚒ Young men   ⚒ Young women

Figure 10.4 Gender distribution of employees in high-prestige occupations in Sweden (1968–2010)

Source: LNU 1968, 1974, 1981, 1991, 2000, 2010.

The Gender Wage Gap

These analyses clearly indicate that young women increased their labour force participation as well as their share of high-prestige occupations. The next step is therefore to investigate the gender wage gap in high compared to low/middle-prestige occupations, and how this has evolved over time. Figure 10.5 shows women's earnings relative to men's (in per cent), given educational attainment, work experience, and sector of employment. It is obvious that during the late 1960s and early 1970s the gender wage gap was much smaller among men and women in high-prestige occupations compared to the gap in low/middle-prestige occupations—that is, approximately 13% compared to 24%. In the early 1980s, the gender wage gap in low/middle-prestige occupations decreased substantially to approximately 13%. The corresponding wage gap in high-prestige occupations was, however, surprisingly stable during the same period. This means that the gender wage gap did not appear to vary much by occupational prestige in the early 1980s. However, after 1981, the gender wage gap in low/middle-prestige occupations continues to decrease, but at a slower pace. Even so, this means that in 2010, the gender wage gap is smaller in low/middle-prestige occupations than in high-prestige occupations. It also indicates that the wage gap in high- prestige occupations has increased slightly since the 1970s. Thus, these findings provide no

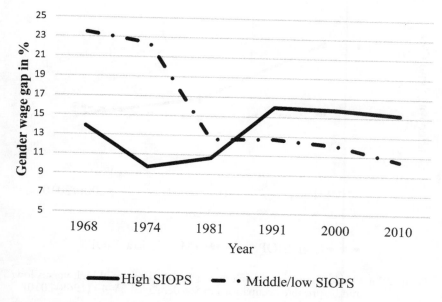

Figure 10.5 Gender wage gap among workers in high versus low/middle-prestige
occupations in Sweden, aged 18–65[a] (1968–2010)

Source: LNU 1968, 1974, 1981, 1991, 2000, 2010.

Notes: Controlled for education, work experience, squared work experience, and employment sector (public versus private).

Notes: Occupational prestige is measured by Treiman's Standard International Occupational Prestige Scale (SIOPS).

[a] In the first three waves of LNU (1968, 1974 and 1980) the lower age bound was 15.

evidence suggesting that the gender wage gap in high-prestige occupations is smaller today than it was in the late 1960s.

While the analysis showed how gender wage differentials evolved for
all men and women in the labour market, Figure 10.6 shows the corresponding trend for young men and women. One problem here is that
relatively few young men and women are employed in high-prestige
occupations. Therefore, to obtain a sufficient number of observations, we
pool the LNU survey data pairwise: 1968–74, 1981–91, and 2000–10.

The analysis presented in Figure 10.6 shows that in 1968–74, the
wage gap among young men and women was much larger in low/middle-
prestige occupations than in high-prestige occupations. Thus, this result
follows the same pattern as that of all employees in the labour market.
The gender wage gap among individuals in low/middle-prestige occupations decreases substantially thereafter, and is not statistically significantly different than the gender wage gap in high-prestige occupations.

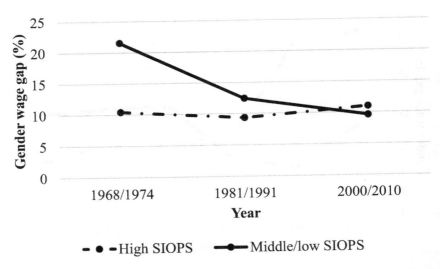

Figure 10.6 Gender wage gap among young female workers in high versus low/
middle-prestige occupations in Sweden, aged 25–40 (1968–2010)

Source: LNU 1968, 1974, 1981, 1991, 2000, 2010. Controlled for education, work experience, squared work experience, employment sector (public versus private), and survey year.

The gender wage gap in high-prestige occupations is rather stable over the period studied. Thus, in terms of wages, young women, compared to young men, do not fare better today than in the early 1970s.

The category of high-prestige occupations is broad and includes occupations in both the public and private sector, across different fields. To analyse whether the gender wage gap differs within the category of high-prestige occupations, we carry out separate analyses on five specific high-prestige occupational groups. The specific professions (divisions are based on ISCO-88 two-digit) are corporate managers (ISCO-88 = 12), physical, mathematical, and engineering science professionals (21), life science health professionals (22), teaching professionals (23), and other professionals (e.g., business, legal, and social science professionals) (24).[6] Figure 10.7 reveals the gender wage gap in 2000–10 among five professional groups. The largest gender wage difference is found in managerial positions. The gender wage gap among physical, mathematical, and engineering science is the smallest and is not statistically significant. Overall, the gender wage gap is relatively equal among other professionals, except for a tendency toward a smaller gap among teaching professionals.

Finally, to get a sense of women's economic power in society, we describe the allocation of women among top earners and how this has changed over time (see Figure 10.8). Young women constitute a somewhat

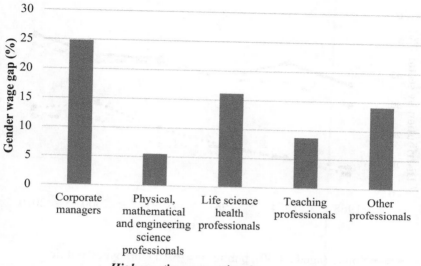

Figure 10.7 Gender wage gap among workers belonging to five high-prestige occupational groups, aged 18–65 (2000–2010)

Source: LNU 1968, 1974, 1981, 1991, 2000, 2010. Controlled for education, work experience, squared work experience, and survey year.

Notes: High-prestige occupational groups are classified according to the International Standard Classification of Occupations (ISCO-88 two-digit).

larger share of top earners in the public sector compared to the share of all employed women, and the share of young women among top earners is more or less identical to the average share.

The allocation of women among top earners has increased over time, both in the public and private sector. In 1968, the share of women among top earners in the private sector was approximately 9%, and in 2010, this share had increased to approximately 24%. The corresponding figures in the public sector increased from approximately 30% to 50%. It is worth remembering that in 2010, almost 68% of all employees in the public sector were women. Thus, women are still underrepresented among top earners in the public sector. Women's share in the private sector was 35%. Among top earners, women account for 24% in the private sector in 2010.

Concluding Remarks

The purpose of this chapter was to study changes in the gender wage gap in high-prestige occupations over time, particularly among young men

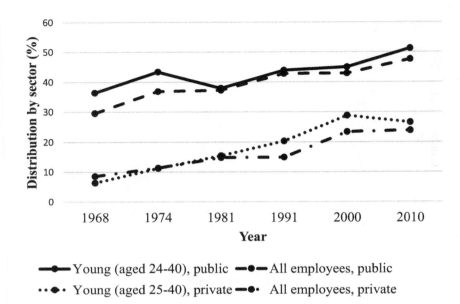

Figure 10.8 Distribution of women among top earners by employment sector
(1968–2010)

Source: LNU 1968, 1974, 1981, 1991, 2000, 2010

and women. The presented findings indicate that women in general, and especially young women, have improved their positions in the labour market over time, both regarding allocation in high-prestige occupations and among top earners. They have also increased their work time in paid labour and consequently increased their relative wages over time. From this point of view, the labour market is clearly more gender equal today than in the late 1960s.

The inflow of women in high-prestige occupations has, however, not resulted in a decrease in the gender wage gap in these occupations. The wage gap among men and women in high-prestige occupations is about the same today as it was in the late 1960s and the early 1970s. The analysis of the wage gap in some specific high-prestige occupations indicates that the wage inequality among men and women is especially wide in managerial positions. Thus, it is both a gender difference in terms of women's disadvantage in holding a managerial position and in the wages they receive in such a position.

In line with prior research (e.g., Boye et al. 2017), we find a decrease in the gender wage gap in low/middle-prestige occupations among all employees as well as among young employees. The decrease in the gender wage gap in low/middle-prestige occupations is most likely related to the centralised wage setting processes in Sweden (a 'solidaric wage policy'), which has stemmed general wage inequality and therefore wage inequality between men and women. During the 1980s, the centralised and collective wage agreements in Sweden were largely replaced by negotiations at the industry level. It appears that this structural change led to an increased overall wage inequality (le Grand 1994). However, while the gender wage gap decreased in low/middle-prestige occupations, the gap between men and women in high-prestige occupations has been more or less stable over time. A simple interpretation of these findings is that none of the structural changes in paid and unpaid labour that have occurred during the last 40 years have had a significant influence on the gender wage gap in high-prestige occupations.

On the one hand, the presented findings support criticism of the Swedish welfare policies in one respect, since the gender wage gap is larger among men and women in high-prestige occupations. On the other hand, the gender wage gap has not decreased substantially since the late 1960s. Thus, gender inequality in high-prestige occupations has not decreased since the implementation of family-friendly policies or since the large inflow of mothers in paid labour. Accordingly, it is difficult to ascribe much of the wage inequality among men and women in high-prestige occupations to changes in the welfare system. Given that the gender wage gap appears to be rather stable over time in high-prestige occupations, it is also difficult to ascribe changes in the composition of the labour force as the most important factor behind the persisting wage gap. If the increase of female employment increases the share of less productive women, one would expect the gender wage gap in high-prestige occupations to be smaller in the 1960s, that is, at a time when the female supply was lower. We find no support for this assumption. Whether changes in the gender wage gap are due to structural changes in paid and unpaid work is, as noted, a complex question and is obviously difficult to answer with the presented analyses. If anything, the presented analyses may be interpreted as if the welfare system and other structural changes may have contributed to a reduction of the wage gap between men and women in low- to middle-high prestige occupations.

Finally, despite all changes in paid and unpaid labour—including fathers on parental leave walking with strollers down the street—the gender wage gap is rather stable. However, being on parental leave and taking time off from paid work to take care for children is only one caregiver function. Increased gender balance in all caregiver functions—such as more men working part-time, performing unpaid work, and taking care of sick children—would probably increase gender equality to a larger degree. Thus, a welfare state characterised by a universal caregiver model could be a possible solution.

190   *Charlotta Magnusson and Magnus Nermo*

Notes

1 Today, two months of paid parental leave, the so called 'daddy months', cannot be transferred to the other parent (Duvander and Viklund 2014).
2 The principle of statistical discrimination is that employers treat female employees as a group to save time and money, basing their judgements on women's average productivity and not on an individual's characteristics (Phelps 1972). Employers may be less prone to hire or promote a female worker (compared to a male worker) because employers know that women are generally more likely than men are to interrupt their work life, to take parental leave or to reduce their paid work hours (Ibid.).
3 For 1968, 1974, and 1981 the respondents are between the ages of 15 and 65.
4 The following estimation is used to calculate the percentage change: 100(exp(b)–1).
5 The gender differences have been tested with two sample t-tests.
6 It is worth remembering that that even if the occupations in these categories are similar to each other, the occupational groups based on broad two-digit ISCO-88 categories include occupations with varying degrees of qualification requirements. As the number of observations is low, we can only look at the overall gender wage gap, not divided by age categories.

References

Albrecht, J, Björklund, A and Vroman, SB (2003) 'Is There a Glass Ceiling in Sweden' 21 *Journal of Labor Economics* 145. doi:10.1086/344126
Allison, P (1999) *Multiple Regression: A Primer* (Thousand Oaks, Pine Forge Press).
Blau, F and Kahn, L (2017) 'The Gender Wage Gap: Extent, Trends, and Explanations' 55 *Journal of Economic Literature* 789. doi:10.1257/jel.20160995
Boye, K and Evertsson, M (2014) 'Vem Gör Vad När? Kvinnors och Mäns Tid i Betalt och Obetalt Arbete' in M Evertsson and C Magnusson (eds), *Ojämlikhetens Dimensioner: Uppväxtvillkor, Arbete och Hälsa i Sverige* (Stockholm, Liber Publishing).
Boye, K, Halldén, K and Magnusson, C (2017) 'Stagnation Only on the Surface? The Implications of Skill and Family Responsibilities for the Gender Wage Gap in Sweden, 1974–2010' 68 *The British Journal of Sociology* 595. doi:10.1111/1468-4446.12252
Duvander, A-Z and Johansson, M (2012) 'What Are the Effects of Reforms Promoting Fathers' Parental Leave Use?' 22 *Journal of European Social Policy* 319. doi:10.1177/0958928712440201
Duvander, A-Z and Viklund, I (2014) 'Kvinnors och Mäns Föräldraledighet' in K Boye and M Nermo (eds), *Lönsamt Wrbete—Familjeansvarets Fördelning och Konsekvenser*, (Stockholm, Fritzes, Statens Offentliga Utredningar). www.regeringen.se/49baec/contentassets/283b9cb9b0414c3abf46aea24798476b/lonsamt-arbete—familjeansvarets-fordelning-och-konsekvenser-sou-201428
England, P (2010) 'The Gender Revolution: Uneven and Stalled' 24 *Gender and Society* 149.
Försäkringskassan (2011) *Socialförsäkringsrapport* 7. www.forsakringskassan.se/wps/wcm/connect/84cb4254-0889-4a51-9601-e4bc82931872/socialforsakringsrapport_2011_17.pdf?MOD=AJPERES

——— (2016) *Föräldrapenning och Yrke* (Korta Analyser 1). www.forsakrings kassan.se/wps/wcm/connect/da6e8823-eef8-4d18-aeb4-991e726e2d18/korta_ analyser_2016_1.pdf?MOD=AJPERES

Fraser, N (1994) 'After the Family Wage: Gender Equity and the Welfare State' 22 *Political Theory* 591. doi:10.1177/0090591794022004003

Gash, V (2009) 'Sacrificing Their Careers for Their Families? An Analysis of the Penalty to Motherhood in Europe' 93 *Social Indicators Research* 569. doi:10.1007/s11205-008-9429-y

Grönlund, A and Magnusson, C (2016) 'Family-Friendly Policies and Women's Wages—Is there a Trade-Off? Skill Investments, Occupational Segregation and the Gender Pay Gap in Germany, Sweden and the UK' 18 *European Societies* 91. doi:10.1080/14616696.2015.1124904

Gupta, ND, Smith, N and Verner, M (2008) 'Perspective Article: The Impact of Nordic Countries' Family Friendly Policies on Employment, Wages, and Children' 6 *Review of Economics of the Household*, 65. doi:10.1007/ s11150-007-9023-0

Halldén, K (2014) 'Könssegregering Efter Yrke på den Svenska Arbetsmarknaden år 2000–2010' in A Kunze and K Thorburn (eds), *Yrke, Karriär och lön— Kvinnors och Mäns Olika Villkor på den Svenska Arbetsmarknaden* (Stockholm, Fritzes, Statens Offentliga Utredningar (SOU)), 81.

Jurajda, Š and Harmgart, H (2004) 'IZA DP No. 985: When Are 'Female' Occupations Paying More?' 35 *Journal of Comparative Economics* 170. www.iza. org/publications/dp/985/when-are-female-occupations-paying-more

Korpi, W, Ferrarini, T and Englund, S (2013) 'Women's Opportunities Under Different Family Policy Constellations: Gender, Class, and Inequality Tradeoffs in Western Countries Re-Examined' 20 *Social Politics: International Studies in Gender, State and Society* 1. doi:10.1093/sp/jxs028

Lanninger, AW and Sundström, M (2014) *Part-Time Work in the Nordic Region: Part-Time Work, Gender and Economic Distribution in the Nordic Countries* (TemaNord, 2014), 503. http://norden.diva-portal.org/smash/get/ diva2:707663/FULLTEXT01.pdf

le Grand, C (1994) 'Löneskillnaderna i Sverige: Förändring och Nuvarande Struktur' in J Fritzell and O Lundberg (eds), *Vardagens Willkor: Levnadsförhållande i Sverige Under Tre Decennier* (Stockholm, Bromberg).

le Grand, C, Szulkin, R and Tåhlin, M (2001) 'Lönestrukturens Förändring i Sverige' in J Fritzell, M Gähler and O Lundberg (eds), *Välfärd och Arbete i Arbetslöshetens Årtionde* Kommittén Välfärdsbokslut (Stockholm, Fritzes, Statens Offentliga Utredningar (SOU)), 53.

Magnusson, C (2009) 'Gender, Occupational Prestige, and Wages: A Test of Devaluation Theory' 25 *European Sociological Review* 87. doi:10.1093/esr/ jcn035

Magnusson, C and Nermo, M (2017) 'Gender, Parenthood and Wage Differences: The Importance of Time-Consuming Job Characteristics' 131 *Social Indicators Research* 797. doi:10.1007/s11205-016-1271-z

Nermo, M (2000) 'Models of Cross-National Variation in Occupational Sex Segregation' 2 *European Societies* 295. doi.org/10.1080/146166900750036295

——— (1999) 'Structured by Gender: Patterns of Sex Segregation in the Swedish Labour Market. Historical and Cross-National Comparison' PhD dissertation (Institutet för Social Forskning (SOFI), Stockholm).

192 Charlotta Magnusson and Magnus Nermo

Mandel, H and Semyonov, M (2005) 'Family Policies, Wage Structures, and Gender Gaps: Source of Earnings Inequality in 20 Countries' 70 *American Sociological Review* 949. doi:10.1177/000312240507000604

Olivetti, C and Petrongolo, B (2014) 'Gender Gaps Across Countries and Skills' 17 *Review of Economic Dynamics* 842. doi:10.1016/j.red.2014.03.001

Petersen, T, Penner, AM and Hogsnes, G (2014) 'From Motherhood Penalties to Husband Premia: The New Challenge for Gender Equality and Family Policy, Lessons from Norway' 119 *American Journal of Sociology* 1434. doi:10.1086/674571

Phelps, ES (1972) 'The Statistical Theory of Racism and Sexism' 62 *The American Economic Review* 659.

Schettkat, R and Yocarini, L (2006) 'The Shift to Services Employment: A Review of the Literature' 17 *Structural Change and Economic Dynamics* 127. doi:10.1016/j.strueco.2005.04.002

Schofer, E and Meyer, JW (2005) 'The Worldwide Expansion of Higher Education in the Twentieth Century' 70 *American Sociological Review* 898. doi:10.1177/000312240507000602

SOU (2004) *Den Könsuppdelade arbetsmarknaden Statens offentliga utredningar.* www.regeringen.se/49baef/contentassets/533a8d5e46bf409cb3c0e7710e 85c141/den-konsuppdelade-arbetsmarknaden-a-2004

Statistics Sweden (2018) *Women and Men in Sweden. Facts and Figures 2018.* www.scb.se/contentassets/4550eaae793b46309da2aad796972cca/le0201_ 2017b18_br_x10br1801eng.pdf

Thévenon, O (2011) 'Family Policies in OECD Countries: A Comparative Analysis' 37 *Population and Development Review* 57. doi:10.1177/0003122 40507000602

Treiman, D (1977) *Occupational Prestige in Comparative Perspective* (New York, Academic Press).

Universitetskanslersämbetet (2016) *Kvinnor och Män på Högskolan* (Universitetskanslersämbetet, Rapport 16). www.uka.se/download/18.5d85793915 901d205f9a852/1487841854015/rapport-2016-10-14-kvinnor-och-man-i-hogskolan.pdf

Wegener, B (1992) 'Concepts and Measurement of Prestige' 18 *Annual Review of Sociology* 253. doi:10.1146/annurev.so.18.080192.001345

Williams, J (2000) *Unbending Gender: Why Family and Work Conflict and What to Do About It* (Oxford, Oxford University Press).

11 Age–Gender Relations in the Academic Profession

Putting the Challenges of Early Career Academics Into Context

Jeff Hearn and Liisa Husu

Introduction

To understand the academic profession, and indeed many other professions, questions of age, gender, and the relations of age and gender need to be foregrounded. This is what we seek to do in this chapter, through a specific focus on early career academics making their way—or not—in the academic profession. The academic profession, or professions, comprises those occupational groupings and their individual and collective professionalisation projects that derive their professional power and status specifically from academic study, research, and higher education teaching. Academic professions are located primarily and collectively in universities and other institutions of higher education, though many individuals and group members also work elsewhere, often as researchers, in the private, public, or third sectors, yet continue to identify with academic professional associations and identities.

In addition, broad distinctions can be made: the overall academic profession as a more or less inclusive whole; particular academic disciplinary professions, such as historians or bioscientists; academic researchers as a profession; and professions that cross over between research, education, policy, and practice, such as engineering, medicine, law, and education itself. Inevitably, there are overlaps between these various forms of professions. Moreover, and lying largely outside our concern here, are those other professions, the majority of whose members are located mainly outside academia, such as architecture, nursing, or social work, and that are linked to academia by way of professional education and training as a means of entry to the profession.

The academic profession provides an especially interesting case to examine early professional careers, for three reasons. First, the academic profession(s) are both historically long established and also currently exposed to major processes of organisational, social structural, and technological change. As such, they are characterised by some archaic, very hierarchical, patriarchal, neo-feudal, and at times ritualistic practices, along with a meritocratic ethos and ideology, and late modern transformations spurred by managerial, surveillance, and information communication and related technologies. They are both persistently aged and gendered, despite being sites of widespread assumptions and claims of objective neutrality.

Second, academic professions are both intensely national and increasingly international. Their foundation and development has often been closely related to the nation-state project. In some European countries, such as in Sweden, universities are public authorities, and university employees have the status of civil servants. Yet universities are also highly and increasingly international and transnational in form, content, and staffing. This latter feature, while increasing in intensity, is not wholly new: for example, many of the early women pioneers entering the male bastions of universities in the nineteenth century did so only by travelling from their home country to study and graduate elsewhere (Czarniawska and Sevón 2008).

A third reason why the early careers of academic profession(s) are of special interest follows from their very long period of professional qualification, education, and socialisation—an issue to which we will return.

In this chapter, following some brief historical and conceptual contextualisation, including the complexity of the academic profession(s), we discuss the plight of early career researchers and academics, empirical studies of gendered early careers in academia and research, and recent policy developments around early career academics, defined by academic age. While age and ageing more generally cannot be separated from the body and biology, they are also partly social and cultural. Social constructionist approaches to age and ageing include, for example, cognitive age, which is based on subjective feelings of age (Barak and Schiffman 1981), and cultural ageing (Twigg and Martin 2015). Rather than being strictly based in chronological age, academic age primarily concerns professional position, for example, in relation to doctoral studies or years after doctorate. Such academic positioning intersects with generational position, as with changing, often gendered caring responsibilities. To analyse early academic careers necessarily entails engaging with interrelations of age and gender, age–gender relations, and sex-ageism or gendered ageism in academic professions and institutions. What is especially interesting is how age–gender relations in early academic careers have shifted historically from formal exclusion of women to formal gender neutrality, along with continuing discrimination, academic intensification, and proactive policies for gender equal early careers.

Academic Professions in Historical Contexts

The gender neutrality of academia is often assumed, despite men's historical and contemporary domination of the power structures of higher education, research, and science. Still, women have been involved in academic activities and tasks throughout the history of higher education, research, academia, and science, but became excluded with its institutionalisation (Schiebinger 1999). For example, in the late eighteenth century women were hired as 'professional' astronomical 'computer' women on low pay and with no opportunities for career advancement: observatories, such as Harvard College Observatory, hired numerous women as 'computers' to perform star observation and arithmetic work (Rossiter 1982). The historical literature on women pioneers in the professions, in their modern form, and the obstacles and prejudice they faced is extensive (for example, Rossiter 1982; Adams and Tancred 2000; Chung 2010). The position of women entering or re-entering medicine in nineteenth-century United States of America has been recorded by Elisabeth and Emily Blackwell (1860) in *Medicine as a Profession for Women*. A classic account of the persistence of pioneering women and the resistance they encountered is found in the autobiography of Agnes Sjöberg, the first woman veterinary surgeon in Europe, and the first woman in Europe to obtain a doctorate in veterinary medicine (Sjöberg 1964). A major early overview of women's entry into professional associations in the US is found in the report, *Women in the Twentieth Century* (Breckinridge 1933). Women initially formed parallel women's professional associations, such as the Medical Women's National Association. Such processes can now be reconceptualised in terms of women's early academic careers seen at the structural historical level.

Well-developed arguments for and against women serving in the professions have been and still are put forward, often tending to emphasise either sexual/gender difference or gender/sexual sameness. Difference arguments against women's inclusion in the late nineteenth century could rely on forms of essentialist age-related biologism, such as the argument that intellectual work may damage women's reproductive organs, as reported in such medical journals as the *Norwegian Journal of Medicine* in 1892 (see Husu 2001: 33). Such thinking might appear archaic, but it has not vanished—even among current science leaders, as when Harvard's previous president, Lawrence Summers, justified the under-representation of women in some natural science fields on biological grounds, creating a strong counter-reaction in the scientific community:

> It does appear that on many, many different human attributes—height, weight, propensity for criminality, overall IQ, mathematical ability, scientific ability—there is relatively clear evidence that whatever the difference in means—which can be debated—there is a difference in the standard deviation, and variability of a male and a female population.
>
> (Summers 2005)

This example highlights the question of men's responses, discrimination, and resistance to women's entry, from both gatekeeping and peer positions, and the arguments articulated for and against women entering the professions. Arguments for women's inclusion have included women's special contributions (for example, in midwifery) that might thus benefit from women's contribution, and the more fundamental argument of justice for women in broadening their own occupational choices. These twin arguments of gender complementarity (difference) and gender comparability (sameness) are paralleled by arguments for diversity in various occupational fields, and in relation to gendered, and sometimes intersectional, labour markets. For example, increasing women's representation in STEM fields (natural science, technology, engineering, and mathematics) can be justified (or indeed opposed) in relation to women's choices, women's contribution and potential, industrial and labour market demands, and justice and equality. Likewise, gender or intersectional equality can be framed in different ways: individual choice, potential, and contribution; organisational, occupational, and labour market dynamics; or the structuring of (professional) knowledge itself, and what counts as (professional) knowledge (Hearn and Husu 2011; Schiebinger 1999). This last approach might be rather easily understood in professions such as law and medicine, but may be less obvious in, say, physics or mathematics.

The Professions in Contemporary Academia

The status of academic and research professions is, in comparative cross-national terms, highly variable. In the Soviet Union the medical profession tended to be coded as women's work, rather than as a male bastion into which women sought entry. In some countries veterinary medicine has been a men's arena, which women are entering in greater numbers (Lofstedt 2003), while in Finland it has long been numerically (currently almost totally) dominated by women. Dentistry in Finland has traditionally been a female-coded profession, in contrast with other Nordic countries (Haavio-Mannila 1975). Child psychiatry has been more a women's specialism in Finland than in Scandinavia; medicine has generally been more male-dominated in Denmark than other Nordic countries, but this is not the case in radiology (Riska 1998).

Different combinations of such professions are found within different research institutes and university departments. Academic and research organisations typically house professions and professional groupings defined by and in relation to their specific home organisation, such as the specific university or institute, but often also by and in relation to the relevant academic discipline or its associated professional association. Arguably, the location and employment of research professionals and professional researchers in organisations outside universities, including in business, government, and non-governmental organisations, is becoming more important, quantitatively and qualitatively. Meanwhile, universities are in many countries becoming more marketised—that is, more subject to demands for funding of research from non-public sources. In such various ways, the classic tensions between bureaucratic and professional organising and commitment are being changed through restructuring, if not ameliorated.

Some academic and research professions are clearly strongly established and institutionalised. The professions of medicine and law, in different ways, span university and practitioner milieux. In the first case, research is integral to the professional project; in the latter, canonical university teaching is especially powerful. Some academic professions are less thoroughly institutionalised. For example, professions such as sociology are much more recently established, and, in some countries at least, more porous in terms of welcoming researchers and teachers not originally educated therein. Psychology is, in a sense, in between medicine and sociology, especially in the chartering and certification of specific specialisms in psychology, such as clinical or occupational. An interesting, more unstable example is the relatively recent discipline of gender studies that has developed since the 1970s. For a start, gender studies scholars have very diverse academic backgrounds. In addition, the political acceptance of and/or resistance to gender studies can be both very varied and highly intense, both within and beyond universities, even from neighbouring academic disciplines. Professionalisation of the discipline has been relatively slow, perhaps partly due to ambivalence in some feminist circles around formalisation in organising. Thus, there is wide variation in the extent of correspondence between academic *disciplines* and the development of specific academic *professions*.

Moreover, academic and professional boundaries are not fixed, and new academic and disciplinary professions arise (for example, information science, environmental studies, and cultural studies); also crossovers and redefinitions occur between academic and disciplinary professions. This latter process may well be gathering pace, with the increase in multi-, trans-, and post-disciplinary scholarship (for example, digital humanities and computational art and design). New and emerging academic professions mirror changes in the labour market more generally, as in the 'gig economy', and the expansion of turker jobs, hybrid occupations, and composite skills (Webster and Randle 2016). Such changes within and beyond academia create more organisational uncertainty and challenges, such as devising robust managerial, faculty, and departmental structures, and educational programmes. For example, certain academic professions and professional groupings, such as communication studies, could be located in very different faculties and departments: management, psychology, social psychology, sociology, information science, media studies, and/or cultural studies. These complexities make for highly variable, and at times flexible and changing—and thus also unpredictable over time—conditions for academic professions. This raises practical and career challenges, particularly for early career academics, as disciplines and specialisms are reformulated and relocated.

Gendered and Aged Characteristics of Academic Professions

As with the established professions more generally, both the historical and contemporary academic and research professions are structured through clear social divisions: academic and research professions show clear gendered and aged features and characteristics, including vertical and horizontal divisions. Academic research organisations and professions are heavily gender and age differentiated, with age–gender structures, segregations, and hierarchies often taken for granted. Women have made great gains in higher education globally, but academia and research remain persistently male-dominated in most parts of the world. Globally, only around one-third of all researchers are women (UNESCO 2015). Gender and age patterns operate somewhat differently in different societies, according to historical contingencies, and variations in supply of and demand for specific research expertise, rates of relatively rapid expansion or decline in disciplines, and the presence of aged, gendered, and further exclusionary/inclusionary practices in those professions, organisations, and societies. For explanatory purposes, we first outline some gendered patterns, before considering intersections of age and gender.

Gendering occurs in gendered distributions and gendered practices, and even when professions and professional organisations, including academic professions, comprise only men or indeed only women (Boni-Le Goff and Le Feuvre 2017; Hearn et al. 2016; Riska 2014; Witz 1992). We emphasise that gendering applies as much to men and masculinities as to women and femininities: 'gender' is not a synonym for 'women'. Gender and sexual categories are multiple, as with LGBTIQ+ (lesbian, gay, bisexual, transgender, intersex, queer, and further non-normative gender and sexual positions) and expanding numbers of online identifications. Gender is thus much more than cisgender. Typical patterns of gendering of academic professions include the following:

- *Gendered divisions, inclusions and exclusions of professional labour and authority*, including between academic professions and other occupations: women and men tend to become specialised in particular types of professional labour, creating horizontal and vertical gendered divisions, between and within disciplines, and across academic hierarchies. Gendered valuations of work, formal authority, and informal standing vary within and between academic professions, and in forms of tenure and contracts. Women are more likely to do, and to be encouraged and expected to do, more teaching, pastoral care, and relatively invisible 'academic housekeeping' tasks, that often continue to be valued less than research when assessing academic performance and potential. They are more likely to face contradictory messages about gender-appropriate professional behaviour, both sustaining gendered divisions and providing possible flexibility in responding to gendered professional norms (Pierce 1995).

- *Gendered valuing of academic work over care work in the private domains:* academic work is 'greedy' and easily becomes all-consuming, with academic work valued over unpaid work. Women typically do more childcare and unpaid domestic work than men, and care for dependents, older people, and people with disabilities.
- *Gendered processes between the centre and margins of academia*: these may be literally or metaphorically spatial in distributions of power and activity between centres and margins of academic professions. The 'main aim' and priorities of organisations tend to be defined by men (Cockburn 1991).
- *Gendered disciplinary, departmental, and research group cultures*: for example, the concept of a 'chilly climate' has been used to describe subtly hostile academic culture affecting women's well-being and advancement (Britton 2017).
- *Gender bias in evaluation and assessment, and gendered careers*: experimental studies have demonstrated that gender bias is operating in the evaluation and assessment of academic capacity, performance, and future promise (Moss-Racusin et al. 2012).
- *Gendered processes in sexuality, harassment, bullying, and physical violence*: most professions have reproduced heterosexual norms, ideology, and practices, impacting and influencing academic activities, such as sexual dynamics in supervisory and mentoring relations.
- *Gendered processes in interactions and individuals' mental work* maintain or disrupt other gendered patterns, and concern how gendering is made sense of.
- *Gendered academic symbols, images, stereotypes* (of researcher and academic as assumed male), *identities, and forms of consciousness* include the props of academic expertise, academic titles (for example, 'master', 'fellow'), portraits of famous men on walls, and names of buildings and lecture halls.

All of these organisational issues are highly relevant in academic and research professions, professional organisations, and their relations with other professions and occupations, including aspiring professions. Significantly, similar conclusions on the gendered patterns of academia were summarised by Veronica Stolte-Heiskanen (1991) in the early 1990s in reviewing comparative European research on women in science:

1. The higher the position, the fewer women.
2. Recruitment base to academic careers is feminising.
3. Academic culture has gendered elements.
4. There are contradictions between the academic/research system clock and the biological clock.
5. Women are relatively invisible to male colleagues in the scientific community as colleagues.
6. The more a scientific arena is linked to power, the smaller the share of women.

Despite the growing awareness of these issues and increased gender equality interventions, these features are persistent today (Caprile et al. 2012; Husu 2001; Massachusetts Institute of Technology 1999). Even with the feminisation of the career base, major gender structurings, discriminations, and biases still exist throughout the educational, schooling, and student experience: for example, bias in student evaluations of teachers (MacNell et al. 2015; Moss-Racusin et al. 2012).

Academic professions are characterised by comparable processes in relation to and in intersection with other social divisions, such as age and racialisation. This becomes especially clear when locating professions in international, comparative, and transnational contexts. In some post-socialist countries, and also in Turkey, there is a significantly higher proportion of women in the university professoriate and STEM research than in some Western Europe countries (European Commission 2016). Indeed, much of the historical development of professions has been influenced by processes of imperialism and colonialism, for example, in the Anglophone world, professions have historically been more often white and educated in the metropole(s) (for example, Johnson 1972; Annisette 2000). More recently, some professions, notably medicine, have become more diversified by ethnicity and skin colour, whilst at the same time Black and minority ethnic professionals often continue to face discrimination and barriers to hierarchical advancement (Saggar et al. 2016).

A clearly important aspect of intersectional analysis in considering early career development of academics and researchers is age, and what we call age–gender relations. Mirroring the gender divisions, typical aged features of academic organisations and professions include the following: aged divisions of hierarchy, authority, and resources (often with those of older academic age being more powerful); aged divisions of labour (younger research assistants or casualised teachers working for older project leaders and professors); aged relations of care and related responsibilities (interlinking generation, gender, and career); aged processes between centres/margins (between and within disciplines); aged cultures and careers (that may reproduce or subvert [sex-]ageism); aged organi-sational/bodily/sexual processes (combining formality, informality, and intense emotional dynamics); and aged interactions, mental work, sym-bols, images, and forms of consciousness. These patterns typically favour older people and older men, especially older white men (depending on national, regional, and cultural contexts), while older women may be subject to gendered ageism.

The age–gender structure of European academia has been mapped by the European Commission's gender and science compilation, *She Figures:*

> There appears to be a generational effect whereby women research-ers are more likely than men to be found in the youngest age groups (in all countries except Latvia), whilst the opposite is observed in the oldest age groups. . . . In 2009, in all countries, a higher per-centage of the population of women researchers was concentrated in the under-35 category as compared to men researchers. . . . in 2012, this situation generally holds, although in Latvia the reverse is true, meaning men are more likely to work in the <35 age cat-egory compared to women. Unlike in 2009, in 2012 women were also more likely than men to be in the 35–44 years category, in all countries except Cyprus. However, in most countries men are more likely than women to be found in the 45–54 years category, with the largest difference being found in Cyprus. . . (7.3 percentage points). Furthermore, in all countries the proportion of men in the 55+ age group was higher than the proportion of women. The largest differ-ences in this age group are found in Poland and Romania, where the proportion of men exceeds that of women by 14.8 and 13.1 percent-age points respectively.
>
> (European Commission 2016: 77)

The normalised age–gender structure of academic organisations is reinforced by the structure of education and knowledge formation in universities and age–gender structures of science. Universities are slow to change, especially at the senior levels. A more fixed layer of senior academics and professors, mainly men, inhabit the same organisations as shifting, temporary populations of women and men members. Such insti-tutionalisations of hierarchical age, gender, and indeed sexual dynamics provide opportunities for both women and men to conform, and occa-sionally to subvert.

> Striking gender inequalities persist when it comes to career advance-ment and participation in academic decision-making. . . . In 2013, women made up only 21 % of the top-level researchers in Europe (grade A), showing very limited progress compared to 2010 (20 %). Despite significant progress in their level of education relative to men

over the last few decades, women are increasingly under-represented as they move up the stages of an academic career. At grade C level, the difference with men stands at 10 percentage points, while at grade A level it reaches 58 percentage points. This effect is even more pronounced in the field of science and engineering, where women represented only 13 % of grade A staff in 2013. A generational effect exists amongst grade A researchers, in that women tend to occupy a higher proportion of positions in the youngest age group (49 %) relative to the older age groups (22 %).

(European Commission 2016: 6)

Overall, this situation brings a heavy correlation between being male, being older, and being in a higher position in the academic hierarchy: if one is male, one is more likely to be older and higher in academic hierarchy; if one is older, one is more likely to be male and higher in the academic hierarchy; and, if one is higher in the academic hierarchy, one is more likely to be male and older. In this situation, a key issue for professional development and advancement is: which women do men sponsor?

Having said that, there are two major qualifications to these broad patterns. First, there is an absolute or relative cut-off and/or decline in power with older age—more so for women, but also for men. Indeed, there is sometimes a favouring of or an advantage granted to younger scholars (especially men), in terms of potential 'new blood' appointments (as some UK appointments were earlier labelled) and less expensive hirings. Such age processes are also often gendered, with far more 'young men in a hurry' than 'young women in a hurry' appointed to senior positions, even professorships, at a relatively young age. Younger women academics are still more likely to be referred to as 'girls' or mistaken as secretaries. Second, in some countries there have been some relative changes in recent decades in gender structure, especially in middle management, and lower and middle academic ranks. With greater numbers of women academics in the work environment, men who do rise up the ranks may consider this is even more dependent on their own ability than was experienced previously.

Having charted some of the complex historical, gendered, aged contexts of academia and research, we now focus on early career academics and researchers more specifically. We highlight three main sets of data and development: experiences and empirical research, resources, and policy development.

The Plight of Early Career Academics and Researchers: Experiences and Survey Research

A particularly important aspect is the long time span of entry and early career, and increasingly, the lack or scarcity of permanent professional positions. The entry phase can include bachelors, masters, doctoral, and postdoctoral studies—sometimes more than one postgraduate qualification—as well as teaching and supervisory qualifications and experience, participation in research projects, and extensive publications, all of which are increasingly subject to specified evaluative criteria. All of these may take between 10 and 30 years, and even then, for many there is no guarantee of a permanent tenured professional job in either academic or professional organisations.

There is now a rather well-developed literature on the first-hand experiences of early career academics and researchers. These also include reports of exclusion, marginalisation, and discrimination, especially of women, Black and/or minority ethnic, and working-class students, academics, and researchers (for example, Byrne 2015; Käyhkö 2015; Mirza 1995, 2014/2015; Reay et al. 2009; Silverstein 1977). Many early career female academics navigate simultaneously between career demands and starting a family; the discrimination they experience in academia may be both work related and family related (Husu 2005). Additionally, there is the plight of the older, non-tenured academic who remains in an 'early career' phase (see Associations of Departments of English/Association of Departments of Foreign Languages 2013, especially Weinbaum 2013).

Academic precarity can mean temporary, casualised, hourly paid, and short-term contracts in teaching and research, sometimes in more than one institution. The UK university union 'UCU estimates that most UK higher education institutions use hourly paid teachers for between 15 and 40 per cent of their teaching, with an average of 27 per cent' (Inge 2018). Insecurity and vulnerability in early career is not limited to the doctoral phase, but for many continues during the postdoctoral years, often with complex (inter)national career movements that are disruptive of personal and family life. These conditions do not only concern early career academics, as examined by Preston (2004) and discussed by Caprile et al. (2012: 91):

> One of the few comprehensive studies about leavers is that of Preston (2004), who surveyed about 1,700 scientists (not including social scientists) and engineers in the US. Her study confirms that women leave science careers in greater numbers than men . . . withdrawal from the scientific career by a person who has finished their doctorate forms part of the possible risks that exist in an academic career and quite often it is a frustrating situation in which it is difficult to distinguish empirically the 'push' and 'pull' effect. However, the study provides evidence of both types of factors, as well as of certain gender differences in the reasons portrayed: men complain more about low salaries and the lack of promotion perspectives, while women refer to a more complex set of reasons, including difficulties in balancing work and family life and a women-unfriendly environment.

204 Jeff Hearn and Liisa Husu

In this situation, some very established academics may also choose to leave or be forced to leave (see Caprile et al. 2012: 189; Husu 2001). Even very well recognised academics and researchers may remain on temporary contracts all their working life, or gain a permanent position only in their later career. Empirical studies indicate gender bias in recruitment of students and researchers (Moss-Racusin et al. 2012), as well as further bias in assessing evidence on gender bias itself (Handley et al. 2015). Career entry and early careers of academics and researchers have to be placed into this aged–gendered hierarchical context.

More specifically, both the doctoral and postdoctoral phases are crucial for early careers in academia. Some of the most detailed data on the former phase is from Sweden, where the experiences of doctoral students have been monitored by three extensive national surveys in 2003, 2008, and 2016 (Högskoleverket 2003, 2008; University Chancellor's Office 2016). Sweden is a country with high overall gender equality, as well as advanced provisions for childcare and parenting, but nonetheless high levels of gender segregation in education and working life (see, for example, World Economic Forum 2017). Women make up nearly half of Swedish doctoral students, with a clear male majority in natural sciences and technology, but a female majority in other disciplinary fields (Swedish Higher Education Authority 2018). Drawing from the most recent survey of doctoral researchers in Sweden in 2016, the majority of Swedish doctoral students rated their doctoral education as overall as 'good' (64%) or 'very good' (22%) (UKÄ 2016). However, gender differences were found to be related to health, stress, parenthood, discrimination, sexual harassment, integration in the academic environment, doctoral work, and career coaching. Most differences were in men's favour, indicating more positive and supportive doctoral educational environments for men than for women. When asked whether they would choose to take on doctoral studies again, 13% of men but 16% of women responded 'probably not' (UKÄ 2016).

Female doctoral students in Sweden had more often been on longer sick leave (beyond two weeks) and had been working when ill more often than men. Women also reported more stress and pressure with negative effects than men. Sweden has among the most generous provisions for work–life balance, including parental leave provisions for both parents, and the system allows doctoral students to take time off for parental leave and return to their studies. Female doctoral students had under 18-year-old children more frequently than their male counterparts; interestingly, male doctoral students more often reported that parental leave was accepted in their work environment to a high or very high degree. Discrimination experiences among female doctoral students were related to both gender and age, whereas their male peers reported more discrimination related to ethnicity and religion. Women reported more frequent sexual harassment by teaching staff, supervisors, other doctoral students, and/or administrative staff than men did; the figures are, however, low (UKÄ 2016). It should be noted that the survey was conducted before #MeToo discussions highlighting sexual harassment experiences in Sweden in numerous sectors, including academia.

Regarding doctoral supervision, gendered patterns included men having most often male supervisors and co-supervisors, women (more often than men) having female supervisors and co-supervisors. Male doctoral students reported receiving more supervision hours than their female counterparts. More female than male doctoral students had made an initiative to change their supervisors. Men reported that they experience their institutional milieu as creative, and feel like accepted members in their research community, more often than women. Men reported more career support from their institution, for a career inside or outside of academia; women reported being worried about possible unemployment after the doctorate more than men. The survey results in aggregate suggest female doctoral students feel less integrated and accepted in their academic environments, which doubtless has relevance for their career prospects and aspirations, as well as general well-being (UKÄ 2016).

Resources for Early Career Academics and Researchers

In part as a response to structural conditions, a spate of books, articles, blogs, webfora, and other collective resources on early careers have appeared over the last 20 years or more. A genre of self-help books or guidebooks advising how to navigate or survive in academia has emerged since the 1990s. More recently, this genre has developed into subgenres aimed at women academics, and then younger women academics, postdoctoral, and doctoral researchers. Many of these have a feminist orientation rather than adopting a 'lean in' (Sandberg 2014) approach advising women how to fit in. In some ways, this genre mirrors the much earlier 'how-to' books in business and management that later shifted into 'how to get on' for women in those fields. Such texts, whether directed to business or academia, tread a thin line between, on the one hand, sharing information in a democratic and empowering mode, and on the other hand, reinforcing not just individual instrumentalism but dominant organisational cultures, hierarchies, and power relations without challenging them.

An early German roadmap for women guiding them on how to work within the patriarchal higher education system was *Uni-Knigge für Frauen: Wegweiser durch den patriarchalischen Hochschuldschungel* [*University Etiquette for Women: A Roadmap Through the Patriarchal*

Higher Education Jungle] (Katz and Vieland 1993). An important contribution to this literature is Diana Leonard's (2001) very thorough *A Woman's Guide to Doctoral Studies*, which draws on solid gender research expertise and a sober feminist approach. It gives women practical advice for different stages of the doctoral process, stressing the importance of 'understanding the rules of the game', discussing the chilly climate, sexual harassment and violations, intimate relations between staff and students, and 'how to access work on gender if your supervisor doesn't know what he (or she) doesn't know'. Advice for the postdoctoral phase is the focus of the Swedish book *Efter festen [After the Party]*, subtitled 'A survival guide for postdoctoral existence' (Eldén and Jonsson 2014). This book advises on many basic academic skills in a gender-neutral way, including in relation to gender equality and the complex gendered dynamics of academia, suggesting ways academics can act for change (Husu 2014). A recent collection on and for feminist early career academics presents reflective accounts of the postdoctoral and lecturer experience, but surprisingly not the doctoral phase (Thwaites and Pressland 2017).

Policy Development on Early Career Researchers and Academics

In many countries there is increasing awareness and policy development focusing on the entry level in academic careers, including the doctoral and postdoctoral levels: for example, by the network of research-intensive European universities, LERU (League of European Research Universities) and EPWS (European Platform of Women Scientists), by disciplinary field organisations, such as EMBO (European Molecular Biology Organisation), and by leading research funders, such as the European Research Council. Many national, and some international, research funders earmark funding for early career researchers: for example, in the three- or five-year postdoctoral period. These policy developments are crucial for understanding the current age–gender relations of early careers.

A key policy development was the European Commission's adoption in 2005 of the *European Charter for Researchers* and the *Code of Conduct for the Recruitment of Researchers*. These two documents, addressing researchers as well as research employers and funders in both the public and private sectors, are key elements in the EU's policy to boost researchers' careers. By August 2018, 1,040 organisations had endorsed the principles of the *European Charter for Researchers* and *the Code for the Recruitment of Researchers* (2005). The *European Charter for Researchers* is a set of general principles and requirements specifying roles, responsibilities, and entitlements of researchers, employers, and research funders (see Box 1).

Box 11.1 *European Charter for Researchers* and *Code of Conduct for Recruitment of Researchers* specify that employers and/or funders should do the following.

- Aim for gender balance at all staff levels, including the supervisory and managerial levels. Selection and evaluation committees should have an adequate gender balance.
- Draw up a specific career development strategy for researchers at all career stages, regardless of contractual situation, including those on fixed-term contracts. It should include the availability of mentors involved in providing support and guidance for personal and professional development of researchers, motivating them, and contributing to reducing insecurity in their professional future. All researchers should be made familiar with such provisions.
- Ensure career advice and job placement assistance, in the institutions concerned, or through collaboration with other structures, is offered to researchers at all stages of their careers, regardless of contractual situation.
- Ensure that a person is clearly identified to whom early stage researchers can refer to for performance of their professional duties. Such arrangements should clearly define that proposed supervisors are sufficiently expert in supervising research, have the time, knowledge, experience, expertise, and commitment to offer the research trainee appropriate support and provide for necessary progress and review procedures, as well as necessary feedback mechanisms.
- Ensure entry and admission standards for researchers, particularly at the beginning of careers, are clearly specified and facilitate access for disadvantaged groups or researchers and teachers returning to a research career.

The *Charter* and the *Code* include numerous references to how early career researchers should be treated and supported. Employers should also aim to provide working conditions to allow both women and men researchers to combine family and work, children and career. Particular attention should be paid, *inter alia*, to flexible working hours, part-time working, teleworking, and sabbatical leave, as well as necessary financial and administrative provisions.

Contemporary Reflections

In this chapter we have discussed experiential accounts, empirical studies, developing resources, and policy developments on and about aged–gendered early careers in academia and research. The long extended career entry phase in academia, with its built-in insecurity, is in contemporary contexts complicated further with moves to greater regulation and monitoring of university research and teaching, financialisation and neoliberalisation of academia, and increasing competition for research funding. In some universities, there are direct financial rewards for research funding success and publishing in, for example, journals whose impact factor is more than 1.0; such rewards may influence career decisions on short-term financial grounds, especially for early career academics.

In many parts of the world there is a significant narrowing of the criteria for academic appointment and promotion, with greater surveillance of teaching, and greater value placed on student evaluation and publication in high-ranking and high-impact English language journals with low acceptance rates—even to the extent that such articles can count for more than a whole book with a prestigious international publisher. These moves increase pressures on early career academics and researchers, especially those in universities, to mould their careers accordingly, often away from teaching, professional development, pastoral care, outreach, and promotion of societal impact. Increasingly, early academic careers necessitate very complex planning and decision-making, including around personal and family life, and (inter)national movements and migrations.

Importantly, even with the 'feminisation' of academia—specially numerically at the student and lower academic levels—gender dominance, principally of men of middle and older years, persists, with the caveat that ageism against older people also continues, especially for women, but also for some men too. Thus to understand the situation of early career academics one must consider the wider contexts of ageism, sexism, and age–gender relations, both societally and within specific organisations, professions, and disciplines. Taking all of these factors into account sheds light on the broader relations of age, gender, power, and professions at a time of their restructuring and reconfiguration in many arenas.

References

Adams, A and Tancred, P (2000) *Designing Women: Gender and the Architectural Profession*, (Toronto, University of Toronto Press).

Annisette, M (2000) 'Imperialism and the Professions: The Education and Certification of Accountants in Trinidad and Tobago' 25 *Accounting, Organizations and Society* 631.

Associations of Departments of English [ADE]/Association of Departments of Foreign Languages [ADFL] (2013) *Non-Tenure-Track Faculty Members in*

English and the Other Modern Languages: Issues and Directions (ADE Bulletin 153, ADFL 42.3).

Barak, B and Schiffman, LG (1981) 'Cognitive Age: A Nonchronological Age Variable' in KB Monroe (ed) *Advances in Consumer Research* 8 (Ann Arbor: Association for Consumer Research), 602–606.

Blackwell, E and Blackwell, E (1860) *Medicine as a Profession for Women* (New York, New York Infirmary for Women).

Boni-Le Goff, I and Le Feuvre, N (2017) 'Professions from a Gendered Perspective' *Oxford Research Encyclopedia of Business and Management*. doi:10.1093/acrefore/9780190224851.013.89.

Breckinridge, SP (1933) *Women in the Twentieth Century: A Study of their Political, Social and Economic Activities* (New York, McGraw-Hill).

Britton, DM (2017) 'Beyond the Chilly Climate: The Salience of Gender in Women's Academic Careers' 31 *Gender & Society* 5.

Byrne, G (2015) 'Coming to Terms with Being a Working Class Academic' *Sociology Lens* 22 22 April 2015, updated 12 April 2017. www.sociologylens.net/article-types/opinion/coming-to-terms-with-being-working-a-working-class-academic/14799

Caprile, M, Addis, E, Castaño, C, Klinge, I, Larios, M, Meulders, D, Müller, J, O'Dorchai, S, Palasik, M, Plasman, R, Roivas, S, Sagebiel, F, Schiebinger, L, Vallès, N and Vázquez-Cupeiro, S (eds) (2012) *Meta-analysis of Gender and Science Research* (Luxembourg, Publications Office of the European Union), 91, 189. doi:10.2777/75176

Cockburn, CK (1991) *In the Way of Women: Men's Resistance to Sex Equality in Organisations* (London, Palgrave Macmillan).

Chung, K-T (2010) *Women Pioneers of Medical Research* (Jefferson, NC, McFarland).

Czarniawska, B and Sevón, G (2008) 'The Thin End of the Wedge: Foreign Women Professors as Double Strangers in Academia' 15 *Gender, Work & Organization* 235. doi:10.1111/j.1468-0432.2008.00392.x.

Eldén, S and Jonsson, A (eds) (2014) *Efter festen: Om konsten att utvecklas från doktor till docent eller en överlevnadsguide för den postdoktorala tillvaron* [*After the party: On the skill to develop from doctor to docent or a survival guide for postdoctoral existence*] (Lund, Studentlitteratur AB).

The European Charter for Researchers & the Code for the Recruitment of Researchers (2005) 25 August 2018. https://euraxess.ec.europa.eu/jobs/charter

European Commission (2016) *She Figures 2015* (Luxembourg, Publications Office of the European Union), 6, 77. doi:10.2777/744106

Haavio-Mannila, E (1975) *Sex Roles Among Physicians and Dentists in Scandinavia* (Helsinki, University of Helsinki Institute of Sociology, Research Report 206).

Handley, IM, Brown, ER, Moss-Racusin, CA and Smith, JL (2015) 'Quality of Evidence Revealing Subtle Gender Biases in Science is in the Eye of the Beholder' 112 *Proceedings of the National Academy of Sciences of the United States of America* 13201. doi:10.1073/pnas.1510649112.

Hearn, J, Biese, I, Choroszewicz, M and Husu, L (2016) 'Gender, Diversity and Intersectionality in Professions and Potential Professions: Analytical, Historical and Contemporary Perspectives' in M Dent, IL Bourgeault, J-L Denis and

210 *Jeff Hearn and Liisa Husu*

E Kuhlmann (eds), *The Routledge Companion to the Professions and Professionalism* (London, Routledge).

Hearn, J and Husu, L (2011) 'Understanding Gender: Some Implications for Science and Technology' 36 *Interdisciplinary Science Reviews* 103.

Högskoleverket [HSV] (2003) 'Doktorandspegeln 2003 [The Doctoral Mirror 2003]' (HSV Rapport 2003: 28 R).

——— (2008) 'Doktorandspegeln 2008 [The Doctoral Mirror 2008]' (HSV Rapport 2008: 23 R).

Husu, L (2001) *Sexism, Support and Survival in Academia: Academic Women and Hidden Discrimination in Finland* (Helsinki, University of Helsinki), 33.

——— (2005) 'Women's Work-Related and Family-Related Discrimination and Support in Academia' in MT Segal and V Demos (eds), *Gender Realities: Local and Global* (Amsterdam, Elsevier JAI).

——— (2014) 'Att verka på lika villkor i akademin—om jämställdhet och likebehandling' ['To Act on an Equal Footing in Academic—On Gender Equality and Equal Opportunities'] in S Eldén and A Jonsson (eds), *Efter festen: Om konsten att utvecklas från doktor till docent eller en överlevnadsguide för den postdoktorala tillvaron* [*After the Party: On the Skill to Develop from Doctor to Docent or a Survival Guide for Postdoctoral Existence*] (Lund, Studentlitteratur AB).

Inge, S (2018) 'UK Universities Rely on Casual Staff "for up to half of teaching"' *Times Higher Education* 6 March 2018. www.timeshighereducation.com/news/uk-universities-rely-casual-staff-half-teaching

Johnson, T (1972) 'Imperialism and the Professions: Notes on the Development of Professional Occupations in Britain's Colonies and the New States' 20 *The Sociological Review* 281. doi:https://doi.org/10.1111/j.1467-954X.1972.tb03222.x

Katz, M and Vieland, V (1993) *Uni-Knigge für Frauen. Wegweiser durch den patriarchalischen Hochschuldschungel* [*University Etiquette for Women: A Roadmap Through the Patriarchal Higher Education Jungle*] (Frankfurt am Main, Campus Verlag GmbH).

Käyhkö, M (2015) 'Working-Class Girls in a Foreign Land: Social Class and Settling into University in a Cross-current between Two Cultures' 27 *Gender and Education* 445. doi:10.1080/09540253.2015.1028900.

Leonard, D (2001) *A Woman's Guide to Doctoral Studies* (Buckingham, Open University Press).

Lofstedt, J (2003) 'Gender and Veterinary Medicine' 44 *The Canadian Veterinary Journal* 533.

MacNell, L, Driscoll, A and Hunt, AN (2015) 'What's in a Name: Exposing Gender Bias in Student Ratings of Teaching' 40 *Innovative Higher Education* 291. doi:10.1007/s10755-014-9313-4.

Massachusetts Institute of Technology [MIT] (1999) *A Study on the Status of Women Faculty in Science at MIT* (Committee on Women Faculty in the School of Science, MIT). www.web.mit.edu/fnl/women/women.pdf

Mirza, HS (1995) 'Black Women in Higher Education: Defining a Space/Finding a Place' in L Morley and V Walsh (eds), *Feminist Academics: Creative Agents for Change* (London, Taylor and Francis).

——— (2014/2015) 'Decolonizing Higher Education: Black Feminism and the Intersectionality of Race and Gender' 7/8 *Journal of Feminist Scholarship* 1.

Moss-Racusin, CA, Dovidio, JF, Brescoll, VL, Graham, MJ and Handelsman, J (2012) 'Science Faculty's Subtle Gender Biases Favor Male Students' 109 *Proceedings of the National Academy of Sciences of the United States of America* 16474.

Pierce, JL (1995) *Gender Trials: Emotional Lives in Contemporary Law Firms* (Berkeley, University of California Press).

Preston, AE (2004) *Leaving Science: Occupational Exit from Scientific Careers* (New York, Russell Sage Foundation).

Reay, D, Crozier, G and Clayton, J (2009) ' "Strangers in Paradise?" Working-class Students in Elite 43 Universities' *Sociology* 1103. doi:10.1177/0038038509345700

Riska, E (1998) '*Further Rationalization* of Medicine: The Reconfiguration of the *Medical* Profession' 15 *Research in the Sociology of Health Care* 111.

—— (2014) 'Gender and the Professions' in WC Cockerham, R Dingwall and SR Quah (eds), *The Wiley Blackwell Encyclopedia of Health, Illness, Behavior, and Society* (Chichester, West Sussex: Wiley-Blackwell). doi:10.1002/9781118410868.wbehibs007

Rossiter, MW (1982) *Women Scientists in America: Struggles and Strategies to 1940* (Baltimore, MD, John Hopkins University Press).

Saggar, S, Norrie, R, Bannister, M and Goodhart, D (2016) *Bittersweet Success: Glass Ceilings for Britain's Ethnic Minorities at the Top of Business and the Professions* (London, Policy Exchange).

Sandberg, S (2014) *Lean In: For Graduates* (New York, Alfred A. Knopf).

Schiebinger, L (1999) *Has Feminism Changed Science?* (Cambridge, MA, Harvard University Press).

Silverstein, M (1977) 'The History of a Short, Unsuccessful Academic Career (with a postscript update)' in J Snodgrass (ed), *A Book of Readings for Men Against Sexism* (Albion, CA, Times Change Press).

Sjöberg, A (1964) *Euroopan ensimmäinen naiseläinlääkäri* [*The First European Woman Veterinary Surgeon*] (Vaasa, Vaasan kirjapaino; reprinted 2000, Helsinki, Lasipalatsi).

Stolte-Heiskanen, V (1991) 'Handmaidens of the "Knowledge Class": Women in Science in Finland' in V Stolte-Heiskanen and R Fürst-Dilić (eds), *Women in Science: Token Women or Gender Equality?* (Oxford, Berg).

Summers, L (2005) 'Harvard President Summers' Remarks About Women in Science, Engineering'. www.pbs.org/newshour/science/science-jan-june05-summersremarks_2-22

Swedish Higher Education Authority (2018) *Higher Education in Sweden 2018 Status Report* (Swedish Higher Education Authority Report 10).

Thwaites, R and Pressland, A (eds) (2017) *Being an Early Career Feminist Academic: Global Perspectives, Experiences and Challenges* (London, Palgrave Macmillan).

Twigg, J and Martin, W (eds) (2015) *The Routledge Handbook of Cultural Gerontology* (London, Routledge).

UNESCO (2015) *Women in Science* (UNESCO Institute of Statistics). unesdoc.unesco.org/images/0023/002351/235155E.pdf

University Chancellor's Office [UKÄ] (2016) 'Doktorandspegeln 2016. En enkät om studenternas studiesituation [The Doctoral Mirror 2016: A Survey on Students' Study Situation]'. (UKÄ Rapport 2016), 18.

Webster, J and Randle, K (eds) (2016) *Virtual Workers and the Global Labour Market* (London, Palgrave Macmillan).

Weinbaum, B (2013) *Expropriation of the Professoriat: View of an Untenured Radical* (Associations of Departments of English Bulletin 153/Association of Departments of Foreign Languages 42.3). www.ade.mla.org/content/download/7945/225708

Witz, A (1992) *Professions and Patriarchy* (London, Routledge).

World Economic Forum (2017) *The Global Gender Gap Report 2017* (Geneva, World Economic Forum).

12 A Young Man's Game
Age and Gender in Technology Jobs

Christianne Corbett

Introduction

Much has been made of the differences between Americans born after 1980, identified as members of the Millennial generation or 'Millennials', and those who came before them (Fry et al. 2018; Lebowitz 2018). In answer to the question of whether Millennials are really that different, a recent report states: 'The answer is yes—profoundly so. Millennials will change the world more decisively than any other generation. . . . Millennials are altering the very social fabric of America and the world' (Gallup 2016: 2). Compared to previous generations, young adult Millennials are more educated, marry and have children later, carry more student debt, and are more likely to be living with their parents. Millennial women are more likely to be in the labour force compared to previous generations of women at the same life stage (Vespa 2017), and Millennials have a reputation for requiring stimulating work and workplace flexibility, leaving their jobs if these elements are missing (Finn and Donovan 2013). Indeed, a 2016 survey of U.S. workers found that Millennials were more likely than members of other generations to change jobs and to look for the 'opportunity to learn and grow' through their work, ranking this as the most important factor when they consider applying for a job (Gallup 2016).

The field of high technology came of age in tandem with the Millennial generation. With the widespread use of the internet starting in the early to mid-1990s, many Millennials learned to use technology as young children, developing a familiarity with technology earlier in life than previous generations. Although technology workers are found throughout the economy and in nearly every professional workplace, they are often associated with jobs in technology startups or dedicated technology companies. These jobs are known for providing stimulation—often both in terms of work tasks and the social/physical environment (think free cafeterias, ping pong tables, and happy hours)—as well as flexible work arrangements. Given the traits associated with the Millennial generation, technology jobs seem tailor-made for them. Indeed, one international study concluded that small to mid-sized information technology (IT) firms are staffed primarily by men under the age of 35, and workers age 40 and over are widely viewed as past their prime and possessing technological knowledge that is out of date (McMullin 2011).

It is important to note that this study found that IT firms are staffed primarily by *men* and not *people* under age 35. Scholars have written for decades about the embedded masculinity in many technology workplaces (Britton 2000; Demaiter and Adams 2009; Peterson 2007; Peterson 2010; Wright 1996). As Acker (1990) argued, women are marginalised in most organisations because masculinity is incorporated into most organisational processes. Because technology organisations are more male-dominated than most others, one might expect that women would be even more marginalised in technology than in many other industries, and there are a number of indicators that this is the case. A longitudinal study found that women working in science, technology, engineering, and mathematics (STEM) fields—primarily engineering and technology jobs—are more likely to leave their jobs, compared to women working in other types of professional jobs (Glass et al. 2013). A survey of mid-level scientists and engineers in high-tech companies found that women are more likely than men to suffer poor health and to delay or forgo getting married and having children as a result of work demands (Simard et al. 2008). Other research has found that women are less likely to work in STEM occupations than men with comparable educational credentials (Xie and Shauman 2003) and are more likely than men to leave STEM jobs, and engineering jobs in particular (Frehill 2012; Hewlett et al. 2008; Hunt 2016; Preston 1994, 2004). Over the past few years, harassing and discriminating cultures in technology companies have been exposed and highlighted in the mainstream media, leading to outcomes such as anti-harassment initiatives and high-level resignations, including that of Uber's founder and former CEO and a number of high-profile venture capitalists (Isaac 2017; Benner 2017).

Despite the fact that technology jobs have been described as best suited to younger workers and also to men, few studies have looked at the ways in which age and gender interact to influence workers' experiences in technology jobs. Do younger men and women report more positive experiences than their older counterparts? As the current literature suggests, do younger men report the most positive experiences in technology jobs while older women report the least positive experiences? Perhaps most importantly, are gender disparities narrower among younger technology workers than among older technology workers, suggesting that conditions are improving for women in technology jobs? This chapter explores these questions.

Hypotheses

Based on previous research, this chapter proposes and tests the following hypotheses:

H1. Among technology workers, Millennials report more positive work experiences than Generation X/Baby Boomers do.

H2. Overall, and within generations, women report more negative workplace experiences in technology jobs compared to their counterparts who are men.

H3. Among technology workers, younger men report the most positive workplace experiences.

H4. Among technology workers, older women report the least positive workplace experiences.

H5. Gender disparities in technology workplace experiences are not lessening among younger workers compared to older workers.

Defining Generations

In 2015, the U.S. adult population under age 70 was divided roughly evenly into three generations: the Millennial generation, born after 1980 (age 18–34); Generation X, born between 1965 and 1980 (age 35–50); and Baby Boomers, born between 1946 and 1964 (age 51–69) (Pew Research Center 2015). These parameters define the generations in the background descriptive analyses of individuals in the U.S. with highest degrees in computer science/mathematics using the National Survey of College Graduates. In the main analyses of the Tech Workplace Experience Survey, the Millennial generation includes respondents born after 1981 (under age 35 in 2016), and Generation X/Baby Boomers includes respondents born in 1981 or earlier (age 35 and older in 2016).

Population

The population of interest for this study is the population of technology workers in the U.S. Unfortunately, a nationally representative survey of U.S. technology workers does not exist. However, an analysis of U.S. Census Bureau American Community Survey data (U.S. Census Bureau 2011, 2013) estimates that approximately one-third of U.S. technology workers have a bachelor's degree or higher in a technical field like computer science. Another one-third have bachelor's degrees or higher in other fields like business or the social sciences, and the remainder have less than a bachelor's degree (Corbett and Hill 2015). Because technology workers with computer science degrees tend to fill the highest-status positions in technology workplaces, the demographics of this group shape the overall technology sector. As a result, understanding the demographics of those individuals whose highest degree is in computer science, by generation, is a useful basis for understanding the population of technology workers overall, by generation.

Individuals With Computer Science Degrees

Table 12.1 presents nationally representative statistics about the population of college graduates whose highest degree is in computer science or mathematics, using the 2015 National Survey of College Graduates, disaggregated by gender and generation. In 2015, women made up just under one-third (31%) of individuals in the U.S. whose highest degree was in computer science or mathematics, and this percentage did not vary significantly across generations, which is consistent with other reports (National Center for Science and Engineering Statistics 2017). Millennials were less likely than older respondents to have advanced degrees, with 28% of Millennials holding a master's or doctoral degree, compared to 40% among Baby Boomers, but this may be because Millennials have yet to obtain graduate degrees. Women and men are largely similar in their educational attainment levels in computer science/mathematics, with the one exception of Baby Boomer men, who are more likely than women in their age group to hold a PhD.

Among individuals whose highest degrees are in computer science/ mathematics, Millennials are more racially and ethnically diverse than previous generations, and this is especially true among women. Among Baby Boomers, 80% of men and 75% of women whose highest degrees are in computer science/mathematics are white, but among Millennials with those credentials, just 54% of men and 41% of women are white. The bulk of this increase in diversity is due to higher percentages of Asian Americans among the younger population. The proportion of Hispanic and multiracial men has grown too, although the representation of African Americans has remained steady at around 7%.

Millennials with highest degrees in computer science/mathematics are very likely (92%)—and just as likely as members of Generation X—to be in the labour force. Millennials in this population are significantly less likely than members of Generation X to have children living at home, especially Millennial men (23% of Millennial men, compared to 71% of Generation X men have children at home) (see Table 12.1). This is not surprising given that Americans are having children later, and many Millennials are under the average age of first childbirth in the U.S., which in recent years has risen to 28 years among women and 31 years among men (Khandwala et al. 2017; Mathews and Hamilton 2016).

Table 12.1 Selected characteristics of individuals with highest degree in computer science/mathematics, 2015, by generation and gender

	All Generations				Millennial (39%)			
	Overall	Men 69%	Women 31%	Gender Difference	Overall	Men 72%	Women 28%	Gender Difference
Highest degree level								
% Bachelor's	65	65	66	n.s.	72	72	72	n.s.
% Master's	31	31	31	n.s.	26	26	26	n.s.
% PhD	4	4	3	n.s.	2	2	2	n.s.
Race/Ethnicity								
% White	63	66	57	***	50	54	41	*
% Asian	22	20	28	***	32	28	44	**
% Hispanic	6	6	7	n.s.	8	8	9	n.s.
% African American	7	7	7	n.s.	7	7	6	n.s.
% Multiple race	2	2	1	*	3	3	1	*
% Native Hawaiian/Other Pacific Islander	0.3	0.4	0.04	n.s.	0.1	0.1	0.1	n.s.
% American Indian/Alaska Native	0.1	0.1	0.03	n.s.	0.04	0.04	0.03	n.s.
% Have children living at home	48	47	51	n.s.	27	23	38	**
Average age (years)	45	44	45	n.s.	29	29	29	n.s.
% In labour force	85	88	76	***	92	96	82	**
% Full-time	74	79	62	***	80	85	67	**
% Part-time	8	6	12	**	9	8	13	n.s.
% Unemployed	3	3	3	n.s.	3	3	1	n.s.
Unweighted N	7,419	4,886	2,533		2,890	1,992	898	
Weighted N	2,878,873	1,976,242	902,631		775,908	557,073	218,835	

(Continued)

Table 12.1 (Continued)

	Generation X (32%)				Baby Boomer (29%)				Overall Millennial–Generation X Difference	Overall Millennial–Boomer Difference
	Overall	Men 68%	Women 32%	Gender Difference	Overall	Men 67%	Women 33%	Gender Difference		
Highest degree level										
% Bachelor's	66	66	64	n.s.	60	57	65	*	*	***
% Master's	31	30	33	n.s.	35	36	32	n.s.	*	**
% PhD	3	4	3	n.s.	5	6	3	**	n.s.	***
Race/Ethnicity										
% White	59	63	50	**	78	80	75	n.s.	*	***
% Asian	25	23	31	*	11	9	13	n.s.	*	***
% Hispanic	7	6	9	n.s.	4	3	5	n.s.	n.s.	***
% African American	7	6	9	n.s.	6	7	6	n.s.	n.s.	n.s.
% Multiple race	1	2	1	n.s.	1	1	1	n.s.	n.s.	*
% Native Hawaiian/Other Pacific Islander	1	1	0.01	n.s.	0.03	0.03	0.05	n.s.	n.s.	n.s.
% American Indian/Alaska Native	0.1	0.1	0.03	n.s.	0.1	0.1	0.04	n.s.	n.s.	n.s.
% Have children living at home	71	71	73	n.s.	38	38	36	n.s.	***	***
Average age (years)	43	42	43	n.s.	60	60	60	n.s.	n/a	n/a
% In labour force	92	96	83	***	70	73	65	n.s.	n.s.	***
% Full-time	84	90	71	***	57	62	47	***	n.s.	***
% Part-time	5	3	8	*	10	8	14	*	*	n.s.
% Unemployed	4	4	4	n.s.	3	3	3	n.s.	n.s.	n.s.
Unweighted N	2,353	1,505	848		2,176	1,389	787			
Weighted N	1,137,703	773,990	363,714		965,262	645,179	320,082			

Source: 2015 National Survey of College Graduates

Individuals Working Full-Time in a Job Related to Their Computer Science Degree

Women made up around 25% of individuals working full-time in a job related to their highest degree in computer science/mathematics in 2015, and this percentage is constant across the three generations. As one would expect, Millennials earn less than Generation X members and Baby Boomers in this group, presumably because they are not as far along in their careers (see Table 12.2). Millennials stand apart from previous generations in that there is no statistically significant pay gap between men and women working full-time in jobs related to their computer science/mathematics degrees. Rather than an actual generational change, though, this may be due to the earlier career stage of Millennials, which is typically a time when the pay gap between men and women is smaller or nonexistent (U.S. Bureau of Labor Statistics 2017). Among members of Generation X and Baby Boomers, despite similar levels of education, age, and weekly hours worked, men reported being paid approximately $25,000 and $16,000, respectively, more per year than women ($111,238 compared to $86,135 among Generation X, and $110,521 compared to $94,250 among Baby Boomers). In a sign of potential generational change, Millennials in this group report working slightly (but significantly) fewer hours per week than older generations (43 compared to 45 average hours per week).

The data presented so far provide a basis for understanding the demographics of the portion of the population of U.S. technology workers who have at least four-year computer science degrees, many of whom occupy leading roles in the overall population of technology workers. The rest of the chapter presents an analysis of survey responses from a sample of technology workers that includes some workers with computer science degrees and some without.

Data

The 2016 Anita Borg Institute Workplace Experience Survey for Top Companies, referred to throughout this chapte as the 'Tech Workplace Experience Survey', is arguably the best dataset currently available for analysing the experiences of men and women in technology jobs. The survey was conducted by the Anita Borg Institute (now AnitaB.org), a non-profit organisation focused on women in technology, in the summer of 2016. It is based on a random sample of men and women technology employees at six companies that together employ more than 34,000 technology workers. Four of the companies are dedicated technology companies and two are not, reflecting the widespread nature of technology jobs in today's workplaces across industries. Each of these companies has more than 5,000 employees in total (technology workers and others), and has been in existence for more than 20 years. In addition, each has

Table 12.2 Salary and work hours among individuals with highest degree in computer science/mathematics working full-time in a job related to that degree, 2015, by generation and gender

	Overall	Men	Women	Gender difference	Difference From Millennials Overall	Difference From Millennials Among Men	Difference From Millennials Among Women
Average salary ($)	97,737	101,977	85,579	***			
Millennials	80,265	81,529	76,224	n.s.			
Generation X	104,528	111,238	86,135	***	***	***	*
Baby Boomers	106,178	110,521	94,250	*	***	***	*
Average hours worked (per week)	44	44	44	n.s.			
Millennials	43	44	43	n.s.			
Generation X	45	45	44	n.s.	*	n.s.	n.s.
Baby Boomers	45	45	44	n.s.	*	n.s.	n.s.
Unweighted N	5,422	3,815	1,607				
Weighted N	1,912,381	1,417,969	494,413				

Source: 2015 National Survey of College Graduates

Notes: ***$p < 0.001$; **$p < 0.01$; *$p < 0.05$ (two-tailed test). 'n.s.' means 'not significant'. Table includes respondents who indicated they work in a job 'somewhat related' or 'closely related' to their highest degree.

made a commitment to provide metrics of their technology workforce, including the representation of women at entry, mid, senior, and executive levels each year, to AnitaB.org, suggesting some level of commitment to achieving gender equity in their organisation. Because of this commitment, and because these companies are well-established organisations with human resources departments and processes for addressing discrimination claims (rather than small startup technology firms that often do not have such structures in place), the findings presented from the Tech Workplace Experience Survey may represent a better than average scenario for women in technology jobs and a conservative estimate of gender differences in technology workplace experiences.

For the Tech Workplace Experience Survey, AnitaB.org sampled either 1,000 technology employees or 20% of the technology workforce at each organisation, whichever number was higher. As much as possible, equal numbers of men and women were sampled within each company, and respondents varied in age from their early 20s to over age 65. The response rate was approximately 32%,[1] yielding a sample of 2,813 responses, divided nearly evenly between men and women: 1,477 men and 1,336 women. Because the main goal of this chapter is to understand how the experiences of Millennial men and women in technology jobs vary from the experiences of men and women of previous generations, the analysis of the Tech Workplace Experience Survey compares just two groups: Millennials, on one hand, and a combined category of Generation X/Baby Boomers, on the other hand. Around two-thirds of the sample (1,855 respondents) falls into the Generation X/Baby Boomers category and approximately one-third (958 respondents) falls into the Millennials category (see Table 12.3).

Table 12.3 Age distribution of tech worker survey respondents, by gender

Generation	Age (%)	Overall	Men (53%)	Women (47%)	Gender Difference
Millennial	Under 35	34.1	32.7	35.5	
	18–24	2.6	2.6	2.5	n.s.
	25–34	31.5	30.1	33.0	n.s.
Generation X/Baby Boomer	35+	65.3	66.5	64.1	
	35–44	26.9	27.5	26.2	n.s.
	45–54	25.6	25.6	25.7	n.s.
	55–64	12.8	13.4	12.2	n.s.
	65+	0.6	0.7	0.5	n.s.
N		2,813	1,477	1,336	

Source: 2016 Anita Borg Institute Workplace Experience Survey for Top Companies

Notes: ***$p < 0.001$; **$p < 0.01$; *$p < 0.05$ (two-tailed test). 'n.s.' means 'not significant'.

AnitaB.org used stratified sampling to include men and women workers similar in terms of age, tenure at organisation, career level, and manager status. Men and women respondents were similar in terms of age and tenure at their organisations overall and within generational categories (see Table 12.4). Respondents' tenure at their organisations varied substantially across generations, as would be expected. Over half of the sample of Millennials (59%) had spent a year or less at their organisation, compared to just 7% of Generation X/Baby Boomer respondents. In contrast, just over half of Generation X/Baby Boomer respondents (50%) had spent ten or more years at their organisation, compared to 2% of Millennial respondents. As a result, Millennial respondents are clustered in entry-level (47%) and mid-level (49%) jobs, while Generation X/Baby Boomers are concentrated in mid-level (60%) and senior-level (26%) jobs. As is often the case, women are clustered at lower job levels than men within each generation category. Women are more likely than men to be entry-level employees in both generation groups (17% of women compared to 11% of men among Generation X/Baby Boomers, and 51% of women compared to 43% of men among Millennials). At the same time, women are less likely than men to be mid-level employees among Millennials (45% compared to 52%, respectively), but among Generation X/Baby Boomers women are more likely than men to be mid-level employees (65% compared to 55%, respectively) and less likely than men to be at senior levels (18% compared to 32%, respectively). Women are also more likely than men to be managers (20% compared to 16%, respectively).

Methods

I first conducted a descriptive analysis of means by gender and generation from the Tech Workplace Experience Survey data. I distilled the 25 Tech Workplace Experience Survey items of interest into 11 underlying factors of technology workers' workplace experiences, using a principal-component factor analysis with varimax orthogonal rotation (the factor analysis results, including the 25 original survey items, are shown in Table 12A1 in the appendix). I then calculated the mean responses to each of the 11 factors for men overall and women overall and in each generational group (Millennials and Generation X/Baby Boomers), and tested whether the differences in means by gender and generation were statistically significant.

Next, I conducted a series of OLS regression analyses to explore the impact of generation and gender on workplace experiences, after adjusting for length of time at an organisation, career level, and managerial responsibilities. I ran one regression analysis with each of the 11 factor variables serving as the dependent variable. Generation and gender are the explanatory variables of interest, and organisation tenure, career

Table 12.4 Selected job characteristics of U.S. technology worker survey respondents, by generation and gender

	Overall				Millennial				Generation X/Baby Boomer			
	Overall	Men	Women	Gender Difference	Overall	Men	Women	Gender Difference	Overall	Men	Women	Gender Difference
Tenure												
% 0–6 months	16.1	15.2	17.1	n.s.	39.5	38.0	40.9	n.s.	4.1	4.1	4.1	n.s.
% 6–12 months	8.4	7.9	9.0	n.s.	19.7	19.2	20.3	n.s.	2.6	2.4	2.8	n.s.
% 1–2 years	7.7	7.6	7.9	n.s.	10.4	11.0	9.9	n.s.	6.3	5.9	6.7	n.s.
% 2–5 years	18.4	18.9	17.9	n.s.	19.4	20.7	18.1	n.s.	17.9	18.0	17.8	n.s.
% 5–10 years	15.5	16.3	14.6	n.s.	8.9	8.9	8.9	n.s.	18.9	19.8	17.8	n.s.
% 10+ years	33.8	34.1	33.5	n.s.	2.1	2.3	1.9	n.s.	50.2	49.7	50.9	n.s.
Managers	14.3	12.9	15.9	***	7.4	6.6	8.2	n.s.	17.9	15.9	20.2	*
Career Level												
% Entry	25.0	21.7	28.7	***	46.9	43.0	50.8	*	13.8	11.4	16.5	**
% Mid	56.0	54.4	57.8	n.s.	48.9	52.3	45.4	*	59.7	55.4	64.6	***
% Senior	18.5	23.3	13.2	***	4.3	4.8	3.8	n.s.	25.8	32.3	18.3	***
% Executive	0.5	0.6	0.4	n.s.	0.0	0.0	0.0	n.s.	0.75	0.9	0.6	n.s.
N	2,813	1,477	1,336		958	484	474		1,855	993	862	

Source: 2016 Anita Borg Institute Workplace Experience Survey for Top Companies

Notes: ***$p < 0.001$; **$p < 0.01$; *$p < 0.05$ (two-tailed test). 'n.s.' means 'not significant'.

level, and management responsibilities serve as control variables for each of these analyses. I then created dummy variables based on the interaction of gender and generation that identified Millennial men, Millennial women, Generation X/Baby Boomer men, and Generation X/Baby Boomer women. I ran analyses with each of the 11 factor variables serving as the dependent variable, first with Millennial men as the reference group and next with Generation X/Baby Boomer women as the reference group, and measured how other age–gender groups rated the dependent variables, compared with how the reference group rated it.

Results

Finding 1: Among Technology Workers, Millennials Report More Positive Work Experiences Than Do Generation X/Baby Boomers

Comparing mean values of workplace experiences between generations and within gender shows that, in general, men and women Millennial technology workers reported more positive workplace experiences than did older men and women respectively (see Table 12.5).

Workplace experiences did not always differ by generation, but when they did, Millennials nearly always rated workplace factors more positively than did older workers. Millennial workers (men and women) were more positive than Generation X/Baby Boomer workers about advancement and development opportunities, challenge and growth opportunities, and the presence of a culture that supports gender diversity. Millennial men were more likely than older men to report that the stress they experienced in their work role was manageable and to rate their organisation as having a strong reputation as well as a culture built for innovation. Millennial women expressed more satisfaction than did older women with their salary and benefits package. According to the raw mean values, the only factor by which older workers—men or women— expressed more positive experiences compared to Millennial workers was flexible work options: Generation X/Baby Boomer women more strongly agreed that they had opportunities for flexible work arrangements than Millennial women did. Importantly, this advantage among older women disappears after controlling for organisation tenure, career level, and management responsibility, suggesting that women may 'earn' flexible work opportunities over time at their organisation, as they gain seniority (see Table 12.7, Model 6b).

One might reasonably expect that most of the differences between Millennial and older workers would disappear after controlling for factors related to tenure and seniority. As with flexible work opportunities, this does happen with some workplace experience measures. For example, after adjusting for organisation tenure, career level, and managerial

Table 12.5 Workplace experiences among U.S. technology workers, by generation and gender

Factor		Mean Value Men	Mean Value Women	Gender Difference	Difference From Millennials among Men	Difference From Millennials among Women	N
1	**Sense of purpose a = .82**	0.75	0.74	n.s.			2,813
	Millennials	0.75	0.73	*			958
	Generation X/Baby Boomers	0.75	0.75	n.s.	n.s.	n.s.	1,855
2	**Advancement and development opportunities a = .89**	0.64	0.60	***			2,813
	Millennials	0.69	0.64	**			958
	Generation X/Baby Boomers	0.62	0.58	**	***	***	1,855
3	**Stress: In my role, the amount of stress I deal with is manageable.**	0.68	0.64	***			2,813
	Millennials	0.70	0.65	**			958
	Generation X/Baby Boomers	0.66	0.63	**	**	n.s.	1,855
	Scale: 0 = Strongly disagree; 0.25 = Disagree; 0.5 = Neutral; 0.75 = Agree; 1 = Strongly agree						
4	**Challenge and growth opportunities a = .82**	0.63	0.61	**			2,235
	Millennials	0.66	0.63	n.s.			811
	Generation X/Baby Boomers	0.62	0.60	*	**	**	1,424
5	**Critical mass of one's gender a = .85**	0.76	0.60	***			2,812
	Millennials	0.78	0.61	***			958
	Generation X/Baby Boomers	0.75	0.60	***	**	**	1,854
6	**Culture that supports gender diversity a = .89**	0.76	0.68	***			2,813
	Millennials	0.79	0.72	***			958
	Generation X/Baby Boomers	0.75	0.66	***	***	n.s.	1,855
7	**Manager: A supportive manager.**	0.79	0.72	***			1,491
	Millennials	0.79	0.71	**			464

(Continued)

Table 12.5 (Continued)

Factor		Mean Value		Gender Difference	Difference From Millennials among		N
		Men	Women		Men	Women	
	Generation X/Baby Boomers	0.79	0.72	***	n.s.	n.s.	1,027
8	**Reputation:** An organisation with a strong reputation and name recognition.	0.81	0.78	**			2,321
	Millennials	0.84	0.80	**			795
	Generation X/Baby Boomers	0.79	0.78	n.s.	***	n.s.	1,526
9	**Flexibility:** Opportunities for flexible work arrangements.	0.78	0.76	*			2,321
	Millennials	0.77	0.72	*			795
	Generation X/Baby Boomers	0.79	0.78	n.s.	n.s.	***	1,526
10	**Salary:** A good salary and benefits package.	0.65	0.65	n.s.			2,235
	Millennials	0.67	0.69	n.s.			811
	Generation X/Baby Boomers	0.65	0.63	n.s.	n.s.	***	1,424
11	**Innovation:** A culture built for innovation.	0.67	0.68	n.s.			2,321
	Millennials	0.69	0.69	n.s.			795
	Generation X/Baby Boomers	0.66	0.67	n.s.	*	n.s.	1,526
Intent to stay	I see myself working at my organisation a year from now.	0.75	0.72	**			2,813
	Millennials	0.76	0.72	*			958
	Generation X/Baby Boomers	0.74	0.72	n.s.	n.s.	n.s.	1,855

Scale: 0 = Very absent from my organisation; 0.25 = Absent from my organisation; 0.5 = Neutral at my organisation; 0.75 = Present at my organisation; 1 = Very present at my organisation

Scale: 0 = Strongly disagree; 0.25 = Disagree; 0.5 = Neutral; 0.75 = Agree; 1 = Strongly agree

Source: 2016 Anita Borg Institute Workplace Experience Survey for Top Companies

Notes: *** $p < 0.001$; ** $p < 0.01$; * $p < 0.05$; two-tailed test. 'n.s.' means 'not significant'.

responsibilities, Millennials no longer report more manageable levels of stress at work than older workers (see Table 12.6, Model 5a). Nevertheless, some generational differences remain after adding the controls mentioned earlier. Net of these factors, Millennials are still more positive about their advancement and development opportunities and challenge and growth opportunities (see Table 12.6, Models 1a and 2a). This suggests that Millennials' more positive perception of technology workplaces is not due solely to fewer responsibilities and less time on the job. Instead, these differences suggest that age or generation has an additional independent effect on perceptions of possibilities for growth among technology workers.

Finding 2: Women Report More Negative Workplace Experiences Than Do Men in Technology Jobs, Across and Within Generations

Comparing mean values of workplace experiences by gender shows that both across and within generational groups, men reported more positive experiences than women did, according to a number of measures (see Table 12.5). Importantly, having a supportive manager is one of the larger gender differences (8 points on a 100-point scale), and is found in both generational groups. Overall, this disparity remains and is only slightly reduced after controlling for organisation tenure, managerial responsibilities, and career level (see Table 12.6, Model 4b), suggesting that women in technology jobs face a troubling disparity in access to supportive management, independent of tenure and seniority.

Across generations, women also indicated significantly less access to advancement and development opportunities and challenge and growth opportunities, and were less likely to agree that the stress in their jobs was manageable, even after adjusting for tenure and seniority (see Table 12.6, Models 1b, 2b, and 5b). In line with other research (Funk and Parker 2018), men in this sample also perceived the culture in their organisation as more supportive of gender diversity than women did (see Table 12.6, Model 3b).

Within generations, women also reported more negative experiences compared to men. After adjusting for career level, tenure, and managerial responsibilities, compared to Millennial men, Millennial women reported less access to advancement and development opportunities, less agreement that the stress they encountered in their work roles was manageable, less agreement that their workplace culture supported gender diversity, less access to a supportive manager and flexible work arrangements, and less of a sense of purpose in their work (see Table 12.7, models 1a, 2a, 4a, 5a, 6a, 7a). Likewise, compared to Generation X/Baby Boomer men, women age 35 and older were less likely to agree that their organisation provided advancement and development opportunities,

Table 12.6 OLS regression predictors of U.S. technology workers' workplace experiences

Independent Variables	Model 1a	Model 1b	Model 2a	Model 2b	Model 3a	Model 3b	Model 4a	Model 4b	Model 5a	Model 5b
	Advancement and Development Opportunities		Challenge and Growth Opportunities		Culture That Supports Gender Diversity		Supportive Manager		Manageable Stress	
Millennial (Ref. group: Baby Boomer/Generation X)	0.0536***		0.0290*		0.0177		-0.00384		0.0209	
	(0.0126)		(0.0126)		(0.00959)		(0.0193)		(0.0123)	
Woman (Ref. group: men)		-0.0359***		-0.0219*		-0.0834***		-0.0645***		-0.0324***
		(0.00905)		(0.00921)		(0.00670)		(0.0137)		(0.00879)
Organisation tenure	-0.0113***	-0.0192***	-0.00777*	-0.0119***	-0.0131***	-0.0153***	-0.0102*	-0.00929*	-0.00763*	-0.0106***
	(0.00326)	(0.00265)	(0.00329)	(0.00270)	(0.00248)	(0.00196)	(0.00482)	(0.00394)	(0.00317)	(0.00258)
Managerial responsibilties	0.00401	0.00880	-0.0272	-0.0243	0.0123	0.0232*	-0.0286	-0.0205	-0.0629***	-0.0586***
	(0.0134)	(0.0134)	(0.0142)	(0.0143)	(0.0102)	(0.00995)	(0.0190)	(0.0190)	(0.0130)	(0.0131)

Career level	0.0290***	0.0183*	0.0268***	0.0205**	0.00201	-0.0104	0.0530***	0.0457***	0.0338***	0.0273***
	(0.00764)	(0.00758)	(0.00784)	(0.00777)	(0.00581)	(0.00561)	(0.0115)	(0.0113)	(0.00744)	(0.00736)
Constant	0.583***	0.663***	0.587***	0.632***	0.755***	0.830***	0.689***	0.728***	0.619***	0.663***
	(0.0192)	(0.0154)	(0.0194)	(0.0155)	(0.0146)	(0.0114)	(0.0292)	(0.0236)	(0.0187)	(0.0150)
R-squared	0.025	0.024	0.014	0.014	0.026	0.076	0.016	0.030	0.017	0.020
N	2813	2813	2235	2235	2813	2813	1491	1491	2813	2813

Source: 2016 Anita Borg Institute Workplace Experience Survey for Top Companies

Notes: $*** p < 0.001$; $** p < 0.01$; $* p < 0.05$ (two-tailed tests). Standard errors in parentheses. Scale for advancement and development opportunities and manageable stress: 0 = Strongly disagree; 0.25 = Disagree; 0.5 = Neutral; 0.75 = Agree; 1 = Strongly agree. Scale for all other dependent variables: 0 = Very absent from my organisation; 0.25 = Absent from my organisation; 0.5 = Neutral at my organisation; 0.75 = Present at my organisation; 1 = Very present at my organisation.

230   *Christianne Corbett*

manageable levels of stress, a culture that supports gender diversity, and access to supportive managers (see Table 12.7, models 1b, 2b, 4b, and 5b).

Finding 3: Younger Men Report the Most Positive Experiences and Older Women Report the Least Positive Experiences in Technology Jobs

Given the previous two findings, it is perhaps not surprising that Millennial men report the most positive work experiences in their technology jobs. In terms of raw means, Millennial men rated none of the 11 workplace factors less positively than even one of the other groups, and this remains true after adjusting for career level, organisation tenure, and managerial responsibilities (see Tables 12.5 and 12.7). After controlling for these factors, Millennial men agreed more strongly than all three other groups (Millennial women, Generation X/Baby Boomer men, and Generation X/Baby Boomer women) that they had access to advancement and development opportunities and that the amount of stress they dealt with in their jobs was manageable (see Table 12.7, models 1a and 2a). Millennial men reported significantly greater levels of challenge and growth opportunities than did older men and women (see Table 12.7, Model 3a), and were more likely than women of either generation to say they had a supportive manager and that their organisational culture supports gender diversity (see Table 12.7, models 4a and 5a).

On the other side of the coin are Generation X/Baby Boomer women, the group that reports the most negative work experiences in their technology jobs. After adjusting for career level, organisation tenure, and managerial responsibilities, Generation X/Baby Boomer women rated none of the workplace factors more positively than even one other group (see Table 12.7, 'b' models): Generation X/Baby Boomer women reported significantly fewer advancement and development opportunities than all three other groups (Millennial women, Millennial men, and Generation X/Baby Boomer men), and agreed less strongly than men of either generation that the amount of stress they dealt with in their jobs was manageable, that they had a supportive manager, or that their organisation's culture supported gender diversity (see Table 12.7, models 1b, 2b, 4b, and 5b).

Finding 4: Gender Disparities in Workplace Experiences Are Not Lessening Among Younger Workers

Given the presence of gender disparities in the workplace experiences of technology workers identified here, it is worth asking whether disparity levels are lower among younger workers, because this would suggest that conditions are improving for women overall in technology jobs. The data

Table 12.7 OLS regression predictors of U.S. technology workers' workplace experiences

Independent Variables	Advancement and Development Opportunities		Manageable Stress		Challenge and Growth Opportunities		Culture That Supports Gender Diversity	
	Model 1a	Model 1b	Model 2a	Model 2b	Model 3a	Model 3b	Model 4a	Model 4b
Millennial men	Ref. group	0.0919***	Ref. group	0.0559***	Ref. group	0.0506**	Ref. group	0.0976***
		(0.0156)		(.0152)		(.0156)		(.0116)
Millennial women	-0.0525***	0.0393*	-0.0483**	0.00758	-0.0258	0.0249	-0.0753***	0.0223
	(0.0153)	(0.0159)	(0.0149)	(0.0155)	(0.0151)	(0.0160)	(0.0113)	(0.0118)
Generation X/baby boomer men	-0.0656***	0.0262*	-0.0322*	0.0236*	-0.0317*	0.0190	-0.0103	0.0873***
	(0.0155)	(0.0111)	(0.0151)	(0.0108)	(0.0155)	(0.0116)	(0.0115)	(0.00826)
Generation X/baby boomer women	-0.0919***	Ref. group	-0.0559***	Ref. group	-0.0506**	Ref. group	-0.0976***	Ref. group
	(0.0156)		(.0152)		(.0156)		(.0116)	
Organisation tenure	-0.0114***	-0.0114***	-0.00765*	-0.00765*	-0.00776*	-0.00776*	-0.0128***	-0.0128***
	(0.00325)	(0.00325)	(0.00317)	(0.00317)	(0.00329)	(0.00329)	(0.00242)	(0.00242)
Managerial responsibilties	0.00802	0.00802	-0.0592***	-0.0592***	-0.0246	-0.0246	0.0234*	0.0234*
	(0.0134)	(0.0134)	(0.0131)	(0.0131)	(0.0143)	(0.0143)	(0.00995)	(0.00995)
Career level	0.0251**	0.0251**	0.0302***	0.0302***	0.0242**	0.0242**	-0.00871	-0.00871
	(0.00771)	(0.00771)	(0.00751)	(0.00751)	(0.00794)	(0.00794)	(0.00573)	(0.00573)
Constant	0.669***	0.577***	0.669***	0.614***	0.632***	0.581***	0.825***	0.728***
	(0.0163)	(0.0196)	(0.0159)	(0.0191)	(0.0164)	(0.0199)	(0.0121)	(0.0146)
R-squared	0.031	0.031	0.022	0.022	0.016	0.016	0.077	0.077
N	2813	2813	2813	2813	2235	2235	2813	2813

(Continued)

Table 12.7 (Continued)

Independent Variables	Supportive Manager		Flexible Work Arrangements		Sense of Purpose	
	Model 5a	Model 5b	Model 6a	Model 6b	Model 7a	Model 7b
Millennial men	Ref. group	0.0602*	Ref. group	0.0100	Ref. group	0.00914
		(.0237)		(.0165)		(.0115)
Millennial women	-0.0738**	-0.0136	-0.0369*	-0.0269	-0.0239*	-0.0148
	(0.0242)	(0.0245)	(0.0160)	(0.0166)	(0.0113)	(0.0117)
Generation X/baby boomer men	0.000147	0.0603***	-0.0121	-0.00204	-0.0110	-0.00187
	(0.0238)	(0.0166)	(0.0165)	(0.0117)	(0.0114)	(0.00820)
Generation X/baby boomer women	-0.0602*	Ref. group	-0.0100	Ref. group	-0.00914	Ref. group
	(.0237)		(.0165)		(.0115)	
Organisation tenure	-0.0103*	-0.0103*	-0.000333	-0.000333	-0.00525*	-0.00525*
	(0.00479)	(0.00479)	(0.00344)	(0.00344)	(0.00240)	(0.00240)
Managerial responsibilities	-0.0206	-0.0206	-0.0259	-0.0259	0.0154	0.0154
	(0.0190)	(0.0190)	(0.0141)	(0.0141)	(0.00988)	(0.00988)
Career level	0.0453**	0.0453***	0.0616***	0.0616***	0.0281***	0.0281***
	(0.0116)	(0.0116)	(0.00812)	(0.00812)	(0.00568)	(0.00568)
Constant	0.732***	0.672***	0.669***	0.659***	0.715***	0.706***
	(0.0250)	(0.0295)	(0.0171)	(0.0205)	(0.0120)	(0.0144)
R-squared	0.030	0.030	0.035	0.035	0.014	0.014
N	1491	1491	2321	2321	2813	2813

Source: 2016 Anita Borg Institute Workplace Experience Survey for Top Companies

Notes: ***$p < .001$; **$p < .01$; *$p < .05$ (two-tailed tests). Standard errors in parentheses. Scale for advancement and development opportunities, manageable stress, and sense of purpose: 0 = Strongly disagree; 0.25 = Disagree; 0.5 = Neutral; 0.75 = Agree; 1 = Strongly agree. Scale for challenge and growth opportunities, culture that supports gender diversity, supportive manager, and flexible work arrangements: 0 = Very absent from my organisation; 0.25 = Absent from my organisation; 0.5 = Neutral at my organisation; 0.75 = Present at my organisation; 1 = Very present at my organisation.

suggest this is not the case. The absolute value of the coefficients on 'Millennial women' in the 'a' models and 'Generation X/Baby Boomer men' in the 'b' models in Table 12.7 represent the difference in responses to the various workplace factors between men and women among Millennials ('a' models) and Generation X/Baby Boomer members ('b' models). In most cases, the absolute value of the 'Millennial women' coefficient in the 'a' model is greater than the 'Generation X/Baby Boomer men' coefficient in the 'b' model, suggesting perhaps *greater* gender differences in workplace experiences among younger technology workers. According to a Z test for coefficient equivalence (Clogg et al. 1995), however, none of the coefficients for Millennial women and Generation X/Baby Boomer men, for any workplace factor, are significantly different from one another, indicating that gender differences in workplace experiences in technology jobs may not be growing but are not shrinking either.

Together, the data support hypotheses one through five. Net of tenure and seniority, Millennials and men report more positive experiences in technology jobs. Younger men report the most positive experiences and older women the least positive, and gender disparities in workplace experiences are as large and significant among younger workers as among older workers.

Discussion

The findings from this study suggest that indeed the technology sector seems to be a good fit for Millennials, but much more so for Millennial men than Millennial women. Millennial men reported more positive workplace perceptions and experiences than any other group. Given that overall job satisfaction tends to increase with age (Dobrow et al. 2016), it is somewhat remarkable that Generation X/Baby Boomer men did not report even one more positive workplace perception or experience in their technology jobs than Millennial men did.

There is reason to suspect that it is younger people, especially younger men—rather than something particular about the Millennial generation—who have more positive experiences in technology jobs, and that as Millennials age into the 'older' category, their experiences in technology jobs will become less positive. This seems likely to be true for two reasons: first, organisation scholars have argued that the characteristics of work have become conflated with the actual working practices enacted in professional spheres (Gascoigne et al. 2015). Because most of the people working in technology jobs are young men, the unencumbered availability of these workers becomes taken for granted and expected, a 'requirement' of the jobs (Acker 1990). In a kind of self-perpetuating cycle, because so many technology workers are young men, high-technology jobs favour 'ideal workers' who are constantly available and have few outside-of-work demands, perhaps more than many other industries (Perlow 1998).

As they age, Millennial men are unlikely to remain as free from caregiving and household responsibilities as many of them are now, and, as a result, may experience less of a good fit with their technology jobs. Second, in tandem with a preference for ideal workers, biases against older workers may play a role. Despite evidence to the contrary (Kock et al. 2018), there remains a widespread perception that older adults perform less well than younger adults on technology tasks (Czaja 1995; Perry et al. 2003), and age discrimination in technology jobs has been identified as a significant barrier for older workers (Visier 2017). If biases against older workers in technology persist as Millennials age, Millennials will likely feel it and their workplace experiences will become less positive.

Biases against older workers and in favour of younger workers may help to explain why, even after controlling for career level, organisation tenure, and managerial responsibilities, Millennial men express more agreement that their organisation provides advancement and development opportunities, manageable levels of stress, and challenge and growth opportunities than do older workers. It is possible to provide growth and development opportunities for workers at all ages, and organisations that focus on building human capital by providing development opportunities related to technical, interpersonal, and leadership skills have been found to be more rewarding and fulfilling for employees than those that do not (Haviland et al. 2010). The data presented here show that older workers in technology jobs are less likely than younger workers to report having these development opportunities.

Perhaps the most interesting finding from this analysis is that differences in the workplace experiences of men and women technology workers are not going away. Gender differences among Millennials in technology jobs are quite similar to those found among older generations of technology workers. Like Generation X/Baby Boomer women, Millennial women in technology jobs did not report the rosy picture of the workplace that Millennial men did, and in fact were not very different from older women in their perceptions and experiences of their technology jobs. After adjusting for tenure and career level, the only measure by which Millennial women assessed their workplace experiences more positively than older women did was in terms of advancement and development opportunities. Millennial women were less positive than Millennial men about a range of factors, including access to supportive managers, opportunities for flexible work arrangements, advancement and development opportunities, and manageable stress. By no measure did Millennial women report a more positive view of their workplace than Millennial men did. Many of the gender differences between Millennial men and women are small, but they are statistically significant—and small differences accumulate to become larger disparities (Martell et al. 1996). In addition, it is important to remember that all of the companies included in the Tech Workplace Experience Survey had made a commitment to work toward gender equity, so these gender differences may represent close to a best case scenario for technology jobs.

Importantly, women from Generation X and the Baby Boomer generation also reported lower levels of many of these same factors, compared to Generation X/Baby Boomer men. Generation X/Baby Boomer women were less likely than men of their generation to agree that their organisations provided supportive managers, advancement and development opportunities, manageable stress, and a culture that supports gender diversity. Because of this common gender disparity among Millennials and Generation X/Baby Boomers, this analysis finds no evidence that gender disparities in the technology sector are declining. To the contrary, this study finds that gender disparities in workplace perceptions and experiences in technology jobs remain substantial among the youngest generation of U.S. workers. Combined with the finding that women do not make up a higher proportion of those with highest degrees in computer science/mathematics in the U.S. in the Millennial generation compared to prior generations, this study suggests a trend of stagnation for women in technology.

In addition to signs of stagnation, the analyses presented here provide a few hopeful signs for increasing diversity among technology workers as well. The population of individuals whose highest degrees are in computer science or mathematics has become more racially and ethnically diverse among Millennials, compared to previous generations. In addition, those Millennials with the highest degrees in computer science/ mathematics who are working full-time in a job related to those degrees are working slightly fewer hours than previous generations, potentially opening the door to workers with more responsibilities outside of work, including caregiving, to participate in the technology workforce on a more level playing field.

Conclusion

The results of this study do not paint a promising picture for increasing gender diversity in technology jobs. Although the population of individuals with the highest degrees in computer science has become more racially and ethnically diverse among Millennials compared to Generation X and the Baby Boomer generation (largely because of an increase in Asian American men and women with highest degrees in computer science/mathematics), the representation of women has not increased. In addition, gender differences in workplace experiences among technology workers found among Generation X/Baby Boomers persist among Millennials. A particularly troubling disparity is the lower likelihood of women having a supportive manager, compared to men, among younger as well as older workers. The workers who express the most positive experiences in their technology jobs are Millennial men, pointing to the continuation of the reality of 'gendered jobs' that Acker described nearly three decades ago (1990), as well as a preference for unencumbered 'ideal workers' in technology jobs.

These analyses suggest that technology jobs are not going to gradually become more gender balanced without intentional efforts to make them so. To level the playing field, organisations that employ technology workers must create working conditions that provide similar experiences for men and women. The results presented here point to some concrete steps that organisations can take to achieve this end. First, they can identify why women are less likely than men to perceive their workplace culture as one that supports gender diversity and address the issues. Second, they can provide women in technology jobs with more advancement and development opportunities to match those offered to men. Third, they can shape jobs so that workers find the amount of stress entailed in doing their jobs to be manageable, which includes providing opportunities for flexible work arrangements. If we are to reduce occupational gender segregation, organisations must address the ways in which technology jobs have become tailor-made for young men and less appealing to older men and to women of all ages.

Note

1 There is some evidence that lower response rates observed in recent years compared to past years are not necessarily associated with significant declines in sample representativeness (Curtin et al. 2000; Keeter et al. 2000). For example, Chang and Krosnick (2009) found that a sample with a 25% response rate was just as representative of a population as a 43% response rate sample.

References

Acker, J (1990) 'Hierarchies, Jobs, Bodies: A Theory of Gendered Organizations' 4 *Gender & Society* 139. doi:10.1177/089124390004002002

Benner, K (2017) 'Women in Tech Speak Frankly on Culture of Harassment' *New York Times* 30 June.

Britton, DM (2000) 'The Epistemology of the Gendered Organization' 14 *Gender & Society* 418. doi:10.1177/089124300014003004

Chang, L and Krosnick, JA (2009) 'National Surveys Via RDD Telephone Interviewing Versus the Internet: Comparing Sample Representativeness and Response Quality' 73 *The Public Opinion Quarterly* 641. doi:10.1093/poq/nfp075

Clogg, CC, Petkova, E and Haritou, A (1995) 'Statistical Methods for Comparing Regression Coefficients Between Models' 100 *American Journal of Sociology* 1261. doi:10.1086/230638

Corbett, C and Hill, C (2015) *Solving the Equation: The Variables for Women's Success in Engineering and Computing* (Washington, DC, American Association of University Women). www.ehu.eus/documents/2007376/3500574/solving_the_equation.pdf

Curtin, R, Presser, S and Singer, E (2000) 'The Effects of Response Rate Changes on the Index of Consumer Sentiment' 64 *The Public Opinion Quarterly* 413. doi:10.1086/318638

Czaja, SJ (1995) 'Aging and Work Performance' 15 *Review of Public Personnel Administration* 46. doi:10.1177/0734371X9501500205

Demaiter, EI and Adams, TL (2009) ' "I really didn't have any problems with the male-female thing until . . .": Successful Women's Experiences in IT Organizations' 34 *Canadian Journal of Sociology* 31.

Finn, D and Donovan, A (2013) *PwC's NextGen: A Global Generational Study* (PricewaterhouseCoopers, University of Southern California, and London Business School). www.pwc.com/gx/en/hr-management-services/pdf/pwc-nextgen-study-2013.pdf

Frehill, LM (2012) 'Gender and Career Outcomes of U.S. Engineers' 4 *International Journal of Gender, Science and Technology* 148.

Fry, R, Igielnik, R and Patten, E (2018) 'How Millennials Today Compare with Their Grandparents 50 Years Ago' *Pew Research Center* 16 March 2018. www.pewresearch.org/fact-tank/2018/03/16/how-millennials-compare-with-their-grandparents

Funk, C and Parker, K (2018) 'Women and Men in STEM Often at Odds Over Workplace Equity' *Pew Research Center* 9 January 2018. www.pewsocialtrends.org/2018/01/09/women-and-men-in-stem-often-at-odds-over-workplace-equity/

Gallup (2016) *How Millennials Want to Work and Live* (Washington, DC, Gallup). www.gallup.com/workplace/238073/millennials-work-live.aspx

Gascoigne, C, Parry, E and Buchanan, D (2015) 'Extreme Work, Gendered Work? How Extreme Jobs and the Discourse of "Personal Choice" Perpetuate Gender Inequality' 22 *Organization* 457. doi:10.1177/1350508415572511

Glass, JL, Sassler, S, Levitte, Y and Michelmore, KM (2013) 'What's So Special about STEM? A Comparison of Women's Retention in STEM and Professional Occupations' 92 *Social Forces* 723. doi:10.1093/sf/sot092

Haviland, SB, Morgan, JC and Marshall, VW (2010) 'New Careers in the New Economy: Redefining Career Development in a Post-Internal Labor Market Industry' in JA McMullin and VW Marshall (eds), *Aging and Working in the New Economy: Changing Career Structures in Small IT Firms* (Cheltenham, Edward Elgar Publishing Limited).

Hewlett, SA, Luce, CB, Servon, LJ, Sherbin, L, Shiller, P, Sosnovich, E and Sumberg, K (2008) *The Athena Factor: Reversing the Brain Drain in Science, Engineering, and Technology* (Boston, MA, Harvard Business Publishing).

Hunt, J (2016) 'Why Do Women Leave Science and Engineering?' 69 *Industrial and Labor Relations Review* 199. doi:10.1177/0019793915594597

Isaac, M (2017) 'Uber Founder Travis Kalanick Resigns as C.E.O.' *New York Times* 21 June.

Keeter, S, Miller, C, Kohut, A, Groves, RM and Presser, S (2000) 'Consequences of Reducing Nonresponse in a National Telephone Survey' 64 *The Public Opinion Quarterly* 125. doi:10.1086/317759

Khandwala, YS, Zhang, CA, Lu, Y and Eisenberg, ML (2017) 'The Age of Fathers in the USA Is Rising: An Analysis of 168 867 480 Births from 1972 to 2015' 32 *Human Reproduction* 2110. doi:10.1093/humrep/dex267

238   *Christianne Corbett*

Kock, N, Moqbel, M, Jung, Y and Syn, T (2018) 'Do Older Programmers Perform as Well as Young Ones? Exploring the Intermediate Effects of Stress and Programming Experience' 20 *Cognition, Technology & Work* 489. doi:10.1007/s10111-018-0479-x

Lebowitz, S (2018) '11 Things Millennials Do Completely Differently from Their Parents' *Business Insider* 12 March 2018. www.businessinsider.com/millennials-habits-different-from-baby-boomers-2018-3

Martell, RF, Lane, DM and Emrich, C (1996) 'Male-Female Differences: A Computer Simulation' 51 *The American Psychologist* 157. doi:10.1037/0003-066X.51.2.157

Mathews, TJ and Hamilton, BE (2016) *Mean Age of Mothers Is on the Rise: United States, 2000–2014* (Hyattsville, MD, National Center for Health Statistics (NCHS) data brief no. 232). www.cdc.gov/nchs/data/databriefs/db232.pdf

McMullin, JA (ed) (2011) *Age, Gender, and Work: Small Information Technology Firms in the New Economy* (Vancouver, University of British Columbia Press).

National Center for Science and Engineering Statistics (2017) *Women, Minorities, and Persons with Disabilities in Science and Engineering: 2017* (Arlington, VA, National Science Foundation, Special Report NSF 17–310). www.nsf.gov/statistics/2017/nsf17310/static/downloads/nsf17310-digest.pdf

Perlow, LA (1998) 'Boundary Control: The Social Ordering of Work and Family Time in a High-tech Corporation' 43 *Administrative Science Quarterly* 328. doi:10.2307/2393855

Perry, EL, Simpson, PA, NicDomhnaill, OM and Siegel, DM (2003) 'Is There a Technology Age Gap? Associations Among Age, Skills, and Employment Outcomes' 11 *International Journal of Selection and Assessment* 141. doi:10.1111/1468-2389.00237

Peterson, H (2007) 'Gendered Work Ideals in Swedish IT Firms: Valued and Not Valued Workers' 14 *Gender, Work & Organization* 333. doi:10.1111/j.1468-0432.2007.00347.x

——— (2010) 'The Gendered Construction of Technical Self-Confidence: Women's Negotiated Positions in Male-Dominated, Technical Work Settings' 2 *International Journal of Gender, Science and Technology* 65.

Pew Research Center (2015) 'The Whys and Hows of Generations Research' *Pew Research Center* 3 September 2015. www.people-press.org/2015/09/03/the-whys-and-hows-of-generations-research/

Preston, AE (1994) 'Why Have All the Women Gone? A Study of Exit of Women from the Science and Engineering Professions' 84 *The American Economic Review* 1446.

——— (2004) *Leaving Science: Occupational Exit from Scientific Careers* (New York, Russell Sage Foundation).

Riza, SD, Ganzach, Y and Liu, Y (2016) 'Time and Job Satisfaction: A Longitudinal Study of the Differential Roles of Age and Tenure' 44 *Journal of Management* 2558. doi:10.1177/0149206315624962

Simard, C, Henderson, AD, Gilmartin, SK, Schiebinger, L and Whitney, T (2008) *Climbing the Technical Ladder: Obstacles and Solutions for Mid-Level Women in Technology* (Stanford, CA, Michelle R. Clayman Institute for Gender Research, Stanford University, and Anita Borg Institute for Women and

Technology).   www.anitab.org/wp-content/uploads/2013/12/Climbing_the_
Technical_Ladder.pdf

U.S. Bureau of Labor Statistics (BLS) (2017) *Highlights of Women's Earnings in 2016* (Washington, DC, US BLS Report 1069). www.bls.gov/opub/reports/womens-earnings/2016/pdf/home.pdf

U.S. Census Bureau (2011) *2006–2010 American Community Survey.*

—— (2013) *2012 American Community Survey.*

Vespa, J (2017) *The Changing Economics and Demographics of Young Adulthood: 1975–2016* (Washington, DC, US Census Bureau). www.census.gov/content/dam/Census/library/publications/2017/demo/p20-579.pdf

Visier (2017) *Visier Insights Report: The Truth About Ageism in the Tech Industry* (Visier).   www.visier.com/wp-content/uploads/2017/09/Visier-Insights-AgeismInTech-Sept2017.pdf

Wright, R (1996) 'The Occupational Masculinity of Computing' in C Cheng (ed), *Masculinities in Organizations* (Thousand Oaks, CA, Sage Publications).

Xie, Y and Shauman, KA (2003) *Women in Science: Career Processes and Outcomes* (Cambridge, MA, Harvard University Press).

Appendix

Table 12A1 Rotated factor loadings from principal-component factor analysis on tech workplace experience survey responses

Survey items	Factor 1: Purpose α = 0.82	Factor 2: Advancement & development opportunities α = 0.89	Factor 3: Challenge and growth opportunities α = 0.82	Factor 4: Critical mass of one's gender α = 0.85	Factor 5: Culture that supports gender diversity α = 0.89	Factor 6: Reputation	Factor 7: Stress	Factor 8: Salary	Factor 9: Flexibility	Factor 10: Innovation	Factor 11: Manager	Uniqueness
My work gives me a sense of personal accomplishment	0.7846	0.1910	-0.0199	0.0462	0.0939	0.0576	0.1250	-0.1112	-0.0052	0.0482	-0.0165	0.3016
I generally find my work meaningful	0.6574	0.2201	-0.1309	0.0464	0.0732	-0.0394	-0.1101	0.0795	0.0709	-0.0931	0.1232	0.4407
I am proud to work at my organisation	0.5986	0.2535	-0.0435	0.0652	0.1354	0.3122	0.2027	0.1856	-0.0756	0.0171	-0.0310	0.3693
I have opportunities to advance in my organisation	0.2089	0.7377	0.1009	0.2076	0.1554	0.0292	0.0215	0.0620	0.0145	-0.0179	0.0421	0.3259
The development opportunities I'm offered make me optimistic about my career trajectory at my organisation	0.3315	0.7265	0.0864	0.1293	0.1868	0.1267	0.1299	-0.0456	-0.0014	0.0206	0.0097	0.2664

Clearly defined opportunities for advancement and professional growth	-0.0906	0.0450	0.8139	0.0218	-0.1390	0.0065	-0.0157	0.0207	-0.0109	-0.0114	-0.0360	0.3028
Available mentors and sponsors	-0.0492	0.0386	0.7324	-0.0765	-0.0781	-0.0435	0.0768	0.0072	-0.0019	-0.0380	-0.0749	0.4298
A challenging position that utilises my technical knowledge	0.0899	0.0916	0.6410	0.0294	0.0899	0.0052	-0.1413	-0.0560	0.0286	0.0628	0.1256	0.4967
The percentage of technical workers of your gender in the organisation	0.0127	0.0197	-0.0563	0.8464	0.2255	0.0188	-0.0065	-0.1161	0.0129	0.0284	0.0388	0.2108
A critical mass of your gender in the workplace	-0.0061	0.1416	0.0906	0.8057	0.2426	-0.0251	0.0513	0.1025	-0.0298	-0.0834	0.0374	0.2352
A network of colleagues of your gender	0.0751	0.0978	-0.0192	0.7228	0.2815	0.1075	0.0667	0.0611	0.0429	0.1116	-0.0882	0.3057
A strong presence of role models of your gender at every level in the organisation	0.1459	0.1947	0.0150	0.5436	0.3495	0.0389	0.0780	0.0245	-0.0285	-0.0492	0.0333	0.4162
The job satisfaction of technical workers of your gender in the organisation	0.2527	0.2288	-0.1743	0.4870	0.3363	0.1851	0.0730	-0.0083	0.0203	0.0629	0.3747	0.3148

(*Continued*)

Table 12.7 (Continued)

Survey items	Factor 1: Purpose α = 0.82	Factor 2: Advancement & development opportunities α = 0.89	Factor 3: Challenge and growth opportunities α = 0.82	Factor 4: Critical mass of one's gender α = 0.85	Factor 5: Culture that supports gender diversity α = 0.89	Factor 6: Reputation	Factor 7: Stress	Factor 8: Salary	Factor 9: Flexibility	Factor 10: Innovation	Factor 11: Manager	Uniqueness
Institutional commitment to diversity and gender equality	0.0488	0.1340	-0.0405	0.3199	0.7844	0.1663	0.0725	-0.0969	-0.0177	-0.0339	-0.1019	0.1917
Leaders who are held accountable for gender equity in their department	0.1281	0.1422	0.0048	0.2919	0.7522	-0.0672	0.0865	0.1064	-0.0751	0.1207	0.1378	0.1896
A work culture that supports gender diversity	0.1075	0.0407	-0.0516	0.2331	0.7334	0.0984	-0.0296	-0.0224	0.1565	-0.0361	-0.0367	0.3258
Pay equity between men and women with the same job	0.0229	0.1366	-0.1003	0.2573	0.6221	0.0050	0.1164	0.1146	-0.0493	-0.1871	0.2304	0.3860
Allies of the opposite gender who support gender diversity in the workplace	0.0595	0.0273	-0.1034	0.1290	0.5940	0.1415	-0.0013	0.0216	-0.0012	0.3691	0.0595	0.4533
A CEO who openly supports gender diversity	0.1953	0.2241	-0.1434	0.3978	0.5550	0.0505	0.1247	0.0042	0.0165	-0.0508	-0.0430	0.2701

An organisation with a strong reputation and name recognition	0.2709	0.2177	-0.0404	0.1262	0.3035	0.5577	0.0362	-0.0246	0.0019	0.0304	0.0602	0.4519
In my role, the amount of stress I deal with is manageable.	0.2158	0.2506	-0.0922	0.1192	0.2126	0.1312	0.4692	0.0524	0.0129	-0.1507	0.1331	0.5347
A good salary and benefits package	-0.1450	0.1386	0.3524	-0.0104	-0.0078	0.1284	-0.0839	0.2621	0.0165	0.0296	0.0307	0.7083
Opportunities for flexible work arrangements	0.2399	0.0850	0.0840	0.1067	0.1617	0.3436	0.2301	0.0132	0.2246	0.0198	-0.0126	0.6633
A culture built for innovation	0.4221	0.2723	0.0099	0.0271	0.1760	0.3160	-0.0137	-0.0445	-0.0163	0.1250	-0.0672	0.5426
A supportive manager	0.3286	0.2359	-0.0245	0.2299	0.2945	0.0111	0.4822	-0.0236	0.2176	0.0053	0.1837	0.4398

Source: 2016 Anita Borg Institute Workplace Experience Survey for Top Companies

Notes: α = scale reliability coefficient. Although "A supportive manager" and "In my role, the amount of stress I deal with is manageable" appear to vary together, a correlation analysis found a scale reliability coefficient of just 0.5, so they are treated as independent factors

13 Women in Engineering

Experiences of Discrimination Across Age Cohort

Tracey L. Adams

Introduction

Over the last 30 years a sizeable body of academic research has identified challenges faced by women engineers. Discrimination in hiring and promotion, gender wage gaps, hostile work environments, and difficulty combining engineering work with family life are just some of the challenges women face in the profession (Devine 1992; Evetts 1994; Hatmaker 2013; Herman 2015; Katawazi 2017; Sharp et al. 2012). In Canada, women comprise only 13% of licensed professional engineers nation-wide (Engineers Canada 2018). Nevertheless, there are signs of positive change. In many Canadian engineering schools, women make up one-quarter to one-third of all engineering students (Engineers Canada 2018), and Engineers Canada has established a '30 by 30' initiative to bring 'the percentage of newly licensed engineers who are women to 30% by the year 2030' (Engineers Canada 2018). In line with this initiative some engineering workplaces are taking steps to encourage retention of female engineers, and to promote employment equity (Engineers Canada 2018; Sharp et al. 2012). Policies are being implemented to make the Canadian engineering profession more female-friendly than ever before.

In light of these efforts, this chapter explores women engineers' experiences with discrimination across age cohort, drawing on survey and interview data. Previous research has documented sexism in engineering, but changing gender norms and professional equity initiatives could result in more positive work experiences for female engineers. Young women who have recently embarked on an engineering career might find a more welcoming environment than their predecessors did. The result may be varying experiences of discrimination and professional practice across age cohort. Do younger female engineers report less discrimination and more opportunities than their predecessors? Or because of their youth, are younger women even more vulnerable to discrimination and marginalisation than their older counterparts? Analysis of survey and interview data on women engineers in Ontario, Canada finds evidence that age and gender do intersect to shape experiences of discrimination, and to some extent, women's strategies for coping with it.

Gender, Professions, and the Life Course

Professions—like other occupations and organisations (Acker 1990; Wright 1996)—are gendered (Adams 2000; Davies 1996; Evetts 1994; Tancred 1999). Historically, professions like medicine, dentistry, law, and engineering were defined by men, for men. They have masculine cultures and structures (Dryburgh 1999; Tancred 1999), which inhibit women's opportunities for entry-to-practice, skill acquisition, and promotion (Davies 1996; Tancred 1999; Evetts 1994). Historically, women were both formally and informally excluded from many high-status professions, through processes of social closure (Witz 1992). Yet, as Celia Davies (1996) has argued, the gendering of professional work may be revealed less through women's exclusion than through the manner of their inclusion. Traditionally, professional work was masculine and male-dominated, requiring extensive education, skill, rationality, and detachment (Davies 1996). Women were clustered in support roles, where they provided care and offered emotional support, both to clients and male professionals (Davies 1996; Adams 2000). The discourses around this division of labour have tied professional skill and competence to masculinity, while simultaneously linking women with emotion and care. Even as women enter male-dominated professions, such ideas have shaped perceptions of their practice. When competence is tied to masculinity, women are at an inherent disadvantage (Hinze 1999; Guinier et al. 1997; Tancred 1999). Women in male-dominated professions may be cast as less competent and may be relegated to support roles; the skills they possess may be discounted.

The gendering of professional work has been a historical process. When modern professions took their current form—in the West, predominantly in the nineteenth century—prevailing gender inequalities were embedded within them (Adams 2000). Over time the gendering of professions has shifted, as women have made inroads into male-dominated professions—sometimes in large numbers (Adams 2010; Boulis and Jacobs 2008; Le Feuvre 2009). Professional work may still be gendered, but there is reason to believe that the experiences of women entering male-dominated professions today may differ in meaningful ways from those entering in decades past (Boulis and Jacobs 2008; Donley and Baird 2017).

The life course paradigm offers a way for researchers to understand these historical shifts in the gendering of professional work, and people's experiences of pursuing professional careers. This approach sheds light on the 'social pathways of human lives, particularly in their historical time and place' (Elder et al. 2003: 4). Scholars using the life course paradigm often focus on the norms and social-historical and individual circumstances surrounding key life transitions—significant changes that typically bring shifts in status and identity (such as leaving school and embarking on a career) (Elder et al. 2003; Shanahan and Macmillan 2008). Some transitions can have lifelong consequences, as they may set in motion cumulative advantages and disadvantages that influence individuals' life trajectories and opportunities (Shanahan and Macmillan 2008: 78–81). Not everyone experiences such transitions and trajectories the same way, since human beings have agency and varying life experiences (Elder et al. 2003; Elder 1994); however, transitions and trajectories are patterned by social norms, institutions, and historical events. As a result, people who share an age cohort may have distinct experiences of major life transitions, which might lead to life course trajectories that are distinct from those experienced by people in other age cohorts (Elder et al. 2003; Shanahan and Macmillan 2008). Applying these insights to women in professions, life course theory suggests that the social-historical context in which women enter a profession could profoundly shape their career experiences. Further we would expect different generations or cohorts of women to have different career experiences. In this manner, the experiences of women who entered engineering in the 1980s and 1990s may be markedly different than those who entered in the 2000s, in light of changing social attitudes to women working, and rising social and legal penalties for discrimination.

Women in Engineering: Past and Present

Engineering has long been a male-dominated endeavour. Historically, apprenticeship training for entry to practice effectively barred women (Walby 1986). When formal education in the field was introduced in the early twentieth century, women gained a toehold, but their presence was quite rare (ibid). Women's participation in engineering education was discouraged by a 'strongly masculine' culture, emphasising not only hard work, discipline, and respect for authority, but also pranks, parties, and occasional rowdiness (Heap and Scheinberg 2005: 193–194). Engineering workplaces were also heavily male dominated, and employers were reluctant to hire women. Some women who were trained as chemical engineers found jobs, but others had to seek opportunities outside the engineering profession. In the mid-twentieth century, women engineers reported gender discrimination in hiring, pay, and promotion opportunities (Heap and Scheinberg 2005: 204–205).

Research exploring women's experiences in engineering training and professional practice in the 1980s and 1990s provides similar accounts of engineering culture and discrimination. For example, Dryburgh's (1999) study of women at an Ontario, Canada engineering school, finds a culture emphasising masculinity, hard work, and discipline, combined with an emphasis on pranks and parties. Women tended to accept and blend in with this culture; some were 'just one of the guys' (Dryburgh 1999: 674). When they entered the engineering workplace, however, women often met with more blatant discrimination (Dryburgh 1999; Robinson and McIlwee 1989). Diversity initiatives opened up employment opportunities for women in this era, but hostility against women in the field lingered (Evetts 1994; Devine 1992). Once hired, women were concentrated in the lowest job levels, and opportunities for promotion were limited (Robinson and McIlwee 1989). Women engineers found it difficult to navigate gendered bureaucratic structures (Evetts 1994). Few women were able to break through the barriers and enter management. When women engineers had children they were often put on a 'mommy track' and were no longer viewed as promotable (Devine 1992). The women engineers whom Devine (1992) spoke with also talked about having to push hard for training opportunities, mentorship, and promotion consideration, unlike their male counterparts. As one of her study participants explained, 'you have to be better at your job, and you have to make yourself more known and be seen to be better at your job than a man' (Devine 1992: 568).

Since the early 2000s, there have been many initiatives to recruit young women to study engineering, and to encourage their persistence in the profession after graduating (Gill et al. 2008; Sharp et al. 2012). However, research suggests that the masculine structure and culture of engineering perpetuates sex segregation and discrimination in the field. In engineering programs, female engineering students often find success, but their first placements in industry are eye-opening, as many experience sexism from older male workers (Seron et al. 2016). Realising that 'sexism is not just an annoyance, but may be part of [their] everyday workplace experiences after graduation', some female engineering students begin to question their career choices (Seron et al. 2016: 203). Such experiences can reduce women engineering students' confidence that they can fulfil professional roles well, which in turn is associated with attrition out of the field (Cech et al. 2011).

Women who enter engineering practice typically quite enjoy their work, but they report several challenges (Gill et al. 2008). On the job, they can experience marginalisation (Hatmaker 2013). They are the focus of sexist comments (ibid). Their ideas can be ignored, and their competence can be questioned (Hatmaker 2013: 386–387). In these situations there may be a tendency for women to blame themselves (Gill et al. 2008), and they may seek individual solutions to these problems. For some women, the strategy to achieve success and prevent marginalisation is to downplay femininity and try to blend in with the men, becoming 'one of the guys' (Fortier 2002; Gill et al. 2008; Hatmaker 2013; Powell et al. 2009; Ranson 2005); however, this strategy may be difficult to maintain when engineers become mothers (Ranson 2005). Women whose competence is drawn into question respond by emphasising their technical skills: they do their research, gather evidence to support their decisions, and endeavour to work harder than their male counterparts to enhance their credibility (Hatmaker 2013; Powell et al. 2009). Some women are cast in stereotyped female roles and asked to take on gendered tasks (such as getting food and coffee, and taking meeting notes) (Gill et al. 2008; Hatmaker 2013). Women engineers resist this sex typing, but often find it difficult to battle against assumptions that their status as wives and mothers affects their ability to focus on their careers. Women may not challenge biases and discrimination outright to avoid further alienation and hostility from their colleagues (Powell et al. 2009). When the local labour market contains many opportunities, women in engineering may be able to resist poor working environments by job-hopping to more friendly firms (Shih 2006), but this strategy is not always available.

Although engineering firms have established diversity programs and policies, these have not been entirely effective (Sharp et al. 2012). Leaders may accept that the number of women in engineering should be increased (Ibid); however, there has been resistance among both men and women engineers to diversity initiatives (Sharp et al. 2012). Moreover, organisational cultural change has not accompanied such initiatives, and sometimes leadership has been ineffective at invoking change (Sharp et al. 2012).

What have been the implications for women entering engineering in recent years? In many respects, the literature suggests their experiences may be similar to their predecessors: discrimination, sex typing, and challenges navigating a masculine culture. Yet there is reason to believe their experiences may differ, as the engineering profession is committed to bringing about change, family-friendly policies are more established, and there are earlier cohorts of women engineers who have already blazed trails. Diversity initiatives may open up more opportunities for advancement. The literature on women in engineering rarely considers the significance of age cohort in shaping experience.

Methodology

To understand age and cohort differences in experiences of discrimination among Ontario, Canada women engineers, I use mixed methods. Data analysed in this chapter come from a larger study on the changing nature of work in Canada. Research on changes in Ontario engineering was conducted in partnership with the Ontario Society of Professional Engineers (OSPE). The case study of engineering involved three phases: (1) interviews with key informants who were experienced engineers with at least 15 years of practice experience; (2) an on-line survey conducted between October 2016 and February 2017; and (3) follow-up interviews with survey respondents. University ethics approval was obtained for all three phases. This chapter draws on both interview and survey data.

The on-line survey was lengthy and focused on work, learning, and attitudes to professional and social issues. The focus in this chapter is on responses to questions related to discrimination and discounting of skills. Only about 18% of the 700 survey respondents were women. Interview data are taken from eight key informant interviews with mid-career and late-career women engineers, and 13 interviews with women at various phases of their careers that were conducted after the survey was completed. In-depth, one-on-one interviews were conducted in person, over the phone, or via Skype. All 21 interviews were recorded and transcribed. Transcripts were analysed thematically, with a focus here on women's experiences of sexism and discrimination. While the main focus of the interviews was to discuss professional experiences generally, the women frequently raised gender issues unsolicited, and if they did not they were asked if they wanted to comment on the experiences of women in their profession. The majority recounted experiences of sexism and discrimination. In the analysis that follows, I address the following research question: do women's experiences of discrimination and their career opportunities vary across age cohorts?

Survey Findings

The survey asked respondents, 'In the last year, at work, have you been discriminated against, in any way, by anyone you have had contact with?' Over 51% of women said 'yes'. In contrast, only 12% of men indicated they had experienced discrimination. Women also reported receiving less credit for the work they completed: 66% of women respondents agreed or strongly agreed with the statement, 'At my workplace, men get more credit for their contributions and skills than women do'. In contrast, only 12% of men engineers agreed there was a gender imbalance. Women also believed they made less money than their male counterparts. Most women (81%) agreed or strongly agreed that 'men make more money in engineering than women do even when completing similar work'; however, 24% of men concurred. Generally, then, women in engineering report experiencing discrimination, wage inequality, and having their skills discounted.

To determine if women's experiences vary by age cohort, respondents were divided into three age categories: 35 and under, between 36 and 50, and 51 and over. These age categories were chosen because they approximate different generations of workers identified in the literature: those 35 and under are Millennials, while those 36–50 fall into 'Generation X', and many in the older group are Baby Boomers (see Choroszewicz and Adams 2019, this volume). Despite fairly low sample sizes, some age cohort differences were statistically significant. Table 13.1 shows the percentage of women in each age group indicating they had experienced discrimination, and agreeing or strongly agreeing with the statements on credit for work and wage bias.

As this table shows, younger female engineers were more likely to report problems than their older counterparts. Most women agreed that

Table 13.1 Women's experiences of discrimination by age cohort

Statement	35 and Under	36–50	51 and Older	Total
Discriminated against in last year. (% [and number] saying yes)	60.1% (28)	37.5% (9)	42.9% (6)	51.2% (43)
Men get more credit for their contributions and skills than do women. (% [and number] agree)	67.9% (36)	60.7% (17)	68.5% (13)	66% (66)
Men make more money than women even for similar work. (% [and number] agree)	85.8% (42)	80.0% (20)	68.4% (13)	80.7% (75)

men at their workplace got more credit for their work contributions and skills, but the women most likely to *disagree* with this statement were over 36. Roughly one-third of women 36–50, and 26% of those 51 and over, indicated this was not true in their workplace, while only 20% of younger women disagreed. This age difference among women is statistically significant ($X^2 = 16.6$, $p < .05$). Age differences were also apparent in responses to the statement concerning men making more money than women. Here again, younger women were more likely to agree than older women ($X^2 = 16.6$, $p < .05$).

Table 13.1 suggests small differences in discrimination, as well, with 60% of women under 35 reporting discrimination, compared to less than half of those over 35; however, the difference is not statistically significant.

Women elaborated on their experiences with discrimination, sexism, having their skills discounted, and other challenges in the in-depth interviews.

Experiences of Discrimination and Sexism

In interviews, women talked about being denied opportunities, getting passed over for jobs and promotions, and losing their jobs. Women in all age groups relayed stories of discrimination and sexism. In general, amongst the women, there was a clear understanding that they had to navigate male-dominated environments and masculine cultures. Margaret (51+) summed it up well:

> The workplace was kind of designed for an alpha male, for alpha men and if you don't take on those characteristics, whether you're

a man or a woman, you won't be successful. . . . You know, this is a problem of our profession not having an inclusive work environment.

On a day-to-day basis, women engineers of all ages might face sexist comments and micro-aggressions from people they worked with. In interviews, it was the youngest women who provided the most examples. For them, sexism was clearly intertwined with ageism:

I'd have guys telling me, 'well, you didn't test that right', 'you didn't do that right', 'you didn't do this right'. You know, 'I've been doing this since you were'—well, a few rude things, but essentially a twinkle in your dad's eye. And, you know, that kind of stuff frequently. . . 'You don't know your ass from your armpit'. 'Whoever gave you a book should be shot'. 'Who gave you shoes? You should be barefoot and pregnant and chained to the stove'. Like [they said] just horrible things.

(Raina, < 35)

Cheryl (< 35) indicated that she had 'experienced both sexism and ageism' in the form of 'older men kind of talking down the younger generation and women'. Younger women also had to deal with sexual comments and harassment:

I think it's unfortunate that if you're like, attractive, you're expected to accept the harassment, and if you're ugly, you're told to appreciate it.

(Elizabeth, < 35)

Some older women also referred to harassment, especially earlier in their careers, such as Julia (51+):

I could tell you a whole story about being a woman engineer out in the construction sites—300 men and me—that could take up another two hours of your time. I call it character building experience, in the 80s—you can imagine. Them talking about sexual harassment with the brochures and I was living the dream. I'd go in there and say, 'Excuse me, nice brochure but I need some help here!'

Negative interactions with co-workers were shocking, and yet women had come to expect them:

Everything you do, especially in a male dominated field, is always going to have some sort of sexism spin. It's never going to be completely equal. Well, maybe it will be one day, but at the time right now it's not.

(Elizabeth, < 35)

Although older women provided fewer examples of micro-aggressions, many did continue to experience them:

Like, I've been working for 27 years, and I've heard the same comments that I heard the first day I stepped in an engineering role, which is unfortunate. And a lot of the young people, they are experiencing that. And I say, where is the evolution in the profession? It's not there!

(Shawna, 51+)

For the most part, the women I spoke with successfully navigated these masculine work environments by demonstrating considerable resilience and determination:

I'm not the kind of person who would let something this piddly get in my way.

(Madelyn, 36–50)

You have to get toughened up so fast. I call it positive rebellion. They'd say, 'Oh women don't belong in construction'. That used to really bother me. I'd say 'well, I'll decide where I'm going to be. I wanna learn out here'.

(Julia, 51+)

I have never considered gender difference as a problem. Well, I will go into a meeting in a construction site, and I am the only female on the site. But it's no big deal. You are with six to eight other guys. It's no big deal. I have been in the field for years.

(Hannah, 51+)

Such resilience helps women cope with everyday sexism and micro-aggressions, but it cannot protect them from blatant discrimination, such as being denied opportunities:

I was the only engineer in my company, the only female . . . So, yeah, you're definitely treated differently. We were doing a lot of international work back there. The boss came right out and told me 'I'm not sending a woman [overseas]. Sorry, you're not going'.

(Kimberly, 36–50)

When I first started I didn't have a family or anything and I wanted to travel and I wanted to be involved in exciting projects and so on.

And [when I asked] they would just look at me with these dumb-founded faces and no answer.

(Delilah, 51+)

During an economic downturn, Margaret was let go by her engineering company:

I was told. . . 'we're laying you off because you have a husband who works'.

(Margaret, 51+)

Her boss had to choose between her and a male colleague, and he had a stay-at-home wife, so he got to keep his job.

Ruth (51+) was semi-retired at the time of her interview. Over the course of her career she had not only been denied jobs because of her gender, but also overlooked for promotion opportunities after having children:

In terms of advancement, me and my group [cohort at her firm] . . . we had children, and um . . . and that doesn't do much for your career. At least it didn't at that time. So um my sort of group . . . of people, we had our kids, we took the maternity leave, we . . . in fact, we job-shared or did reduced hours of work. And um we were stigmatised for that. We were all, you know, 'you're on the mommy track'.

Raina (< 35), one of the younger women in the study, had worked out-side of Canada and found it difficult to find work. For 'fun' she altered her resume:

I just put my initial as my first name, and I'd get way more phone calls. It was fun, because it would be like 'Oh, I'm looking for Mr. ----'. 'Speaking'. And they're like, 'Oh, we're looking for Mr. ----, the engineer from Canada'. 'Yeah, you're talking to her'. 'Oh, I'm sorry, you're not what we're looking for'.

Skills/Knowledge Discounted

Many interview participants reported having their skills and knowledge discounted. While this experience was shared by the majority of study participants, it was especially highlighted by the youngest and very oldest women interviewed, suggesting—as in the survey findings—that gender and age interact to shape experiences.

For Elizabeth (< 35), having skills discounted is

the only normal I've ever experienced. So, to be talked down to, to walk into a meeting room and have people look at you to take notes in the meeting every single time, just because you're the youngest and the female person in the room, is really challenging.

Ying (< 35) reported that her experiences have been generally good in engineering:

like I guess I haven't been mistreated badly or something, but there are sometimes little funny things that happen.

More specifically, she finds that when people have questions about something she has designed they first approach her male co-worker 'that had nothing to do with the project' with their questions. Clients are slow to recognise her technological expertise.

Raina (< 35) also reported that some of her colleagues refused to recognise her skills:

There's a few engineers that I work with . . . who won't recognise the fact that I am an engineer, that I am trained, that I have experience, that I have the technical knowledge. It just doesn't even register with them.

This can be especially challenging for young women who have to try to direct the work of older men:

To try to be authoritative in a project engineering role, telling . . . a man your father's age, to get their work done quicker. I'm not going to get anywhere.

(Elizabeth, < 35)

When working with other engineers, Elizabeth (< 35) felt her ideas were not being recognised or appreciated, and she had to be strategic to get her ideas to be heard:

Anytime you do say something, or suggest an idea, or something like that, you have to make the managers or the other engineers there feel like they came up with it themselves, in order to get it done. So, it's like . . . you have to be like, super manipulative, even to get them on your side. And so, it's one of those . . . things . . . making older men and older engineers feel like the idea was theirs, because then they will actually do it, even though it was yours all along. And, you have to be, 'Oh wow, I wonder if we could, you know, devise a system that would work in this way. Oh, that would be so cool'. And . . . then have them come up with like the idea that you're like, feeding them.

Women aged 36–50 reported mixed experiences. Some felt that their skills were still devalued, despite the experience they had accumulated. In Kimberly's (36–50) words,

> Probably the worst thing is your opinion isn't valued on a construction site regardless of your experience.

In contrast, Gemma (36–50) felt that she had an easier time on-site, because even if workers did not like listening to her, they had to do so because of her position. She had a tougher time among those she worked with more closely:

> Amongst the engineers it is harder. I've been in a place that we have a technologist and he's drafting and it's me and another EIT [engineer-in-training] at the same level, the same position, the same level, the same project. He's a man. I'm a woman. So I'm telling him that what he's drafting we don't need it because they decided it's not going to be fitted in the project. And he got frustrated. He didn't say anything and he turned and asked in front of me the man engineer to ask him like I didn't talk.

Madelyn's (36–50) experience was different. She believed that since she had proven her competence, she experienced fewer problems, although upon reflection she indicated the problems had not completely disappeared:

> I don't ever face problems because of it. You know, it's . . . I find that people are pretty . . . once they realise that you're competent and you know what you're doing, they will respect that. So, you know, there may be a bit of a 'Oh, it's a woman' initial reaction, probably less now than I faced ten years ago, but, it still happens every once in a while . . . But, yeah. I don't know if anything's changed. It's always kind of been the same, which is again, kind of depressing.

Zoe (36–50) believed that even senior women engineers did not get the respect they deserved, arguing that women—unlike their male counterparts—'would have to prove themselves, each and every time' they encountered a new client, customer, or team.

Most of the women aged 51 and over did not mention having their knowledge discounted, suggesting that with experience (and as we will see later, workplace change), their skills may have been more respected. Nevertheless, there were hints that older women could face some problems. Consider these comments from Ruth, who was semi-retired:

> Women's skills are belittled a little bit. I have another friend who is working for another company in the industry. She's been working

since about 1985. She's an engineer, and she was recently . . . her supervisor changed, and her new supervisor treats her as if she's, you know, from the clerical pool. No acknowledgement of her degree and her 30 years of experience.

It appears that the youngest and possibly the oldest women are most vulnerable to having their skills discounted, while many mid-career women feel that their experience and skill is more often recognised.

Coping Strategies

Women have developed numerous coping strategies to succeed in their careers despite these masculine work environments and sexism. In the previous sections it is clear that women have become resilient and found ways to navigate these environments. Tolerance is emphasised by many. For example, Ying (< 35) says she tries to keep an open mind:

Usually people don't do it purposely, right. Like they're not trying to kick all women out. That's not what they want. It's just a habit. Like their intentions are good, so I think just understanding that it's totally fine. It's just like the way they act, and you can't like directly say, you're acting rude. You don't do that.

She continued to explain, 'You can't just stop people and say, "hey, stop doing that; you're being sexist" '. This is not simply an excuse. Margaret (51+) told a story of trying to intervene when one of her colleagues experienced sexism on the job.

I ended up bringing it to the attention of our director of the group and because I did that, I lost—like it was clearly limiting for me.

Margaret's experience suggests that speaking out can have negative repercussions.

This is not to say that women did not fight sexism and discrimination. A number of older women talked about fighting for flexible working hours, family-friendly policies, sexual harassment policies, and other important policies in their workplaces. They established associations and supported each other, and attempted to mentor junior women entering the profession. At the same time, many women found that the best response to a negative work environment was to seek another job:

A lot of women have said, 'just leave' you know? There's nothing you can do. Go find another company. I heard one woman, she did very, very well. She moved up. She moved from company to company. She said she hit a brick wall, she left, you know? She didn't wait around, you know, hitting her head against the wall.

(Ruth, 51+)

[The] women engineers that were not being treated properly . . . I would say typically what they did is they left the job. And sometimes they left the profession, which was really problematic.

(Heather, 51+)

Many of the women I spoke with had run into problems and had changed jobs as a result. Elizabeth (< 35) endured workplace harassment and lost her job when she complained. She found a fulfilling job that enabled her to use her engineering skills, even though she was not working as an engineer. Kimberly (36–50), Veronica (51+), Delilah (51+), Shawna (51+), and Heather (51+) started their own companies to find work that was fulfilling, challenging, and enjoyable. Others worked for various companies until they found workplaces that were flexible, and female-friendly. Some lucked into such positions early in their careers.

Women's tendency to move around until they find work that is more female-friendly—whether in engineering or not—illuminates the survey findings presented earlier. Older women may report less discrimination, and fewer instances of skill downgrading, because over the course of their careers they have actively sought workplaces where they feel accepted and appreciated. If they have the opportunity, younger women may do the same over time. Many are hopeful, though, that the environment for women in engineering will soon get better:

To be honest I think in the next generation that'll phase out . . . when a lot of the, I want to say Baby Boomers, retire.

(Cheryl, <35)

I think if more women come into the industry, or more women engineers are educated and hired, eventually it changes.

(Ying, <35)

Conclusion

Both the survey and interview data reveal that women in engineering today continue to face discrimination. Across age cohorts, women report experiencing sexism and the discounting of their skills. Yet, differences across cohorts are evident. Younger female engineers are more likely to report receiving less credit for their skills. They indicate they earn less than their male colleagues. They appear to be more vulnerable to sexism and gender bias than their older female counterparts. Professional initiatives and social change have not yet succeeded in creating environments where young entrants into the engineering profession can thrive. Older women report less recent discrimination, but in interviews most recounted having to overcome many obstacles during their careers, including blocked opportunities, sexism, and harassment. Many mid-career and late-career women intentionally sought, and eventually found, work environments that provided opportunities for challenging and fulfilling work, and were more female-friendly. The challenges they experienced in engineering fostered resilience, and encouraged a career trajectory that sometimes took them into non-traditional practice areas, and into jobs outside of engineering.

It is not yet clear whether younger cohorts of engineers will traverse career paths similar to their predecessors over time. New initiatives to make engineering workplaces more female-friendly may open up opportunities for younger women within engineering. Women may find less of a need to move from firm to firm, and even out of the profession to advance their careers. At the same time, however, the labour market prospects for newer engineers are less positive than in the past, leading many young engineers into jobs outside of engineering (OSPE 2015); hence younger engineers may face some challenges their predecessors did not. Younger cohorts of women engineers may experience more difficulty getting established in the profession, but once they are established, they may have more opportunities for promotion and advancement. Although engineering workplaces are still gendered masculine, they appear to be shifting. Nevertheless, the long-term impact of organisational and labour market change is difficult to predict. It is important that future research continue to explore the importance of cohort and age to professional experiences, in order to understand better shifts in gendered professional work over time.

Clearly the engineering profession, and engineering workplaces, still have some work to do to create less hostile work environments. Given concerns over retention in engineering, it is notable that women's search for positive work environments sometimes takes them out of traditional engineering. More work remains to be done to plug the leaky pipeline. At the same time, however, if the goal is to improve women's representation in engineering, the profession may also want to consider broadening its definition of engineering to include more non-traditional, and female-friendly work settings. Many women who leave engineering continue to identify as engineers, and they use engineering skills in their jobs. They *are* engineers, even if not counted as such. Expanding narrow conceptions of engineering practice, along with restructuring engineering workplaces, may be required to undermine the traditional (masculine) gendering of engineering practice, and to create environments in which new cohorts of engineers, regardless of gender, can thrive.

References

Acker, J (1990) 'Hierarchies, Jobs, Bodies: A Theory of Gendered Organizations' 4 *Gender & Society* 139. doi:10.1177/089124390004002002

Adams, TL (2000) *A Dentist and a Gentleman: Gender and the Rise of Dentistry in Ontario* (Toronto, University of Toronto Press). doi:10.3138/9781442670297

—— (2010) 'Gender and Feminization in Health Care Professions' 4 *Sociology Compass* 454. doi:10.1111/j.1751-9020.2010.00294.x

Boulis, AK and Jacobs, JA (2008) *The Changing Face of Medicine: Women Doctors and the Evolution of Health Care in America* (Ithaca, NY, Cornell University Press).

Cech, E, Rubineau, B, Silbey, S and Seron, C (2011) 'Professional Role Confidence and Gendered Persistence in Engineering' 76 *American Sociological Review* 641. doi:10.1177/0003122411420815

Choroszewicz, M and Adams, T (2019) 'Introduction' in M. Choroszewicz and T. Adams (eds), *Age, Gender, and Inequality in Professions* (New York, Routledge).

Davies, C (1996) 'The Sociology of Professions and the Profession of Gender' 30 *Sociology* 661. doi:10.1177/0038038596030004003

Devine, F (1992) 'Gender Segregation in the Engineering and Science Professions: A Case of Continuity and Change' 6 *Work, Employment and Society* 557, 568. doi:10.1177/0950017092006004003

Donley, S and Baird, CL (2017) 'The Overtaking of Undertaking? Gender Beliefs in a Feminizing Occupation' 77 *Sex Roles* 97. doi:10.1007/s11199-016-0699-6

Dryburgh, H (1999) 'Work Hard, Play Hard: Women and Professionalization in Engineering—Adapting to the Culture' 13 *Gender & Society* 664, 674. doi:10.1177/089124399013005006

Elder Jr, GH (1994) 'Time, Human Agency, and Social Change: Perspectives on the Life Course' 57 *Social Psychology Quarterly* 4. doi:10.2307/2786971

Elder Jr, GH, Johnson, MK and Crosnoe, R (2003) 'The Emergence and Development of Life Course Theory' in JT Mortimer and MJ Shanahan (eds), *Handbook of the Life Course* (New York, Kluwer Academic/Plenum Publishers), 4.

Engineers Canada (2018) *Women in Engineering* (Ottawa, Engineers Canada). https://engineerscanada.ca/diversity/women-in-engineering

Evetts, J (1994) 'Women and Career in Engineering: Continuity and Change in the Organisation' 8 *Work, Employment and Society* 101. doi:10.1177/0950017094008001007

Fortier, I (2002) 'Pouvoir, compétence et féminité: Expérience d'ingénieures en gestion' 15 *Recherches Féministes* 65.

Gill, J, Mills, J, Franzway, S and Sharp, R (2008) ' "Oh you must be very clever!" High-Achieving Women, Professional Power and the Ongoing Negotiation of Workplace Identity' 20 *Gender and Education* 223. doi:10.1080/09540250801968990

Guinier, L, Fine, M and Balin, J (1997) *Becoming Gentlemen: Women, Law School, and Institutional Change* (Boston, Beacon Press).

Hatmaker, DM (2013) 'Engineering Identity: Gender and Professional Identity Negotiation Among Women Engineers' 20 *Gender, Work & Organization* 382, 386–387. doi:10.1111/j.1468-0432.2012.00589.x

Herman, C (2015) 'Rebooting and Rerouting: Women's Articulations of Frayed Careers in Science, Engineering and Technology Professions' 22 *Gender, Work & Organization* 324. doi:10.1111/gwao.12088

Heap, R and Scheinberg, E (2005) ' "Just one of the gang": Women at the University of Toronto's Faculty of Applied Science and Engineering, 1939–50' in R Heap, W Millar, and E Smyth (eds), *Learning to Practise: Professional Education in Historical and Contemporary Perspective* (Ottawa, University of Ottawa Press), 193–194, 204–205.

Hinze, S (1999) 'Gender and the Body of Medicine or at Least Some Body Parts: (Re)Constructing the Prestige Hierarchy of Medical Specialties' 40 *The Sociological Quarterly* 217.

Katawazi, M (2017) 'Gender Pay Gap Persists, Census Data Shows' *Toronto Star* 29 November 2017. www.thestar.com/news/canada/2017/11/29/gender-pay-gap-persists-census-data-shows.html

Le Feuvre, N (2009) 'Exploring Women's Academic Careers in Cross-National Perspective: Lessons for Equal Opportunity Policies' 28 *Equal Opportunities International* 9.

Ontario Society of Professional Engineers (OSPE) (2015) *Crisis in Ontario's Engineering Labour Market: Underemployment Among Ontario's Engineering-Degree Holders* (Toronto, OSPE). www.ospe.on.ca/public/documents/advocacy/2015-crisis-in-engineering-labour-market.pdf

Powell, A, Bagilhole, B and Dainty, A (2009) 'How Women Engineers Do and Undo Gender: Consequences for Gender Equality' 16 *Gender, Work & Organization* 411. doi:10.1111/j.1468-0432.2008.00406.x

Ranson, G (2005) 'No Longer "One of the Boys": Negotiations with Motherhood, as Prospect or Reality, Among Women in Engineering' 42 *Canadian Review of Sociology* 145. doi:10.1111/j.1755-618X.2005.tb02459.x

Robinson, JG and McIlwee, JS (1989) 'Women in Engineering: A Promise Unfulfilled?' 36 *Social Problems* 455. doi:10.2307/3096812

Seron, C, Silbey, SS, Cech, E and Rubineau, B (2016) 'Persistence Is Cultural: Professional Socialization and the Reproduction of Sex Segregation' 43 *Work and Occupations* 178, 203. doi:10.1177/0730888415618728

Shanahan, MJ and Macmillan, R (2008) *Biography and the Sociological Imagination: Contexts and Contingencies* (New York, WW Norton and Co), 78–81.

Sharp, R, Franzway, S, Mills, J and Gill, J (2012) 'Flawed Policy, Failed Politics? Challenging the Sexual Politics of Managing Diversity in Engineering Organizations' 19 *Gender, Work and Organization* 555. doi:10.1111/j.1468-0432.2010.00545.x

Shih, J (2006) 'Circumventing Discrimination: Gender and Ethnic Strategies in Silicon Valley' 20 *Gender and Society* 177. doi:10.1177/0891243205285474

Tancred, P (1999) 'Outsiders/Insiders: Women and Professional Norms' 14 *Canadian Journal of Law and Society* 31. doi:10.1017/S0829320100005913

Walby, S (1986) *Patriarchy at Work* (Cambridge, Polity Press).

Witz, A (1992) *Professions and Patriarchy* (London, New York, Routledge).

Wright, R (1996) 'The Occupational Masculinity of Computing' in C Cheng (ed), *Masculinities in Organizations* (London, Sage).

Conclusion

Conclusion

14 Conclusion

Findings, Future Research, and Policy Recommendations

Tracey L. Adams and Marta Choroszewicz

Introduction

There is a substantial body of research exploring the significance of gender to both the organisation of professional work and the prospects, opportunities, and experiences of professional workers (Adams 2010; Davies 1996; Witz 1992). Many traditional professions in the West were defined by men, for men, and women have faced discrimination and marginalisation as a result (Adams 2000; Davies 1996). Although women have entered professions in large numbers over the last few decades, there is evidence that there are gender differences in practice and opportunities for advancement and promotion (Hearn et al. 2016; Riska 2014). Nevertheless, in this volume, we have argued that a gender lens is not sufficient to understand the experiences of women and men engaging in professional work. Adopting an intersectional approach reveals that gender interacts with age cohort and the life course (as well as race, ethnicity, nationality, and other identities and structured sets of social relations) to shape social experience.

The chapters in this volume focus on different professions and touch on a variety of experiences from career entry through work–family conflict and career trajectories, to social media activities, emotional capital, discrimination, and income. Each one provides insight into how gender and age cohort/generation intersect to shape experiences. The chapters reveal that men and women in different generations or age cohorts can experience professional work differently, and that life stage can profoundly shape professional work and careers. The chapters also highlight the importance of time and place: experiences vary by era and country, as not only social-historical context but also gender regimes and policy environments shape professionals' opportunities.

In the introduction we provided a theoretical lens for bringing age into intersectional research. Intersectional theory has tended to focus on the intersection of gender with race/ethnicity and class (Acker 2006; Glenn 2002; Holvino 2010); there has been less attention to the intersection of gender and age (McMullin 2011). In fact, some scholars argue that age is not as 'thoroughly embedded in organizing processes' as other dimensions of inequality, like gender and race (Acker 2006: 445). This has left a theoretical gap and perhaps discouraged intersectional research linking age and gender. We have suggested that adopting a life course perspective (Elder 1994; Shanahan and Macmillan 2008) provides an avenue to advance intersectional research. Blending intersectional research with a life course perspective illuminates how gender in interaction with class and race/ethnicity structures social pathways, and how experiences along these pathways vary not only across time and place, but also for individuals as they age. Furthermore, incorporating a life course perspective allows us to explore generational differences in experience of gender inequalities within professions. It is through a life course lens that we can better understand the intersection of age and gender at work.

While the chapters in this volume adopt such a lens to varying degrees, we argue that all enhance our understanding of the intersection of gender with age cohort/generation to shaping inequalities within professions. In this concluding chapter we summarise the main findings of the research presented in this volume, and consider their significance for understanding and theorising age and gender inequalities in professions. We then discuss the implications of these findings for research on professions, and identify promising directions for future research. At the end of the chapter, we build on the insights of the research presented in this volume and provide some policy recommendations for organisations, professions, educational institutions, and governments.

Main Themes and Findings

The chapters in this volume explore different professions—including Medicine, Nursing, Law, Academia, Information Technology, and Engineering—in different Western countries, in the present and over time. Despite this broad lens, several themes recurred: the challenges experienced by Millennials and others embarking on careers, work–family conflict and its impact on career trajectories, and the shifting significance of gender to professional work across generations. The exploration of each of these themes reflects the ways in which gender and age converge to confer privilege and produce disadvantage, and the ways in which gender inequality is reproduced, and disrupted, through the activities of professionals on the job.

Recent research has highlighted the challenges facing a growing segment of the labour force in labour markets characterised by precarity (Kalleberg 2009). Although professional work has long been more secure and stable than other types, professionals are not immune from these trends (Barley and Kunda 2004). However, positive change is evident as well, as states and organisations have endeavoured to advance gender equality in Western countries in a manner that would appear to reduce gender barriers in professional employment (Boulis and Jacobs 2008; Magnusson and Nermo in this volume). Thus, new practitioners entering professions today face a very different labour market than those who preceded them. Nevertheless, the studies in this volume suggest that Millennials embarking on professional careers still face many challenges.

Young women entering professions appear more likely than their male counterparts to work in precarious and/or lower-status jobs (Adams in this volume; Kay in this volume). They may find it difficult to obtain training opportunities in an institution that allows them to balance their work and life commitments (Adams and Kwon in this volume; Corbett in this volume). They face discrimination from teachers, mentors, and sometimes senior colleagues (Adams in this volume; Adams and Kwon in this volume). They have less supportive managers, and fewer opportunities for advancement (Corbett in this volume). They earn, on average, less money (Magnusson and Nermo in this volume). They are subject to more intensive negative emotions and uncertainty on the job than older practitioners (Cottingham and Dill in this volume). Moreover, even when working in professions that are feminised or feminising, they have to conform to traditional (masculine) gendered assumptions about career commitment and constant availability, which not only prevent work–life balance, but also can limit career advancement (Olakivi and Wrede in this volume).

Combined, these studies reveal that new entrants face many challenges when entering professions, and that these challenges are gendered. Young women are expected not only to be professional at all times, but also to conform to cultural expectations of femininity that leave them vulnerable to work–life conflict, emotional pressures, and discrimination. Young men face pressures as well, but gender norms and cultural scripts may insulate them from some of the emotional demands, discrimination, and work–family conflict experienced by young women. Gender and age combine in particular ways to shape the early career experiences of men and women embarking on professional careers. These early career challenges have implications for career trajectories.

The impact on career trajectories is evident in studies exploring work–family conflict within professions. Studies in this volume highlight how professions' cultures of long work hours lead to work–family conflict for both men and women. This conflict appears to be experienced differently across generation and gender. Research on the legal profession reveals how the structure of law careers renders law difficult to combine with raising children. Some women resolve this conflict by leaving practice altogether, or taking on less demanding work in the legal field (Boni-Le Goff et al. in this volume). However, it must be noted that opportunities for work–life balance are significantly shaped by the structure of firms, professions, and policy, such that experiences can differ significantly across country (ibid). Men also face challenges with work–life balance, and these challenges may be felt more by younger generations of men who expect to be more involved in child-rearing than men of the Baby Boomer generation (Choroszewicz in this volume). Work–family conflict can have a significant impact on professional careers. Firms may discriminate against individuals because of actual (or even presumed) family responsibilities, negatively impacting women's career opportunities (Plickert in this volume). The impact of discrimination on this basis is different and distinguishable from gender discrimination, which can ebb and flow across the life course (ibid).

Work–family conflict challenges are evident in other professions as well. Olakivi and Wrede (in this volume) show how these problems can be individualised by professionals such as medical doctors. The doctors in their study recognised work–family conflict, yet did not see this as an organisational or professional issue, but rather as a private challenge for individuals to work out in a manner that would not affect their work. Professionals did not recognise these challenges as ones shaped by gender, age, and life course stage. The result can be an acceptance of the status quo and a failure to recognise how professional practices reproduce gender inequalities, especially during particular life course stages. Thus, despite the presence of national and firm-based policies aiming to minimise work–family conflict, it persists and continues to perpetuate gendered inequalities in professions—especially during child-rearing years—with lasting impacts on career trajectories.

While the gendered nature of professions and persistent work–family conflict place women—especially younger women—at a disadvantage in professions, there is evidence of change over time. The experiences of men and women in one generation are not the same as those in another. Men and women who enter professions under different labour market conditions, gender regimes, and policy contexts have different experiences of working (Boni-Le Goff et al. in this volume; Magnusson and Nermo in this volume). The gendering of professional work can also shift over time. Age differences are certainly evident, as older women professionals experience different emotional demands (Cottingham and Dill in this volume) and report different experiences with discrimination (Adams in this volume). In information technology (IT), they report lower levels of satisfaction than do their younger counterparts (Corbett in this volume), but in other professions this may be reversed. Today, younger women are well-represented in high-prestige occupations; however, wage inequalities among young men and women are largely unchanged since the late 1960s (Magnusson and Nermo in this volume). Furthermore, technological change—for example the rise of social media—has altered the landscape, providing different mechanisms through which gender inequalities can be reproduced and challenged (Neville in this volume). All of these trends point to the changing significance of gender to professional work.

Professions remain gendered, but precisely how they are gendered has changed over time.

This latter finding reveals how professionals, through their actions, can challenge and change the structure of professional work. While gender and age continue to combine to produce privileges and disadvantages for men and women pursuing professions, there are continual opportunities for positive change. Impactful change is already evident, leading to an increase in women's participation in male-dominated professions and more policies that support work–family balance. However, gender differences in early career opportunities and support, as well as experiences of work–family conflict and discrimination, suggest that more change is needed. As Olakivi and Wrede (in this volume) suggest, perhaps the first step towards change is realising that differences by gender, age (and ethnicity, race, and many other factors) exist, and that these problems are structural and institutional, not private and personal. This book, in drawing attention to the significance of gender and age cohort/generation to inequality in professions, has identified many areas in which important changes can be made to foster greater inequality in professions. Such changes promise to improve the lives and work of professionals, which—given the important services they provide to society—could have a significant benefit for clients, customers, and society more generally.

To promote positive change, we provide policy recommendations at the end of the chapter.

Professionals' 'Meta-Work' Within Traditional Professional Structures

The chapters provide ample examples of strategies and tactics that young and female professionals use to cope with structural inequalities. For example, new lawyers who are older than the typical graduate are more likely to enter the public sector as well as solo practice and small firms (Kay in this volume). Women lawyers are more likely to change their work schedules due to experiences of discrimination (Plickert in this volume). Women's most common response to discrimination across professions is to exit workplaces or professions (Adams in this volume; Boni-Le Goff et al. in this volume), which results in their underrepresentation in male-dominated work environments (Corbett in this volume). Young female professionals in particular feel pressure to find ways to cope with stress, discrimination, and feelings associated with being young and inexperienced (Cottingham and Dill in this volume; Hearn and Husu in this volume; Kwon and Adams in this volume; Olakivi and Wrede in this volume), as well as building new narratives of themselves, for example as involved fathers (see Choroszewicz in this volume).

These professionals spend extra time and energy to develop individual strategies and tactics. We call this 'meta-work' because it is hidden

268   Tracey L. Adams and Marta Choroszewicz

and invisible to others—especially to those in privileged positions. This 'meta-work' is linked to professional roles and identities and more specifically to the traditional ideals of becoming and acting as a professional. These ideals, as the chapters in this volume show, rest upon strong assumptions around sex/gender, race/ethnicity, class and age, yet they are hardly recognised. These ideals are deeply embedded within professional structures and cultures; thus, they are considered 'obvious' and 'natural', especially for the privileged members of professional communities. These ideals still prevail even though professional communities are much more diverse today than when these professional ideals were formed. 'Meta-work' is laborious as it touches on young and female professionals' sense of self and their belonging to their professional communities. While some 'meta-work' is inherent to the development of professional identity and thus needs to be performed by all professionals, it may place particular strains on young professionals from less traditional socio-demographic backgrounds who need to do more 'meta-work' to present themselves as competent professionals. The chapters in this volume provide insightful evidence of how extensive 'meta-work' can be for women and young professionals in contemporary professions. Burdening these professionals with responsibility for finding their way and developing strategies to cope with professional pressures on and around their work and work–family reconciliation cannot be seen as the only remedy for making professions more equal and diverse.

While 'meta-work', and the tactics and strategies that result from it, are important coping mechanisms for some professionals, enabling them to deal with rapidly changing work realities and the lack of collegial support, they are resource-consuming and thus they may further disadvantage professionals in their careers. What is more, they are also expressions of varying forms of agency experienced specifically by professionals from less traditional socio-demographic backgrounds. While we do not deny the importance of this 'meta-work' for disrupting and changing the old gender-, age-, and race/ethnicity-related inequalities, it does not always lead to the creation of permanent fissures in patterns of professional practice and career trajectories. Instead, some chapters in this volume show that the extra burden of meta-work may result in professionals becoming disillusioned with their chosen careers, prompting them to leave their jobs, organisations, sectors, and even their professions. This is why we argue that this 'meta-work' needs to be supplemented with structural changes to create long-lasting alterations to the professions.

However, meaningful structural change is currently hindered by the neoliberal ideology that is prevalent in the professions. This ideology—with its emphasis on competition, individualism, productivity, performance, and entrepreneurship—hampers recognition of gender-, age-, and race/ethnicity-related structural inequalities. It operates as the catalyst for structural inequalities as it is used to normalise career outcomes as expressions of individual freedom, free will, and hard work. While equality and diversity programs and policies within contemporary professions and organisations are popular, they appear to have limited impact on changing social structures (McLaughlin and Deakin 2011). These programs and polices often stay at the level of image management within companies. In addition, they are usually consistent with the neoliberal ideology—from which they are derived—to the extent that overcoming discrimination is seen as an individual phenomenon (ibid). The key question remains whether neoliberal subjects such as young and female professionals have the resources to dissolve the old hierarchies in professional work.

Concluding Thoughts and Suggestions for Future Research

This book has explored age and gender inequalities within professional work, arguing for an intersectional approach and introducing the concept of meta-work to capture the activities that individuals pursue to adapt to, and challenge, existing professional hierarchies. Still, much work remains to be done in this field. In this section, we highlight several areas for future research. We have chosen to highlight a few key areas: the day-to-day experiences of professionals, longitudinal research to capture trends over time (and life course transitions and trajectories more accurately), emotions, the work–family interface, and technology. More broadly, there is also a need for further theoretical work, to incorporate age cohort and generation into intersectional research.

While there is a large body of research on the significance of gender to professional employment, we know more about gendered career outcomes than we do about the day-to-day struggles and experiences of professionals on the job, and the significance of gender, age, and other dimensions of inequality to these experiences. A few chapters in this book have touched on the emotional lives of practitioners, as well as their identities and outlooks. There is clearly more work to be done here to capture the emotional experiences of men and women in professions. Professions have long been conceived as work predicated on science and reason, leading to a relegation of emotion to subordinate workers (Davies 1996). However, emotions are a part of professional practice, and we need more research on how emotions and emotion work are shaped by the intersection of gender and age. Research on the day-to-day experiences of professionals should also focus on social interactions at work, to enhance our understanding of the conditions needed for sharing professional skills, knowledge, and experience—within and across generations—as well as building positive professional identities.

Furthermore, more research on professional work should be longitudinal. Such research will enhance our understanding of how practitioners' coping strategies and tactics differ as they age and as they progress in their careers, and how these strategies are influenced by everyday interactions at work. Longitudinal research is essential if we are to embrace a life course perspective and consider the significance of key transitions for the long-term career trajectories of men and women.

Several chapters in this volume highlight the importance of traditional family norms and family policies, such as parental leave, to inequality within professions. Such policies differ across countries, but increasingly include a non-transferable parental leave for fathers. We encourage more comparative research to explore the impact of policy on professional careers more thoroughly. This research should take age and generation into account. Young professionals are more likely to experience contradictions between their expectations and realities for gender equality in family and in work (McDonald 2018). Research in this volume and elsewhere has illuminated women's experiences, but there is a need for more research examining men's experiences and career impacts. There is also a need for more attention to cases, practices, and policies that challenge traditional gender norms, both in family and in work, to elucidate conditions and factors facilitating these. Research in this area is also needed on the intersection between professional and parenting identities, and shifts in these identities across the life course—not only for women but also for men. Specifically, further research could examine heterogeneity within age cohorts and generations, in terms of career goals and patterns, as well as gender relations in constructions of parenthood.

A few chapters in this volume call for broadening traditional definitions of professional work to include new environments and non-traditional work settings. New practitioners, and those otherwise marginalised, may gravitate to new settings, whether due to a desire for innovation or a lack of opportunities in traditional sectors. Research on practitioners in these less traditional work settings may provide important insights into professional work and careers, and how these are shaped by the intersection of gender, age cohort, and other dimensions of inequality. These insights may also shed new light on traditional settings and challenge accepted divisions between the traditional and non-traditional. Incorporating young women into traditionally male-dominated professions may, at times, involve expanding our conception of what professional work is.

Although few chapters touched on technology, it is clear that this is another important area for future research. Technological advances have changed professional expectations of work availability. Moreover, they facilitate the development of new mechanisms through which gender inequalities can be reproduced and challenged. Still, we know little about the ways in which professionals engage in online activity, and how their use of technology informs their professional roles and identities. Future research could focus further on professionals' social media use, and how experiences differ across occupational groups and age cohorts/

generations. The issue of professional behaviour in online spaces may emerge as central to professional education and training in the future. Finally, there is a need for further critical research on generational and cohort differences in workplaces and professions. Earlier research shows the ways in which generational discourse can be deployed to legitimise generational conflicts and tensions and thus hinder visibility of shared concerns (Pritchard and Whiting 2014). In addition, future research might need to merge the literature on generation and age cohorts, which remains to a large extent separate, to better distinguish between differences and changes that occur due to generation and age cohort.

Policy Recommendations

The chapters in this volume have highlighted the many ways in which gender, age cohort, and other factors intersect to shape experiences of working in professions, and the ways in which these experiences are related to the life course. Each of these chapters not only contributes to our general knowledge of age, gender, and the professions, but they also point attention to numerous policy implications. Next we provide a list of policy recommendations based on the research findings. We have aimed to keep these brief to enhance their readability and relevance to various stakeholders. We have divided the recommendations by audience, even though several recommendations are relevant for, and of relevance to, multiple groups and organisations.

For Workplaces and Employing Organisations

1. New recruitment methods are necessary to increase diversity in employing organisations. Women, racial minorities, and professionals entering practice at later ages are disadvantaged under traditional recruitment methods, and they face barriers more traditional professional entrants do not. Firms should commit to greater monitoring and regulation with respect to equity, work–family balance, and the pursuit of social justice.
2. Firms need to legitimate paternity and parental leave policies, and demonstrate greater support for non-linear career patterns (including part-time work, flexible working hours, remote work, and telework) by making these options available to all professionals working within them. Creating clear incentives for fathers to take time off to devote to family life will most likely decrease the current stigma associated with parental leaves.
3. Workplace cultures should change so that mothers and fathers feel that they can use their parental benefits without harming their career prospects. Currently, parental leaves and cutting back on overtime and on-call hours can hurt careers and prospects for advancement,

resulting in professionals rejecting these mechanisms. Only the truly desperate take advantage of them—to their detriment. The current culture reproduces gender and age inequalities at work.

4. Family responsibilities should be recognised not as private concerns, but as professional and political concerns. These responsibilities are widely held by professionals during a particular life course stage, and these responsibilities are a predictable and common part of the life course. The structure of careers, overtime expectations, and promotion norms should be revised to take into account the fact that many professionals, especially those in their thirties, have these responsibilities. Generalised policies should be established, rather than creating ad hoc arrangements only when individual professionals request them.

5. Firms should recognise that heavy work responsibilities combined with family responsibilities lead to burnout, overwork, sick days, and other challenges. By providing workers with supports to achieve work–family balance, they are likely fostering an environment with lower turnover and fewer days lost.

6. It is important for workplaces to create safe spaces in which professionals and employers can discuss current life situations, work expectations, and workers' abilities to meet them, and what kind of accommodations are needed from employers. Such discussions should be systematic and occur regularly as part of career development and evaluation discussions, without senior staff imposing their own perspectives, assumptions, and expectations.

7. Firms should prioritise equity, appreciating that equity does not mean that everyone has the same experiences (working hours, overtime expectations, and so on). Equality—treating everyone the same regardless of their circumstances—results in the reproduction of structural inequalities.

8. Organisations employing professionals should pay attention to social media usage and recognise implicit and unconscious gender, age, and racial biases embedded within organisational structures. Doing so will help to create a more inclusive work environment.

9. Firms should take a more active role in establishing formal organisational rules and expectations regarding the work-related use of mobile technologies by their employees outside of work hours and workplaces.

10. Organisations should create safe spaces for the intergenerational transfer of knowledge, open dialogue, and support. Special attention should be paid to endorsing non-discriminatory and non-judgmental styles of communication in interpersonal interactions among employees.

11. Workplace cutbacks appear to have resulted in a deterioration of mentorship opportunities. Older workers should be provided with

the time and opportunity to mentor others, without compromising their own work tasks or extending their own work day. Increased mentorship of the young should result in increased work satisfaction (across generations), as well as decreased burnout and turnover.

12. Training in gender sensitivity, and intergenerational and cross-cultural communication, should be expanded. Leaders should be given training to equip them with the skills to recognise and revise their gender and age biases, especially with respect to the use of flexible work arrangements and parental leaves, family responsibilities, and career progress.

13. There should be zero tolerance for sexual harassment and workplace discrimination, which disproportionately affect young women (and in some instances, minority women) entering professions, increasing stress and negatively affecting their work and career advancement. It is recommended that workplaces establish contact persons for matters relating to sexual harassment and workplace discrimination.

14. Companies should consider helping to arrange and purchase services that could facilitate their employees' everyday lives, such as child- and eldercare, food delivery, cleaning, and shopping services.

For Professional Groups

1. Professional associations should advocate on behalf of professional workers, and other workers, in light of evidence of deteriorating working conditions and intensified work–family conflict, stress, and burnout. They should work with employers to change the culture towards one that appreciates diversity and sees work–family conflict not as a personal issue, but as a set of circumstances experienced by most workers at certain points across the life course.

2. Professions should continue to advocate for expanded opportunities for on-the-job professional training—for instance, medical residencies. An undersupply of opportunities not only leads to stress and mental health challenges, but also can reproduce existing inequalities by age, gender, and race/ethnicity.

3. Professions should recognise that young workers are under particular strains as they enter practice. These strains may be practical, emotional, and skill based, and can lead to feelings of incompetence, burnout, and stress, as well as turnover. Additional supports for young workers, especially increased formal mentorship programs, should be implemented. Mentoring should not only focus on enhancing job skills and dealing with work challenges, but also cover issues like asking for pay raises and dealing with challenging work assignments, and should provide rapid and continuous feedback.

4. Definitions of professionalism should be adjusted to adapt to changing social circumstances, especially around social media use. Violations of professionalism on and through social media should be taken seriously as a violation of professional conduct and be subject to sanctions. At the same time, professions should encourage uses of social media to enact positive change.

5. 'Emotional mentorship' should be provided. This involves moving beyond the unidirectional transfer of skills from the older generation to the younger, by providing safe spaces for dialogue between generations to improve cross-generational relations, and potentially challenge some taken-for-granted expectations.

6. Professions and professional associations should work towards making career structures and occupational structures more diverse, inclusive, and flexible, with respect to combining work in different work settings and sectors. The professions could benefit from the development of 'bridges' between different sectors and work settings, which would facilitate entry, exit, and returns to the professions.

7. Professions and professional associations should establish Equal Opportunities Committees and/or info-lines and networks for matters relating to harassment, bullying, and discrimination in the professions. Such committees could also deal with cases of harassment, bullying, and discrimination, which are difficult to solve at the workplace level, and thereby serve as powerful agents in promoting equal opportunities and in lowering the threshold to report discriminatory behaviours in the professions.

For Professional Education Programs

1. Professional education programs should take note of the added pressures that young workers face as they embark on professional careers, and should take steps to prepare new professionals so that they expect that the first few years may be particularly challenging but that certain aspects of their work should get easier over time. Better preparation could decrease feelings of incompetence, burnout, and stress, and ultimately reduce turnover.

2. More training in gender sensitivity, and intergenerational and cross-cultural communication, should be implemented in professional education programs.

3. Faculty and clinical leaders/practicum supervisors should practice positive mentorship, and not channel women—especially young, minority women—into specialties traditionally deemed more appropriate.

4. Mentorship seems particularly important for young women (and perhaps minority women). Effort to provide professionals-in-training

with mentorship, from those who share their gender and race/ethnicity as well as those who do not, should be enhanced.

5. Professional education programs should adjust traditional definitions of professionalism to encompass changing social circumstances, especially around social media use, and work–life balance.

6. Student codes of conduct should include rules around social media use and standards of professionalism. Violations of professionalism on social media should be taken seriously. At the same time, programs should encourage use of social media to enact positive change.

7. Within educational institutions, younger and minority workers should not be forced into precarious jobs, but should be given opportunities for secure and stable careers, skill development, and research opportunities.

8. Professional education programs should provide a wide and gender- and ethnicity-neutral overview of potential work settings including non-traditional practice areas for young professionals.

For Governments

1. Governments could do more to extend and legitimate paternity and parental leave policies, and encourage organisations in the public sector (and private sector) to demonstrate greater support for non-linear career patterns (including part-time work, remote work, and telework).

2. Family responsibilities should be recognised not as private concerns, but as political concerns. These responsibilities are widely held by workers during particular life course stages. These responsibilities are a predictable and common part of the life course and of professional careers. Governments should provide incentives for companies who take these responsibilities into account and provide workers with flexibility, as well as to those firms that are willing to promote individuals and not deny them certain assignments because of their family responsibilities.

3. Governments should take steps to eradicate the gender wage gap. More support for men's part-time and unpaid work (in addition to women's) may provide a solution. Thus, a welfare state characterised by a universal caregiver model should be considered.

4. Governments should recognise that heavy work responsibilities combined with family responsibilities lead to burnout, overwork, sick days, and other challenges.

5. Support for expanded opportunities for on-the-job professional training—for instance, medical residencies—should be provided. An undersupply of opportunities not only diminishes the supply of professionals providing needed services, but it also leads to stress and

mental health challenges; it can also reproduce existing inequalities by age, gender, and race/ethnicity.

6. Steps should be taken to encourage firms to take on and invest in younger workers' training, mentorship, and skills development. A focus on developing junior talent benefits society and the economy in the long run.

7. Governments should establish an equity or ombudsperson office to process complaints concerning harassment and discrimination, and to advise and assess what employers, professional associations, and education institutions should do to prevent discrimination on the grounds of gender, age, and race/ethnicity.

Finally, we advocate for more joint efforts between and among the various stakeholders to build more inclusive work environments for women and nascent generations of professionals.

References

Acker, J (2006) 'Inequality Regimes: Gender, Class, and Race in Organizations' 20 *Gender & Society* 441, 445. doi:10.1177/0891243206289499

Adams, TL (2000) *A Dentist and a Gentleman: Gender and the Rise of Dentistry in Ontario* (Toronto, University of Toronto Press). doi:10.3138/9781442670297

――― (2010) 'Gender and Feminization in Health Care Professions' 4 *Sociology Compass* 454. doi:10.1111/j.1751-9020.2010.00294.x

Barley, SR and Kunda, G (2004) *Gurus, Hired Guns, and Warm Bodies: Itinerant Experts in a Knowledge Economy* (Princeton, NJ, Princeton University Press).

Boulis, AK and Jacobs, JA (2008) *The Changing Face of Medicine: Women Doctors and the Evolution of Health Care in America* (Ithaca, NY, ILR Press).

Davies, C (1996) 'The Sociology of Professions and the Profession of Gender' 30 *Sociology* 661. doi:10.1177/0038038596030004003

Elder Jr, GH (1994) 'Time, Human Agency, and Social Change: Perspectives on the Life Course' 57 *Social Psychology Quarterly* 4. doi:10.2307/2786971

Glenn, EN (2002) *Unequal Freedom: How Race and Gender Shaped American Citizenship and Labor* (Cambridge, MA, Harvard University Press).

Hearn, J, Biese, I, Choroszewicz, M and Husu, L (2016) 'Gender, Diversity and Intersectionality in Professions and Potential Professions: Analytical, Historical and Contemporary Perspectives' in M Dent, IL Bourgeault, J-L Denis and E Kuhlmann (eds), *The Routledge Companion to the Professions and Professionalism* (London, Routledge).

Holvino, E (2010) 'Intersections: The Simultaneity of Race, Gender and Class in Organization Studies' 17 *Gender, Work & Organization* 248. doi:10.1111/j.1468-0432.2008.00400.x

Kalleberg, AL (2009) 'Precarious Work, Insecure Workers: Employment Relations in Transition' 74 *American Sociological Review* 1. doi:10.1177/000312240907400101

McDonald, PK (2018) 'How "Flexible" Are Careers in the Anticipated Life Course of Young People?' 71 *Human Relations* 23. doi:10.1177/0018726717699053

McLaughlin, C and Deakin, S (2011) *Equality Law and the Limits of the "Business Case" for Addressing Gender Inequalities* (Centre for Business Research, University of Cambridge). www.cbr.cam.ac.uk/fileadmin/user_upload/centre-for-business-research/downloads/working-papers/wp420.pdf

McMullin, JA (ed) (2011) *Age, Gender, and Work: Small Information Technology Firms in the New Economy* (Vancouver, University of British Columbia Press).

Pritchard, K and Whiting, R (2014) 'Baby Boomers and the Lost Generation: On the Discursive Construction of Generations at Work' 35 *Organization Studies* 1605. doi:10.1177/0170840614550732

Riska, E (2014) 'Gender and the Professions' in WC Cockerham, R Dingwall and SR Quah (eds), *The Wiley Blackwell Encyclopedia of Health, Illness, Behavior, and Society* (Chichester, West Sussex: Wiley-Blackwell). doi:10.1002/978111 8410868.wbehibs007

Shanahan, MJ and Macmillan, R (2008) *Biography and the Sociological Imagination: Contexts and Contingencies* (New York, WW Norton and Co).

Witz, A (1992) *Professions and Patriarchy* (New York, Routledge).

Index